M000273849

Disasters: A Sociological Approach

Disasters:
A Sociological Approach

KATHLEEN TIERNEY

polity

Copyright © Kathleen Tierney 2019

The right of Kathleen Tierney to be identified as Author of this Work has been asserted in accordance with the UK Copyright, Designs and Patents Act 1988.

First published in 2019 by Polity Press
Reprinted 2020 (twice)

Polity Press
65 Bridge Street
Cambridge CB2 1UR, UK

Polity Press
101 Station Landing
Suite 100
Medford, MA 02155, USA

All rights reserved. Except for the quotation of short passages for the purpose of criticism and review, no part of this publication may be reproduced, stored in a retrieval system or transmitted, in any form or by any means, electronic, mechanical, photocopying, recording or otherwise, without the prior permission of the publisher.

ISBN-13: 978-0-7456-7101-7
ISBN-13: 978-0-7456-7102-4(pb)

A catalogue record for this book is available from the British Library.

Library of Congress Cataloging-in-Publication Data

Names: Tierney, Kathleen J., author.
Title: Disasters : a sociological approach / Kathleen Tierney.
Description: Medford, MA : Polity Press, [2018] | Includes bibliographical references and index.
Identifiers: LCCN 2018029797 (print) | LCCN 2018031922 (ebook) | ISBN 9781509535699 (Epub) | ISBN 9780745671017 (hardback) | ISBN 9780745671024 (pbk.)
Subjects: LCSH: Disasters–Social aspects. | Disasters–Research.
Classification: LCC HV553 (ebook) | LCC HV553 .T54 2018 (print) | DDC 363.34/1–dc23
LC record available at https://lccn.loc.gov/2018029797
Typeset in 10 on 13pt Swift by
Servis Filmsetting Ltd, Stockport, Cheshire
Printed and bound in the United States by LSC Communications

The publisher has used its best endeavours to ensure that the URLs for external websites referred to in this book are correct and active at the time of going to press. However, the publisher has no responsibility for the websites and can make no guarantee that a site will remain live or that the content is or will remain appropriate.

Every effort has been made to trace all copyright holders, but if any have been inadvertently overlooked the publisher will be pleased to include any necessary credits in any subsequent reprint or edition.

Every effort has been made to trace all copyright holders, but if any have been overlooked the publisher will be pleased to include any necessary credits in any subsequent reprint or edition.

For further information on Polity, visit our website:
politybooks.com

Contents

Detailed Contents

Tables

Figures

Acknowledgments

I owe thanks to many people for their help with this book. My partner of over thirty years, Peter Park, died in April 2014, just as I was finishing my last book. He remains an inspiration to me, and he is never far from my thoughts. Thank you, Peter, for all those wonderful years, for your integrity, and for your important intellectual contributions to my work. I remain in awe.

In the years that followed, I benefitted enormously from the support—both personal and professional—provided by colleagues and dear friends, especially Liesel Ritchie, Nnenia Campbell, Chip Clarke, Brandi Gilbert, Duane Gill, Jim Kendra, Wee-Kiat Lim, Jamie Vickery, and Tricia Wachtendorf. Thanks are also due to the staff of the University of Colorado Natural Hazards Center, where I served as director from August 2003 to January 2017, and to Lori Peek, my brilliant successor. Special thanks to staff member Jeff Gunderson for the figures in Chapter 7. Many other colleagues and friends, too numerous to acknowledge here, made this journey possible. All of you helped me keep it together throughout this process, and for that I am grateful.

There are no friends like old friends, and my deepest thanks for your unfailing support go to Maggie Andersen, Sheila Balkan, Valerie Hans, Elizabeth Higgenbotham, and Ruth Horowitz. Thanks also to the Late Great Kate—Kathleen Connors, my oldest friend, who was taken from us in January 2018. Trips to Las Vegas and Sayulita will never be the same without you, Katie.

I am fortunate to live in a close-knit neighborhood—a place where social capital is strong—and I am grateful to all my neighbors, who since the early 2000s have hosted monthly potluck dinners, holiday parties, and (last but not least) the viciously competitive summer croquet tournament. We went through the 2013 flood together, and that experience made our bonds even stronger.

To Jonathan Skerrett, my editor at Polity, and to editorial assistant Karina Jákupsdóttir, thank you for your patience and for your wise counsel. You are both models of kindness, understanding, and probity. I am especially grateful to Manuela Tecusan, who went over the manuscript word by word and line by line and made many suggestions that improved the clarity and quality of the text. I also wish to thank the anonymous reviewers of earlier versions of the manuscript for your sage guidance.

Very special and heartfelt thanks are due to Jamie Sedlacko, my assistant on this book project. Jamie, I literally could not have completed the project without your help. Sorry for those all-nighters!

Finally, I want to thank my extended family: On my side, dearest Justin, Amy, Violet, and Rita; Barbara and Jerry; Mary, Lori, Lynn, Matt, Ava, Rowan, Michael, and Emily; and Erin, Jeremy, and Katherine. On Peter's side, Susy, Ben, Bea, and Roland; Sam; Phoebe, Tom, Lulu, Tommy, and Gus; and my dearest nieces, nephew, and grand-nieces and grand-nephews. How very, very fortunate I am to have all of you in my life.

1

The Social Significance of Disasters

Introduction

Disasters are a frequent occurrence across the globe and, despite organized efforts to reduce disaster losses, those losses continue to grow. Between 1996 and 2005, an estimated 1.5 million people were killed in disasters worldwide, and many more were affected by injuries, disaster-related illness, homelessness, and economic loss. Deaths and injuries are more common in low- and middle-income countries by several orders of magnitude, while economic losses are significantly higher in wealthier nations (Centre for Research on the Epidemiology of Disasters (CRED) 2016). According to studies carried out by Munich Reinsurance, worldwide disaster losses for 2017 totaled $330 billion, only half of that amount being covered by insurance. A significant share of those losses is attributable to three major hurricanes that struck the United States in 2017—Harvey, Irma, and Maria—making 2017 the second-highest year for overall losses, after 2011, when losses amounted to approximately $354 billion in current dollars.

In addition to causing deaths, injuries, and economic losses, disasters have other profound social impacts that we will explore in this volume. According to a recent report by the World Bank Group (2017), disasters are a key factor in driving people into poverty and keeping them there. Disasters can lead to short- and long(er)-term mental health problems as well as to threats to physical health. Experiencing a disaster can be a major stressor for households and business owners. The extensive damage and disruption that disasters cause can result in the breakup of neighborhoods and in the loss of significant sources of social support for disaster survivors, some of whom may never be able to return to their homes, while others will never recover from these experiences. Many who survive disaster may find themselves living in temporary accommodations for months or even years, their daily routines disrupted and their plans for recovery stalled. After disasters, children's development may suffer as a result of interruptions in schooling, residential dislocation, and parental stress.

Key societal institutions also experience difficulties in the aftermath of disasters, as schools, churches, charitable organizations, and agencies that provide health and welfare services see their burdens increase. Communities face challenges associated with the disruption and restoration of key lifelines such as water, electrical power, transportation, and other critical infrastructure systems. Local jurisdictions may experience population decline and tax losses. A disaster is a once-in-a-lifetime experience for most communities, and they often struggle to understand what they need to do to respond and recover.

Large economies, such as those of the United States and other developed countries, experience temporary economic setbacks in the aftermath of disasters, but there is little evidence to date that disasters cause significant economic downturns in more developed nations. However, this is not the case for smaller, less developed countries; in those cases, disasters can have significant economic impacts, particularly when they affect key sectors of those economies. For a nation seeking to improve its level of economic development, a disaster can be a major setback. In both large and small countries, the need to respond to and recover from disasters drains financial resources that could otherwise be employed more productively. In the United States, as billion- and multibillion-dollar disasters continue to occur with alarming frequency, taxpayers, insurance companies, and disaster survivors themselves are forced to foot the bill. For households and businesses, disasters can result in increased debt and an inability to take advantage of opportunities for financial advancement. In many instances, particularly of catastrophic and near-catastrophic disasters, it can take years or even decades for social and economic recovery to take place, as communities, families, and businesses struggle to cope over the long term.

As we will see throughout this volume, disaster impacts and losses are not random, nor are the burdens of disasters borne equally by all members of affected populations. Rather, the impacts of disasters often fall most heavily on those who are most vulnerable: the poor, racial and ethnic minorities, and other marginalized groups. Many current inquiries in the sociological study of disasters center on how various axes of inequality such as class, race, gender, and other aspects of social stratification contribute to shaping the patterns of disaster victimization and recovery.

Media attention typically focuses on the immediate impacts of disasters and fades away in days or weeks. As a result, the public is generally unaware of the cascading effects of disasters and of the struggles that survivors endure over time. In Hurricane Harvey in 2017, floodwaters surged over many facilities that contained toxins, such as landfills and agricultural and petrochemical plants. Those waters, too, contained biological hazards, for example fecal matter, E. coli bacteria, shigella, and even Vibrio vulnificus, a deadly bacterium. When Hurricane Maria struck the US territory of Puerto Rico that same year, the island's electric power infrastructure was essentially destroyed. Among other impacts, the loss of power threatened the lives of those who were dependent on kidney dialysis treatments and on medical devices that required a supply of electricity. Wildfires denude landscapes and set the stage for flooding and landslides later, when it rains, as happened for example in 2017, when major fires in central California were followed by deadly debris flows. After the devastating 2010 earthquake in Haiti, Nepalese troops providing relief under the auspices of the United Nations brought cholera to the island. As of 2016, an estimated 770,000 people, or about 8 percent of the population, have been infected with cholera and over 9,000 people have died—and those numbers are thought to be underestimates (Knox 2016). In 2011 in Japan, when the Great Tohoku earthquake triggered a deadly tsunami that caused a triple meltdown at the Fukushima nuclear power plant, the media covered that sensational story, but now there is little coverage of the ongoing effects of the large-scale population displacement and long-term nuclear contamination that this massive disaster caused.

Also neglected are the ways in which hazards and disasters can erode the sense of community and the sense of place, and also lead to conflict among those who are affected. Disasters can result in the loss of important cultural assets, as happens for example when historic structures are destroyed and traditional livelihoods are disrupted. Decades ago sociologist Kai Erikson (1976) showed how a flash flood that occurred in 1972 in Buffalo Creek, West Virginia as a result of negligence on the part of a coal company that failed to maintain a dam effectively destroyed community cohesion and triggered widespread mental health problems in the affected communities. In a subsequent book entitled *A New Species of Trouble*, Erikson (1995) documented how technological disasters and toxic threats can cause collective trauma for Native Americans and other disadvantaged groups. As the title suggests, technological advances achieved in contemporary societies have a dark side, which manifests itself in the form of heretofore unacknowledged hazards. Other research illustrates how such threats and the lawsuits they often engender can lead to the formation of contentious factions and to decline in social connectedness and trust.

Disasters can also provoke challenges to the legitimacy and competence of governments and institutions. In one historic example, the dictatorial government of Nicaragua appropriated and mishandled international aid after the 1972 Managua earthquake and subsequently fell from power seven years later, largely as a result of public indignation. The 2003 epidemic of severe acute respiratory syndrome (SARS), which originated in China, created a legitimacy crisis for the ruling Communist Party, which had attempted to cover up the outbreak even as it spread worldwide. In 2005 the response to the Hurricane Katrina catastrophe was so inexcusably inept that it permanently tarnished the record of the Bush administration. In the aftermath of the 2009 L'Aquila earthquake in Italy, six scientists and one public official were found guilty of manslaughter for not adequately informing the public, in the days leading up to the disaster, about the impending danger—an episode that bears evidence of the eroding confidence in science and government in the face of disaster.

Governments that depend on international aid in order to respond to and recover from disasters may find their countries overrun and their authority bypassed by outside entities that pursue their donors' interests rather than the needs of disaster victims. The provision of large amounts of disaster aid also tends to breed and feed corruption, particularly in already corrupt societies, and this leads to public distrust and disillusionment.

The impacts of disasters, and in many cases their likelihood, are amplified by ongoing global trends. Rapid and uncontrolled urbanization and intensified development in hazardous areas put ever larger populations at risk. The proliferation of global supply chains means that disasters that affect suppliers in one country have ramifications for businesses in distant nations. Climate change leads to ocean warming and sea-level rise, which in turn result in more extreme atmospheric events and greater impacts from those events in coastal areas. As climate change progresses, societies around the world will be forced to grapple with more frequent heat waves, the spread of infectious disease agents, land loss in coastal areas, and a host of other climate change-induced effects.

Given the societal significance of disasters, it is not difficult to see why sociologists and other social scientists find these events and the efforts to reduce their impacts endlessly fascinating. As we have already seen, disasters have economic, political and policy, health and mental health dimensions. They frequently bring to the fore issues of inequality and social justice, shining a light on the problems experienced by marginalized and vulnerable populations. At the same time, social behavior in disasters also reveals the human capacity for altruism and creativity. We will explore together these and other themes in the chapters that follow.

Key Concepts and Definitions in the Study of Disasters

To ensure that we are working from a common set of definitions in the discussion that follow, in this section I introduce concepts that are commonly used in the sociological study of disasters and that will be employed in later chapters. Obviously one key concept is the idea of *disaster* itself. An important takeaway point is that disasters are by their nature social events, not merely physical ones. If a major volcanic eruption were to occur in an area where human settlements did not exist or remained unaffected, that eruption would be a significant geophysical event, but not a disaster. In keeping with sociological conceptualizations, disasters involve the juxtaposition of physical forces—geological, atmospheric, technological, and other forces—and vulnerable human communities. The severity of a disaster is measured not by the magnitude of the physical forces involved, but rather by the magnitude of its societal impacts.

As subsequent discussions will show, disasters were previously seen as discrete events, concentrated in time and space, that disrupt the social order and interfere with the ability of a community or society to continue to operate, for example by interfering with governmental functions, economic activities, utility services, education, transportation, telecommunications, and housing. While acknowledging such impacts, more recent social science formulations see disasters as arising not so much from the physical forces that trigger them at specific times as from longer-term global and societal processes, which in turn result in an increase of the potential for loss. Much of the discussion that follows will focus on those processes, making the point that the potential for disasters and disaster victimization builds up over long time periods.

While media accounts and commonsense views of disaster tend to gloss over differences in event severity in a search for commonalities among events, sociological formulations are attentive to such differences because of their social implications. Sociologists typically classify events into *emergencies, disasters,* and *catastrophes* (see Quarantelli 1996). As shown in Table 1.1, these different types of occurrences are associated, among other things, with differences in spatial scope, the severity of their impacts, which entities respond and how, the degree of public participation in providing assistance, and

Table 1.1 How emergencies, disasters, and catastrophes differ.

Emergencies	Disasters	Catastrophes
Impacts localized	Impacts widespread, severe	Devastating physical and societal impacts
Response mainly local	Response is multi-jurisdictional, intergovernmental, but typically bottom-up	Response is initiated by central government because localities and regions are devastated
Standard operating procedures sufficient to handle event	Response requires activation of disaster plans; significant challenges emerge	Response challenges far exceed those envisioned in disaster plans
Vast majority of response resources are unaffected	Extensive damage to and disruption of key emergency services	Response system paralyzed at local and regional levels
Public generally not involved in response	Public extensively involved in response	Public only source of initial response
No significant recovery challenges	Major recovery challenges	Massive recovery challenges and very slow recovery process

SOURCE: Compiled from data in Quarantelli 1996 and Tierney 2008.

recovery challenges. Emergencies include events such as multi-vehicle traffic accidents, large structure fires, and minor industrial accidents—incidents that may cause deaths and injuries but that are localized, do not create large-scale disruption, and are typically handled by public safety agencies such as fire and police departments. Emergencies are more or less everyday occurrences in large urban areas. Disasters are much less common and much more serious; they have severe consequences that include deaths, injuries, and large-scale social disruption. In disasters, members of the public join responding organizations in dealing with these and other effects. Unlike emergencies, disasters can damage and degrade the very resources that are meant to respond to them. Catastrophes are larger still; they involve massive repercussions, which greatly exceed the capacity of stricken communities to respond—including long-lasting impacts that require protracted recovery efforts. Examples of catastrophes include the Indian Ocean tsunami of 2004, Hurricane Katrina in 2005, the 2010 Haiti earthquake, and the triple catastrophe that struck Japan in 2011. In its history, the United States has experienced only four true catastrophes: the 1900 Galveston Hurricane, the 1906 San Francisco earthquake, the Great Mississippi flood of 1927, and Katrina. As indicated in the table, emergencies, disasters, and catastrophes are qualitatively different. A disaster is not just a big emergency, and a catastrophe is not just a big disaster; rather the three occurrences are accompanied by differing effects, response patterns, and challenges.

The term *extreme event* is sometimes used interchangeably with *disaster*. Here the reference is to events that are out of the ordinary or outside the norm—that is, rare or unlikely. The term is more appropriately applied to physical phenomena such as rainfall or wind speed than to disaster events. This is because disasters can result from events that are technically not extreme in the physical sense, but that nonetheless overwhelm a community's or society's capacity to cope. The United Nations International Strategy for Disaster Reduction recently developed a consensus set of terms and definitions that are meant to be applied to disaster-related phenomena. *Extreme event* was not among them. I mention it here because it is a term that is commonly in use in some scientific circles.

The term *hazard* refers to an ongoing condition that has the potential for causing a disaster. Many regions around the world are exposed to earthquake hazards; many coastal areas are exposed to hurricanes and coastal flooding; flood hazards exist along rivers and streams; areas adjacent to nuclear and chemical facilities are exposed to those technological hazards; and so on. The terms *hazard* and *disaster* are not interchangeable. The former refers to the *potential* for a disruptive event to occur, while the latter refers to what happens *when that potential is actualized*. Various scientific disciplines—geology, seismology, atmospheric science, and others—conduct research to better understand and characterize hazards, and communities and societies worldwide seek to use that knowledge to improve their understanding of the hazards to which they are exposed and the ways they can respond to such threats.

The concept of *vulnerability* refers to the potential for experiencing adverse impacts from disasters and having poorer outcomes after the occurrence of disasters. The concept is applied to both physical systems and individuals and social groups. For physical systems such as buildings, transportation networks, dams, and utility services, vulnerability consists of the potential for destruction, damage, or loss of function. For individuals and groups, it represents the potential for dying, being injured, losing property, being displaced, and experiencing other negative disaster impacts, as well as for having difficulty recovering after disasters. Like the term *hazard*, vulnerability relates to the *potential* for the occurrence of adverse experiences and outcomes—a potential that may or may not be realized in any particular disaster. Like hazards, vulnerabilities can be assessed in non-disaster contexts; the field of vulnerability science is devoted to improving such measurements.

Disaster resilience is a concept that has risen to prominence over the past twenty years and that will be discussed in greater detail in Chapter 7. Based as it is on ideas from fields as diverse as engineering, psychology, and ecology, the concept refers to the ability of social units at different scales (e.g., societies, communities, households, and organizations) to absorb disaster shocks, to cope with disaster impacts, and successfully to adapt and in some cases even improve their functioning in the aftermath of disasters. Research has revealed significant differences in disaster resilience at various levels of analysis, and here again poverty and marginality are often (though not necessarily) associated with low capacities.

Risk is a term that is also used extensively in the study of disasters. Risk has been defined as "a situation or event in which something of human value (including humans themselves) has been put at stake and where the outcome is uncertain" (Jaeger, Renn, Rosa, and Webler 2001: 17). The idea that entities that have human value are "at stake" means that losses may occur. Although the term is commonly used to refer to the possibility of losses, the concept also includes the potential for positive outcomes. People risk their money when they play the stock market, which has the potential for yielding gains as well as losses. People also engage in risky activities such as skydiving and extreme sports because, even though these are dangerous, they hold the possibility of rewards such as excitement and a sense of accomplishment. As the definition indicates, risk is always accompanied by *uncertainty*. We know that losses may result from taking risks, but we can only estimate their likelihood. The fields of risk analysis and risk management focus on clarifying those probabilities to the greatest extent possible and on taking steps to reduce the risks.

Emergence is a concept used to refer to new patterns of individual, group, and organizational behavior that are formed during and after the occurrence of disasters. Disasters are occasions that call into being novel social group-ings and collaboration and coordination networks whose structures grow and change in response to newly identified needs. Disasters and catastrophes always contain an element of surprise—occurrences that were not, even could not, have been foreseen. Essentially, if an event does not produce surprises, it is not a disaster; it is merely a small or larger emergency. Emergence is common in disaster situations because so much of what happens in disasters is unanticipated.

At different points in this book I will use the term *disaster agent*. A disaster agent is a physical force that leads to the occurrence of a disaster. Here again, the agent and the disaster are not the same thing; a disaster occurs when an agent damages and disrupts human societies and the sorts of things that humans value. A partial list of disaster agents includes hurricanes or tropical cyclones, riverine and flash floods, tornadoes, wildfires, earthquakes, tsuna-mis, droughts, and various types of chemical or nuclear agents that can be released as a result of facility accidents or as a result of impacts caused by other disaster agents—as happened in the 2011 Japan triple disaster, where, as noted earlier, an earthquake triggered a tsunami, which in turn caused core meltdowns in nuclear facilities.

Historically, researchers have distinguished disaster agents along several dimensions: whether they occur with or without warning; how long a warning period they allow for; the duration of impact; the scope of impact (localized disasters vs. disasters with broader impact areas); whether impacts are singu-lar or repetitive; and whether the agent is familiar or unfamiliar and exotic. Using these distinctions, an earthquake is characterized as a disaster agent that creates impacts without warning,[1] is relatively brief in duration, lasting seconds or minutes, typically has a large geographic scope of impact, and car-ries the potential for repetitive impacts in the form of aftershocks. Earthquake hazards are familiar and well understood in many regions of the world, and many major earthquake faults have been mapped, but earthquakes also occur unexpectedly, on unmapped faults and in places where residents are not aware of the hazard. These features make this particular disaster agent chal-lenging in terms of societal and community ability to respond. Other types of disaster agents also present distinctive challenges. Droughts are slow-onset occurrences, and often drought conditions and their adverse impacts are not recognized until a drought is well advanced, deaths begin to occur, and liveli-hoods are disrupted. Chemical and nuclear incidents may be so unfamiliar that members of the public may not know what risks they pose or how to protect themselves. In the presence of those kinds of agents the public will be especially reliant on authorities to communicate effectively regarding what they need to do to avoid danger.

Some disaster agents are able to produce very severe and widespread impacts and thus can be more likely to lead to catastrophes, particularly when vulnerability is high in the affected areas. In this century, for example, a number of catastrophes and near-catastrophes have resulted in the death of tens to hundreds of thousands of people. Examples include the 2001 Gujarat earthquake in India (over 20,000 fatalities), the 2004 Indian Ocean earthquake and tsunami (over 200,000 deaths), an earthquake in Pakistan-administered Kashmir in 2005 (over 73,000 fatalities), Cyclone Nargis in Myanmar in 2008 (more than 130,000 killed); the 2008 Wenchuan earthquake in China (nearly 88,000 deaths), the 2010 Haiti earthquake (an estimated 220,000 killed), and the 2011 earthquake and tsunami in Japan (approximately 20,000 deaths). Earthquakes and tropical storms are not the only disaster agents that have brought about high mortality in this century; in the summer of 2003 a heat-wave that struck Europe resulted in the deaths of an estimated 70,000 people. (All statistics are based on CRED 2016.) Note that, with the exception of the 2003 heat wave and the 2011 Japan disaster, all the events listed here took place in less developed countries. In this volume I will explore why death tolls are so high in those kinds of societal settings.

Climate change is a hazard that stands virtually in a category of its own. Outside scientific and policy circles, its characteristics and effects are largely unfamiliar. Its onset has been and continues to be relatively slow and, for many people, its effects to date have remained unseen, while other people are already experiencing them. It currently affects nations and communities around the world primarily through its interaction with other hazards and through its influence on the likelihood and severity of certain disaster agents. Although scientists note that it is difficult to attribute specific disaster events to climate change, it is widely recognized that, when climate change causes sea-level rise, this makes the storm surges associated with hurricanes, cyclones, and typhoons larger and that, when it increases ocean temperatures, it contributes to more intense rainfall events. With climate change, we will see more periods of extreme heat, which can contribute to the occurrence of deadly heat waves and wildfires. Climate change will be discussed throughout this volume, but especially in Chapter 8.

At various points in the book, I will also use the term *hazards cycle*, which refers to activities that can be undertaken before disasters, during and immediately after disaster impact, and during the longer-term recovery period to reduce losses and hasten recovery. The hazards cycle consists of four elements: mitigation, preparedness, response, and recovery. *Mitigation* refers to measures that can be taken in advance of disasters, with a view to reducing their impacts.[2] Such measures include planning and zoning activities that direct development away from hazardous areas; building codes that require disaster-resistant construction; and strategies for retrofitting structures, so that they can resist being damaged when disasters strike. These types of measures are typically undertaken either by governments or as part of governmental requirements. Another important aspect of mitigation involves strengthening the natural defenses that reduce the impacts of disaster agents, for example restoring wetlands so that can they absorb hurricane-force winds. Private property owners often engage in disaster mitigation activities on their own—for example, when homeowners in earthquake country bolt their homes to their foundations so that those structures would not slip off their foundations when an earthquake strikes.

Insurance is sometimes considered a mitigation measure, but that is not entirely accurate. Insurance does not so much reduce risk as identify other parties (insurance and reinsurance companies) that will pay for damages in the event of a disaster. Insurance can be used to spur mitigation actions, however, as happens when insurance coverage is tied to the implementation of mitigation measures. In the US National Flood Insurance Program (NFIP), for example, flood insurance premiums paid by property owners are lower if the communities where those property owners live undertake flood control projects. Following the NFIP's Community Rating System, the more the communities do to reduce flood hazards, the less property owners have to pay.

The second stage in the cycle, *preparedness*, consists of activities taken in advance of disasters that strengthen the ability of communities, households, and individuals to respond effectively when disaster strikes. Preparedness measures cover the development of disaster plans at various governmental levels, ranging from local to national and international, as well as household and business disaster planning. Such measures also include knowing what to do when a disaster threatens or strikes—for example, being aware of evacuation routes and knowing what self-protective measures to carry out in the event of a chemical or nuclear accident or other type of disaster. Drills and exercises are other common preparedness activities that are undertaken by emergency responders to ensure disaster readiness, as well as by institutions such as schools and hospitals and by private sector organizations. Governmental agencies seek to improve public preparedness through various forms of messaging, such as by communicating with the public about hazards and risks through a range of media or by educating the public about what to do in the event of a disaster. Other kinds of preparedness activities are developing disaster-warning systems, marking evacuation routes and providing evacuation maps, providing training experiences for members of at-risk populations so that they can assist in the event of a disaster, and integrating hazards knowledge into school curricula.

Response, the third stage of the hazards cycle, takes place when disasters occur and consists of activities undertaken by individuals, households, businesses, and governmental and nongovernmental organizations and aimed at coping with the impacts of disaster. Response activities are multifaceted; examples include implementing expedient self-protective measures such as evacuating and seeking emergency shelter; activating disaster plans; searching for and rescuing persons in distress; caring for the injured and making arrangements for those who have been killed; containing immediate threats associated with cascading disaster effects, such as agent-induced fires and hazardous materials releases; and taking additional measures to ensure public safety, such as issuing information about particularly hazardous areas and evolving threats. As discussed earlier in this chapter, as disasters unfold, new dangers emerge, and part of the response to disasters consists of informing the public about those dangers. Entities that respond to disasters encounter challenges of their own. For example, they must be able to assess the disaster situation and identify and prioritize critical needs. They also must be able to communicate and coordinate their activities.

As we will see later, particularly in Chapters 4 and 7, responding to disasters involves implementing disaster plans—but other measures as well. Response activities include improvising in various ways when plans fail to anticipate realities on the ground. While we tend to think that disaster response consists of the activities of so-called "first responders"—such as fire services, police, and emergency management personnel—actual disaster responses are diffuse and decentralized, as members of the public and entities that had not been included in planning activities spur into action and new groups emerge to address pressing needs. Sometimes such public-based responses are well coordinated with those of official entities; other times they are not. Viewing disaster response as "what first responders do" misses the point that, as noted earlier in Table 1.1 and the discussion around it, the public is, typically, extensively involved in a range of response activities in the aftermath of disasters and catastrophic events. It is only in emergency incidents that public safety agencies are the main ones to handle response activities.

Finally, disaster *recovery* consists of all the activities that encompass efforts on the part of those affected by disasters to overcome disaster disruption and continue to thrive. Here again, recovery activities take place at different levels: individuals, households, businesses, communities, regions, and in some cases entire societies. Recent scholarship and practice emphasize the idea that recovery activities can be planned even before disasters occur, in order to smooth the recovery process.

Disaster recovery is often incorrectly equated with restoring and reconstructing the built environment. However, as we will see in more detail later, many other processes unfold during post-disaster recovery, for example processes associated with recovering from trauma, reestablishing disrupted livelihoods and economic activity, and regaining a sense of community. Too often after disasters governments hasten to reconstruct and rebuild, but without attending to other, less tangible but still essential aspects of recovery. As a result, communities are left with rebuilt and often attractive physical spaces that fail to meet their social and cultural needs.

In keeping with the *disaster cycle* concept, recovery activities should, and often do, incorporate new mitigation measures, bringing the cycle full circle.

The recovery period after a disaster can open up new opportunities to increase the safety of affected communities through implementation of mitigation strategies. This is the period when disaster-stricken communities can make progress in areas such as hazard-aware land use policies and stricter building codes, as interest groups that may have previously opposed such measures recognize and embrace mitigation as a pressing need. Governments can help in this respect. For example, US post-disaster assistance frameworks allow for setting aside funds, proportionate to the size of aid packages, specifically for mitigating the impacts of future disasters. Unfortunately, however, even though the recovery period presents possibilities for future risk reduction, those possibilities frequently go unrealized, leaving disaster-stricken areas vulnerable to future events.

Chapter Themes

This book provides an introduction to the sociology of disasters and at the same time seeks to advance the field, particularly with respect to theories concerning the causes of disasters. Many of the issues discussed in this volume are covered in greater detail in more specialized publications that deal, for example, with topics such as disaster vulnerability and resilience. In those cases, my task is to present an overview of the current scholarship and point readers to those additional sources for more in-depth analyses. In addition and perhaps more importantly, what I hope to do in this volume is advance new ideas about the societal origins of disasters. Much of the discussion in the chapters that follow delves more deeply into ideas that I began to develop in an earlier book, *The Social Roots of Risk* (Tierney 2014). As that title suggests, disasters and their impacts are produced to a much greater extent through the workings of social forces than of natural or technological ones. Put more directly, the arguments I make here show that disasters are socially produced, not produced by natural or technological forces external to society, and that those societal forces constitute the means by which disasters take their toll on human lives and livelihoods. The root causes of disasters are to be found in the social order itself—that is, in social arrangements that contribute to the buildup of risk and vulnerability. As subsequent chapters will show, those interacting and mutually reinforcing arrangements include processes that operate within the global political economy, actions undertaken by state actors for their own purposes that ignore and increase hazards and risks, processes that contribute to social vulnerability by further marginalizing disadvantaged social groups, and local growth-machine politics that elevate so-called "economic development" as a major priority while ignoring increasing risks.

Chapter 2 provides an overview of the history of disaster research in sociology and other social sciences. It shows how systems thinking in sociology and the idea of "adjustments" to hazards in geography formed the basis for early research in the field. In Chapter 2 we also see how both theory and research on disasters have changed over time. New theoretical approaches such as the pressure and release (PAR) model have come to the fore that place greater emphasis on the social production of disaster vulnerability than on the physical events that cause societal disruption. While the early tradition in disaster research focused mainly on the impact and response periods of disasters, later research has begun to concentrate on other phases of the hazards cycle, including mitigation and recovery.

The boundaries around what constitutes the sociology of disasters are fuzzy; other social science disciplines have made significant contributions to the sociological understanding of disasters, their causes, and their impacts. In Chapter 3 I focus on some of the most important contributions from fields such as economics, geography, psychology, and mental health.

In Chapter 4 I present an overview of general theoretical perspectives that can be applied to better understand disasters, as well as middle-range theories that explain different aspects of disaster-related phenomena. The chapter shows how perspectives such as that of world systems theory, along with insights from environmental sociology, reveal the social roots of disasters, as well as how constructivist perspectives help us understand what shapes our thinking on disasters—and what shapes our ignorance of hazards. Also discussed are theoretical perspectives that help explain phenomena such as self-protective behaviors and group and network emergence.

Chapter 5 provides an overview of disaster research methods. This chapter is not intended to be a primer on research methods, or even on all the methods that disaster researchers employ. Rather the discussion centers on what is distinctive about conducting research in disaster settings, including challenges to applying conventional research approaches in disrupted social environments. This chapter also focuses on the special operational and ethical challenges that accompany the efforts to carry out research in disaster contexts. For example, unlike researchers who plan their studies over months and even years, those who study disaster response activities may be required to mobilize—which often means going to unfamiliar places—at very short notice. Ethical issues always arise in research involving human subjects, but are those issues the same or different in disasters? Do disaster survivors warrant special ethical protections? We will explore these and similar questions in Chapter 5.

The concept of disaster vulnerability is discussed in many places in this volume, but Chapter 6 delves more deeply into it, focusing on global and historical trends that make particular populations and groups more vulnerable than others and on the intersectional nature of vulnerability, given that factors such as race, ethnicity, class, and gender combine to produce differential levels of vulnerability. Age and disability are among other factors explored as sources of vulnerability, as are citizenship and linguistic competence. A key point emphasized in this chapter, and indeed throughout the volume, is that individuals and groups are not born vulnerable: they are rendered vulnerable through processes of social marginalization and exclusion. This chapter also reviews efforts to measure disaster vulnerability.

Chapter 7 focuses on disaster resilience: what it is, what factors contribute to it, and why it is relevant to our understanding of why some segments of society are able to cope successfully with disasters while others are not. Discussions in this chapter focus a good deal on the concept of social capital as it relates to disaster resilience. Like Chapter 6, this chapter provides an overview of efforts to measure resilience as well as to improve it by reducing disaster vulnerability (among other strategies). Although the concept of resilience is ubiquitous in disaster research and practice, it is also contested, and in this chapter we will review critiques of it.

Chapter 8 offers ideas about what we can expect in the future in the way of future disasters, as processes of global environmental change inexorably proceed. New threats are emerging, including threats associated with our growing dependence on an increasingly vulnerable power grid and cyber-infrastructure.

2

Disaster Research in Historical Context

Early Insights and Recent Trends

Introduction

In this chapter I offer a general overview of the field of disaster research, with an emphasis on contributions from sociology and geography. I then move on to discuss major critiques that were launched against classic disaster and hazards research. This discussion is followed by an overview of subsequent trends in the evolution of the field—especially the growing emphasis on vulnerability as a central topic for research, the introduction of perspectives highlighting power and inequality in the genesis of disasters and in disaster victimization, and the recognition of the importance of axes of inequality such as class, race, and gender in producing disaster impacts and outcomes. We will see how an international network of researchers has formed over time and how the field has matured, as indicated by the growing number of research centers devoted to the social dimensions of hazards and disasters as well as by that of specialist journals in the field. Chapter narratives will also emphasize how particular disaster events shaped sociological research over time. The themes discussed in this chapter are meant to introduce readers to key ideas in the sociological study of disasters that will be explored in the main body of this book.

Disaster Research: Origins and Early Years

Notwithstanding important early research by Samuel Prince (1920) and Lowell Carr (1932), disaster research began as an organized discipline in the United States in the late 1940s. The original impetus for research on disasters came from the US military. The United States' use of nuclear weapons against Japan in World War II and the Soviet Union's successful nuclear test in August 1949 ushered in a period in which the two enemy states and the world at large were forced to contemplate the possibility of nuclear war. One topic of interest was how members of the public would react in the face of nuclear destruction. War planners were wondering whether panic and hysteria would result, whether collective demoralization would set in, or whether residents in bomb-stricken areas would be psychologically willing and able to cope with the terror of nuclear war and begin to rebuild their communities; and this was not the first time that such concerns were being addressed. Findings from the World War II Strategic Bombing Surveys in Europe and Japan suggested that even the most intensive bombing campaigns were unsuccessful in destroying community morale; the bombing actually improved morale. However, those findings were downplayed by military leaders who championed air power and bombs as a way to win wars (Quarantelli 1987; Knowles 2011).

Initial research into the societal dimensions of disasters focused on an event that resembled what might take place in wartime. In August 1948 an air inversion in Donora, Pennsylvania resulted in a toxic smog that killed twenty residents and sickened approximately 7,000—about half of the population in that community. The Army Chemical Center (ACC), which played a role in US chemical warfare planning, sent a team of psychiatrists to look into the deadly smog episode, in an effort to better understand the psychological effects it had on the population; the idea was that such a study could provide insights into possible public reactions to the use of chemical weapons. One finding was that residents who were not exposed to the toxic smog exhibited reactions similar to those of residents who had been directly exposed. This suggested that psychological as well as physiological factors were at play and that chemical weapons could in principle cause panic or other adverse effects in exposed populations.

The ACC asked the National Opinion Research Center (NORC) at the University of Chicago to conduct a more in-depth study of the Donora episode, but it proved difficult for the center to recruit and train enough field staff to collect all the needed time-sensitive data on public responses. The ACC went on to establish a contract with NORC whereby the latter would train University of Chicago social science graduate students and send them into the field, on a quick-response basis, after major disasters. More than a dozen students were recruited and trained in field methods. Emergencies that took place in and around Chicago were used as training opportunities.

NORC subsequently conducted several quick-response studies on different types of community emergencies, and in 1952 it undertook its first large-scale research project following a deadly tornado that struck White County, Arkansas. The study, which involved face-to-face interviews with 342 residents, yielded a large amount of data on public responses immediately before the tornado struck; the respondents' perceptions of threat at the time of impact; their observations about the behavior of others during the impact period; psychological and behavioral responses after impact, including participation in search and rescue activities; and their emotional responses and behavior in the days and weeks after the disaster. Enrico (Henry) Quarantelli, who was among the original NORC team members, later noted that the findings from this seminal study were replicated many times in subsequent research. For example, the White County study found that

[s]elf control is maintained in extreme threat situations. Panic or wild flight, hysterical breakdown, affective immobility are almost non-existent . . . Those in danger try to help one another. Because persons are very frightened or afraid does not mean that they will fail to try and take protective actions . . . Passivity is not characteristic of the immediate post-impact period. The initial and by far the greatest amount of search and rescue is undertaken on the spot by survivors . . . Severe mental health problems are not occasioned on any scale by disasters . . . Convergence on a disaster site is a major problem . . . There may be widespread stories of looting, but actual cases of looting are very rare in post-impact situations. (Quarantelli 1988: 305)

These findings contradicted war planners' expectations about public reactions under conditions of extreme stress. Rather than revealing pathological or antisocial patterns of behavior, the early NORC studies characterized disaster victims as levelheaded (even though fearful) and willing to engage in a variety of pro-social behaviors.

The pioneering NORC studies were significant for their contributions to the subsequent growth of the field. Charles Fritz, who played an important role in establishing the NORC disaster teams, went on to direct studies that were conducted by the Committee on Disaster Studies and the Disaster Research Group at the National Academy of Sciences and became a central figure in disaster-related activities at the Academy. Under Fritz's direction, the Academy carried out approximately 160 disaster studies during the 1950s (for more detail, see Quarantelli 1987). It was also Fritz who formulated what is probably the best-known definition of disaster:

[a]n event, concentrated in time and space, in which a society, or a relatively self-sufficient subdivision of a society, undergoes severe danger and incurs such losses to its members and physical appurtenances that the social structure is disrupted and the fulfillment of all or some of the essential functions of the society is prevented. (Fritz 1961: 655)

Henry Quarantelli went on to become one of the founders of the Disaster Research Center (DRC), which was the first place of its kind in the world: a center devoted to the study of the social and behavioral aspects of disasters. Established in 1963 at Ohio State University, DRC moved in 1985 to the University of Delaware, where it continues to operate. In 1962, Quarantelli and DRC co-founders Russell Dynes and J. Eugene Haas—who, like Quarantelli, were professors in the sociology department at Ohio State University—submitted a proposal to the National Science Foundation requesting support for disaster studies. Somehow—and the three sociologists never did find out how this happened—the proposal made its way both to the Air Force Office of Scientific Research and to the US Office of Civil Defense. Significant funding followed. What had originally been a request for $50,000 for a project designed to take up eighteen months subsequently became a five-year $1,000,000 grant from the Office of Civil Defense—nearly $8 million in 2017 dollars (Knowles 2011).

At the time of its founding, the DRC conducted both laboratory and field studies. A key focus of the center's laboratory research, which was funded by the US Air Force, was on organizational responses to stress. In one laboratory study, groups of police dispatchers were brought into the lab and asked to respond during a simulated plane crash. In this scripted simulation study, DRC staff members relayed messages to the dispatchers that were designed to increase their stress levels. The objective was to learn how communication and decision-making patterns change when organizations are faced with excessive demands (Drabek and Haas 1969).

Initial DRC field studies focused on a variety of different disaster types, including floods, fires, a dam break in Italy, and major explosions. The 1964 Great Alaska earthquake gave the DRC its first opportunity to conduct fieldwork in a truly major disaster. DRC field teams carried out research beginning in the immediate post-earthquake period and continuing until nearly two years later; they conducted over 500 tape-recorded interviews and collected numerous reports and other materials in various earthquake-stricken communities (Anderson 2014). When the National Academy of Sciences established a committee on the Alaska earthquake, DRC researchers were represented on the committee and made a number of contributions to the Academy's reports. Much of DRC's research on the earthquake focused on organizational performance, adaptation, and change following the earthquake, but there was also an emphasis on groups made of up community residents that formed spontaneously in the earthquake's aftermath. Dubbed "emergent groups," these informal responders became a continuing area of interest for DRC and for other disaster researchers (Brouillette and Quarantelli 1971; Stallings and Quarantelli 1985). The Great Alaska earthquake studies were also marked by a focus on community recovery; the Alaska case was subsequently included in the volume *Reconstruction Following Disaster* (Haas, Kates, and Bowden 1977). Notwithstanding this concern with longer-term recovery issues, the Alaska study and many of the studies that followed placed significantly more emphasis on response patterns during the immediate post-impact period.

The general conceptual model that guided these early studies was based on two related theoretical perspectives that were influential at the time: structural functionalism and systems theory. As emphasized in Fritz's original definition of disaster, communities were seen by early researchers as consisting of systems and subsystems organized around the performance of key functions such as socialization, economic activity, and education. A disaster is a damaging event that disrupts the operations of these subsystems, making such functions impossible to perform. Because communities are systems, excessive demands such as those created by disasters result in a search for ways of returning to equilibrium—in this case, they stimulate efforts to enhance community capabilities so that those demands are met. The term "demand/ capability ratio" was employed to convey the idea that disasters happen when demands exceed capabilities; under such conditions, organizations and communities must devise ways of coping. The use of the systems framework thus necessitated a focus on how organizations and service delivery systems adapt and change in the face of disaster-related demands, as well as on group emergence as a spontaneous strategy intended to cope with those demands. Researchers documented how responding organizations increase in size by taking on volunteers, how resources converge from outside disaster-stricken areas, how entities that previously had no disaster-related responsibilities get involved in disaster response, and how community-based groups emerge to carry out various response activities because official public safety agencies, which would normally carry out those tasks, are overwhelmed.

Originating as it did at the University of Chicago, early disaster research was also influenced by symbolic interactionism, as formulated by Chicago sociology professor Herbert Blumer. An important methodological tenet of symbolic interactionism was the notion that, in order to gain access to the common understandings and interpretations that members of a social setting develop through interaction, it is necessary to observe that interaction directly (Blumer 1969). This was part of the reason for entering the field as rapidly as possible after disaster impact. Early fieldworkers were not interested in retrospective interpretations of response activities—as presented, for example, in after-action reports and other official documents. Instead, they sought to get as close to the "action" as possible in actual disaster situations and to gather information from those engaged in response activities before memories had a chance to fade. They found that entrée was not difficult during crises and that agency staff members were often surprisingly candid during the post-disaster emergency period, as opposed to weeks or months later. The symbolic interactionist approach also influenced field teams' data collection methods in other ways. Open-ended face-to-face interviews were favored over closed-ended surveys, because they allowed interviewees to raise issues and offer explanations in their own words. Interviews were recorded, transcribed, and coded as a way of ensuring that the study participants' own accounts were preserved for analysis.

In addition to developing the symbolic interactionist perspective in social psychology, Herbert Blumer was a founder of the sociological subfield of collective behavior—that is, the study of the social behavior that emerges in conditions of social disruption and normative uncertainty; this subfield examines behaviors such as extreme crowd enthusiasm, crowd violence, panic, and social movements (Blumer 1939). Blumer's collective behavior scholarship influenced Quarantelli, who as a graduate student set out to conduct research on panic behavior and found that panic was difficult to study because it occurred so infrequently, even in dangerous, terrifying situations like disasters (Quarantelli 1954). However, early DRC studies did identify many other types of emergent behavior, such as the spontaneous formation of search and rescue groups, and a focus on emergence remained a part of the DRC research repertoire (for a discussion of the focus on collective behavior in early disaster research, see Wenger 1987).

From the mid-1960s to the early 1970s, the DRC branched out to conduct studies on episodes of urban unrest such as the 1965 Watts riots. Research again focused on organizations involved in responding during those disturbances, for example fire and police departments, but also emphasized innovative organizations that often developed to deal with civil unrest, for example rumor control centers, or emergent groups, for example counter-rioters, or groups that organized themselves to discourage violence. In addition to findings on organizational responses, DRC research yielded important insights regarding the selective and symbolic nature of looting and arson during civil disturbances, and these contradicted popular images of riots as involving irrational acts and behavioral contagion (Quarantelli and Dynes 1970).

During the 1970s, DRC research began to focus not only on individual organizations undergoing stress but also on service delivery systems, or collections of organizations that seek to coordinate their activities in order to provide the services needed in the aftermath of disasters. Important among these were mental health and emergency medical service systems. Following the deadly 1974 tornado in Xenia, Ohio, which took place not far from DRC's base in Columbus in the same state, field and survey research methods were employed to gain a better understanding of the ways in which mental health services were provided in a post-disaster context (Taylor, Ross, and Quarantelli 1977). Public Law 93-288 (now known as the Robert T. Stafford Disaster Relief and Emergency Assistance Act, or the Stafford Act), which was passed in 1974, specified that crisis counseling services should be made available following disasters, but little was known about how programs were being implemented on the ground; nor was much known at that time about the extent to which disasters caused mental health problems. Mental health services for underserved rural communities were also a focus in DRC research during that period.

The decade of the 1970s also saw federal government efforts to improve emergency medical services, for example through the Emergency Medical Service Systems Act of 1973 (Public Law 93-154), and here again the DRC undertook a series of studies to determine how such systems functioned in disasters and large-scale emergencies. The study involved rapid response fieldwork in twenty-nine mass casualty events, including both natural disasters and human-caused or technological events such as bombings, explosions, and toxic chemical releases. The DRC also conducted fieldwork in events where the crowds were so large that the possibility of greater-than-usual demands on emergency care systems was high, for example the Mardi Gras celebrations in

New Orleans, the Kentucky Derby, and the large bicentennial celebrations that took place in Washington, DC and in Philadelphia in 1976 (see Quarantelli, Taylor, and Tierney 1977; Tierney and Taylor 1977).

Several research themes are evident in this brief review. Although pre-event preparedness and recovery were not totally ignored, the overwhelming focus of these studies was on the immediate post-crisis period. Most of the research centered on the performance of organizations that were officially designated as having disaster-related responsibilities—although there was also an emphasis on emergence. To a large extent, the research topics that were addressed were consistent with the needs of federal policymakers and planners. This connection may have been more explicit at the time of the field's founding, but, for at least the first thirty years, there was invariably some linkage between the research that was conducted and federal government policy, whether centering on war planning, urban unrest and riot control, disaster mental health, emergency medical care, or some other topic.

Finally, the desire to debunk both official and commonsense beliefs about human behavior in disasters was evident in early disaster studies. Beginning with some of the first post-disaster studies such as the one conducted in White County, myths surrounding panic, "disaster shock," collective demoralization, negative mental health sequelae, and looting and other antisocial behavior were contradicted by empirical studies of disasters and replaced by images of widespread pro-social behavior and organizational problem-solving. Positive aspects of community responses were highlighted: disasters were characterized as giving rise to "therapeutic communities," as being accompanied by "status leveling" and a reduction in community conflict, and as leading to positive outcomes such as increased feelings of self-efficacy. The message emerging from pioneering studies is perhaps best summed up in the title of an article that appeared in 1977 in *Psychology Today*, which was "Good News About Disasters" (Taylor 1977). As I have noted elsewhere (Tierney 2007) this "good news" frame masked important aspects of disaster, such as intergroup conflict, that came to the fore in later studies.

The Natural Hazards Tradition

The second major strain of research in the United States also had its origins at the University of Chicago, in the work of geographer Gilbert White. White's 1945 Chicago dissertation focused on what he termed the "human adjustment to floods," and the concept of alternative adjustments in the face of hazards was central to his analytic approach. The dissertation is probably best known for White's assertion that "floods are acts of God, but flood losses are largely acts of man. Human encroachment upon the flood plains of rivers accounts for the high annual total of flood losses" (White 1945: 2). In other words, it is human decisions and actions that mainly determine the extent to which naturally occurring events become damaging and disruptive.

According to White's framework, developed in collaboration with Robert Kates of Clark University, Ian Burton of the University of Toronto, and others, communities, societies, and social actors in general can choose among a range of adjustments when confronting hazards. These alternative adjustments include engineered works such as levees and dams, hazard-specific adjustments such as raising properties so as to avoid floods, land use controls, warning systems, emergency response measures, disaster relief programs, and risk-spreading through insurance. This emphasis on the spectrum of possible adjustments was in sharp contradiction to US flood management policies, which emphasized engineering solutions to the flood problem. White was deeply suspicious of the nation's overreliance on technological solutions to flood-related problems and was convinced that such measures were solutions in name only, as indicated in a 1958 report on which he was the senior author, which showed that federal investments in engineered flood control works subsequent to the 1936 Flood Control Act had actually resulted in increased rather than decreased flood losses.

Countering such policies and advancing the idea that adjustments are an appropriate topic for study, White and his colleagues emphasized that there are multiple ways of reducing flood losses and that how that objective is achieved is a matter of choice. For hazard managers, following Herbert Simon's formulation, bounded rather than strict rationality shapes these choices. Far from being perfectly rational human beings who weigh the costs and benefits associated with their decisions and who have complete information about alternative choices, actual human beings are "bounded" in their decision-making by their own cognitive limitations and by incomplete information. Following that logic, White made a key distinction between the theoretical range of choice—that is, all the adjustments that have been, or could feasibly be, carried out in a given setting—and the practical range of choice, which is always more narrow, owing to lack of awareness and various other social and cultural constraints (Burton, Kates, and White 1978). At the individual level, choices are influenced by such factors as hazard perception, experience, personality traits, and social roles. At low levels of hazard perception, it is likely that no adjustments will be considered, but above that threshold choices are influenced by knowledge about available adjustments and evaluations regarding their suitability in light of criteria such as technical feasibility and the possibility of economic gain. Community-level decisions regarding hazard adjustments can shape individual choices, just as nationally adopted loss-reduction policies shape choices at the community level.

In emphasizing the concept of adjustments, White was following Harlan Barrows, an influential mentor at the University of Chicago. Earlier on Barrows had made a strong case for viewing geography as the study of human ecology, a field that, in his words, attempts to

> make clear the relationships existing between natural environments and the distribution and activities of man. Geographers will, I think, be wise to view this problem in general from the standpoint of man's adjustment to environment. (Barrows 1923: 3)

Barrows's insistence that geography should be reframed as the study of human ecology was consistent with the emphasis that later came to be placed on human ecology within other disciplines at the University of Chicago, most notably in the sociology of Robert E. Park (1936). In addition to advocating for a definition of geography as human ecology, Barrows also argued that the field should deemphasize subspecialties such as physiography and climatology in favor of social, economic, and historical studies, and also that geographers should get out of the library and into the field. White heeded these admonitions in every respect.

White gained many of his insights into the causes of flood disasters while working in water resource and other agencies in Washington, DC during the New Deal period. He became president of Haverford College in 1946, at the age of thirty-five, then in 1956 moved back to the University of Chicago, where he began a systematic program of research that focused primarily on flood hazards, but later branched out to consider in more detail different adjustments to natural hazards (Hinshaw 2006).

White's research on natural hazard adjustments expanded further, both before and after his move to the University of Colorado in 1970. Between 1968 and 1972, under the auspices of the International Geographic Union and with funding from the National Science Foundation, he organized and led a series of studies on the characteristics of and responses to nearly a dozen different hazards in different societal settings and communities. His main collaborators in this research were Ian Burton and Robert Kates. The results of these investigations appeared in a volume edited by White and entitled *Natural Hazards: Local, National, Global* (White 1974) and in a number of articles. In addition to its focus on specific hazards, the *Natural Hazards* volume contained sections on hazard perceptions and decision processes, general summaries of the human response to tropical cyclones, floods, and earthquakes, and reviews of hazard loss reduction policies in New Zealand, Canada, Japan, and the Soviet Union. At around the same time, with funding from the National Science Foundation, White and J. Eugene Haas, who had moved to the University of Colorado, launched an assessment of hazards research in the United States. The assessment project had several goals: to document the significance of hazards in national life; to explore the social, economic, and policy consequences of the adoption of different hazard adjustments; to identify areas in which new research on hazards would yield benefits to society; and to propose a program for future research.

A key theme in the final project report for the assessment was that "[n]atural hazards research in our nation is spotty, largely uncoordinated, and concentrated in physical and technological fields" (White and Haas 1975: 5). The assessment report made a strong case for the need for more research expenditures on the social, economic, and political dimensions of hazard adjustments: they should be comparable, for example, to expenditures in the engineering disciplines. In particular, the report emphasized the need for research on five adjustments that are common to most hazards that the nation faced: relief and rehabilitation, insurance, warning systems, technological aids such as engineered works, and land use management. Among the report's other recommendations were calls for "post-audits"—that is, systematic comparative studies of disasters that would be conducted by multidisciplinary teams—as well as for longitudinal studies of disaster recovery processes.

The report also called for the establishment of a clearinghouse service that would facilitate communication among the people involved in studying different adjustments to hazards and the practitioners involved in developing and implementing adjustments. That recommendation became a reality with the founding of the Natural Hazards Research and Applications Information Center (NHRAIC) at the University of Colorado in 1976. With funding from the National Science Foundation and under the leadership of White and Haas, the NHRAIC became the second major center in the United States that was devoted to research and training in the field of hazards and disasters.

In line with what White and Haas had recommended in the assessment, the NHRAIC was staffed by graduate students from different disciplines. And, in line with White's original vision, much of the research conducted in the early years of the NHRAIC continued to center on specific hazard adjustments. For example, among the first generation of NHRAIC trainees, Dennis Mileti, who was a graduate student in sociology, then a faculty member at Colorado State University and, later, director of the NHRAIC, specialized in research on hazard warnings and warning systems, then branched out into the study of risk communication more generally, including communications to the public concerning earthquake predictions (Mileti 1975; Mileti and O'Brien 1992; Mileti and Fitzpatrick 1993; Mileti and Darlington 1997). Geographer Eve Gruntfest also specialized in hazard warnings and warning responses, particularly in the context of flash flooding. Psychologist Michael Lindell focused on a variety of topics, including warning and evacuation, but a substantial portion of his research investigated the adoption of adjustments to different types of hazards (Lindell et al. 1997; Lindell and Perry 2000; Lindell, Arlikatti, and Prater 2009).

Gilbert White is considered among the most influential geographers of the twentieth century, not only for his work in the area of natural hazards but also for his research on water resources and other environmental issues and for his influence on public policy in the areas of flood plain management and flood insurance. His emphasis on human adjustments to hazards provided a useful complement to the DRC's focus on disaster events and subsequent responses. To an even greater extent than the DRC's founders, White was interested in the practical implications of his work for policy, particularly federal government policy. His ideas had a major impact on the US National Flood Insurance Program (NFIP), although he was also a major critic of that program. He wanted the insights from his and others' research to influence science policy and even went as far as to suggest what levels of funding should be allocated to different hazard-related issues. Beyond policy, White also believed that the purpose of geography and other fields of study was to enroll science in the service of the broader good and to bring about positive social change (Kates 2011).

The "good news about disasters" theme and White's emphasis on choice and on the study of alternative adjustments to hazards reflected both broader disciplinary tendencies and personal ways of viewing the world. Adherence to the "good news" frame, which contradicted official and popular notions of what happens when disasters strike, was consistent with the idea that sociology should be a debunking science (Berger 1963). Disaster and hazards research developed in a functionalist intellectual milieu that emphasized the smooth (if occasionally disrupted) operation of social systems and eschewed Marxian or other conflict-oriented theories about society–environment relations. Both White's Quaker faith and his intellectual projects emphasized the need for harmony with and adjustments to nature, as opposed to control over nature through technological means (Hinshaw 2006).

Ways of seeing are also ways of not seeing; by illuminating certain aspects of hazards and disasters, the activities of these pioneering centers also created blind spots. In the early decades of the field, neither center paid much attention to the role of political power or social inequality in disaster victimization. In foregrounding organizational and group responses to disasters, DRC research elided the ways in which community and supracommunity factors affect disaster responses. White's vision of individuals and hazard managers exercising rational choice—albeit bounded by cognitive and other limitations—was influenced by emerging research in behavioral economics (for a discussion, see Kunreuther and Slovic 1986), but without much recognition that many at-risk groups have essentially no choice about shielding themselves from hazard-related risks, because those risks are imposed on them.[1]

Both centers were active in the training of subsequent generations of disaster researchers, including several who went on to found and direct research centers. Because the centers were so prolific, their output—both of ideas and of human resources—helped foster a kind of disaster orthodoxy. However, over time classic perspectives began to be supplanted by new and heterodox approaches to understanding the causes and consequences of disasters.

Trends in the Study of Hazards and Disasters

Critiques of disaster orthodoxy

Disaster orthodoxy began to be seriously challenged during the 1980s. Elsewhere (Tierney 2007; 2014) I have written about the significance and subsequent influence of the multicontributor volume *Interpretations of Calamity*, which was published in 1983 (Hewitt 1983b). Two chapters in *Interpretations* were especially important in terms of their critique of the reigning hazards and disasters frameworks. In the first chapter, Kenneth Hewitt opened with a broadside against what he termed the "dominant consensus" in the field of disaster research. Observing that contemporary disaster research was "certainly rich in the results of scientific enquiries" (Hewitt 1983a: 3), he went on to argue that

> [t]he applications of scientific research are not, however, its definitive feature. It may have internal coherence or at least conviction. That does not alter my sense that it capitalizes rather arbitrarily upon scientific discovery. Indeed it accords with "the facts" only insofar as they can be made to fit the assumptions, development and social predicaments of dominant institutions and research that has grown up serving them. (Hewitt 1983a: 3)

For Hewitt, disaster orthodoxy could best be understood as reflective of, and also as being in the service of, the social context in which it had developed: the technocratic, bureaucratic, managerial state. Drawing upon Foucault's (1965) *Madness and Civilization*, which analyzed how "madness" was socially constructed and managed, Hewitt argued that "[n]atural calamity in a technocratic society is much the same sort of pivotal dilemma as insanity for the champions of reason" (1983a: 9). Disasters constitute a challenge to the state's claims regarding its ability to manage and control, and the response of dominant institutions to this threat is to categorize disaster as separate from and discontinuous with "normal" social life and human–environment relations. Thus sequestered,

> [t]he geography of disaster is an *archipelago* of isolated misfortunes. Each is seen as a localized *dis*organization of space, projected upon the extensive map of human geography in a more or less random way due to independent events in the geophysical realms of atmosphere, hydrosphere, and lithosphere. More specifically, each disaster is an unplanned hole or rupture in the fabric of *productive* and orderly human relations with the habitat or "natural resources." (Hewitt 1983a: 12–13)

In Hewitt's telling, the discursive creation of disaster as an archipelago that is distinct from normal everyday life serves the interests of the state and dominant institutions by absolving them of any responsibility for creating disasters. To be consistent with the materialist and utilitarian ideology of the state and its agents, disaster must necessarily arise from outside the social order itself, as an accident or unanticipated event; in Hewitt's words, "to argue that government, business, science, or other institutions create disaster has been in a sense outlawed from rational discourse" (Hewitt 1983a: 17). This was the view that the dominant consensus uncritically supported.

A second and equally fierce critique was launched in a chapter by Paul Susman, Phil O'Keefe, and Ben Wisner entitled "Global disasters: A radical interpretation" (Susman, O'Keefe, and Wisner 1983). In these authors' view, disaster does not represent a disruption of normal life, as the dominant consensus would contend, but rather is a part of normal life, the consequence of political–economic processes within the dominant capitalist world system that result in marginalization and increased vulnerability. Following critiques of the concept of underdevelopment formulated by Andre Gunder Frank (1969), Tamas Szentes (1971), and others, the authors characterized underdevelopment not as a condition characteristic of countries in the so-called third world that have yet to "develop," but rather as the direct result of the processes by which nations at the core of world economy—that is, the United States, other western industrialized nations, and Japan—exploit nations outside that core. Because the core exercises hegemony over nations situated at the periphery, economic exchanges invariably result in negative impacts for peripheral nations, for example extreme poverty and poor governance, that are seen as characteristic of underdevelopment. Among the other effects of that hegemony are the increased marginalization of people living in peripheral countries and their increased vulnerability to environmental stressors, including environmental extremes.

The authors used the impact of Hurricane Fifi in Honduras to illustrate how these processes work. In the mid-twentieth century, US banana companies developed land in northern Honduras around the San Pedro Sula Valley, building roads and railways, clear-cutting forests, and attracting labor. The indigenous population could not live in the valley because that land was owned by the banana companies and used for irrigation. Instead, the population was forced to live and farm on hillsides that were deforested and subject to erosion. When the hurricane struck in 1974, it triggered flooding and numerous landslides, some of which buried entire villages. An estimated 5,000 people were killed.

Patterns such as these are reproduced across the world as exploitive exchanges originating at the core of the world system and make everyday life more tenuous for those who live in nations outside the core. As the processes that create underdevelopment intensify, the ability of populations to adapt to change decreases, which leaves them vulnerable to both chronic stressors and the occurrence of environmental extremes such as hurricanes.

The "discovery" of vulnerability

One of the key contributions of these authors was their effort to make the concept of vulnerability central to the study of disasters. They defined disaster vulnerability as

> the degree to which different classes in society are differentially at risk, both in terms of the probability of occurrence of an extreme physical event and [in terms of] the degree to which the community absorbs the effects of extreme physical events and helps different classes to recover. (Susman et al. 1983: 264)

This emphasis on class as a factor in differential risk was in part a reflection of the authors' Marxian theoretical commitments, but was also indicative of the extent to which other contributors to vulnerability, such as gender and race, had not yet been theorized. As discussed later in this chapter, those analyses were still to come.

Just over ten years after *Interpretations*, another volume was published that was written in a similar vein. *At Risk: Natural Hazards, People's Vulnerability, and Disasters* (Blaikie, Cannon, Davis, and Wisner, 1994; see also Wisner, Blaikie, Cannon, and Davis 2004) made the case that the production of vulnerability should be central to the study of disasters. Both the editors and the contributors characterize the vulnerability of individuals and groups as the result of a series of macro-, meso-, and microlevel economic and political processes, organized into what they called the "pressure and release" (PAR) model of disaster. Macrolevel factors, termed *root causes*, consist of broad global and national forces that affect the access to political power and economic resources and result in social, political, and economic inequities. Another set of factors, *dynamic pressures*, consists of the more immediate factors that represent the manifestation of root causes in particular social and historical contexts. For example, the structural adjustment programs and debt that have been forced on many countries at the global periphery are an instantiation of macrolevel globalization and neoliberalization processes. Other dynamic pressures can include such factors as the imposition of export-oriented agricultural practices and rapid urbanization. Dynamic pressures lead in turn to *unsafe conditions* within particular contexts. Thus structural adjustments and burdensome debt lead to decreased national investments in health, education, and welfare. Export-oriented agriculture leads to food insecurity and, potentially, to livelihood loss and migration. And rapid urbanization results in overcrowding, slum conditions, development of settlements in unsafe areas, and depletion of natural resources. Such factors contribute to vulnerability, which, if not offset by increases in coping capacity and access to resources that serve to release vulnerability-generating pressures, will disproportionately expose vulnerable populations to potential losses. One key point emphasized in *At Risk* is that individuals and groups are made vulnerable through linked sets of conditions that operate at different levels of analysis. It only takes a geophysical, atmospheric, or other kind of event of magnitude for disastrous losses to occur—losses that are disproportionately borne by the most vulnerable. Another point is that it is not the physical event itself that produces those losses. The event is merely a trigger; the losses are the result of processes that are internal to the social order.

The critiques of conventional disaster research advanced in *Interpretations* and *At Risk* began to subtly shift the field of hazards and disaster in several ways. First was the notion that disasters should be thought of not as discrete "unscheduled events" but rather as part of the social fabric itself—occurrences that are characteristic of the social settings in which they occur. Second was the related idea that the conditions that set the stage for disaster are the consequence of long-term political, economic, and environmental processes, such as unequal exchanges between core and peripheral nations in the world system, the exploitation of the natural resources of "underdeveloped" countries in the interest of capital accumulation, and subsequent resource depletion and environmental problems. Seen in this light, disasters are among the many negative consequences of the operations of global political economy. Third was the idea that processes that are pervasive within that global system push populations in exploited regions to the margins of their societies, force them to live in increasingly unsafe conditions, and undermine their capacity to adapt, making them vulnerable to disasters. As disaster scholar Steve Matthewman puts it, "events are merely processes made visible" (2015: 136). More generally, these conceptual and analytic shifts indicated an openness to using alternative paradigms such as world systems theory and Marxian critiques of global capitalism for the purpose of challenging fundamental assumptions not only about the social aspects of disasters but also about the practice of disaster research itself.

Geographers and development scholars were the main contributors *Interpretations* and *At Risk*, and the focus of those volumes was overwhelmingly on vulnerability, hazards, and disasters in less developed countries. However, during the decade of the 1990s, sociologists and other social scientists began to focus increasingly on issues related to disaster vulnerability within the US context. During that period and under the leadership of Dennis Mileti, the NHRAIC carried out a second assessment of research on natural hazards. That multi-year effort was funded in part by the National Science Foundation but mainly carried out by over one hundred researchers who volunteered, on their own time, to inventory knowledge on a range of hazards- and disaster-related topics. In tune with the center's historical roots, parts of the second assessment were concerned with research on hazard adjustments such as land use planning (Burby 1998), hazard insurance (Kunreuther and Roth 1998), the geographic dimensions of disasters (Cutter 2001), and disaster preparedness and response (Tierney, Lindell, and Perry 2001). However, other scholars who worked on the second assessment focused on factors associated with differential disaster vulnerability such as gender (Fothergill 1996; 1998), race and ethnicity (Fothergill, Maestas, and Darlington 1999), and poverty (Fothergill and Peek 2004). The influence of earlier critiques of disaster orthodoxy and of work highlighting the centrality of vulnerability is clear in many of the analyses produced by the second assessment. For example, in their article on poverty and disaster vulnerability, Fothergill and Peek argue that

> there has been a false separation of hazards and the social system because of the lack of widespread recognition of connections between the daily risks people face and the reasons for their vulnerability to hazards and disasters. Indeed, disasters are the products of the social, political, and economic environment, as well as the natural events that cause them. (Fothergill and Peek 2004: 89)

During this same time period, a series of urban disasters and crisis events took place in the United States that further revealed the ways in which societal diversity can translate into differential vulnerability to disasters. In particular, research on the societal dimensions of the 1989 Loma Prieta earthquake, of the 1992 Los Angeles uprising, of Hurricane Andrew in 1992, which struck parts of Miami and southern Dade County, and of the 1994 Northridge earthquake uncovered patterns of unequal exposure to the potential for loss and poor recovery outcomes, as well as differences in coping capacity and access to the resources needed for recovery; and all these were associated with social class, race and ethnicity, citizenship status, and gender (Bolin and Stanford 1990; 1993; 1998; Phillips 1993; Tierney 1994). As researchers studied these and other US disasters, the need to focus on difference and diversity in disaster research became increasingly clear.

Space, place, and disaster

During the 1990s decade, researchers also began to couple a sensitivity to the role of diversity and inequality in structuring disaster vulnerability and outcomes with an awareness of the importance of understanding the forces that shape urban forms and help determine which populations are disproportionately exposed to hazards. For example, the multicontributor volume *Hurricane Andrew: Ethnicity, Gender, and the Sociology of Disasters* (Peacock, Morrow, and Gladwin 1997) contained research on axes of vulnerability such as gender, as well as studies that reflected insights from the fields of political ecology and critical urban studies—a synthetic approach that Peacock referred to as "sociopolitical ecology." In that volume, Peacock and Ragsdale argued, for example, that "[the] extraordinary influence exerted by powerful economic interests on government policy, land use patterns, and construction has important implications for disaster research ... pro-development interests can dramatically alter attempts to regulate development, financial decisions, and building practices" (Peacock et al. 1997: 29) and that understanding how these interests operate in different settings can tell us a lot about how and why events become disastrous and who suffers most when they do. Urban centers like Miami are shaped by these kinds of political–economic forces and by other social processes such as waves of migration and immigration and intergroup conflict and marginalization.

The *Hurricane Andrew* volume marked a return to the field's origins in the study of human ecology, but with a difference: spatial relations and patterns of settlement were highlighted, while conflicting political and economic interests and power differentials were identified as sources of disaster vulnerability and loss. The contributors to the volume discussed how Miami at the time of Andrew had been shaped over time by political, economic, and demographic forces in ways that had enabled a vibrant Cuban and Cuban American enclave to establish itself, marginalized the city's African American community, and allowed a white elite to maintain control over many of the city's most important institutions. When Andrew struck, disparities between those who possessed political and economic power and those who lacked it were reflected not only in patterns of damage and destruction but also in differential trajectories and outcomes of recovery. These disparities were traceable to such factors as residential segregation by race and ethnicity, the relegation of poor residents to hazardous residential structures, discriminatory practices in homeowner insurance coverage, and inequities in the provision of post-disaster assistance.

The *Hurricane Andrew* book also brought to the fore issues of gender and disaster vulnerability. In a chapter called "A gendered perspective," Elaine Enarson and Betty Hearn Morrow pointed out that

> [t]he effects of gender and gender relations have been virtually ignored in most disaster research, with few sources addressing women's wide range of involvement in disaster-stricken households and communities. Women and gender still remain largely absent even as organizing categories in the disaster literature. While sex as a bipolar variable is sometimes analyzed in quantitative studies, a complex gendered analysis is rare. (Enarson and Morrow 1997: 117)

The chapter then went on to provide composite profiles of women whose lives were disrupted by Andrew: a white social worker, an African American woman who was the head of a multigenerational family, a poor woman of Haitian descent, and a Cuban American businesswoman. Through these brief case studies, the authors showed how women's experiences of disaster were strongly shaped by gender, but also by race, ethnicity, and class—a treatment of gender issues that directly incorporated intersectionality. The year after the

Andrew volume came out, these same scholars edited *The Gendered Terrain of Disaster: Through Women's Eyes* (Enarson and Morrow 1998), which again argued strongly for placing gender on the disaster research agenda.

Institutionalizing a discipline

The history of disaster research has also been marked by growing ties among researchers in different countries and by international collaborations. As Dynes (1988) notes, there were episodic contacts between US investigators and ones in other countries as far back as the early 1950s. However, collaborations became more common in the 1970s and 1980s. Examples include collaborative research on public responses to volcano eruptions in the United States and Japan (Perry and Hirose 1983), mass media reporting in disasters in the United States and Japan (Hiroi, Mikami, and Miyata 1985; Quarantelli, Wenger, Mikami, and Hiroi 1993), and the public response to the 1985 Mexico City earthquake (Wenger and James 1994). This period also saw exchanges between US and Italian disaster researchers regarding theory and research (Dynes, De Marchi, and Pelanda 1987). Later on, the first edition of *What Is a Disaster? Perspectives on the Question* (Quarantelli 1998) included contributions by researchers from the United States, France, Germany, Russia, Canada, and the Netherlands.

The international dimension of social science disaster research was strengthened with the formation of the International Sociological Association's Research Committee on Disasters (RC 39) in 1986. The membership of the research committee includes not only sociologists but representatives from other social sciences. The research committee meets every four years at the World Congress of Sociology and also holds annual research sessions in the United States. It is the sponsor of one of the field's leading journals, the *International Journal of Mass Emergencies and Disasters (IJMEAD)*.

Earlier discussions focused on two pioneering research centers in the United States. Over time, many other centers have been established in the United States and around the world. Table 2.1 lists a selected group of centers and programs whose research focuses primarily on the societal aspects of hazards, disasters, and risk. The table is meant to provide a snapshot of research activities and does not include all the social–scientific institutions and programs that currently exist, or the many centers worldwide whose research activities focus on the physical science and engineering aspects of hazards and disasters, or those that conduct research in related areas, such as climate change and the environment more generally.

Another indicator of the field's maturity is the proliferation of professional journals devoted to social–scientific aspects of disasters. Disaster researchers frequently publish in key journals in their respective fields—anthropology, economics, geography, psychology and mental health, sociology, and so

Table 2.1 Examples of hazard-, disaster-, and risk-related centers and programs.

Center or Program	Location
Center for Public Health and Disasters University of California, Los Angeles	United States
Centre for Research on the Epidemiology of Disasters School of Public Health, Catholic University of Louvain	Belgium
Copenhagen Center for Disaster Research University of Copenhagen	Denmark
Disaster Research Center University of Delaware	United States
Hazard Reduction and Recovery Center Texas A&M University	United States
Hazards and Vulnerability Research Institute University of South Carolina	United States
Institute for Catastrophic Loss Reduction Western University	Canada
Joint Centre for Disaster Research Massey University	Australia
National Center for Disaster Preparedness Earth Institute, Columbia University	United States
Natural Hazards Center University of Colorado Boulder	United States
Population Impact, Recovery, and Resilience Program College of Global Public Health, New York University	United States
Red de Estudios Sociales en Prevencion de Desastres en America (Network for Social Studies on Disaster Prevention In Latin America)—LA RED	Panama
Research Center for Disaster Reduction Systems Disaster Prevention Research Institute, Kyoto University	Japan
Resilient Organisations	New Zealand
Risk and Resilience Program International Institute for Advanced Systems Analysis (IIASA)	Austria
UCL Institute for Risk and Disaster Reduction University College London	United Kingdom
Wharton Risk Management and Decision Processes Center University of Pennsylvania	United States

on—but they also publish extensively in specialty journals in the disaster field. Examples of such journals are the aforementioned *International Journal of Mass Emergencies and Disasters*, *Disasters*, the *Journal of Disaster Studies, Policy, and Management*, the *Journal of Contingencies and Crisis Management*, *Natural Hazards Review*, the *Journal of Homeland Security and Emergency Management*, *Prehospital and Disaster Medicine*, *Global Environmental Change, Part B: Environmental Hazards*, the *International Journal of Disaster Risk Reduction*, the *Journal of Disaster Research*, *Disaster Prevention and Management*, and the *International Journal of Disaster Risk Science*.

Watershed Events: 9–11, Katrina, the Indian Ocean Tsunami, and the 2011 Japan Triple Disaster

The first five years of the twenty-first century marked the occurrence of large-scale and even catastrophic disasters. For sociologists, the September 11 attacks on the World Trade Center called attention to various forms of emergent activity and organization at different levels of analysis. The unprecedented nature of the attacks created the demand for the performance of a variety of tasks for which there were no plans, such as evacuating tens of thousands of people from Lower Manhattan, reconstituting a big-city emergency operations center literally from the ground up, conducting search and rescue while attempting to preserve a crime scene, and simultaneously removing massive amounts of debris and searching for and identifying human remains. In the face of these and other challenges, responding agencies were forced to improvise, and researchers sought to understand how such improvisation came about. Improvisational activities had been studied before by disaster sociologists, most notably Gary Kreps (1985), but Kreps's research had relied primarily on archival material collected in past disasters. The September 11 disaster gave researchers the opportunity to observe improvisation unfolding essentially in real time, as responders grappled with the fact that, while emergency plans provided guidance for the performance of some tasks, there were literally no plans in place for others.

The largest terrorist attack in US history by many orders of magnitude, the World Trade Center disaster was followed by a massive convergence of uniformed responders, some of whom came literally from across the country, volunteers, donations of all types, and groups and organizations with no designated disaster responsibilities that simply wished to provide assistance. This large-scale response resulted in extensive emergence at the network level, as official and unofficial responders established communication, coordination, and information-sharing linkages that grew and evolved over time and space. Here again, the study of emergent response networks was not entirely new in disaster sociology; Thomas Drabek and his collaborators had studied search and rescue networks in the 1980s (Drabek, Tamminga, Kilijanek, and Adams 1981). What was new was the systematic application of network-analytic methods, including specialized computer software and analysis techniques, to an extremely large and dynamic response network. These types of methods were subsequently used in the study of other disaster events.

The 9–11 attacks ushered in a period that was marked by what many consider extreme reactions to the terrorist threat on the part of the Bush administration, Congress, and officialdom at large. Of interest in the context of sociological disaster research are such trends as the massive bureaucratization of emergency management that accompanied the creation of the US Department of Homeland Security; the framing of terrorism as a major risk to the nation, which superseded concern with hazards and disasters; and a tilt toward a stricter "command-and-control" approach to managing large-scale events. Prior to 9–11, sociological and other social science research had been somewhat successful in influencing emergency management policies and practices, as evidenced, for example, by its incorporation into widely used textbooks and training materials in the emergency management field, for example the courses offered by the Federal Emergency Management Agency (FEMA)'s Emergency Management Institute. Sociological research had provided information on such topics as how the public responds in disaster situations—that is, in non-panicky, pro-social ways—and why more decentralized response systems that are capable of accommodating emergency are preferable to hierarchical command-and-control structures. However, many of these research lessons were lost and many disaster myths were revived after 9–11, which led to critical responses on the part of some sociologists and other social scientists.

If researchers and the general public needed a reminder of the catastrophic potential of disasters, that reminder came on December 26, 2004, when a massive earthquake measuring approximately 9.0 on the Richter scale caused a tsunami that propagated throughout the Indian Ocean, killing an estimated 230,000 people in fourteen countries. Coastal areas in Indonesia, Sri Lanka, India, and Thailand were the ones hardest hit, as entire villages and their inhabitants were washed away. The tsunami catastrophe raised important questions regarding the need for effective warning systems and what should be done to assist at-risk populations in responding to disasters such as the Indian Ocean tsunami, in which warning periods may be very short. With so much devastation, the tsunami also shed light on issues related to disaster recovery, including questions about population relocation and the recovery of livelihoods for those affected.

Then came the event that marked a sea change in the sociological study of disasters: Hurricane Katrina in August 2005. While federal agencies were still in the process of devising plans for responding to terrorism, including attacks that employed all manner of exotic chemical, biological, and nuclear weapons, Katrina brought death and devastation to a wide swath of the Gulf region. Katrina's impacts shocked the nation and the world, but sociologists were not particularly surprised by what they saw during and after the catastrophe. It was well understood that hurricane-buffering natural protections such as wetlands had been depleted and that Louisiana levees would not be able to withstand the storm surge that a major hurricane would produce. It was also understood that New Orleans is essentially a "bowl" that would rapidly flood once the levees were breached. The racial and class disparities in access to self-protective measures such as evacuation were not a surprise, nor were the disparities in death rates. What perhaps did come as a shock was the sheer incompetence of responding agencies and the viciousness of the racially motivated attacks against Katrina survivors.

Many sociologists were drawn to conduct research on Katrina and its aftermath—both those who were experienced disaster researchers and those for whom disasters were a new topic of study. Studies were conducted by disaster specialists, but also by environmental and urban sociologists, demographers, gender scholars, and researchers from other sociological specialty areas. This influx of researchers from outside the disaster research community was valuable by bringing new theories, concepts, and methods into the study of disasters.

As it had after the September 11 attacks, the Social Science Research Council (SSRC) established a special website that featured scholarly commentary on Katrina from sociologists and other social scientists. The SSRC and several private foundations provided funding to a group of social scientists worked on a project called the Katrina Bookshelf—a series of books that have been or will be published by University of Texas Press. To date, five books have been released, focusing on the experience and impacts of post-disaster displacement (Weber and Peek 2012), the role of culture and connection in the recovery of a large African American extended family (Browne 2015), Katrina as collective trauma (Eyerman 2015), children's experiences and recovery (Fothergill and Peek 2015), and the recovery of African American neighborhoods (Kroll-Smith, Baxter, and Jenkins 2015). Other funding agencies, in particular the National Science Foundation, were also active in funding research on the sociological dimensions of the Katrina catastrophe.

The body of sociological research that was developed in the aftermath of Katrina represents the culmination of several of the trends discussed earlier in this chapter. More than before, Katrina research brought home the notion that the origins of disaster are endogenous, not exogenous, to the social order, and showed how these endogenous political and economic forces inscribe themselves on landscapes over time. The Katrina catastrophe provided stark examples of the ways in which processes of marginalization and vulnerability production operate at local and regional scales. And research highlighted as never before the ways in which class, race, and gender get imbricated in particular social settings and produce differential patterns of loss and recovery. Perhaps more so than other recent disaster events, Katrina pointed the way forward for subsequent sociological research.

In March 2011 the Great Tohoku earthquake caused a massive tsunami, which killed approximately 20,000 people and triggered a triple core meltdown at the Fukushima Daichi nuclear power plant—one of only two Level 7 nuclear plant disasters since the inception of that technology (the other Level 7 event was the 1986 Chernobyl disaster). Taking into account the entire cascade of events, this was the most costly disaster in history, and its many dimensions have raised important questions for sociological research. Some of the most important ones relate to the causes of catastrophic failures in risky technologies. It has been more than thirty years since the publication of Charles Perrow's (1984) influential book *Normal Accidents: Living with High-Risk Technologies*, and much has been written about the ways in which organizations and institutions can discount hazards and drift into practices that cause risks to proliferate—and how they can cause disasters that in hindsight appear to have been entirely avoidable. The Fukushima disaster was a stark reminder that such pathologies continue to operate, even in advanced industrial societies that pride themselves on being safety-conscious.

Hurricanes that occurred in the United States in 2012 and 2017 highlighted the interaction between climate change and extreme events. In 2012 Hurricane/Superstorm Sandy struck the greater New York City area at high tide, causing a storm surge that was made more intensely damaging by the sea-level rise. In 2017, three major hurricanes—Harvey, Irma, and Maria—caused extensive damage respectively in Texas, Florida, and US territories in the Caribbean. In all three cases, hurricanes formed and strengthened because of warming waters in the Atlantic Ocean and Gulf of Mexico. Climate change was also a factor in the extreme rainfall that accompanied Harvey. These events added further to discussions about the relationship between slow-onset phenomena associated with climate change and disaster events, and about the relationship between climate change adaptation and disaster mitigation.

In this chapter I focused first on the origins of social science disaster research in the United States, with an emphasis on research in the fields of sociology and geography, as embodied in the work of pioneering research centers. In addition to describing the conceptual frameworks that guided early studies, I also traced the history of critiques that were launched against those frameworks, beginning with perspectives in critical geography in the early 1980s. The field evolved as a consequence of these critiques and of new formulations such as those presented in the seminal volume *At Risk*, but also as a consequence of disaster events whose impacts on diverse populations raised fundamental questions regarding the inequality–vulnerability nexus. Shifts in emphasis in the sociology of disasters also mirrored trends in the larger field of sociology, albeit slowly. Originating at a time when conflict-oriented perspectives such as Marxism had reached the nadir of their influence in US academia, sociological disaster research eventually followed the broader trend of increasingly incorporating ideas influenced by those perspectives, such as political economy and political ecology. The emphasis on gender issues in disasters was also a reflection of broader trends in sociology. In the chapter that follows, we turn to the ways in which research in other social science fields has contributed to sociological disaster research.

3

Sociological Research on Disasters
Key Contributions from Other Disciplines

Introduction

The ingredients necessary for the sociological study of disasters do not reside solely within the discipline itself. Sociology and its various subfields are so broad that they often merge into adjacent or complementary fields. Cross-fertilization is also evident in the area of methods; for example, while originally developed by geographers, various types of spatial analysis are now widely employed by sociologists and other social scientists. As fields have become increasingly multi- and interdisciplinary, disciplinary boundaries have become more porous. This is particularly true in problem-focused fields such as disaster research (and environmental studies more generally), which can involve teams of researchers from different subject matter areas and a good deal of borrowing and synthesis across disciplines.

Additionally, sociologists who study disasters almost always find that they must have some familiarity with the scientific and engineering aspects of different disaster agents, both to understand how and why those agents cause harm and loss and to have their work viewed as credible in those disciplines. They also have to be knowledgeable about public policies that are relevant within the disaster context as well as about private-sector approaches to reducing disaster losses, such as insurance.

For these reasons, we should take a broad view of what constitutes the sociology of disasters. Disaster sociology can best be considered a sociological subfield that draws upon research conducted in other social and policy sciences and that is catholic with respect to methods. Within this big tent, the sociology of disasters has evolved both by employing perspectives that are sui generis and by borrowing creatively from ones developed in other disciplines. For the purposes of my discussion, what matters is not so much whether specific disaster studies are carried out by bona fide sociologists, but rather whether their findings are sociologically relevant and rest upon assumptions that are consistent with sociological reasoning. The perspective adopted in this volume, while still arguing for a distinctively sociological approach to the study of disasters, recognizes that sociological research on disasters often relies on findings from other fields.

With those caveats in mind, the present chapter focuses on how perspectives and findings from other disciplines have shaped the knowledge base within the field of disaster sociology. The emphasis is on six fields: anthropology, economics, geography, political science and public administration, psychology, and urban planning. This is not meant to be an exhaustive account of each and every contribution from outside the discipline of sociology; rather the intent is to provide examples of contributions from a select group of disciplines that have had a significant influence on sociological thought on the subject of disasters. A more inclusive and in-depth examination of the contributions of various disciplines to the field can be found in McEntire (2007).

Contributions from Selected Disciplines

Anthropology

Anthropology scholars who study hazards and disasters are relatively few in number, but they have had a significant impact on the sociological study of disasters (for overviews of past and current research in the field, see Oliver-Smith 1996; Oliver-Smith and Hoffman 1999; Hoffman and Oliver-Smith 2002; Barrios 2017). Key strengths of anthropological approaches to the study of disasters are their focus on culture in its various manifestations; their commitment to long-term engagement in communities and societies; their emphasis on societies other than the Western ones in which many other social scientists conduct research; and their related concern with problems of development and underdevelopment. Anthropologists typically specialize in the study of specific societies, cultures, and geographic regions, which means that they bring an awareness of the importance of the broader context to the study of disasters. Additionally, the concept of adaptation has been central to the field throughout its history, which has encouraged a focus on how societies and communities adapt in the face of both environmental change and sudden shocks such as disasters. Anthropologists also remind us that nature and the built environment are imbued with symbolic significance and that it is important in the disaster context to understand the meanings people attach to them.

The use of in-depth ethnographic methods is a hallmark of anthropological research that has enabled anthropologists to develop a nuanced understanding of such topics as variations in the cultural interpretations of hazards and disasters across societies and over time, how cultural beliefs and practices influence adaptation strategies in the face of extreme events, and the role of culture in individual and community disaster experiences and disaster recovery. In an example of the anthropological approach to studying disaster recovery, shortly after the Katrina catastrophe, anthropologist Katherine Browne began following a large extended African American family that was displaced by the hurricane; and subsequently she spent more than eight years documenting their experiences. Her book *Standing in the Need: Culture, Comfort, and Coming Home after Katrina* (Browne 2015) tells the story of how family members were able to sustain their distinctive "cultural cycle" through reliance on family traditions such as cooking and eating special meals together and on institutions such as the black church. Among the other products of Browne's research was a documentary film, *Still Waiting: Life after Katrina*, which showed how during the early recovery period, members of the family struggled to maintain their distinctive culture while living with relatives in Dallas, Texas.

Like sociology, anthropology stresses that the meanings associated with disasters are not given but rather are socially and culturally constructed; and, like sociologists, anthropologists are also interested in how hazards and disasters are framed by different actors and interests. For example, studies on hazard and disaster risk perception are often marked by clashes between producers of "scientific" and producers of "lay" knowledge—where the former is characterized as objective and fact-based and the latter is seen as subjective and emotionally driven. Yet the perspectives of both scientists and non-scientists are shaped by their positions in the social order. For instance, on the basis of more than thirty years of studying accidents and disasters that involve toxic agents—the Exxon and British Petroleum (BP) oil spills, for example—anthropologist Gregory Button (2016) shows how science itself reflects the interests of powerful producers of knowledge and how dominant narratives regarding the impacts of disasters and the concept of scientific uncertainty are constructed by corporations and their public relations allies and disseminated through the media.

Cognitive psychology, behavioral economics, and economics

These three areas of inquiry are discussed together here, although they are in many ways dissimilar. With respect to hazards and disasters, cognitive psychology and behavioral economics, which also form the foundation of the interdisciplinary field of decision science, focus primarily on individual perceptions and decision-making, while the more general field of economics tends to be meso- and macro-oriented, emphasizing for example the impact of extreme events on losses and recovery at business, community, regional, and national levels and on the costs and benefits associated with different strategies for managing hazards.

Decision-making and heuristics

Psychologists Amos Tversky and 2002 Nobel laureate in economics Daniel Kahneman influenced disaster studies primarily through their contributions in the areas of risk perception and decision-making. They are best known for the development of prospect theory, a descriptive theory of decision-making that stands in contrast to expected utility theory—the normative "rational actor" paradigm that is favored by classical economists (Kahneman and Tversky 1979). While expected utility theory argued that people mentally tally the costs and benefits of their decisions and choose the option that secures the greatest amount of value, prospect theory showed that the options that yield identical values can be selected differently depending on how they are framed—for example, whether they are presented to individuals as gains or losses, probabilities or certainties. One insight from this influential theory is that people are more sensitive to the potential for losses than to the potential for gains, a pattern that is referred to as the endowment effect.

In important related work, Kahneman and Tversky demonstrated that, in order to avoid psychic overload, individuals typically take cognitive short-cuts, called heuristics, when forming judgments in uncertain situations (see Kahneman and Tversky 1972; Tversky and Kahneman 1973, 1974). For example, availability, one of the original heuristics they identified, depends on the ease with which information can be drawn from memory. Information can be more readily available if it is recent or vivid and dramatic, but for this reason the availability heuristic can also create perceptual distortions regarding risk. For example, after learning about a horrible airline crash, a person may be unwilling to fly and may drive to her destination instead, even if airline accidents are exceedingly rare and driving is statistically more dangerous.

Tversky and Kahneman identified other heuristics too, such as anchoring and representativeness, and subsequent research has uncovered additional patterns of thinking that often characterize the ways in which we think about risks. For example, status quo bias (Samuelson and Zeckhauser 1988) refers to people's tendency to want things in their lives to remain the same rather than to make choices that involve change. Particularly when faced with many choices, the tendency is to decide not to decide. Optimistic bias (Weinstein 1980; 1989) leads individuals to think that the risks they face in areas such as health and safety are lower than those others face. Another heuristic, myopia, refers to the bias toward short-term thinking—the inability to take the long view when thinking about risk. The affect heuristic (Slovic, Finucane, Peters, and MacGregor 2007; Slovic 2010) refers to the influence emotions have on decision-making; in the words of Paul Slovic and his collaborators, "images, marked by positive and negative affective feelings, guide judgment and decision making" (Slovic et al. 2007: 1335; see also Kahneman 2011). Rooted in experience, judgments involving what is good or bad are accompanied by feelings, and this happens automatically, often at the unconscious level.

A veritable industry has developed around the identification of heuristics, which are too numerous to discuss here. However, the few heuristics I briefly highlighted have clear implications for how people perceive and act with respect to hazards. Status quo bias suggests that, to the extent that people have to make changes in their lives to protect themselves against the potential for disaster by purchasing insurance, by adopting mitigation measures, or perhaps even by relocating, if they live in a hazardous area, they will tend not to do so. Optimistic bias could lead them to downplay the risks they face. Myopia may limit their ability to think in the present about losses they could well experience over the longer term. The affect heuristic may lead individuals to overestimate the likelihood of risks that trigger especially negative feelings (nuclear power and similar "dread" risks are examples; see Slovic, Fischhoff, and Lichtenstein 1979, 1981), while underestimating prosaic but more probable threats.

There is not space here to discuss all the many implications of prospect theory and research on cognitive heuristics, except to note that Kahneman and Tversky's contributions, along with those of other pioneers such as 2017 Nobel laureate in economics Richard Thaler, form the basis for the field of behavioral economics, which focuses not on how an idealized rational actor makes decisions that involve risk and uncertainty, but rather how actual human beings do so (for an overview, see Thaler 2015).

Familiarity with heuristics and behavioral economics is important for understanding perceptions and behaviors related to hazards, and also for shaping them. For example, Zaval and Cornwell (2016) argue that, while certain cognitive heuristics lead to inaction about climate change, people may begin to make different judgments perhaps on the basis of direct, unpleasant experiences with phenomena such as heat waves, which will become more common as climate change progresses. This is an example of the operation of availability. Noting that many types of decisions—for example, not saving for retirement—are not in the best interest of those who make them, Thaler and Cass Sunstein (2008) have advocated for policies that "nudge" decision makers in more prudent directions by changing their "choice architecture." In the hazards area, other behavioral economists have suggested ways of nudging homeowners into protecting themselves against disasters, for example through the purchase of insurance (Kunreuther, Pauly, and McMorrow 2013). Because homeowners have a tendency to purchase flood insurance in the aftermath of a flood (availability) and then drop the insurance after periods without flooding (myopia), one way to nudge them into protecting their property would be to make multi-year insurance policies available, rather than the annual ones that are currently being offered (Kleindorfer, Kunreuther, and Ou-Yang 2012).

Economic impacts of disasters

Another contribution to the sociological understanding of hazards and disasters comes from economists' research on the global, national, and regional economic impacts of disasters. At the global level, economic impacts are highest in developed societies, while death tolls are highest in less developed societies. At the national level, most studies concur that the macroeconomic impacts of disasters are generally small and short-lived (Albala-Bertrand 1993;

2006). Even catastrophic events such as Hurricane Katrina and the 2011 Great Tohoku earthquake, tsunami, and triple nuclear power plant meltdown caused relatively little macrolevel economic disruption, except in the short term. It should be noted however, that these two mega-disasters affected developed societies with very large economies. Some recent studies suggest that disasters can result in economic downturns in certain societal contexts—for example in small island nations with less diversified economies (Hochrainer 2009). However, even in such cases, negative effects on GDP and economic growth may be relatively small and may be offset by external aid, remittances, and investments in reconstruction. Nonetheless, questions still remain concerning the potential for disasters with catastrophic impacts to severely disrupt smaller economies. In 2017, Hurricanes Irma and Maria devastated Caribbean islands such as Barbuda, which is part of the small nation of Antigua and Barbuda, the French/Dutch island of St. Martin/St. Maarten, as well as the US territory of Puerto Rico. Destruction was so widespread that those disasters may have lasting negative consequences on the economies of those islands.

Most studies conducted by economists focus on the economic impacts of disasters on regional economies, the majority of those studies being carried out in the United States and Japan. Economists typically focus on interrelationships among different types of disaster losses. Direct losses are losses associated with damage to or loss of capital stock, other property, and infrastructure. Business interruption losses are indirect losses that are incurred when direct damage causes businesses to be unable to operate. Such losses may be due to physical damage at the business, off-site factors such as utility service and transportation system disruptions, or reductions in the demand for goods and services in the aftermath of a disaster. Other indirect losses, often termed "ripple effects," occur as a consequence of interdependencies among industries and economic sectors, suppliers and customers. Examples of such effects are supply chain disruptions such as those that occurred in the automobile industry after the 2011 Tohoku earthquake in Japan and in automobile and personal computer manufacturing after the 2011 floods in Thailand.

The methods most commonly used in assessing the regional economic impacts of disasters are various types of input–output and computable general equilibrium (CGE) models. A discussion of such models here would take us too far afield, but examples of their use and of their similarities and differences can be found in such sources as Okuyama (2007), Rose and Liao (2005), and Koks et al. (2016). Here again, analyses employing these modeling approaches indicate that the economic losses from disasters in the United States are typically not large in relation to the size of its economy, but that might not be the case for other nations, and also that, even at the regional level, negative impacts are generally short-lived. The capacity to recover from the economic shocks that disasters produce is generally attributed to business resilience strategies such as overcoming lifeline service disruption (e.g., by using generators), making up for lost production, or relocating business operations, as well as to the economic activity generated during the recovery process, for instance the expenditures associated with reconstruction (for overviews of studies on the economics of disasters, see Kunreuther and Rose 2004a, 2004b).

As currently employed, the economic modeling of disaster impacts has four main objectives. First, economic loss estimates are conducted in the immediate aftermath of a disaster to help determine an event's scope and severity—for example as a way of establishing assistance needs, or giving the insurance industry information on potential insured losses. Many rapid economic analyses are carried out by catastrophic modeling firms such as RMS, EQECat, and AIR Worldwide, whose main clients are insurers and reinsurers. The US Geological Survey also employs its Prompt Assessment of Global Earthquakes for Response (PAGER) system to develop rough economic impact estimates for earthquakes around the world. The second and most common types of modeling studies in the academic literature focus on the economic impacts of disaster events, either in the (relatively) short term or over longer periods. The objectives of such studies include understanding economic recovery processes and analyzing how disasters affect economic trends (see, e.g., Chang 2000; Miles and Chang 2006; Chang 2010; Chang and Rose 2012).

Third, economic modeling is also used to estimate losses from disaster events that have not yet occurred, either through the use of probabilistic loss estimation modeling, which takes into account a range or suite of disaster events, or through the analysis of the impacts of scenario events. An example of the latter approach is the US Geological Survey's use of modeling to estimate economic losses in its well-known ShakeOut scenario for southern California. Finally, economic modeling can be used to estimate the costs and benefits of disaster risk reduction programs—for example, by developing loss estimates with and without particular mitigation measures. An example of this type of analysis is the *Natural Hazard Mitigation Saves* project (Multihazard Mitigation Council 2005), which used economic modeling to estimate the savings to the US Treasury that resulted from federally funded post-disaster mitigation projects; that study found that one dollar invested in mitigation resulted in a savings of four dollars.

Business impacts

Moving to the micro- or organizational level, most of what is currently known about disaster effects on businesses has resulted from surveys conducted by sociologists and other social scientists after disasters—as opposed to economists. Post-disaster business surveys, which generally employ large randomly selected samples, have focused on such topics as business and owner characteristics, business adoption of pre-disaster mitigation and preparedness measures, direct damage, business interruption, post-disaster operational problems, forms of disaster assistance sought and obtained, and recovery outcomes. Earlier studies on businesses had tended to focus on surviving businesses—that is, on business enterprises in disaster-stricken communities that could be located at the time when the surveys were conducted because they were still in operation (see, for example, Dahlhamer and Tierney 1998; Webb, Tierney, and Dahlhamer 2000, 2003; Tierney 2007). In such cases the emphasis was on how businesses had fared in the period between the time the disaster struck and the time of the survey, which could be years later. More recent research has endeavored to locate both surviving businesses and businesses that had closed after disasters, whether as a result of disaster impacts or for other reasons.

A persistent urban legend emphasizes the fragility of businesses that experience disasters. The Federal Emergency Management Agency (FEMA) itself promulgates this myth. According to its website, "[a]lmost 40% of small businesses never reopen their doors following a disaster." The US Chamber of Commerce also promotes this idea, stating: "Forty percent of businesses do not reopen after a disaster and another 25 percent fail within one year, according to the Federal Emergency Management Agency . . . similar statistics from the Small Business Administration indicate that over 90 percent of businesses fail within two years after being struck by a disaster." Gosling and Hiles (2010) have documented many other statements of this nature in various publications and note that such reports tend to rely on faulty data or merely quote untrue statements from sources such as the FEMA. The logic behind the dissemination of these inaccurate numbers is unclear, but perhaps the objective is to frighten business owners into preparing for disasters. It could also be that information sources such as the FEMA and the Chamber of Commerce simply have not familiarized themselves with the disaster research literature.

In contrast with this disaster mythology, the empirical literature paints a very different picture. Businesses appear to be remarkably resilient in dealing with disaster-induced disruptions and in undertaking recovery efforts. For example, economist Adam Rose (Rose, Oladosu, Lee, and Asay 2009) found that 95 percent of the businesses and government offices displaced by the 2001 terrorist attacks on the World Trade Center relocated and resumed operations in New York City and northern New Jersey, although it took some businesses longer than others to relocate. Five years after Hurricane Katrina, a research team (Schrank et al. 2013; Marshall, Niehm, Sydnor, and Schrank 2015) studied a random sample of small businesses in the hardest hit counties in Mississippi, including businesses that had closed, and found that 18.9 percent were no longer in operation, but not necessarily because of the Katrina catastrophe. Small businesses, particularly newly established ones, are more vulnerable to failure than large businesses during non-disaster times, so it is safe to assume that some percentage of the firms studied by Schrank and colleagues would have closed anyway, owing to expected attrition. Moreover, business closure can be viewed as a strategic decision both after disasters and in normal times—for example, when an owner chooses to retire.

Overall, researchers note that "businesses and local economies are generally resilient to disasters. Most businesses recover" (Chang and Rose 2012: 172). Yet general patterns can mask differences in business vulnerability that are traceable to such factors as business and owner characteristics, disaster impact severity at the business site, and broader community impacts that can negatively affect post-disaster business functioning. In line with the "liability of smallness" hypothesis, small businesses are more vulnerable to poor recovery outcomes after disasters, as are businesses in the highly competitive retail and service sectors, where turnover rates are high during non-disaster times. In the Mississippi studies cited above, businesses owned by women, minorities, and veterans were more likely than others to experience demise, while older businesses and those with prior disaster experience and prior experience in handling cash-flow problems were less likely to fail, presumably because their owners learned from earlier experiences. Owners' business strategies are also important; some are more innovative and able to cope than others (Alesch, Holly, Mittler, and Nagy 2001). Interestingly, economic anthropologists who studied small and medium-sized enterprises in the Philippines that were affected by disasters found that proprietors were so accustomed to experiencing disaster-related damage and disruption that they considered it almost normal and had little difficulty relocating and resuming business operations (Matejowsky 2015).

Studies indicate that businesses that are located in high-damage areas and ones that experience problems such as restricted customer access and supply-chain disruptions can also experience difficulties as they endeavor to recover (Dahlhamer and Tierney 1998). For example, after the 2013 Colorado floods, which constituted the most severe disaster in the state's history, some communities experienced severe infrastructure damage, including damage to transportation routes, and they were essentially cut off from the outside. Businesses reopened as rapidly as they could, but customers could not reach them.

Geography and spatial social science

As discussed in Chapter 2, geographic research formed part of the foundation for contemporary disaster studies. This involved contributions from US-based researchers like Gilbert White and his collaborators, who emphasized alternative adjustments to natural hazards, as well as from scholars in the United Kingdom and Europe whose primary focus was on the hazards–disasters–development nexus.

Sociological research on disasters is indebted to the work of geographers in several ways. In volumes such as *At Risk*, geographers began to frame disasters

and their impacts as a consequence of world-system dynamics such as globalization and the practices involved in what has been termed the "development
of underdevelopment," whereby historical processes associated with the
global expansion of capitalism, such as colonialism, result in the extraction of
resources and the transfer of wealth from subordinate colonies to colonizing
nations (Frank 1966, 1979). At a time when most sociological research was
focusing on organization and community responses in prosperous societies
such as the United States, geographers were framing disaster vulnerability
as a consequence of economic and power relations between the Global North
and South. And at a time when sociologists tended to focus on *attributes or
characteristics* that made individuals and groups be more at risk from disaster
impacts, geographers showed a somewhat greater tendency to focus on the
processes that result in higher levels of vulnerability—as suggested, for example,
in the "pressure and release" (PAR) model. Geographers also remind us that,
while those processes have much in common across communities, societies,
and regions, space and place matter; processes such as rapid urbanization in
the Global South produce general trends, but different urban agglomerations
have evolved in distinctive ways, which have implications for disaster potential and disaster victimization.

Geographers are uniquely positioned to shed light on the conditions that
make particular places either more or less hazardous. Geographic information science (GIS) and spatial social science introduced important tools for
the study of disasters through their ability to integrate various mapping
layers in order to better understand and compare levels of disaster exposure
and vulnerability—for example, by combining databases containing hazard
maps with those showing built-environment characteristics and census-based
population and community characteristics. GIS analyses form the basis of
hazard-mapping and loss estimation methodologies. The kinds of economic
impact analyses discussed earlier would not have been possible without GIS;
disaster impacts, including economic ones, can be assessed through methods
that incorporate data on various aspects of the natural, built, and socioeconomic environments at different scales and over time. Advances in remote
sensing, such as the use of satellite and radar imagery to map hazards and
assess disaster impacts on the natural and built environment, have further
contributed to geographic understandings of the "hazardousness of place"
(for examples, see Poursanidis and Chrysoulakis 2017).

The best-known and most influential center for the geographic analysis
of hazards and disasters is the Hazards and Vulnerability Research Institute
(HVRI) at the University of South Carolina. Researchers affiliated with HVRI
have conducted research on a wide variety of topics, including spatial patterns of hazard risks and disaster losses (Cutter 2001; Ash, Cutter, and Emrich
2013), the analysis and measurement of social vulnerability (Cutter, Boruff,
and Shirley 2003; Emrich and Cutter 2011; Cutter 2017), disaster resilience

conceptualization and measurement (Cutter, Burton, and Emrich 2010; Cutter, Ash, and Emrich 2016; Cutter 2016), and disaster recovery (Finch, Emrich, and Cutter 2010; Burton, Mitchell, and Cutter 2011; Cutter, Emrich et al. 2016). HVRI research on social vulnerability and resilience will be discussed in more detail in Chapters 6 and 7.

Critical (and earlier radical) geographic perspectives include Marxist theoretical orientations that place a priority on the analysis of capitalism and class as drivers of vulnerability; perspectives that employ intersectional analyses to explain how and why different populations are put at risk; feminist geographies; and inquiries influenced by postmodernism and cultural studies (Harvey 1973, 1993, 2001; Bondi 1990; Rose, 1995; Philo 2005; Rose-Redwood 2006; Moss and Falconer Al-Hindi 2008; Soja 1989, 2009; Glassman 2010). What these approaches have in common is their emphasis on how different forms of domination are expressed spatially and, conversely, how such spatial disparities reinforce power relationships. Critical geography reminds us that patterns we observe with respect to the spatial distribution of populations and social activities are the result of the exercise of political power, both in the present and over time. Following geographer Edward Soja (2009), gerrymandering, redlining in real estate sales and mortgage lending, exclusionary zoning, and apartheid are examples of the "political organization of space." Other examples abound, for instance ones associated with "not in my backyard" mobilizations, the siting of locally unwanted land uses (LULUs) in low-income neighborhoods, and inequities in the provision of environmental and other amenities.

Both spatial social science and critical geographic approaches dovetail with sociological concerns regarding hazard exposure and vulnerability. Spatially based analyses are employed extensively in studies on environmental inequality, disaster vulnerability, and disaster recovery (see Cutter, Boruff, and Shirley 2003; Downey 2006a, 2006b; Downey and Hawkins 2008; Downey, DuBois, Hawkins, and Walker 2008; Chang 2010; Finch et al. 2010). Critical geography provides a lens through which to view these as forms of inequality—that is, as consequences of political processes that are inscribed upon physical and social landscapes.

Political science and public administration

Important foci for political science and public administration research include policy development, agenda setting, policy learning after disasters, and the analysis of the effectiveness of policies and programs aimed at reducing disaster impacts that span pre-, trans- and post-disaster activities.

Regarding policy development, political science research tends to bear out findings from a study conducted more than three decades ago by Rossi, Wright, and Weber-Burdin (1982) that indicated that state and local government officials place a low priority on disaster risk reduction in comparison with many other issues that seem more pressing on a daily basis, such as crime. Other researchers have noted that political leaders are more concerned with daily, recurrent problems that raise public ire than with events that may or may not happen in the near term—a tendency referred to as NIMTOFF ("not in my term of office"). Behavioral economists might call this tendency a combination of optimistic bias and myopia.

Peter May's (1991) discussion of policies with and without publics provides a general framework for understanding policies in the hazards and disasters arena. May characterized hazards and disasters as policy areas without publics—that is, areas that generally lack organized interest groups that take an active role in policy formulation and implementation. Policies without publics generate relatively little interest-group mobilization, and what mobilization does occur is generally limited to technical and scientific groups. Other characteristics of policies without publics are that they tend to involve public risks, as opposed to private ones; to lack a common vision of what is causing the problem, or to have the problem defined by technocrats; to be put on government agendas either without public involvement or in the context of a crisis event; and to appear apolitical. The political context surrounding policies without publics is one that presents challenges for agenda setting, except when some dramatic event occurs. Without such events, issues remain marginal, taking a back seat to other problems around which publics have mobilized. To complicate matters further, while judging government positively when it provides post-disaster relief, the public at large does not reward governmental actions taken during normal times to mitigate hazards and prepare for future disasters (Healy and Malhotra 2009). Those wishing to promote policies under such circumstances must find ways of generating political momentum, for example through the creation of publics. Alternatively, in some cases governmental entities may elect to act on their own, as the federal government did in establishing the National Flood Insurance Program (NFIP) to reduce flood risks.

May (1991) does note, however, that whether a policy has or lacks publics is not set in stone; for example, nuclear power in the United States started out as a policy without a public, but that changed after the Three Mile Island nuclear disaster and the emergence of the environmental movement. Similarly, disaster scholars argue that disasters can act as catalysts or focusing events that raise awareness among both elites and the general public, creating pressure for policy formulation, adoption, and implementation.

Explanations for the emergence of public support and the development of policy often draw upon John Kingdon's framework for understanding political agenda setting, which emphasizes how policy windows can open as a result of focusing events, elevating particular issues and making policy formulation and adoption possible (Kingdon 1995, 2011). Issues compete with one another within different public arenas such as executive and legislative processes, the courts, and the media. Novelty and drama, ongoing organizational routines, elite interests, and the presence of advocacy groups and political operatives that offer policy solutions are among the factors that help determine whether an issue rises to the level of active policymaking (Hilgartner and Bosk 1988).

The need to reduce disaster risks is most likely to gain widespread attention in the immediate aftermath of disasters, as policy windows that were formerly closed are forced open by those events—and particularly by the way they are framed in the media. The immediate post-disaster impact period is a time when the public is most aware of disaster threats and impacts, when Congressional hearings and governmental investigations take place, when advocates for disaster risk reduction come forward with suggested solutions, and when new legislation is proposed and is most likely to pass. As emergency management researcher Claire Rubin has noted on the basis of her analyses of emergency management and homeland security legislation and programs over past decades, "certain focusing events drive changes in laws, regulations, systems, and practices. In fact, virtually all major federal laws, executive directives, programs, policies, organizational changes, and response systems have resulted from major and catastrophic disasters" (Rubin 2012: 6–7).

There are many examples of such connections. The discovery of major toxic pollution in Love Canal, a neighborhood in Niagara Falls, New York in 1978 led to the passage of the CERCLA (Comprehensive Environmental Response, Compensation, and Liability Act), known as Superfund, in 1980. The 1984 Bhopal catastrophe in India, in which a toxic release from a Union Carbide plant killed thousands and injured half a million people, was followed in 1986 by the passage of the Emergency Planning and Community Right to Know Act, an amendment to the Superfund law that required handlers of hazardous materials to make information on their inventories available to the public. After the massive *Exxon Valdez* oil spill, which occurred in 1989, Congress passed the Oil Pollution Act of 1990. The terrorist attacks of September 11, 2001 resulted in the passage of the USA PATRIOT Act and the formation of the Department of Homeland Security (DHS); and, after Hurricane Katrina, Congress passed the Post-Katrina Emergency Management Reform Act and the Pets Evacuation and Transportation Standards Act, known as the PETS Act.

Not all disasters become focusing events—in fact, the majority of them do not. Political scientist Thomas Birkland has identified the conditions under which disasters come to be seen as requiring policy changes. The disaster must be severe and must be framed as representing a failure of policy, and both the lessons learned and candidate policy remedies must be identified. Most disasters and threats never reach this threshold, and even when they do, the policies promoted most strongly by advocates and the media have the greatest chance of being adopted—even if those policies are merely symbolic (Birkland 1997, 2007). Indeed, the crisis-induced tendency to pass legislation and create programs results in ever-shifting policy frameworks and recommendations and often fails to address root causes of governmental dysfunction (Roberts, Ward, and Wamsley 2012). As I discuss in the next chapter, social constructionist perspectives provide important insights into how hazards, disasters, and policies to ameliorate them come to be socially defined.

Even when threats and disasters become focal points for policy advocacy and adoption, policy implementation introduces new complications. In some cases policies are misguided and resources are squandered. Following the terrorist attacks of September 11, for example, policy advocates of many different stripes exaggerated the magnitude of the terrorist threat, which led to controversial legislation such as the PATRIOT Act, along with massive expenditures on homeland security. Approximately ten years after 9–11, John Mueller and Mark Stewart estimated that about $1 trillion had been spent on the terrorism threat, not counting the cost of the wars in Afghanistan and Iraq, even though the likelihood of anyone dying in a terrorist attack remained vanishingly small, as indeed it had been prior to 9–11. As a consequence of hastily adopted laws and policies fueled by the climate of fear generated after 9–11 and by interest groups that wanted to capitalize on that fear, homeland security funds that were allocated were grossly out of proportion with the threat of terror attacks (Mueller and Stewart 2011a, 2011b, 2012). Along those same lines, May, Jochim, and Sapotichne (2011) have referred to homeland security, as it was constructed in the aftermath of the September 11 attacks, as "an anemic policy regime." The creation of the DHS was the largest government reorganization since the Department of Defense was established in 1947. However, that did not mean that the nearly two dozen entities that were merged to create DHS, all with diverse functions (e.g., border protection, transportation safety, emergency management), stopped pursuing their previous agendas or changed their distinctive organizational cultures. More than fifteen years after the 9–11 attacks, DHS remains an expensive patchwork of institutional agendas.

Examples abound of other ways in which risk reduction policies can have unanticipated negative effects. For example, in California there has been long-standing concern about the safety and survivability of hospitals in the event of earthquakes, accompanied by a history of legislation in this area. After the opening of a policy window afforded by the 1994 Northridge earthquake, a stricter law, Assembly Bill 1953, was adopted to raise safety levels by requiring that older hospitals serving as critical care facilities be seismically retrofitted to be brought into compliance with a 1983 hospital seismic safety law. Those facilities that could not comply by a specified target date would have to be demolished or converted to non-acute care facilities. No financial assistance was provided to help hospitals comply, and the law was enacted at a time when California hospitals were experiencing severe financial burdens. Hospitals resisted the law as an unfunded mandate and pressured for longer timetables for compliance. Those most able to comply with the legislation were large investor-owned hospital chains, as opposed to nonprofit and publicly owned hospitals, which disproportionately provide care for indigent and less well-off patients. To some degree, the law also helped to accelerate hospital closures (Alesch, Arendt, and Petak 2012). The formulation and implementation of Assembly Bill 1953 is an example of how hasty policy adoption in one arena (earthquake safety) may have perverse effects in other arenas (health care for the poor).

Like sociologists, public administration scholars are concerned with issues of organizational design and behavior. In the area of emergency manage-ment, for example, decades ago, sociologists at the Disaster Research Center pointed to two contrasting models of emergency management: a top-down or command-and-control model and a more bottom-up emergent human resources model. The latter was thought to be the more appropriate one for organizational responses to disaster (Dynes 1994; Drabek and McEntire 2003). Public administration scholars do recognize this distinction but point to the strengths of a third approach: a network perspective model that

> views the network as a cooperative system between central and local gov-ernment, with the central government establishing national priorities and standards, but local governmental units having broad discretion in interpreting priorities and standards and meeting them within existing capabilities. (Roberts, Ward, and Wamsley 2014: 171)

Scholars are also concerned with policy change over time within the emergency management domain. Over its history, the US emergency manage-ment system has undergone a number of shifts in its policy emphasis. The command-and-control model was adopted as an ideal type of organization in the Cold War years; then the system took more decentralized, collaborative forms under the Clinton administration; then, after the September 11 terror-ist attacks, it returned to top-down approaches, moderated to some degree, during the Obama years, to a slightly more collaborative "whole community" approach (Schroeder, Wamsley, and Ward 2001; Roberts 2016).

Psychology and related fields

An earlier section in this chapter discussed key contributions of cognitive psy-chology to our understanding of risks and threats. This section outlines other contributions made by psychological fields, including social and community psychology and the study of psychological trauma. Among the many topics studied by psychologists, the three that are of greatest interest to sociologists and to which they have contributed along with psychologists are risk percep-tion, risk communication and warning responses, and the psychosocial effects of disasters.

Risk perception and communication

The topic of risk perception has been approached from a variety of disciplinary perspectives, but what has come to be known as the psychometric approach has generally been dominant. As I have discussed elsewhere (Tierney 2014) in greater detail, psychologists' initial interest in the perception of risk was driven by concerns about how the public perceived certain technological risks, particularly the risks associated with nuclear power, and why public perceptions differed so markedly from those of experts, who were thought to be in a better position to understand those risks. The insights into cognitive heuristics provided by the work of Kahneman and Tversky (see pp. 41–3 in this chapter) offered some guidance; people used heuristics or cognitive shortcuts in assessing risks.

Further research within the psychometric paradigm explored how perceived characteristics of risks themselves influenced perception. Among the most important findings from this strain of risk perception research was the conclusion that the perceived severity of risks was influenced by whether those risks were seen as voluntarily accepted or imposed, as commonplace or exotic, as familiar or unfamiliar, as dreaded or not. Other perceived characteristics of risks were their being especially deadly, their affecting large numbers of people, and their having intergenerational negative effects. Such attributes could explain, for example, why people had such an elevated sense of the risks associated with nuclear war and nuclear power (Slovic et al. 1979, 1981).

A further development within the psychometric framework involved taking into account the sociodemographic characteristics of individuals as they related to risk perception. Here both race and gender emerged as important influences on how risks were perceived, women in general and members of minority groups in particular perceiving risks in different ways from Caucasian males (Slovic 1999; Finucane et al. 2000). More recently, other research in this same vein has explored how individual characteristics such as gender, education, and income, combined with other factors such as information seeking, influence the perception of various types of risks (Cummings, Berube, and Lavelle 2013).

A different line of research focuses on the influence of emotions on risk perceptions. While in the past there had been a tendency to contrast "emotional" judgments and decisions with "rational" ones and to view emotions as biasing factors in the perception of risk, current approaches emphasize that perceptions are shaped by a combination of emotions and "slower," more analytic forms of thinking, and also that emotions function in positive, adaptive ways. The large body of research on emotions and risk perception includes work on the affect heuristic, which was discussed earlier (Finucane et al. 2000; Slovic 2010), along with studies of the ways in which specific emotions shape the perception of risk. Negative emotions are generally associated with pessimism and greater concern about risks, while positive ones are associated with optimism and a tendency to downplay risks. However, the picture looks different if the effects of specific emotions are the object of study. For example, focusing on two emotions—anger and fear—Lerner and Keltner (2001) found, somewhat counterintuitively, that anger operates like a positive emotion, inducing optimism and lowered risk perception, while the effects of fear more closely resemble those generated by negative emotions. This focus on specific emotions such as fear, anger, and guilt and on how they operate is called appraisal theory. Experts suggest that appraisal theory has considerable potential for the study of environmental risk perception and for understanding why different people respond differently to the same sets of environmental cues (Keller et al. 2012; for more information on how various attributes of emotions can shape risk perceptions, see Parrott 2017).

Another approach within the psychometric paradigm focuses on the role of people's mental models in shaping perceptions of hazards and other risks. This method seeks to elicit from individuals, through open-ended interviews, their understandings of various aspects of hazards, including how people get exposed to the hazard, how it affects them, and what can be done to reduce or control it. These mental models, which are typically expressed as hierarchically organized influence diagrams, are then compared with models developed on the basis of information obtained from experts on those same risks (for examples of how this is done, see Bostrom, Fischhoff, and Morgan 1992 and Morgan, Fischhoff, Bostrom, and Atman 2002). The analysis of mental models helps to identify areas in which there are misunderstandings about the causal processes that characterize hazards, which can be important for crafting effective risk communication messages. For example, with respect to the consequences of flooding, people may well understand that flood waters represent immediate threats to life safety and property, without understanding other risks associated with floods, such as bacteria and hazardous substances in floodwaters or risks associated with mold inside flooded structures—which indicates the need to provide information about such risks.

Risk communication, which aims at assisting recipients of risk information in making sound choices related to health and safety, can be thought of as a blending of insights from the study of various topics such as risk perception, persuasive communication, social marketing, attitude and behavior change, and organizational crisis communication. The literature on risk communication is vast, spanning both theoretical and practical concerns, but generally with an emphasis on the latter—for example on identifying best practices for communicating information about specific types of risks. Although the focus here is on communication related to hazards and disasters, findings from research that involves other types of risks—for example accidents, communicable diseases and other illnesses, and risks associated with medical procedures—are also relevant. Within the area of hazards and disasters, a distinction can be made between communicating about risks during non-disaster times and communicating in the context of immanent threats—for example, by issuing warnings and providing guidance on necessary protective actions.

Janoske, Liu, and Sheppard (2012) identify several general theories and models of risk communication that are relevant within the disaster context. These include the Centers for Disease Control and Prevention's crisis and emergency risk communication (CERC) model, which focuses on the types of communication that are appropriate in different stages of a disaster or crisis; the situational theory of publics, which is concerned with the factors that influence various publics' information seeking and information uptake; the heuristic–systemic model, which deals with the extent to which people make judgments about risks on the basis of superficial cues contained in messages or on the basis of a more systematic analysis of the information provided; and the deliberative process model, which emphasizes involving stakeholders in fashioning risk communication messages that take into account divergent viewpoints, with the aim of furthering the understanding of risks and of moving toward agreement as to their acceptability. These same authors have also identified other models that are appropriate in different phases of a disaster or crisis.

Walaski (2011) discusses other theoretical models that have informed the practice of risk communication, particularly in the context of crises. The risk perception model, as discussed above, focuses on how the intended audience perceives various dimensions of a given risk, as well as how it views the institutions that are involved in that risk—for example, whether or not they are trustworthy and credible. The mental noise model concerns the extent to which a particular threat induces stress and feelings of anxiety in an audience that may interfere with its ability to process information about the risk involved. A related approach, the negative dominance model, posits that messages that are negative in tone engender unpleasant feelings such as fear, hostility, and anxiety, which interfere with information processing, and that it is important to reduce negative messages in favor of positive ones, which emphasize the benefits of taking recommended actions and increase feelings of control and agency. The trust determination model stresses the need for communicators to build and maintain the trust of audiences. Walaski also calls attention to Peter Sandman's work on risk communication, which puts special weight on a component of risk perception he terms "outrage" and suggests that different risk communication strategies should be used according to the level of perceived hazards and the level of outrage within an exposed population (see Sandman 2012).

Lundgren and McMakin (2009) identify more than a dozen bodies of research that inform risk communication practice. One such model focuses on four dimensions of risk communication—source, message, channel, and receiver—and has been used extensively in the disaster arena. The authors also call attention to the important work carried out by the US National Academies on successful risk communication strategies (National Research Council 1989, 1996). That perspective places special emphasis on the importance of interactions among stakeholders in the risk communication process and eschews the idea of unidirectional risk communication.

Several themes have emerged from the decades-long record of risk communication research and practice. These themes underscore the importance of several factors, for example communicating uncertainty appropriately; framing risks in ways that make it more likely that audiences will understand them—which necessitates understanding the actual information needs of those audiences (as opposed to what communicators think the audiences need); paying heed to the existing barriers to acting on the basis of risk communications; and including in messages information that people need to have in order to take action. Numerous guidance documents have been produced that contain these and other points. But, if there are overarching themes in the risk communication literature, one is that trust is an essential component in all risk communication activities: trust that risk communicators are legitimate, credible, and disinterested; trust that the communication process is fair and being undertaken in the public's best interest; and trust in the institutions that produce and disseminate risk information. Additionally, because publics are heterogeneous, groups will vary in levels of trust attached to different communication sources and institutions. Focusing on trust in science, which is embodied in a set of institutions relevant to this discussion, in the United States high trust is associated with higher levels of education, while trust is lower among political conservatives, women, non-whites, regular churchgoers, people who reside in the South, and people with lower incomes (Gauchat 2012). Beliefs concerning hazards also affect receptivity to risk communications. Believing that climate change is happening is an example, and here again public perceptions vary. A survey conducted in 2016 found that on average 70 percent of Americans believe that climate change is occurring, but percentages varied by state: for example 84 percent of Washington DC residents and 78 percent of residents of Hawaii believe in climate change, but only 60 percent of West Virginia residents share that belief (Marlon, Howe, Mildenberger, and Leiserowitz 2016).

Another theme emphasizes the importance of evaluating risk communication strategies. As Baruch Fischhoff, one of the foremost authorities on risk communication, points out, "[i]t is depressing how often even rudimentary evaluation is missing. Amateurish, unscientific communications can be worse than nothing, by creating the impression that the problem has been addressed" (Fischhoff 2012: 25).

If communicating risk information is difficult during normal, non-disaster times, those difficulties are multiplied in the context of imminent threats. A substantial body of research documents factors that positively and negatively affect warning responses. The length of the warning period associated with different disaster agents is one such factor. Some hazards, such as hurricanes and riverine floods, allow for longer warning periods, while for others, such as tornadoes and hazardous chemical releases, the time available to warn the public is very short or even non-existent, and this presents special challenges. Threats such as wildfires and chemical and nuclear hazards can be very dynamic, requiring rapid warning updates and making the warning process even more complex.

Race, class, gender, and household composition influence how members of the public respond, as does the ability to comprehend warning guidance, which can be affected by language, cultural competence, and cognitive ability. Local knowledge is also important; those unfamiliar with the settings in which they find themselves when warnings are issued, such as tourists, transients, and newcomers to an area, may receive and understand warnings but still not know what to do to reach safety (Tierney, Lindell, and Perry 2001).

Those interested in research and practice on risk communication are also challenged to better understand how technological developments have altered risk communication activities. Particularly with the explosion of social media in recent years, older notions of linear source–message–channel–receiver communication have been supplanted by a recognition that information networks have become increasingly complex, in ways that researchers are only beginning to grasp. This trend, combined with the tendency for members of the public to obtain information of all types—including information on risks and warnings—from an increasingly heterogeneous, fragmented, and polarized information marketplace, also presents challenges for researchers and risk communicators alike. As noted, trust is critical for effective risk communication, but different audiences trust different information sources and many lack trust in the institutions that have traditionally provided risk-related information. The drive to better understand communication processes related to hazards and disasters within the context of new technologies and social media has given rise to a new field of study, crisis informatics, which bridges the fields of social, information, and computer science (Palen et al. 2007; Palen, Vieweg, Liu, and Hughes 2009; Vieweg et al. 2008; Palen and Hughes 2018).

There is a tendency to believe that technology holds the key to improving risk communication, but that is not always the case. For example, research on the US government's terse emergency messaging communications system known as the Wireless Emergency Alert (WEA) system,[1] which was designed to send warning information to mobile phone users, has uncovered problems with the system, which has subsequently undergone upgrades designed to improve its effectiveness (Bean et al. 2015, 2016). Also potentially problematic is the use of systems like WEA in communications for which they were not originally designed, for instance in alerting communities about potential lawbreakers and terrorists—a strategy that could lead to racial profiling and backlash against the system. As new technologies come online, it is important to remember that messaging strategies of all types will only be effective to the extent that they adhere to basic principles of effective risk communication. (For more information on communicating risks, see Arvai and Rivers 2014 and a 2014 special issue of the *Journal of Risk Research*: volume 17, issue 10.)

Mental health aspects of disasters

The third major contribution of the psychological sciences is to improve our understanding of the psychosocial aspects and effects both of disasters and of interventions designed to reduce negative impacts. Historically, sociologists and psychologists have differed in their views on those impacts, sociologists tending to argue that negative psychological effects of disasters are relatively mild and transient and psychologists being significantly more concerned with the capacity of disasters to lead to more serious and lasting psychological problems, including post-traumatic stress disorder (PTSD). Research findings that have accrued over time have painted a more nuanced picture. In 2002, psychologist Fran Norris and her collaborators (Norris, Friedman, Watson et al. 2002; Norris, Friedman, and Watson 2002) published a landmark meta-analysis of 160 empirical studies conducted between 1981 and 2001 that identified the conditions under which disasters are more likely to lead to adverse psychological outcomes ranging from PTSD, major depression, and anxiety disorders to elevated stress, health problems (somatic complaints, excessive drinking), problems in living caused by disasters, increased vulnerability to subsequent stressors, and problems specific to youth. For adults, such adverse outcomes were associated with experiencing more severe disasters, being female, being middle-aged, being a member of an ethnic minority group, experiencing additional stressors after disaster exposure, having had prior psychiatric problems, and having diminished psychosocial coping resources. For youths, the most serious psychological effects were associated with having experienced mass violence, for instance terrorism, rather than a natural or technological disaster, and being from the developing world.

Most prior studies, including those reviewed by Norris and her colleagues, have a number of methodological weaknesses. As these researchers note, post-disaster studies of mental health impacts are often undertaken hastily, in the interest of being able to address victims' problems (Norris, Friedman, and Watson 2002). They tend to be cross-sectional rather than longitudinal studies; to be undertaken at different points in time after disasters; to lack baseline data; and to lack consistency in terms of the variables included for analysis. On the positive side, studies have increasingly employed standardized measures of exposure and of outcomes of interest, such as PTSD and clinical depression.

Since the publication of Norris and colleagues' 2002 review, several major disasters have occurred that have led to extensive research on their mental health consequences, including a few longitudinal studies of different lengths. Chief among these were studies devoted to the terrorist attacks of September 11, 2001 and to Hurricane Katrina. Research on the mental health effects of 9–11 includes both nationwide surveys (Silver et al. 2002) and studies on more severely affected populations. The establishment of the World Trade Center Health Registry, then the most extensive study of its kind, made it possible to track health and mental health outcomes of persons most directly affected by the New York City attacks who volunteered to take part. The Registry contains data on over 70,000 rescue and recovery workers, schoolchildren and school staff members, building occupants and residents of the hardest hit areas in Lower Manhattan, and individuals who happened to be in those areas at the time of the attacks. Most of the data collected focused on physical impacts of exposure, but a portion of the research conducted dealt with mental health outcomes at different points in time (Brackbill et al. 2013). Other research on highly exposed populations focused on the incidence of serious mental health problems such as PTSD (Galea et al. 2003; Boscarino et al. 2011; for a review of studies, see Neria, DiGrande and Adams 2011). Findings are not entirely consistent across studies, but the evidence suggests that an event like the 9–11 attacks in New York can have lasting negative psychological effects on those most directly affected, in this case particularly on responders involved in rescues, remains recovery, and cleanup activities at the site of the attacks (Centers for Disease Control and Prevention 2004; Stellman et al. 2008).

Hurricane Katrina is another disaster that has been studied extensively. In terms of negative mental health consequences, Katrina can be considered something of an outlier among US disasters on account of its catastrophic nature and the protracted length of the recovery period, because so many people lost their social support networks through displacement and relocation, and because many of the victims were already vulnerable owing to factors such as minority racial status and poverty. This does seem to be the case and, in a pattern that is unusual for disasters, for some of those affected mental health problems appeared to increase rather than decrease over time (Kessler et al. 2008).

One long-term study, the Resilience in Survivors of Katrina (RISK) project, has been following and continues to follow the experiences and the health and mental health status of more than 1,000 mostly African American young women for whom baseline data had been collected prior to Katrina. In this case, study results from 2010 show a relatively high incidence of post-Katrina PTSD—around 30 percent—as compared with pre-disaster levels, which are associated with factors such as the loss of housing, trauma experienced in connection with the hurricane, and the death of a family member or friend. This model study also takes into account post-traumatic growth and potential genetic and neighborhood factors that could influence the survivors' mental health (Waters 2016). Unfortunately studies of this quality still remain few and far between.

For these and more recent major disasters such as the BP *Deepwater Horizon* oil spill, Superstorm Sandy, and Hurricanes Harvey, Irma, and Maria, it will be important to continue to track the mental health status of those who have been affected. Much remains to be learned, and well-designed longer-term studies are badly needed. (For more information on mental health research in the context of disasters and terrorism, see Norris, Galea, Friedman, and Watson 2006.)

Urban planning

The field of urban planning is concerned with shaping urban forms through appropriate legislation, policies, and plans. In the context of hazards and disasters, urban planning makes the most significant contributions in the pre-disaster mitigation phase, by employing strategies designed to reduce the negative impacts of future disasters, and in the post-disaster recovery phase, by providing guidance on prudent strategies for redevelopment and reconstruction, with the goal of incorporating disaster risk reduction into those strategies. Urban planners advocate a variety of pre-disaster measures designed to mitigate disaster impacts, primarily through the promotion of risk-aware land use practices. These include directing new development away from hazardous areas; relocating populations, existing structures and land uses to safer areas; advocating for measures that maintain the health and functionality of natural protections against disasters, for example wetlands; and identifying areas where there are opportunities to employ land use policies in order to enhance safety (Godschalk, 2003). Similarly, after disasters, the goal of urban planning is to guide recovery processes in ways that maximize safety in the face of hazards but do not sacrifice other important community values such as livability, access to transportation, and overall quality of life.

The employment of land use measures to manage hazards was a key emphasis of the founders of the disaster research—people like Gilbert White, who counted land use among the key adjustments to natural hazards. Examples exist of a number of successful programs for applying land use measures in this fashion. In the United States, for example, the cities of Boulder, Colorado, and Tulsa, Oklahoma are well known for their efforts to reduce flood losses through the adoption of progressive land use measures. Under White's direct influence, Boulder restricted most development in its floodplain and began using the floodplain for other purposes, such as recreation. Following a series of damaging and deadly floods, Tulsa adopted an ambitious risk reduction program that has involved acquiring land in order to keep it from being developed, moving structures out of harm's way, and creating spaces within the urban environment that could serve as overflow reservoirs in the event of major flooding. The Tulsa case will be discussed in more detail later, in Chapter 7. To bolster such efforts, the National Flood Insurance Program (NFIP) offers communities incentives for flood risk reduction through its Community Rating System, which lowers flood insurance rates for the residents of communities that are pursuing recommended risk reduction policies. Examples also abound of coastal zone management policies that seek to protect people and property from hazards such as hurricane storm surge. With respect to earthquakes, a state law in California, the Alquist-Priolo Act, restricts the construction of multi-family structures near active fault zones, and other legislation has long required the incorporation of seismic safety elements into communities' general plans.

There are, however, significant barriers to the use of planning tools such as those discussed above to reduce disaster losses. First, despite efforts on the part of institutions such as the World Bank to highlight the importance of land use-focused measures as part of the efforts to reduce future risks, such measures may be largely ignored in urban areas of poor countries, where residents and migrants seek to live in proximity to jobs and whatever services are available, without regard for the safety of those locations. Migrants gravitate to whatever areas are available for settlement and, given the economic conditions under which they are forced to live, it is unlikely that they give much thought to whether those areas are exposed to hazards or not (Pelling 2003). For their part, given lax regulations on land use and construction practices, developers have little to fear when they construct shabby dwellings in areas exposed to hazards.

Second, even in developed societies like the United States, training in urban planning generally neglects hazards and disasters as important considerations, focusing instead on concepts such as smart growth, the new urbanism, and transit-oriented development. Few schools of urban planning emphasize the importance of integrating disaster risk reduction into urban planning activities, although the American Planning Association (APA) and its Hazards Planning Center are attempting to move education and practice in that direction. The gulf that exists between planners employed by local communities and community officials in disaster management roles only exacerbates this problem. Put simply, hazards are not a priority for urban planners, and disaster planning and urban planning are typically separate in most US communities. How, then, can we expect community planning to take into account disaster risk reduction objectives?

Third and perhaps most importantly, as I have discussed elsewhere (Tierney 1999; 2014) and will explain again in this volume, efforts to shape urban development in ways that take hazards into account typically incur opposition from real estate and development interests. Proponents of "growth," which is socially defined as beneficial to all community residents, although that is clearly not the case, expect to be able to build whatever, wherever, and whenever they want—and they possess the political power to do so. In the face of these kinds of political constraints, urban planners who place a priority on keeping their communities safe have their work cut out for them.

These challenges are evident in research on the implementation of the Disaster Mitigation Act of 2000. Known as DMA2K, this law required all local jurisdictions in the United States and its territories, as well as tribal governments, to engage in mitigation planning, much of which revolves around assessing hazards and making decisions about how best to mitigate them. The little research that has been done suggests that mitigation plans developed by jurisdictions such as those located in coastal areas are generally of poor quality and do not necessarily result in an increase in hazard reduction activities (Kang, Peacock, and Husein 2010; Lyles, Berke, and Smith 2014a). Perhaps those jurisdictions view DMA2K requirements as unfunded mandates—or perhaps their leaders are simply loath to do battle with powerful development interests.

Researchers affiliated with the Hazard Reduction and Recovery Center at Texas A&M University and other urban researchers have also pointed out that there are, typically, disconnects among plans prepared by different entities for the same jurisdiction(s). General land use plans and the hazard mitigation plans mandated by DMA2K may not be integrated (Lyles, Berke, and Smith 2014b). Planning activities undertaken by various authorities can be inconsistent with one another. Additionally, to the extent that they fail to be based on high-quality data on hazards, they can even increase social and built-environment vulnerability (Berke et al. 2015).

In the future, we can expect to see urban planning tools and strategies increasingly employing climate change adaptation strategies. Many cities around the world are moving in this direction and, as climate change goes inexorably forward, other cities, particularly those in coastal areas, will have little choice but to rethink their urban design practices, including both the preservation and maintenance of existing elements of the built environment and the design and construction of new ones. This will be impossible without the active participation of urban planning disciplines.

Concluding Observations

In this admittedly very selective chapter I have attempted to introduce readers to perspectives from outside sociology that are foundational to an understanding of the societal dimensions of hazards, disasters, and risk. This chapter has not aimed at being comprehensive. For example, I have not touched upon contributions from public health and related disciplines, which focus both on factors that contribute to disaster-induced mortality and morbidity and on how public health-oriented strategies can reduce the pain and suffering associated with disasters. Nor have I emphasized how historical research and its methods can contribute to our understanding of how hazards and disasters have been conceived of and contended with over time. Even in the topical areas that have been discussed, reviews and citations have of necessity been brief. The objective of this chapter has been to show readers who are perhaps new to the sociological study of disasters the ways in which sociological inquiry has been informed by other perspectives outside the core of the discipline. I turn next to an overview of theoretical perspectives that are of more central concern to the sociological analysis of hazards and disasters, keeping an eye on both general theories and theories of the middle range.

4

Theoretical Approaches and Perspectives in the Study of Hazards and Disasters

Introduction

In Chapter 2 I provided an overview of the ways in which social–scientific approaches to studying hazards and disasters have evolved over time, and in Chapter 3 I discussed how perspectives and insights from other social science fields have informed disaster research. This chapter delves more deeply into the theoretical assumptions that drive sociological approaches to disasters. I begin it by discussing three general theoretical orientations that have become increasingly important to the study of disasters: social constructionism, vulnerability science, and political economy. I then turn to a discussion of what can be termed middle-range theories (Merton 1957) of disaster behavior—that is, the blend of theoretical assumptions and empirical generalizations that have been developed to explain particular topics of interest. Although the sociology of disasters advances a number of middle-range perspectives, for reasons I will explain in the relevant chapter sections, I have chosen to focus here on theories of panic, emergence, and public warning responses.

Before discussing theoretical approaches, I wish to warn readers that throughout this chapter I will be using the term "theory" loosely. While it is inaccurate to say that the field of disaster research is atheoretical, it would also be wrong to argue that theoretical reasoning is a hallmark of the field. Because with some exceptions disaster sociology has evolved primarily through the study of individual disasters and specific social settings but with little systematic comparative research, what I call theories of hazard- and disaster-related phenomena more closely resemble inductively developed empirical generalizations than they do theories developed through deductive reasoning and hypothesis testing—although there are exceptions. Classifying some of the perspectives discussed here as "theory" is a bit of a stretch. Moreover, to the extent that disaster sociology *is* theoretical, it is mainly because there has been extensive borrowing from broader theoretical orientations within sociology. Finally, much of what I present in this chapter, particularly in the section on political economy, represents my own efforts to add stronger theoretical reasoning to the field.

General Explanatory Frameworks

In this section I first discuss the influence of social constructionism on the study of hazards and disasters. Next I discuss vulnerability and environmental inequality research and their contributions to the sociology of disasters, with an emphasis on social vulnerability. Finally I draw upon insights from critical urban studies and political economy—particularly the political economy of the environment—in an effort to show how these fields shed light on how hazards and disasters are socially produced.

To better frame the discussions that follow, I want to emphasize that saying that hazards and disasters are *socially constructed* is not the same as saying that they are *socially produced*. Scholars sometimes use these terms interchangeably, but they mean different things, as the subsequent discussion will show. A focus on *social constructionism* emphasizes how ideas and assumptions about hazards and disasters—and our own understandings—are shaped by narratives, discourses, institutional practices, and other factors. By contrast, the analysis of the *social production of disasters* centers on how social structure and social processes operate to create the conditions that make geological, meteorological, and other physical events disastrous.

Social constructionism

Despite having its origins partly in symbolic interactionism, early sociological research took an ontological realist approach to the study of hazards and disasters. As noted in Chapter 2, disasters were conceptualized as "events, concentrated in time and space," that produced damage and human harm and disrupted the existing social order. Like disasters, hazards were also conceptualized as having an objective existence. As social scientists, early researchers in the field did recognize that the meanings people attach to such events shape their responses. Notably, however, early studies predated the publication of seminal works in social constructionism such as *The Social Construction of Reality* (Berger and Luckmann 1966) and, partly owing to the practical nature of early disaster studies, researchers were not particularly interested in problematizing disaster-related phenomena. In the decades since the founding of the field, various forms of constructivism have supplanted realism in sociological inquiry; importantly for this discussion, concepts formerly thought to be part of an obdurate reality, such as nature itself, are now theorized as social constructions. The interpretivist and postmodern turns in the social sciences have also undercut the notion that concepts such as "nature," "hazard," "disaster," and "victimization" are stable, uncontested, and non-problematic. This is not to say that forces such as wind, storm surges, and fault ruptures do not exist in the physical world. Denying the existence of these physical forces would be tantamount to denying the forces of gravity. Rather constructionist, interpretivist, and postmodern perspectives remind us that social processes are fundamental to the framings we attach to such phenomena. In a simple example, coastal communities in Florida are continually being exposed to the effects of climate change and sea-level rise—a physical fact—but key political actors at the state level refuse to recognize climate change and sea-level rise, preferring to use the term "nuisance flooding," which conveys the idea that rising water is episodic and not much of a problem. It has even been reported that state environmental officials have been told not to make reference to climate change or global warming in official communications (Korten 2015). At the same time, other local and regional actors in the state frame flooding as a consequence of climate change and sea-level rise and are responding accordingly.

Elsewhere (Tierney 2007, 2018) I have emphasized the importance of viewing disaster-related phenomena as social constructions. For example, expert models purporting to project the likelihood of disasters, claims regarding the putative causes of disasters, statistics and findings concerning the consequences of disasters (deaths, injuries, mental health problems), and programs purporting to reduce disaster losses and aid disaster victims are all outcomes of social construction practices (Tierney 2018). Framings of these and other disaster phenomena have their origins in a range of sources such as scientific knowledge, professional hierarchies that shape perceptions of expertise, bureaucratic routines, interest group mobilization, policy entrepreneurs, and hegemonic discourses and practices.

Like the larger field of science and technology studies, the new field of disaster science and technology studies (DSTS) is concerned, among other things, with how so-called scientific "facts" regarding hazards and disasters are shaped by social, cultural, organizational, and institutional discourses and practices (Fortun and Frickel 2013). As other scholars have noted, except in the aftermath of particular focusing events, disasters are, typically, not constructed as social problems by the broader society, although scientific elites and a few political actors may advocate for that position (Stallings 1995; Drabek 2007). Even the capacity to acknowledge disasters, both potential and actual, is shaped by organizational cultures and practices (Clarke 1993; Eden 2004; Cerulo 2008). As Eric Klinenberg (2002) has shown in his study on the 1995 Chicago heat wave, even a massive heat event that kills hundreds can escape official recognition. Similarly, Lynn Eden (2004) documented how, owing to their institutionalized routines and practices, organizations involved in planning for nuclear war focused almost exclusively on the blast effects of nuclear weapons while essentially overlooking the massive and deadly firestorms the weapons produce.

The social construction of ignorance

Discussions in the previous chapter centered on the contributions of cognitive psychology and behavioral economics to our understanding of why disaster-related threats tend to be underestimated by individuals. These disciplines emphasize the importance of individuals' cognitive limits and the existence of heuristics such as availability, optimistic bias, status quo bias, and myopia for explaining why public recognition of the likelihood of disastrous events is low. Such formulations clearly help explain some disaster-related beliefs and behaviors. However, if we are to employ a sociological lens, insights from agnotology—which is the study of the social organization of ignorance (Proctor and Schiebinger 2008)—are also relevant here. Knowledge about hazards is socially produced, but so is ignorance, and there is much that the public does not know not because it takes cognitive shortcuts when thinking about hazards and disasters but because information about the ways in which people are at risk can be quite elusive. For example, Frickel and Vincent (2007) point out that the inability to understand fully how Hurricane Katrina might have caused environmental contamination in New Orleans is the consequence of significant gaps in historical knowledge concerning the types of contamination to which the city has been exposed over time. What these researchers are emphasizing is that both knowledge and ignorance are the product of social and historical processes. Examples of what Frickel and Vincent term "the politics of not knowing" are abundant with respect to hazards and disasters. Some hazards fall through organizational cracks (Beamish 2002a, 2002b), while others are intentionally concealed—as happened, for example, when a number of earthquake faults disappeared from seismic hazard maps in California and when maps showed faults literally turning and detouring around certain properties—which earthquake faults do not do (Tierney 2014).

With respect to hazards and disasters, there are countless other examples of socially constructed ignorance, or what Linsey McGoey (2012b) calls "strategic unknowns." In her telling, ignorance, which is widely considered undesirable, becomes a strategic resource in the hands of those who hold political and economic power. There is an extensive literature documenting how powerful corporate actors sow doubt concerning threats; obvious examples include the consequences of toxic pollution (Cable, Shriver, and Mix 2008; Auyero and Swistun 2008) and climate change (Dunlap and McCright 2015). Thinking again about earthquakes, as Mike Davis discusses in *Ecology of Fear: Los Angeles and the Imagination of Disasters* (Davis 1999), real estate developers and other growth boosters promoted southern California as an idyllic setting to live in despite the region's long history of floods, drought, fire, and earthquakes. The imaginary, bucolic Los Angeles that they constructed had no room for these and other perils—such as the persistent, unstoppable debris flows that John McPhee documented so thoroughly in his 1989 book *The Control of Nature*. As is the case with respect to so many other hazards and disasters, in Los Angeles property developers made outsized profits, while taxpayers footed the bill when things went wrong.

Steve Rayner (2012) has identified four strategies that organizations and institutions employ to keep "uncomfortable knowledge," for instance about hazards and disasters, from coming to light. *Denial* is the refusal to acknowledge information even when it is available. This attitude resembles what Kari Norgaard has documented in her research on Norwegians' views on climate change, although she was not dealing with organizations there (Norgaard 2011). The individuals in her study could see with their own eyes that the climate was changing, but walled off that awareness because it was emotionally painful; and one of the reasons for it was that recognition of the threat would also involve acknowledging that Norway owes its prosperity to fossil fuels.

Dismissal is the rejection of available information as "unreliable, not relevant, imprecise, not timely or on the wrong spatial scale" (Rayner 2012: 116). The organized effort to deny or sow doubt about climate change and its impacts is a combination of denial and dismissal—an effort often aided by the media, which give as much emphasis to climate change opponents as they do to the broad scientific consensus on this topic (Boykoff and Boykoff 2004). Currently, even the US federal government seeks to obfuscate the scientific consensus on climate change and has, among other things, cancelled its participation in the Paris Climate Agreement. In August 2017, scientists associated with the US Global Change Research Program were so concerned that climate-related information would be suppressed that they gave the *New York Times* a newly developed draft report on climate change and its impact on the United States (Friedman 2017).[1]

A third strategy, *diversion*, is a "nothing to see here" approach that intentionally directs attention away from unwelcome information, in this case about hazards, and toward considering other issues. In this form of "whataboutism," disaster-related threats remain backstage while other issues are moved to the fore. For example, for many decades, organized owners of unreinforced masonry rental properties in Los Angeles that could prove deadly in an earthquake fought proposed seismic retrofits by arguing that those structures could not be upgraded without diminishing the supply of affordable rental housing or turning poor tenants out of their homes (Alesch and Petak 1986). Opponents of stronger seismic safety regulations also argue that businesses will choose to locate facilities in communities where there are less strict controls, which existing businesses might leave, and that tenants will be turned out of their homes because of seismic upgrades.

Finally, *displacement* focuses attention not on the phenomenon itself but on some substitute or surrogate for the phenomenon. Instead of acknowledging uncomfortable information about the world—in this case, the environment—organizations and institutions focus instead on abstract models of the world that they are more capable of managing. To use the earthquake example again, for nearly two decades earthquake engineers have been developing and refining elaborate models to advance performance-based earthquake engineering, which purports to go beyond existing building codes and to assure owners not just that newly designed buildings will not collapse during earthquakes but that they can be occupied and will maintain functionality after earthquakes. To offer such assurances, modelers must consider structures and local geology in isolation from broader community-level impacts of earthquakes. Scientists and engineers are also fond of creating disaster scenarios, hazard maps, and a wide range of other informational tools; they do so partly out of professionally held beliefs that are based on the information deficit model of disaster risk reduction, which assumes that, once the information is in the hands of the "right people," change will take place. This is not an argument against maps and scenarios; there are of course many important information products that can inform policymakers' and community residents' risk reduction decisions. The point is that they do so only under certain rare circumstances. Here again, hazards are framed not as political issues, but rather as problems of insufficient information that are capable of being remedied through the actions of well-meaning people.

There are many other ways in which ignorance about hazards is socially produced. Hazard insurance is a further example. Ideally, insurance premiums should act as signals that help current and potential property owners understand the risks associated with particular areas. Higher insurance rates should be indicative of higher levels of risk. However, these signals are often intentionally muted, particularly in high-risk areas. In the US National Flood Insurance Program (NFIP), for example, many insurance premiums are subsidized by the federal government and do not reflect risk severity, so property owners have a tendency to view flood risks as lower than they actually are. The Biggart-Waters Flood Insurance Reform Act of 2012 was intended to strengthen risk signals by allowing insurance rates to rise in ways that reflected risk assessments associated with property in flood-prone areas. This caused rates on some policies to increase by orders of magnitude, making insurance essentially unaffordable to many property owners. Outrage was so widespread that Biggart-Waters requirements were weakened in subsequent legislation—the Homeowner Flood Insurance Affordability Act of 2014. Not surprisingly, groups like the National Bankers Association and the National Association of Home Builders lobbied hard against flood insurance reform (Warmbrodt and Meyer 2017). In another example, wildfires are a major hazard in California, yet insurance premiums for property owners in high fire-hazard areas do not necessarily reflect the historical record or expert assessments. This is because those whose properties would be considered uninsurable on the regular market on account of very high wildfire risk can still apply to the Fair Access to Insurance Requirements (FAIR) Program, a special state-regulated risk pool. Maintaining hazard insurance subsidies has two adverse effects. Such subsidies not only shield property owners from full recognition of the perils they face but also encourage development in hazardous areas by downplaying those risks.

Along these same lines, the disclosure of hazards can be seen as a means of reducing powerful actors' construction of strategic ignorance by correcting the information asymmetry between such actors and those who may be at risk. Disclosure and right-to-know policies do help lift the veil of ignorance, particularly when information falls into the hands of well-mobilized publics and social movements. Yet the record is mixed with respect to the kind of hazards considered here. Disclosure of threats is often just that—disclosure—and hoped-for risk reduction actions do not inevitably follow. For example, the city of Seattle, Washington has done little to address earthquake hazards associated with unreinforced masonry buildings, even though the need for action has been under discussion for decades. It took until 2016 for the locations of those collapse-hazard buildings to be made public and for residents of those buildings to be informed about their risks. Seattle has yet to take systematic action to demand seismic safety upgrades. Los Angeles has had an unreinforced masonry retrofit ordinance for more than thirty years, but until very recently information about earthquake hazards associated with older, non-ductile concrete buildings in that city was unavailable. In 2014 engineering researchers at the University of California, Berkeley gave the city government a list of about 1,500 such buildings (Lin, Xia, and Smith 2014), but the general public was informed about those hazards only after the *Los Angeles Times* published maps showing the locations of the structures in question. Los Angeles subsequently passed an ordinance that required owners of dangerous older concrete buildings to carry out seismic upgrades.

Legislation demanding hazard disclosure can be an effective means for combatting ignorance about disaster threats, but here again having laws on the books is no guarantee that information will reach those who need it. The Superfund Amendment and Reauthorization Act, Title III, also known as the Emergency Planning and Community Right-to-Know Act, was passed in the aftermath of the deadly 1984 Bhopal chemical disaster. The Act required facilities that produce and handle hazardous materials to make publicly available the information on their inventories; it also mandated the establishment of local emergency planning committees (LEPCs) charged with reducing and responding to the risks posed by such facilities. However, after an explosion at a chemical plant in the town of West in Texas killed fifteen people, injured approximately 160, and damaged or destroyed about 150 structures in April 2013, hazardous materials inventory data were made unavailable on the grounds that terrorists might get access to the data.[2] More plant accidents followed, and the dangers associated with non-disclosure became even more evident in Hurricane Harvey in 2017, when numerous hazardous materials spills occurred and when fires at chemical facilities released toxic smoke, yet the affected residents were left in the dark about the hazards they were facing.

Legislation may do little to overcome socially constructed ignorance. For example, after experiencing multiple hurricanes in 2004 and 2005, in 2006 the state of Florida passed a law requiring sellers of coastal property designated as subject to coastal erosion and to federal, state, and local coastal regulations to inform purchasers about those regulations. This law applied to properties that were either totally or partly seaward of what was called the Coastal Construction Control Line (CCCL). Clearly this legislation was meant to signal to buyers that the properties they were interested in purchasing were in a coastal hazards zone. However, a study published six years after the law went into effect and based on a survey of those who had bought property in the coastal hazards zone found that the vast majority of buyers did not know that their properties were inside the CCCL and thus subject to strict regulation at the time they purchased them; moreover, they did not know anything about the disclosure requirement. The study's authors concluded bluntly that "Florida's coastal hazards disclosure law is not accomplishing its statutory purpose" (Wozniak, Davidson, and Ankersen 2012: vi). In a society awash with information, including information about hazards, it still appears that uncomfortable truths escape public scrutiny.

Disaster vulnerability and vulnerability science

Differential vulnerability to hazards and disasters has long been a concern for the sociology of disasters, as well as for environmental sociology. The concept of vulnerability encompasses both the probability of suffering the negative effects of hazards and disasters and the likelihood that some groups will be less able than others to navigate the recovery process successfully. As earlier discussions on the history of disaster research have noted, the emphasis on vulnerabilities associated with poverty, inequality, race, ethnicity, and gender increased as a consequence of research on disaster events such as the Loma Prieta earthquake (1989), Hurricane Andrew (1992), and the Northridge earthquake (1994); and such vulnerabilities were also highlighted in the mid-1990s, during the second assessment of research on natural hazards. On the basis of the research record, a report by the National Research Council noted that

> what happens to households during and after disasters can be con-
> ceptualized in terms of vulnerability and resilience. With respect to
> vulnerability, social location is associated with the severity of disaster
> impacts for households. Poverty often forces people to live in substand-
> ard or highly vulnerable housing ... leaving them more vulnerable to
> death, injury, and homelessness ... factors such as income, education,
> and homeownership influence the ability of households to mitigate and
> prepare for disasters. Social structural factors also affect the extent to

which families can accumulate assets in order to achieve higher levels of safety, as well as their recovery options and access to resources after disasters strike. (National Research Council 2006: 159)

More detail will be provided in subsequent chapters on which groups are vulnerable to disasters, how, and why. The purpose here is to reemphasize that, while they may not have been a significant concern in classical disaster research, the social and economic dimensions of vulnerability are now a major research focus.

The idea that the study of environmental and hazard vulnerability should become a specialized field was put forth by geographer Susan Cutter, who coined the term "vulnerability science" to describe that emerging specialty area (Cutter 2003). Cutter characterized vulnerability science as a subdiscipline that "[h]elps us understand those circumstances that put people and places at risk and those conditions that reduce the ability of people and places to respond to environmental risk ... [and] integrates the constructs of risk (exposure) hazard, resilience, differential susceptibility, and recovery/mitigation" (Cutter 2003: 6).

Cutter described vulnerability science as an integrative field, capable of taking into account interactions among physical features of the environment that include hazards, aspects of built environments that render them susceptible to damage and destruction, and characteristics of the inhabitants of those environments that indicate a propensity for experiencing more severe disaster impacts and poorer recovery outcomes after disasters. For Cutter, geography was the ideal discipline to bring about such integration because of its distinctive focus on space and place and its use of geographic information science (GIS). As an initial effort to systematize the study of vulnerability, Cutter and her collaborators identified a set of indicators drawn from secondary sources such as the US Census that could be used to better understand vulnerability in communities across the United States (Cutter, Boruff, and Shirley 2003). These indicators were subsequently combined into a social vulnerability index (SOVI) that provides vulnerability scores for US counties.[3] More recent research has applied SOVI concepts to other nations, such as Portugal (Guillard-Gonçalves, Cutter, Emrich, and Zêzere 2015).

The emphasis in disaster research on differential vulnerability and the emergence of vulnerability science mesh nicely with environmental sociology's concern with the related concepts of environmental justice (EJ), injustice, inequality, and racism, even though the two research traditions have mainly evolved on parallel tracks (Tierney 2007). With origins in two important studies conducted in the 1980s—one by the US General Accounting office (in 1983) and one by the United Church of Christ (Commission for Racial Justice)—EJ research has focused primarily on differential racial, ethnic, and class exposures to and impacts of environmental toxins and hazardous facilities (for early work and literature reviews, see Bullard 1990; Bryant and Mohai 1992; Brown 1995; Szasz and Meuser 1997). Over time, an extensive empirical record has developed, showing that, while both the forms of environmental inequality and the factors that are associated with it show variation across communities, general patterns hold: much more often than not, being poor and otherwise marginalized by axes of inequality translates into increased vulnerability to exposure to toxic substances and other environmental "bads" (for examples, see Bolin, Grineski, and Collins 2005; Downey 2006a, 2006b; Brulle and Pellow 2006; Downey and Hawkins 2008; Mohai, Pellow, and Roberts 2009; Grineski, Collins, Romo Aguilar, and Aldouri 2010).

Despite long-standing recognition of the differential effects of disasters, disaster vulnerability was generally not framed as a form of environmental injustice until the occurrence of Hurricane Katrina. In that disaster it was virtually impossible to ignore the social factors that influenced the ability to undertake self-protective actions like evacuation, the stark disparities in death rates by race and age in New Orleans, the unequal treatment of African American disaster survivors, and differences in return rates and recovery trajectories by race and class. Connections with the EJ tradition began to be made in the immediate aftermath of the catastrophe, both in terms of Katrina's immediate impacts and in terms of the hurricane's production of new toxic hazards that adversely affected people of color (Sze 2006; Allen 2007). Researchers such as the pioneering EJ scholar Robert Bullard and others later documented a range of environmental inequities throughout the impact recovery period (Bullard and Wright 2009; Bates and Swan 2010).

Scholars who study disasters are increasingly framing vulnerability and victimization in EJ terms. Flood risk has been studied through an EJ lens in different community and societal settings (Walker and Burningham 2011; Montgomery and Chakraborty 2015; Chakraborty, Collins, Montgomery, and Grineski 2014; Grineski et al. 2015). Extreme heat is the natural hazard that results in the greatest number of fatalities in the United States and many other nations. Here again, researchers are arguing that heat-related vulnerability is an EJ issue, not unlike exposure to toxic hazards. A number of US studies have documented the association between exposure to extreme heat, heat-related deaths, and low-income and minority populations (Klinenberg 2002; Harlan et al. 2006; Harlan, Declet-Barreto, Stefanov, and Petitti 2013; Wilhelmi and Hayden 2010); and scholars have now begun to frame these patterns in EJ terms (Mitchell and Chakraborty 2015).

Political economy and critical urban studies: a framework for understanding the social production of disaster risk and vulnerability

Advances in the study of vulnerability have led to a greater understanding of the ways in which marginalized groups are disproportionately exposed to hazards and to disaster impacts. Judging from this extensive literature, it is clear that the potential for disaster-induced losses is a form of environmental injustice. While moving the field of disaster research forward in significant ways, the vulnerability literature still has two major weaknesses. First, even as evidence continues to mount, showing that patterns of inequity exist across communities and across hazards, by and large studies do not provide a full explanation as to why this is the case. Many studies of vulnerability are place-specific and tend to involve analyses that center on particular variables, such as locational information on particular toxic facilities or on natural hazards, race, and ethnicity. In consequence, a general theory of vulnerability has yet to emerge. Second and relatedly, as can be seen in efforts to develop vulnerability indicators by using census data and other sources, the tendency in the literature is, with a few notable exceptions, to describe vulnerability as an attribute of particular segments of the population—in other words, as a *state*—when for theoretical purposes vulnerability is more appropriately conceptualized as a *process* in which different groups are affected by changes in the broader political and economic environment that either reduce or increase their propensity for loss. To cite just two examples, point-in-time indicators such as census data cannot capture the extent to which undocumented workers in the United States and even legal immigrants have been made more vulnerable as a result of the 2016 presidential election, or how regulatory rollbacks in hazardous industries will affect worker safety. As climate change advances, more people worldwide will become vulnerable to its negative impacts, and in new ways; these are changes that social indicators can only partially capture. Even though Susan Cutter (2003) emphasized that vulnerability science should take historical processes and broader contexts into account, much of the current literature does not do that (again, with some notable exceptions).

With its emphasis on root causes, dynamic pressures, and unsafe conditions, the pressure and release (PAR) model, which was discussed in Chapter 2, represents an effort to explain disaster vulnerability by pointing to contributing factors at different scales. But, even though PAR is relatively sophisticated by comparison with other explanatory frameworks such as the classical treatments of disasters that are based on systems theory, it is still largely descriptive. With its emphasis on political and economic macrolevel drivers of vulnerability, PAR points in the right direction but lacks both ties to a general theory and sufficient specificity with respect to places and populations at risk. PAR should rightly be thought of more as a heuristic tool than as a theory of disasters. While not wishing to downplay its heuristic value, I believe it can be improved upon by being connected to more general theories. In particular, as I discuss in the sections that follow, it is important to understand how social forces operating at different scales and levels of analysis contribute to the production of disaster vulnerability.

Global scale: the world system and environmental harm

A good starting point is to recognize the applicability of theories that focus on the political economy of the environment to our understanding of disaster risk production, starting at the most general level, with three macrolevel environmental sociology theories that attempt to account for the incidence and severity of environmental problems: treadmill of production, world systems theory, and unequal ecological exchange (for an overview, see Rudel, Timmons, and Carmin 2011). These three theories differ in some respects but still have a good deal in common, especially in their emphasis on negative environmental impacts created by global capitalism. Treadmill theory argues that the continual economic expansion that is imperative under capitalism leads to resource depletion and creates other negative externalities, such as increased pollution and various forms of environmental degradation. Excessive consumption is encouraged as a means of maintaining the treadmill and is made possible, for example, when corporations extend their global reach and credit is made more freely available, so that consumers can spend beyond their means. Nation-states facilitate the operation of the treadmill because it is in their interest to do so—for example, an increasing expansion generates tax revenues (Schnaiberg 1980; Gould, Pellow, and Schnaiberg 2004, 2008).

World systems theory characterizes the capitalist world system as a three-tiered political and economic order consisting of core, semi-peripheral, and peripheral nations. Core nations, the wealthiest and most powerful entities in the system, the United States, Western Europe, and Japan, dominate the ones at the periphery—the so-called "less developed" nations that make up the Global South. Semi-peripheral nations are nations that attempt either to vie for core status or to avoid sliding into peripheral status. The key dynamic of the world system is the exploitation of the labor and resources of peripheral countries by those at the core; and, for the purposes of the present discussion, this exploitation involves compelling those countries to restructure their economies in ways that benefit the core rather than their own citizens and taking advantage of their natural resources.

Unequal ecological exchange theory focuses specifically on the environmental consequences of world-system inequalities. This approach argues that "developed countries with higher levels of resource consumption externalize their consumption-based environmental costs to less-developed [sic] countries, which increase levels of environmental degradation within the latter" (Jorgenson 2006: 691). Core nations extract the mineral and other natural resources of more peripheral countries, in effect robbing those nations of the benefits of their own resources, while also ravaging their environment. Nations at the core are able to enjoy environmental amenities, but they do so at the expense of the less developed countries they have plundered. (For an extensive discussion of the different theoretical traditions that have influenced unequal ecological exchange theory, see Foster and Holleman 2014.)

Global institutions, organizations, and networks

Environmental sociologist Liam Downey has added another dimension to these macrotheoretical approaches by arguing that there is a level of analysis to consider between the world system and the national level that focuses on the role of elite, undemocratic institutions, organizations, and networks in the operations of the global political economy. Here Downey is referring to the power not of nation-states but rather of global institutions such as the World Bank and the International Monetary Fund (known as the Bretton Woods institutions) and other globally oriented major entities such as the World Trade Organization (WTO) and the General Agreement on Tariffs and Trade (GATT). These entities can be thought of as the regulators that make the hegemony of the core possible and enable the environmental exploitation of nations outside the core. According to Downey, elite-dominated institutions accomplish those goals through six major strategies: maintaining monopoly power over decision-making; shifting both environmental and non-environmental costs onto less powerful entities in the global system; thwarting the development of environment awareness in dependent nations; limiting the ability of non-elite actors to engage in environmentally sustainable behaviors; defining what constitute environmentally appropriate policies and practices; and cultivating ignorance by directing people's attention away from the environmental problems created by elite dominance (Downey 2015). What Downey demonstrates is that, within the political economy of the world system, the actions of these institutions are the mechanisms through which core dominance is maintained and unequal environmental exchange takes place.

These macrolevel dynamics set the stage for the occurrence of disasters through the impacts they have on societal and population vulnerability. In discussing the 2010 earthquake in Haiti, for example, Anthony Oliver-Smith discusses how Haiti, once known as "the Pearl of the Antilles," was perhaps the world's most productive colony until it won its independence from France in 1804. Then, treated as a pariah by powerful nations, burdened through most of its history by a debt to France that was finally paid off in 1947, with its natural resources and products exploited by elites aligned with core nations, and ruled by a series of kleptocratic dictatorial regimes, Haiti became the poorest and one of the worst-governed nations in the western hemisphere. In the 1990s its rural economy was destroyed as a result of actions undertaken by the US Agency for International Development (USAID) and by the International Monetary Fund, whose tariff policies destroyed the Haitian rice-growing industry by opening its markets to US rice.[4] Before that, USAID, acting in concert with other international entities, had orchestrated the slaughter of the country's entire pig population to block the spread of the African swine flu.

This essentially wiped out the wealth of many rural farmers, while also taking away an important food source. The impoverished rural population had long been cutting down trees to make charcoal for cooking, which contributed to deforestation and soil degradation. Once rural livelihoods were put at risk, people increasingly migrated to slums in the capital of Port-au-Prince and other cities, in search of employment. Many were unable to find work and became destitute. In Oliver-Smith's words:

> [A]s the year 2010 began, Haiti found itself extraordinarily vulnerable to the natural hazards of its environment. In the previous quarter century, few development efforts, misguided and mismanaged as they were, had privileged the issue of environmental security or hazard mitigation. A lack of building codes, together with informal settlements, widespread undernourishment and hunger, disease, poor access to clean water or electricity, inadequate educational and health facilities and services at the national and municipal levels, and crime and corruption led to the construction of extreme vulnerability. (Oliver-Smith 2010: 35)

This is why a 7.0 magnitude earthquake killed hundreds of thousands of people and crippled a nation.

The macrolevel and institutional approaches to the political economy of the environment discussed above highlight how the neoliberal world order drives the production of vulnerability. Having begun to spread in the late 1970s, neoliberalization, with its emphasis on deregulation, privatization, and so-called free markets and free trade, has become the organizing principle for relations among actors in what is now a global economic and political system. Although neoliberalization regimes show variation across different societies, and although neoliberal practices are continually being resisted and challenged, their basic economic and political principles now go virtually unquestioned. As Downey (2015) has shown, the Bretton Woods institutions and similar entities (regional development banks, trade compacts) steer the fates of all societies, but especially of those at the periphery and semi-periphery. Haiti is a prime example of how neoliberalization operates at the periphery of the world system to increase vulnerability.

As seen in Haiti, neoliberalization is the main force driving rapid urbanization in nations outside the core of the world system. Neoliberal policies make life outside urban areas essentially untenable for many inhabitants of the Global South. In a process that Saskia Sassen (2012) refers to as "agglomeration," cities in Latin America, Asia, and around the globe have become ever-expanding hubs for the global economy and magnets that attract migrants in search of better opportunities. Too often, however, those opportunities fail to materialize for ordinary workers and families because the benefits of neoliberalization accrue to global elites and multinational corporations.

Migration to cities has fueled the growth of slums in the Global South, increasing the vulnerability of both people and the environment. At the same time, structural adjustment policies imposed by the Bretton Woods institutions have led to massive debt in the nations of the periphery and semi-periphery and to declining state capacity in areas such as public health, education, and public welfare. In the words of urban scholar Mike Davis, we now live in a world

> in which the claims of foreign banks always take precedence over the needs of the urban and rural poor ... Everywhere the IMF and the World Bank ... offered poor countries the same poisoned chalice of devaluation, privatization, removal of import controls and food subsidies, enforced cost recovery in health and education, and ruthless downsizing of the public sector. (Davis 2006: 153)

National level: state action

Moving from the global to the national level, additional insights into the social production of vulnerability come from scholarship in critical urban sociology that focuses on the impact of interrelated state and corporate action on the growth of regions and metropolitan areas. Put succinctly, this perspective argues that "the use of geographical space is molded by the intersection of the state's strategic agenda with civilian political and economic processes" (Hooks 1994: 747). In the case of superpowers like the United States, the needs of the military are a critical element on that agenda. As Gregory Hooks (1994) has shown, the US government's defense-related wartime investments, particularly during and after World War II, together with growth-machine politics (discussed below), help explain growth in US regional economies. Because of national defense needs, the region that includes Norfolk, Virginia is home to the largest naval base in the world. The region is now highly vulnerable to climate change impacts such as sea-level rise, stronger hurricanes, and more intense coastal storms. National defense requirements contributed to population growth in southern California (military bases, aerospace, and other defense-related industries), the San Francisco Bay Area (military bases), and cities like Seattle (military installations, aerospace). These are cities and regions that are vulnerable to earthquakes and other hazards, but there is no evidence that hazard exposure influenced the growth of these and other regions that are highly dependent on defense spending.

Along these same lines, a variant of the treadmill of production theory known as the treadmill of destruction argues that militarism and military buildup are at the root of numerous environmental problems (Hooks and Smith 2004, 2005; Clark and Jorgenson 2012). Unlike the treadmill of production, which operates according to the logic of capitalism, the treadmill of destruction originates in geopolitical concerns and in the state's interest in projecting military power and in developing ever more lethal war-making tools.

In the United States, this has turned vast lands into sacrificial zones—locations for testing chemical and nuclear weapons, for example. There is also an EJ element to the treadmill of destruction. For example, much of the land contaminated by the military, such as the huge nuclear weapons complex in the southwestern United States, is adjacent to Native American reservations (Hooks and Smith 2004, 2005). In addition to contaminating large swathes of its own territory, including communities such as Oak Ridge in Tennessee and Hanford in Washington, which were sites for the development of nuclear weapons, the United States also represents a global environmental threat in the form of the approximately 800 military bases it operates in countries around the world (Johnson 2004). Maintaining global hegemony requires an enormous amount of resources, which is why the US military is the world's largest consumer of energy and thus among the world's largest contributors to climate change (Downey 2015).

States have other strategic interests besides defense. For example, as neo-liberalization became the global organizing principle for economic activity, experimentation with the market economy became a driving force in China's regional development. However, that development has in turn resulted in greatly increased hazard exposures. For example, the city of Shenzhen, which is located on the southeastern coast of China, north of Hong Kong, was a small fishing village with a population of around 30,000 in 1979 when Deng Xiaoping declared the area a special economic zone, allowing for the introduction of market-based economic activity and export-oriented economic development. A prime example of agglomeration as described by Sassen, Shenzhen is now a center for finance, high technology, and manufacturing, with a population of more than 10 million. The Pearl River Delta (PRD) region, where Shenzhen is located, is the largest urban agglomeration on earth in terms of both spatial scope and population size, which is estimated at over 43 million. Its recent leadership in the climate change arena notwithstanding, historically China has paid little attention to environmental hazards, and coastal economic expansion and population growth have put increasing numbers of people at risk. Development in the PRD has been accompanied by the expansion of impermeable surfaces and the destruction of natural protections such as mangrove forests, further increasing the region's physical vulnerability. In addition to the environmental damage caused by the numerous polluting industries in the PRD, the region is now at greater risk of coastal and riverine flooding and typhoons, which will continue to be exacerbated by climate change and sea-level rise, as well as of earthquakes. A recent report from Swiss Reinsurance lists the PRD as the urban region with the world's third highest vulnerability to natural hazards, after Tokyo and Manila. The PRD is the first in the world in terms of the sheer number of people exposed to hazards (Swiss Reinsurance 2014).

In recent decades, China has urbanized rapidly and to an unprecedented

degree, and new policies call for even more intense urbanization, in particular in second- and third-tier cities. Urbanization and increased density
can have many positive environmental effects, but density can also increase
vulnerability if growth occurs in hazardous areas. Additionally, building code
enforcement and construction quality are major problems in China, as seen in
the devastating 2008 Sichuan earthquake, which killed an estimated 80,000
people (Tierney 2014). Massive construction projects also generate massive
amounts of debris. In December 2015 a mountain of construction waste collapsed in Shenzhen, killing seventy-three residents.

Local communities and regions

Focusing now on the local level, coalitions known as growth machines
(Molotch 1976; Logan and Molotch 1976), which involve political leaders, real
estate and development interests, and industry, champion economic growth
to the exclusion of other values, such as the safety of those at risk from natural
and technological hazards. Growth machines discursively frame continued
economic expansion as an imperative. To give just one example, intensified
development in coastal areas is the main driver of ever-increasing hurricane
losses in the United States (Pielke et al. 2008), and climate change and sea-level
rise will intensify this trend. In many cases, vulnerability results not only
from exposure to hazards like hurricanes, but also from the fragility of the
built environment. Under the pressure of rapid growth, it is difficult to monitor construction practices and ensure that building codes are enforced. Poor
code enforcement has been identified as contributing to hurricane losses in
Florida; according to one study, up to 40 percent of the insured property losses
in Hurricane Andrew were due to substandard building practices and weak
code enforcement (Bragg 1999).[5]

Under the current neoliberal political–economic regime, communities
compete for private sector investment, typically by offering generous tax
incentives to lure economic activity. The same is the case for state-driven
military and other spending, where competing local communities work
with their political representatives to attract government facilities such as
military installations. In many cases, government investment helps growth
machines achieve their objectives while also helping to increase disaster
vulnerability. For example, federal investments in activities such as levee
building and beach replenishment, along with insurance subsidies, often
result in what Raymond Burby (2006) calls the "safe development paradox":
while ostensibly offering protection from hazards, government investments
make intensified development in hazardous areas possible. Growth-machine
elites demand flood protections like levees because these enable construction
in areas adjacent to the levees, but the end result is that development puts
more people and property at risk. The existence of levees is one key reason
for the explosive population growth that has occurred in the delta region in

northern California, yet many of the delta's levees are in danger of failing and the region is at risk from storms, earthquakes, and sea-level rise (Burton and Cutter 2008). Levees failed to protect New Orleans from catastrophic flooding in Hurricane Katrina. At the behest of growth boosters, the building of canals in New Orleans was made possible by large federal subsidies, as was the construction and continued expansion of the Mississippi River Gulf Outlet (MR-GO). Both the extensive network of canals and MR-GO contributed to Katrina's massive impacts (Freudenburg, Gramling, Laska, and Erikson 2009).

When Hurricane Harvey struck in 2017, bringing with it unprecedented rainfall, Houston and neighboring cities in Texas were inundated in what became one of the most damaging and costly disasters in US history. Disaster researchers who watched Harvey's slow march toward the Houston area feared the worst because they understood the Houston region's vulnerabilities. A classic example of growth-machine politics run amok, Houston had become the fourth largest city in the United States by acting as a magnet for migrants who were looking for jobs and affordable places to live. In the years leading up to the hurricane, Harris County, where Houston is located, had been the second fastest-growing county in the country, and at one point Houston was adding about 2,500 new residents *every week*. As the city grew, new roads and highways were built, adding more impermeable surfaces that increased rainfall runoff, and grasslands that could have absorbed rainfall and floodwaters were paved over. Like the state of Texas in general, Houston didn't believe in zoning, so it was not unusual for residential neighborhoods to be located directly adjacently to industrial facilities. Politically averse to anything that might stand in the way of development, the city allowed new construction in flood plains at an alarming rate in the years prior to Harvey. There had been warnings of what was to come. In 2001, Houston experienced extreme flooding and extensive damage as a result of Tropical Storm Allison, which dropped forty inches of rain on the city, but building in hazardous areas continued unabated after Allison. In May 2015 and April 2016, Houston experienced two "500-year" floods—that is, flood events that supposedly had a 1:500 probability of occurring in any given year.

The greater Houston area is home to the largest petrochemical complex in the United States as well as to other sources of toxic materials such as landfills and Superfund sites. Floodwaters carried and spread toxins, resulting in explosions and fires and exposing those in the impact area to both acute and longer-term safety and health threats. Additionally, as noted earlier, because of actions aimed at suppressing information about hazardous inventories, members of the public and those who came to the city to help with the response had no idea about the hazards to which they were exposed.

Race and place: producing environmental injustice

Growth-machine politics constitutes one set of factors that shape vulnerability at the local level. Going further to examine which groups within exposed populations are especially vulnerable to disasters and environmental toxins requires an understanding of the processes and practices that determine how those groups have come to be distributed spatially, in what types of dwellings they live, and near what types of hazards they find themselves. These are, of course, the kinds of questions environmental inequality research seeks to address—and I will deal with them in greater detail in Chapter 6. The existence of environmental racism is well established in the literature. However, the best research on environmental racism is accompanied by a focus on the causal processes that serve as basis for an inequitable exposure to hazards. This involves exploring the concept of race itself, how racism operates, and how it is maintained.

Current sociological conceptions of race rely heavily on racial formation theory—that is, on the idea that racial categories are produced, changed, and maintained through racial projects, which are practices and processes that mark human bodies as different and unequal, as well as through hegemony, the complex of ruling practices and their cultural justifications (Omi and Winant 1994). Although notions of race and racist attitudes existed well before the development of capitalism, racism is essential to the functioning of capitalism, in particular because it makes it possible to assign differential values to differently racialized groups (Pulido 2016, 2017). As sociologist David Pellow (2007) points out, the normal functioning of capitalist economies requires racial, class, and other forms of inequality. This is because capital accumulation, a driving force within capitalism, cannot take place unless subordinate groups such as people of color and the poor—together with what they own and the places where they live—are robbed of value. As Jodi Melamed argues, accumulation under racialized capitalism must necessarily entail

> loss, disposability, and the unequal differentiation of human value, and racism enshrines the inequality that capitalism provides . . . it does this by displacing the uneven life chances that are inescapably part of capitalist social relations onto fictions of differing human capacities, historically race. (Melamed 2015: 77)

The ways in which racialized capitalism operates differ across places, historical periods, and oppressed groups. In the United States, in relation to African Americans, its manifestations have included slavery, violent attacks on African American communities, lynching, and race riots such as the 1921 riot in Tulsa, Oklahoma, in which whites attacked both residents and important institutions in the African American community.[6] Violent attacks against African Americans continue, but in a variety of forms, as the overt collective violence of the past has been replaced by the slow violence of segregation, discrimination, exposure to natural and environmental hazards, and the harassment and killing of African Americans by agents of social control.

In the United States, slow violence against African Americans and other minority groups was instigated by local growth machines but was also enabled in important ways by the state itself. Redlining for purposes of underwriting loans was initiated in 1933 by the federal government's Home Owners' Loan Corporation (HOLC), which privileged white borrowers while disadvantaging African Americans and other people of color. Further incorporating racism into loan criteria, the Federal Housing Authority (FHA) and Veterans Administration followed HOLC practices, as did private lending institutions. Federally supported urban renewal programs, also known as "Negro removal," disrupted African American communities, and public housing projects were located in neighborhoods that were already majority-minority because white-dominated local power structures wanted it that way. The interstate highway system, originally planned for national defense, intensified the trend toward suburbanization and enabled white flight from cities around the United States (for in-depth discussions, see Massey and Denton 1998).

Actions by the state have been accompanied by other measures that have prevented people of color (and also other groups, such as Jews) from having access to a wider range of places to live. Such measures include restrictive covenants that specify who can and cannot live in particular neighborhoods, as well as various forms of exclusionary zoning. Zoning decisions are made by local governments and thus are subject to local political and economic pressure. For example, certain neighborhoods are zoned only for single-family dwellings, keeping out multifamily and apartment buildings. Others are zoned for the kinds of industries that pollute the environment. Additionally, pressure from "not in my back yard" (NIMBY) groups can also ensure that locally unwanted land uses (LULUs) are not permitted, except in low-income and minority areas.

Historically focused studies of environmental inequalities in Phoenix, Arizona (Bolin, Grineski, and Collins 2005) and in the southern California region (Pulido 2000) show how capitalist economic activity and white privilege put people of color at risk. Phoenix was established by whites, in contrast with other southwestern cities, which had originally been settled by Mexicans. Early in its history, Phoenix was segregated, Mexicans, Mexican Americans, and African Americans being relegated to the southern part of the city. The Ku Klux Klan, vigilante groups, and hyperdiscrimination in education and employment enforced this system of "sunbelt apartheid." Phoenix benefitted from the post-World War II expansion of defense spending, but the benefits of this expansion accrued to whites at the expense of people of color. At the same time polluting industries were attracted to south Phoenix, partly through zoning regulations, and interstate highways were routed through Latino/a neighborhoods, increasing air pollution. As suburbanization spread northward in the city, south Phoenix continued to decline into an area with disproportionate exposure to environmental toxins, with poor housing quality, and without environmental amenities. Later, this was revealed as the area where heat-related deaths were concentrated (Harlan et al. 2013). Bolin, Grineski, and Collins (2005) argued earlier that

> conditions in South Phoenix are not intentionally produced yet they clearly flow from a racist ideologies [*sic*] and practices coupled with a strong political drive to promote growth and development in the city. To promote a century of industrialization adjacent to low-income neighbor-hoods, without concern for the well being of residents or any substantial investment in housing for its residents is environmental racism. (2005: 166)

Laura Pulido (2000) documents similar historical patterns in the Greater Los Angeles region. Like Bolin and his coauthors, Pulido shows how, over time, the exercise of white privilege manifested in segregation, decisions about the siting of hazardous facilities, and state-enabled suburbanization resulted in the disproportionate exposure of African Americans, Latinos/as, other people of color, and low-income whites to hazards associated with polluting indus-trial facilities. Like Phoenix, the Los Angeles area experienced defense-related growth in the aftermath of World War II; but institutionalized racism in the form of redlining, as practiced by the HOLC and the FHA, ensured that segregation would persist. At the same time, the incorporation of suburban areas as new cities made it possible for those cities to use zoning regulations, restrictive covenants, and other means to maintain their "whiteness."

Pulido was primarily concerned with the ways in which white privilege was expressed spatially in Greater Los Angeles, with an emphasis on how the region's evolution exposed minority residents to toxic hazards. It is thus understandable that she did not incorporate exposure to natural hazards such as earthquakes into her analysis. Yet her arguments also apply to earth-quake vulnerability. For example, Los Angeles began to address the issue of collapse-hazard unreinforced masonry (URM) buildings in the mid-1980s, yet little was actually done to mitigate those hazards when the Whittier Narrows earthquake struck in 1987. A large number of multi-family URM buildings were concentrated in neighborhoods in the Pico-Union district just west of downtown Los Angeles. This area, in which rental costs were comparatively low, was home to many Mexican Americans and recent immigrants from Central America. There was extensive damage to URM apartment buildings in Pico-Union and, after the earthquake, frightened residents began to set up improvised outdoor shelters in parks or near their apartments—responses to earthquakes that were common in the earthquake-prone nations of Central America. The 1994 Northridge earthquake did major damage to the housing supply of minority and low-income residents and resulted in the same patterns of outdoor sheltering. Understanding that the safety of damaged buildings was a major concern, city officials who conducted safety inspections after the earthquake were accompanied by translators who were able to inform non-English speakers whether they could reoccupy their buildings.

Middle-Range Theory:
Panic, Emergence, and Self-Protective Actions

Panic

As noted in Chapter 2, the study of the social activities that relate to hazards and disasters was originally influenced by research in the sociological subfield of collective behavior. Henry Quarantelli, who is among the most influential thinkers in the field of disaster studies, began his career studying the conditions that contribute to the emergence of panic (Quarantelli 1954). Because in the early days of disaster studies there was a widespread expectation that mass panic would break out in the event of a nuclear war, Quarantelli went looking for panic in high-threat situations, but did not find it in the vast majority of the cases he studied. Although the panic myth has long been debunked by researchers, the concept of panic remains relevant to the study of disasters, because the public still clings to the idea that disasters induce panic and the media still report that it is widespread (Clarke 2002). For example, after the tragic mass shooting at a music festival in Las Vegas in 2017, which killed fifty-eight people and injured over 400, media accounts reported on the "panic" that gripped concertgoers and on the "stampedes" that ensued, even though video footage of people's attempts to move to safety showed an orderly retreat from the bullets that rained down.

Panic is so rare, Quarantelli argued, because the conditions that give rise to it are almost never present, even under circumstances that involve extreme danger, such as building fires and large explosions. According to his findings, for panic to emerge, there must be shared preexisting beliefs that particular situations, for example airline crashes or fires, are the kinds of situations that give rise to panic. Such beliefs are often based on popular culture framings of the incidents in question. Second, there must be an absence of social ties within the endangered collectivity. Third, as the threat becomes evident, members of the collectivity must develop the perception that entrapment is possible; those who come to the conclusion that they are indeed trapped in a threatening situation do not panic. Individuals must also have a sense of powerlessness and total social isolation. Finally, they must feel that, while escape from danger is possible, the chances for it are dwindling. Even under such conditions, only a small number of those facing highly dangerous situations do panic and, if panic does break out, it is short-lived (Quarantelli 1977).

In his many writings on panic, Quarantelli not only challenged the myth of its frequency but also pointed to errors in the way the phenomenon has been characterized, both by scholars and in the popular media. *Contra* Neil

Smelser (1962), panic is not based on irrational or "hysterical beliefs," but rather on realistic fears of an imminent threat, a sense of social isolation, and the belief that escape is the only option. Panic does not involve contagion; in fact panicky reactions are typically confined to a very small segment of those who are confronting danger. The idea that panic is common is a media creation reinforced by the widespread and uncritical application of the term to a variety of emotions and behaviors. Worry about causing panic can lead to faulty decision-making, as happens for example when authorities resist issuing disaster warnings out of fear of causing panic (Quarantelli 1977, 2001a). Quarantelli argued that, because of its potential for generating misunderstandings, the term should be withdrawn—an argument supported by decision scientist Baruch Fischhoff, who inveighed against the media's use of the word to describe the passengers forced to evacuate after a plane crash and fire in Toronto in 2005—an evacuation that was both rapid and orderly:

> Whatever its source, the myth of panic is a threat to our welfare. Given the difficulty of using the term precisely and the rarity of actual panic situations, the cleanest solution is for the politicians and the press to avoid the term altogether. It's time to end chatter about "panic" and focus on ways to support public resilience in emergency. (Fischhoff 2005)

Despite the frequent misapplication of the term in the media and in public discourse, research continues to bear out the points originally made by Quarantelli decades ago. Those caught in frightening situations may be described as panicky in media accounts and may indeed actually believe that they have panicked, but the empirical record continues to show that social bonds do not break down even in truly frightening situations such as fires, plane crashes, crowd crushes, and the 1993 and 2001 bombings of the World Trade Center (Keating, Loftus, and Manber 1983; Johnson 1988; Johnson, Feinberg, and Johnston 1994; Aguirre, Wenger, and Vigo 1998; Clarke 2002; Kuligowski 2011). The resilience of those bonds and the dominance of prosocial behavior provide protection against the development of panic.

Emergence

A key characteristic of disaster situations is the extent to which they result in a range of emergent social phenomena. Emergence involves the development of norms, social practices, and forms of social organization that are novel in comparison with the established social order. Early ideas concerning emergence were influenced by Chicago School social psychologist Herbert Blumer, by symbolic interactionism more generally, and by Turner and Killian's emergent norm theory of collective behavior. Emergent norm theory, which evolved over a thirty-year period during last century (Turner and Killian 1987), sought to explain three key dimensions of collective behavior phenomena:

- extra-institutionalism, that is, a departure from conventional patterns of behavior enabled, according to the theory, by the development of new norms about what is right and wrong or appropriate and inappropriate in a specific situation;
- a move from collectively shared feelings to action, depending on whether that action is collectively defined as feasible and timely; and
- the formation and maintenance of collectivities committed to carrying out the actions that the new norms require, given that these actions depend on preexisting social relationships and/or on an occurrence that is so unusual that it requires interpersonal interaction in order to be inter- preted as to its meaning and for a collective decision on how to respond to be taken.

Collective behavior is inherently dynamic; collective definitions and courses of action shift as a result of changing conditions and collective apprais- als. For example, appraisals concerning what actions are feasible can shift if attempted action is thwarted (Turner and Killian 1987). Paralleling this reasoning, Quarantelli's theory of emergence in disaster settings cites as conditions a shared perception that a given crisis situation requires urgent action—for example, that there are critical needs that are not being addressed by institutionalized means; a supportive social climate consisting of common norms, values, and beliefs; preexisting social relationships that are defined as relevant to the crisis situation; and the presence of crucial resources, includ- ing material resources and knowledge of how to take action. Two other factors increase the likelihood of emergence: prior planning, which sets at least some parameters around what types of actions are appropriate in crisis situations; and prior experience, which affords some opportunity to "rehearse" uncon- ventional action (Quarantelli 1995).

Emergent groups

Research on emergence in disasters has been influenced by what is known as Disaster Research Center (DRC) typology. This is a fourfold framework that characterizes the activities organized in times of disaster according to the extent to which organizational tasks and structures after disasters differ from their pre-disaster counterparts. One organizational form, called the emer- gent group, involves both new tasks and new structural arrangements. Such groups have no pre-disaster existence; they form only after a disaster and its impact, in order to address crisis-related needs identified by group members. Emergent groups operating after disaster impact are often made up of people in the immediate vicinity of the disaster. For example, it has long been recog- nized that post-impact search-and-rescue activities are typically undertaken by community residents themselves (Tierney, Lindell, and Perry 2001; National Research Council 2006).

Emergent groups have been studied in a variety of pre-, trans-, and post-disaster settings (Drabek 1987; Stallings and Quarantelli 1985). As discussed in a review by Drabek and McEntire (2003), in addition to the DRC typology, studies have identified various other forms of emergence in disaster situations: quasi- or partial emergence, task emergence, emergence based on latent knowledge not previously acted upon, and interstitial emergence in which a new group emerges that establishes linkages with existing organizations (see Quarantelli 1996 for a discussion of some of these forms). These studies argue that several factors facilitate emergence—for example shared values or what Drabek and McEntire (2003: 102) refer to as a "culture of responsibility"; the involvement of faith-based organizations in disaster-related activities; and the scope and severity of the disaster, which has a positive impact on the likelihood of emergence. Post-disaster groups can also spring from preexisting ties with groups that were formed for other purposes. For example, Occupy Sandy, a network that emerged in New York after Superstorm Sandy (2012), to provide assistance to disaster survivors, had its origins in the Occupy Wall Street protests that followed the financial meltdown of 2008.

There is also a gendered dimension to emergent group activities, but the literature on the impact of gender is equivocal. Participation in such activities is often done according to traditional gender roles, as happened for example in the 1985 Mexico City earthquake, when men organized themselves into search-and-rescue groups while women provided supplies and aid (Wenger and James 1994), or when groups composed of women assume "caring" roles in the aftermath of disasters (Fothergill 1996). Concern for children's welfare may partly explain why women are more likely than men to protest against technological hazards (Neal and Phillips 1990). It has also been argued that disasters result in a retreat into traditional gender roles even among those who previously espoused egalitarian values (Hoffman 1998). At the same time, there are examples of women forming their own emergent groups in order to resist being excluded from important disaster-related activities such as reconstruction (Enarson and Morrow 1998; Hoffman 1998). To complicate matters still further, some studies find no relationship between gender and involvement in emergent activities (O'Brien and Mileti 1992), while others question whether past accounts of disaster-related behavior have not been themselves biased, either by overlooking women's role in emergent groups in disasters or by inappropriately employing gender stereotypes to describe disaster-related behaviors (Scanlon 1997).

Like gender, race and ethnicity seem to be related to emergence in complex ways. Because government activities benefit those with economic and political power, in disasters we should expect to see members of racial and ethnic minorities forming emergent groups in order to provide mutual aid and carry out tasks they define as necessary. For example, Hurricane Katrina saw the creation of the Common Ground Collective, originally organized by former

Black Panthers and anarchists, as well as collective mobilization on the part of the Vietnamese Americans in the neglected Village de L'Est and Versailles communities in New Orleans (Solnit 2009; Tierney 2014). The literature also contains examples of minority group members who organize after disasters, to demand services that address their specific needs. This is what happened after the 1989 Loma Prieta earthquake in Santa Cruz County, when Chicano residents protested by refusing to go into official government shelters and set up their own facilities in a local park (Bolin and Stanford 1990). Here again, however, to the extent that racial and ethnic minorities are marginalized and isolated—which includes their linguistic isolation and unfamiliarity with the operations of the disaster management system—they may lack the capacity for collective action. Isolation may be particularly acute among members of racial and ethnic groups who are undocumented and who may be afraid to organize in the aftermath of disasters.

Improvisation

Improvisation is a form of emergent activity that is enacted by both existing organizations and newly formed ones. In this case, new strategies emerge for carrying out disaster-related tasks—typically with new tools, including informational ones—that are collectively defined as appropriate in a given disaster setting. Disasters invariably contain elements of surprise; even the best disaster plans can fall short, because by their nature disasters have unanticipated effects. As described by Tricia Wachtendorf (2004) in her study of the 2001 World Trade Center attacks in New York City, improvisation in disasters ranges from activities that differ from what was originally planned but attempt to reproduce it to entirely new sets of activities, never envisioned in the original plan. For example, as a result of the Trade Center attacks, New York City lost its emergency operations center at the height of the attacks, yet was able through improvisation to reproduce organizational configurations and communication capabilities at a new site, in a matter of days. In other cases, however, such as the search for human remains and crime-scene evidence at the Fresh Kills landfill, procedures and practices had to be improvised on the fly, because there was no preexisting "roadmap" for how such tasks would be performed (Wachtendorf 2004).

Improvisation is a relatively new line of sociological inquiry, and much existing scholarship relies on insights developed from the study of jazz and acting. One key lesson from that body of work is that improvisation is not the completely spontaneous creation of new lines of action on the spur of the moment; it is best carried out by professionals who are highly knowledgeable about different musical forms and performance repertoires. While it may appear spontaneous, jazz improvisation reflects the ability to draw upon knowledge that is both broad and deep (Berliner 1994; Weick 1998). Researchers find that the same is the case with improvised emergency response activities. As Tricia Wachtendorf and James Kendra put it, "an emergency responder—whether a formal or informal responder—must be able to draw upon a repertoire of training or education, experience, knowledge of the community, and a shared vision with other organizations":

> Improvisation also involves the ability to use resources that are on hand (whether or not they have been pre-designated as emergency response resources) as well as the ability to decide how much deviation from previous plans is appropriate. Rigid hierarchical forms of command and the compartmentalization of organizational roles discourage improvisation. In contrast, improvisation thrives when local actors have autonomy when confronting surprise. (Wachtendorf and Kendra 2006)

Emergent multiorganizational networks

Emergence in disasters also occurs at the network level. Emergent multiorganizational networks (EMONs) are novel, complex, heterogeneous forms of organization that consist of a mix of preexisting organizations with designated disaster responsibilities and new entrants, including preexisting entities without prior involvement in disaster-related activities and emergent groups. These different types of organizations may themselves undergo structural changes, such as increases in size as volunteers converge to provide additional assistance. EMONs are an outgrowth of efforts at improvisation, formed out of a common recognition, among network participants, that urgent action is needed, namely action that reaches outside pre-disaster institutional arrangements. Subnetworks typically organize themselves around key tasks (Bevc 2010). One example of such a network is the civilian mariners who coordinated their activities to evacuate Lower Manhattan by water after the 9–11 World Trade Center attacks. In that instance, operators of commercial watercraft of all types self-organized to evacuate hundreds of thousands of people from Lower Manhattan—a waterborne evacuation comparable in size to, or perhaps even larger than, the evacuation of Dunkirk during World War II. Without any central coordinating body, the EMON was able to function effectively owing to a variety of factors. Important among them were mariner culture, which calls for action on behalf of those in distress; a shared vision of what needed to be done; and the mariners' extensive local knowledge (Kendra and Wachtendorf 2016).

The most sophisticated studies on disaster EMONs draw extensively on interorganizational theory and on network theory and analytic methods, but with a major difference: while those fields tend to concentrate on network relationships that develop and operate in relatively stable environments, research on disaster EMONs focuses on network phenomena in turbulent, unstable environments, typically characterized by the rapid emergence of new network relationships and by dynamic change. Still, EMON researchers remain committed to studying central network-analytic topics such as network structure (e.g., centrality, connectedness), brokerage, communication, coordination, influence, and factors that help explain network relationships (e.g., homophily, geographic proximity). The difference is that the emphasis is on the ways in which network attributes and associated behaviors depart from pre-event institutional arrangements, such as disaster plans. One challenge in EMON studies is that this research tends to focus on post-impact networks, without the benefit of having baseline data. (For representative studies and discussions of methodological issues, see Petrescu-Prahova and Butts 2005; Butts, Petrescu-Prahova, and Cross 2007; Bevc 2010; Spiro, Acton, and Butts 2013; Schweinberger, Petrescu-Prahova, and Vu 2014; Kapucu and Garayev 2016).

Online emergence and crisis informatics

The study of online emergence and emergent networks is a new area in disaster research. Often referred to as crisis informatics, this field developed in the early years of the new millenium through collaborations among computer and information scientists, disaster sociologists, and other social scientists. The field had its origins in the study of manifestations of disaster-related collective behavior such as convergence and group emergence; scholars found similarities between these kinds of behaviors in real-world crises and virtual-world activities that employed information and communication technology in the context of disasters and other emergencies (Palen et al. 2007; Palen and Liu 2007; Palen and Hughes 2018). Tracking the rapid evolution of information and communication technologies (ICT) and Web 2.0, crisis informatics is a rapidly evolving field. Because it is so new and because the majority of publications on crisis informatics are descriptive case studies of online activities that involve the use of specific technologies in specific disaster events, systematic theories have not yet been developed. One interesting line of research would be to test to what extent conditions that foster real-world convergence operate in the same way in cyberspace.

Research on crisis informatics spans a wide range of topics. In this section I discuss research involving online emergent activity. The next section will deal with warnings and warning responses. There I will briefly look at research on how and to what effect ICT is changing the way warnings are issued and disseminated. I will leave out the use of social media by established (as opposed to emergent) disaster responders, or ICT-enabled one- and two-way communications between officials and members of the public, which are also addressed in crisis informatics research (see, e.g., Hughes, St. Denis, Palen, and Anderson 2014; Sutton, League et al. 2015; Hughes and Chauhan 2015; Chauhan and Hughes 2017).

Collective sense-making is a critical element in disaster-related collective action. Prior research on sense-making has described how the process develops in real-world situations—or fails to do so (Weick 1993). Crisis informatics research looks at how online convergence, emergence, and collaboration can contribute to sense-making and to situational awareness for participants within and outside disaster-stricken areas. For example, in one early study Leysia Palen and her collaborators described how Facebook was used during and after the 2007 Virginia Tech mass shootings, both as a means to dissemi-nate "I'm OK" messages and in order to arrive at an account of those who had perished in the attacks. Noteworthy in this study were Facebook participants' ability to identify victims more quickly than university authorities and par-ticipants' ongoing editing of posts for accuracy (Vieweg et al. 2008). In other work on sense-making and the use of spatial and visual information, Palen and colleagues studied the role of the photo-sharing platform Flickr in docu-menting the impacts of six different disaster and crisis events (Liu et al. 2008). Among other numerous publications by the Palen group are studies on the use of OpenStreetMap following the 2010 Haiti earthquake (Soden and Palen 2014) and on emergent neogeographic practice, or the use of social media platforms and mash-ups to convey crisis-related information both spatially and temporally (Liu and Palen 2010).

According to collective behavior theory, rumor behavior is a form of collec-tive sense-making that typically emerges in uncertain situations, including disasters. Crisis informatics research has explored various aspects of online rumoring; there are for instance studies on rates of rumor propagation, expressions of confidence in information that is passed on through ICT affordances such as Twitter, the ways in which rumors are corrected and affirmed online, and methodological strategies for increasing the accuracy of research on crisis-related rumoring (see, for example, Starbird et al. 2016; Zeng, Starbird, and Spiro, 2016; Arif et al. 2017; Fitzhugh, Gibson, Spiro, and Butts 2016).

In addition to sense-making, crisis informatics researchers study a variety of other online phenomena. Project HEROIC (the acronym stands for "hazards, emergency response, and online information communication") has developed models of EMONs based on Twitter messaging, for example in the 2013 Boston Marathon bombing (Sutton et al. 2013). In related work that is also based on Twitter messaging, project HEROIC investigators studied the EMON that developed after the 2010 *Deepwater Horizon* oil spill and used network-analytic techniques to explore network attributes such as reciprocity, hierarchy, power, and influence (Sutton et al. 2013). Focusing on the Boston Marathon bombing, Andrea Tapia and her colleagues explored what happened when two online groups (Reddit and Anonymous), interacting with authorities and with "virtual bystanders," attempted to aid law enforcement by finding the perpetrators of the bombing (Tapia, LaLone, and Kim 2014). Along with col-laborators, she also examined how ICT connectivity and network structure affect the performance of humanitarian organizations, finding that network centrality and density are important for effective organizational performance (Tchouakeu, Maitland, Tapia, and Kvasny 2013).

Warning responses

Public responses to disaster warnings are among the best-studied topics in the field of social science disaster research. This body of research, which has spanned nearly five decades, has resulted in the formulation of conceptual models and in a large number of hypothesis-testing studies. Classic research on disaster warnings characterized the process in more or less linear terms, using Lasswell's (1948) source–message–channel–receiver–effect–feedback model. Investigators sought to identify the factors that determine successful transmission at each stage in the chain. For example, for message sources, attributes such as legitimacy, credibility, and believability were identified as important. Similarly, researchers identified attributes of messages, channels, and receivers that were deemed important for message effectiveness. Models of warning response drew heavily on more general principles of risk communication, while recognizing that risk communication challenges are different for imminent threats from what they are during non-disaster times.

Sociological theorizing regarding warning responses relies, either implicitly or explicitly, on the emergent norm theory of collective behavior. As noted earlier, emergent norm theory focuses on how members of collectivities develop new norms or courses of action that depart from conventional everyday activity, typically in conditions of uncertainty and urgency. In a general sense, the process of arriving at decisions on protective actions such as evacuation can be characterized as a form of "milling" (Blumer 1939; Turner and Killian 1987; see also Wood et al. 2018) or intensified collective information seeking in which participants seek to develop new "definitions of the situation" when they perceive that something out of the ordinary and potentially threatening is happening. Milling begins when members of the public become aware of a possible threat by receiving information about it through interpersonal networks or social media, or through official notifications. Once the information is received, milling continues as the public attempts to go through other stages of the response process: understanding the information, believing that it is true, feeling personally at risk, confirming the information, and responding accordingly (Mileti and Sorensen 1987). Research on warning responses makes three key points: an active response will not take place without the satisfactory resolution of those stages; action is never automatic and always depends on social interaction; and message recipients must verify the message with the help of other information sources before taking further action.

The protective action decision model

The protective action decision model (PADM) is the most widely recognized formulation that attempts to explain the public's adoption of a range of protective actions, including evacuation and other warning responses.

Originally developed by psychologist Michael Lindell and sociologist Ronald Perry (Lindell and Perry 1992, 2004), the PADM has undergone revision on the basis of subsequent empirical research. In its most recent version (see Lindell and Perry 2012), the PADM consists of four sets of factors. First, the process of self-protective action is set in motion by environmental cues that indicate danger, such as noxious smells associated with a chemical release, by social cues or indications that others are responding to the threat, and by warning messages disseminated through a wide range of channels, all of which have their own strengths and weaknesses. These cues are potentially available to members of the public ("receivers") who differ in terms of physical, cognitive, and language capabilities, mental models related to hazards, and economic resources and social capital in ways that will influence their responses. Second, the recipients of warning information initiate and complete a series of cognitive steps. Prior to making any decision, message recipients must actually be exposed to cues and warnings; for example, they must be able to hear sirens and loudspeakers, or to receive warning messages on cell phones or through social media. Messages must also be intrusive enough to gain the attention of intended recipients, and recipients must comprehend them, which depends on such factors such as language ability and message clarity. Not all of those who are exposed to cues and warnings will actually reach this stage.

If these conditions are met, those receiving warnings must then feel personally at risk—that is, they must decide that the situation could have negative consequences, for example death or bodily harm. This depends in part on such factors as past experience with and proximity to the hazard. Assuming he or she believes that there is a risk, the warning recipient then draws upon his or her knowledge of protective actions associated with the threat, including knowledge about what actions are needed, their difficulty, and their cost. At this point individuals will also decide who is responsible for taking protective steps; in the case of evacuation, this is typically the individual or household.

Once these cognitive steps have been completed, warning recipients have reached the point of having to decide what they will do. Then they must make up their minds that the perceived threat is one that really requires action and that they have a personal (not just a generalized) sense of risk. They must consider alternative actions that could offer protection against the threat, decide which option is likely to be the best one, and formulate a plan. They then must implement the plan; but, typically, they do not do so immediately. Rather they tend to delay until they believe that they have enough information to act (which can require additional milling) and that the need to do so is urgent. Even then, they may not be able to carry out the intended actions because of situational constraints—as happens, for example, when at-risk households need an automobile to flee from floodwaters but do not have or cannot reach one, or when a mobility-challenged individual is physically unable to escape from a burning high-rise building. The final stage of the model involves feedback—that is, a reiteration of the previous stages, which Lindell and Perry (2012: 624) argue is "extremely common in sudden onset disasters because people seek to confirm or contradict any warnings they have received, typically by contacting different sources using a different channel."

PADM is limited in some respects. Although logically sound and consistent with previous research, the theory itself has not been tested in its entirety. Rather it gains authority through its consistency with a large body of empirical work on various phases of the model. Its approach to decision-making tilts too much in the direction of rational actor theory, and relatedly, although the model does make the point that to generate a response cues must be sufficiently intrusive, the PADM tends to neglect the role of emotion in emergency decision-making. Highly emotionally laden situations—for example, ones involving the safety of infants or other dependants in one's care—may trigger a short-circuiting of some of the cognitive processes that the model highlights, in favor of rapid precautionary "better safe than sorry" action. Although, as mentioned earlier, there is a long research record indicating that panic is extremely rare in emergencies, the PADM should be able to account for panic responses too; but it cannot.

New technologies, new questions

There are other reasons for asking whether the extensive findings on public responses to warnings remain valid. A substantial amount of the research on warning responses and self-protective action was carried out during a period when information sources were significantly fewer than they are today and when information channels were more limited and employed conventional technologies such as radio and television. The communication landscape is now quite different. The public, in the United States and in many other developed societies, is continually awash with media that may contain information on numerous threats, imminent or distant, on which sources, messages, and channels abound, but without necessarily being vetted for their legitimacy. What is more, new technologies are continually coming online to communicate public warnings and advisories, and an increasingly diverse public is accessing information in increasingly diverse ways. The changing landscape in information technology, the new ways in which the public is accessing information, and increasing societal diversity raise a variety of questions for researchers. How intrusive do messages need to be to cut through the noise? Do we actually know how societal diversity operates in crisis situations, or are we making unwarranted assumptions? Does the fact that there are politically polarized publics in the United States and in many other societies, which are characterized by markedly different preferences for consuming information, make a difference to the uptake of threat information? If trust in institutions declines, as it has in the United States, how is that affecting hazard perceptions and behavior?

Even with this changed landscape, human information- and decision-processing needs in times of crisis have not changed appreciably; the cognitive and behavioral processes that operate in responding to threats are still the same. According to studies, in order for warning messages to be effective, message content needs to include clear information about who should take protective action and who should not; what actions need to be taken by those at risk; when to initiate action and when it is no longer necessary to continue; and what entity is providing the guidance. Messages should be clear, specific, accurate, confident, and consistent (Mileti and Peek 2000). This leads to questions about whether new systems of alerting and warning the public can improve warning compliance or are unable to meet the criteria for effective warnings. We tend to assume that more IT affordances make for more and clearer information, but is that actually the case?

Attempts to address these and related questions have been the subject of a number of conferences (see, for example, National Research Council 2013a, 2013b) and empirical studies. One such body of research focuses on "terse messaging" of the kind employed by the Federal Emergency Management Agency (FEMA) in its wireless emergency alert (WEA) system. WEA, which, it should be noted, was developed without significant input from social scientists, is designed to send short (90- or 140-character) SMS warning messages to cell phones and other devices. But are terse messages sufficient to warn effectively? In one study, Bean et al. (2016) developed simulated 90- and 140-character WEA messages involving a nuclear hazard and used interviews and focus groups to determine the responses of study participants. They found that the main initial responses to the messages were fear and confusion; that participants displayed low levels of understanding of messages and expressed frustration about what they saw as incomplete information; that there were varying assessments of the believability of the messages; and that participants had difficulty personalizing the risk. Although results were slightly more positive when the 140-character format was used, this study suggests that WEA messaging has serious limitations in terms of what is required for effectively warning the public about imminent threats.

The Bean et al. (2016) study directly addressed the question of whether WEA meets the conditions necessary for effectively warning the public in emergency situations. Although clearly more research is needed, these findings are not promising. Other studies on different forms of terse messaging have focused on such topics as factors that increase the likelihood that official warnings issued via Twitter will be retransmitted (Sutton et al. 2014b, 2015). Here again, however, while rapid dissemination ("retweeting") of threat information is desirable under many circumstances, there could be situations where extensive retweeting has negative effects. There is still a lot that is not known about the impact of new warning technologies. Moreover, there can be problems in trying to extrapolate from controlled studies such as the one Bean and his collaborators conducted to the real world, where members of the public are flooded with all types of information on a continuous basis.

This chapter has discussed both general theoretical frameworks in sociology and middle-range theories developed in the field of disaster research—specifically, theories of panic, emergence, and warning responses and self-protective actions. With respect to general theory, social construction-ism provides a lens through which one could address questions concerning how hazards and disasters are framed both by members of the general public and by elites. In discussing constructionism, I have placed special emphasis on the social construction of ignorance about hazards—a topic that has received little emphasis in the literature. Awareness of hazards generally peaks imme-diately after disasters, but over time collective memories fade. Importantly, as the example of climate change shows, powerful economic and political interests seek to benefit by sowing doubt about scientific findings on hazard-related phenomena and by diverting attention away from the potential for disaster.

I presented a theory on the social production of disaster—as distinct from the social construction of disaster—that draws extensively on perspectives from environmental sociology, particularly the political economy of the environment, and from critical geography and urban studies. In that part of the chapter, I discussed disaster vulnerability and vulnerability science, with an emphasis on how social forces that operate at different levels create the conditions through which places and people are made vulnerable. In the next chapter I focus on research methods in the field of disaster studies, before returning to discuss disaster vulnerability in more detail in Chapter 6.

5

Confronting Disaster Research Challenges

Introduction

In a review of 225 published studies on the effects of disasters on mental health, conducted between 1981 and 2004, and involving more than 85,000 individuals who had experienced 132 different disaster events, Fran Norris (2006) found that the methods employed in those studies varied, but the most common type of design employed in them was cross-sectional and the studies themselves were conducted only after disasters had occurred (in other words, they did not incorporate baseline data), used convenience sampling, and worked with relatively small samples. Because research subjects tended not to be followed over long periods of time, little was learned about the longer-term effects of disasters. The small sample sizes used in mental health studies tended to rule out the possibility of sophisticated statistical analyses. Moreover, Norris noted, the methods used influenced the results that were obtained: studies employing pre- and post-disaster data showed smaller disaster effects than those that used only post-disaster methods, and smaller effects were also found in the studies that used larger sample sizes and convenience rather than random sampling—perhaps because subjects were chosen according to their accessibility. On top of that, although disasters have larger impacts on communities and societies in the Global South, most studies were conducted in the Global North.

Norris's review is more than ten years old and focuses only on mental health research; but, while there is reason to hope that studies have become more methodologically sophisticated since then, my own sense is that many of Norris's findings still hold. Her own review cautions against assuming that study designs have improved over time. For example, over the lengthy period she studied, sample sizes did not increase; and, although researchers were able to get into the field sooner in studies that were carried out later in the period, the methodological approaches used did not improve significantly—for example, sample sizes were still small, and studies still employed convenience sampling.

I mention Norris's review not to highlight weaknesses in the research record, but rather because some of the shortcomings she identified are a result of the many constraints and challenges that accompany disaster research. For example, while for hazard- and disaster-related research during non-disaster periods funding is available from agencies such as the National Science Foundation, funding levels often increase after major disaster events. However, those kinds of grants tend to favor relatively short-term studies and also contribute to researchers' tendency to focus on large-scale disasters rather than on smaller and more common ones. Particularly for social scientists, research funding may not be substantial enough to support longer-term research, longitudinal and panel studies, or systematic efforts to achieve better response rates and better coverage of populations of concern. For reasons that will become evident in the discussions that follow, in disaster research, any effort to increase research quality typically necessitates large budgets that many funding agencies may be unwilling to support except under special circumstances. That being the case, researchers sometimes have to choose between conducting research that is less than optimal methodologically or conducting no research at all.

Disaster Research Methods: How Distinctive Are They?

The data collection and analysis approaches used by sociologists and other social scientists who study disasters do not differ from those employed in social science research more generally. Disaster research methods include systematic observation, participant observation, interviewing, focus groups, collection and analysis of documentary and archival materials (including web-based studies), survey research, spatial social science methods, participatory research, evaluation research, and other approaches. Like other social scientists, disaster researchers use both qualitative and quantitative data collection and analytic strategies, although the types of qualitative methods that have been used throughout the history of the field still predominate. What differs, however, are the contexts and settings in which research is conducted. Of course, a considerable amount of research on hazards and disasters is carried out in non-disaster contexts; examples include research on risk perception, disaster mitigation and preparedness activities, disaster policy, and historical disasters. In such cases, research practices closely resemble those employed in other kinds of social scientific studies. Complications are much more likely to arise when researchers focus on the actual disaster events and their consequences, largely because those studies have to be carried out in disturbed and turbulent environments. In the words of sociologist Robert Stallings,

> it is the *context* of research not the methods of research that makes disaster research unique ... Disaster researchers, therefore, need two types of training: first, they need training in research methods in general ... and

second, they need training in how, specifically, the circumstances surrounding disaster affect the implementation of these research methods. (Stallings 1997: 7)

Details that are typically taken for granted in research conducted in non-disaster times—for example, that a particular organization is in fact located at the address listed on its website, or that those who conduct telephone surveys will generally be able to reach working numbers—cannot be taken for granted in disaster situations. Disasters disrupt communities in ways that require extra effort and ingenuity on the part of those who wish to conduct research.

This chapter is not intended to be a treatise on disaster research methods. There are many other publications that do a better job of providing detailed guidance on conducting research in disaster settings than is possible here (see Stallings 1997, 2002, 2007; Galea, Maxwell, and Norris 2008; Peek and Fothergill 2009; Henderson et al. 2009; Phillips 2014; Marlowe, Lou, Osman, and Zeba Alam 2015; Substance Abuse and Mental Health Services Administration 2016). Rather, in the sections that follow I highlight what I and other researchers have identified as major challenges for researchers who work in disaster contexts. Although these sets of challenges obviously overlap, for simplicity I will divide them into three areas: practical, research-related and methodological, and ethical.

Practical challenges

With respect to practical considerations, one obvious complication is that disasters arrive largely unannounced, although events like hurricanes may allow for some warning. Studies conducted in non-disaster settings can be initiated and proceed on carefully planned schedules, which are developed in advance and are by and large predictable, but this is not the case for many studies of disasters. Disasters know no respect for teaching schedules, other tasks and deadlines, vacations, or holidays. Researchers who wish to carry out quick-response research and even intermediate-term research must thus be able to confront and solve challenges associated with rapid or relatively rapid deployment in the field. Those whose research priorities require them to go into the field in the immediate aftermath of disasters must always be prepared.

Fortunately, there is a lot that can be done in advance to make post-disaster quick-response research proceed smoothly. Research protocols should be developed as much as possible ahead of time, and those who will be conducting the actual research should be trained in advance and told what to expect, in terms of deployment and issues likely to be encountered in the field, in case a disaster event occurs. This is done regularly at major centers, particularly those that specialize in quick-response studies, such as the Disaster Research

Center, but all researchers who wish to engage in rapid-response disaster research should do the same kind of pre-planning. Ideally, before going out in the field, students who plan to do so should already have taken courses on the qualitative and quantitative methods they plan to employ and should have had all sorts of training on methods specific to disaster research. Other important requirements, which are not specific to disaster research but become more pressing in those situations, include understanding travel policies and requirements for reimbursement and, where applicable, having a passport and obtaining the recommended vaccinations. Additionally, it is important that those who may be deployed to the field on short notice always keep their human subjects certifications current.

Institutional review boards and human subjects concerns

Disaster research is still a small field and many institutional review boards (IRBs) are unfamiliar with disaster research and may have difficulty acting rapidly on requests for protocol approval. One strategy for dealing with such issues is to meet with human subjects officials when a proposal is submitted or before sending protocols for review, to explain the purpose of the research and typical disaster research strategies. A good deal of the work required for developing IRB review requests, such as conducting literature reviews on disaster research methods and writing descriptions of the risks and benefits of participating in disaster studies, can be done ahead of a disaster, and again, to the extent that this is possible, speaking with human subjects officials in advance about their potential concerns is desirable.

Researchers should be aware that IRB officials and committee members may automatically consider anyone who is in a disaster area to be vulnerable to being harmed as a consequence of research involvement and thus may be overly conservative when reviewing protocols. Issues related to the potential vulnerability of all research participants, including disaster survivors, are important and, in submitting protocols to IRBs, researchers will need to provide the best available information about the potential vulnerabilities of research participants and the risks and benefits of taking part in post-disaster studies.

At the same time, the concept of vulnerability can be problematic in all types of social science research. Levine (2004) notes that much has been written about the vulnerability of a wide range of populations, including those identified in US federal regulations as requiring extra protections—children, prisoners, pregnant women, fetuses, and newborns—but also poor people, individuals who are discriminated against, stigmatized, and marginalized, persons without political and economic power, members of minority racial and ethnic groups, people of low intelligence, and individuals who lack basic human and civil rights. Researchers are clearly trying to cover all bases in identifying potentially at-risk groups. However, Levine calls research vulnerability "an extraordinarily elastic concept, capable of being stretched to cover almost any person, group, or situation, and then of being snapped back to describe a narrow range of characteristics like age or incarceration" and warns that, with extensive stretching of the concept's meaning, "[i]f everyone is vulnerable, then the concept is so nebulous that it becomes almost meaningless" (2004: 398). She also notes that there are inherent problems with assuming, in research settings, that entire groups of people are vulnerable simply because they have some trait in common, such as being African American or living in poverty. The reality is that there is likely to be considerable intragroup variation in the risks faced by members of groups who are deemed vulnerable. Respect for the autonomy of research subjects is a cornerstone of human subjects protection policy, and wholesale assumptions about the vulnerability of disaster survivors or of particular groups of survivors can be seen as robbing potential participants of that autonomy.

The current consensus in the research community is that there is no a priori reason for assuming that disaster survivors are so highly vulnerable that they require special protections, beyond those that are provided to other research subjects (Newman and Kaloupek 2004; National Institute of Mental Health 2007; Substance Abuse and Mental Health Services Administration 2016). Researchers can also emphasize to their IRBs that members of disaster-stricken populations are heterogeneous and are also diverse in terms of their disaster experiences, so making blanket assumptions about vulnerability is inappropriate. Of course, there can be exceptions—for example, people who have been exposed to extreme trauma or have lost loved ones—and those should be treated as special cases. Similarly, some disaster survivors, such as refugees fleeing from wars and disasters and persons who are not in their country legally, may face special risks, and how those risks will be managed should be part of the research design and consent process.

IRB applications require analyses of the risks and benefits of participation in research, but here again the costs and benefits of participating in disaster research do not look all that different from those associated with research with individuals who have undergone painful and disruptive experiences in their lives and have experienced various degrees of suffering—or with research subjects in general, for that matter. The small amount of research that exists on groups that have experienced trauma indicates that participation can cause distress to some proportion of those who are asked to discuss their experiences. Interestingly, however, studies have also shown that a large majority of those who indicate that they felt some discomfort during the research process still do not regret participating. Instead, it appears that even those who find it in some ways disturbing to take part in research view their participation as having positive effects, such as gaining insight into their own experiences, improving their own self-esteem, and feeling that they have made a contribution to society (Levine 2004; Newman and Kaloupek 2004).

Collogan and colleagues advise that, in addressing the risks and benefits of research participation,

> [a]dministrators and IRB members who are charged with protecting the interests of human participants in research may be benefited in their considerations by having access to data on the low likelihood of significant risk of research postdisaster when conducted in appropriate settings with sensitivity to the needs of participants ... Evidence of the important benefits that disaster-focused research participants experience may also be useful to reviewers when weighing the risk–benefit ratio of participation. (Collogan et al. 2004: 369)

Again regarding institutional review, researchers should be aware that there may be other IRBs outside their own institutions that will need to give their approval before research can begin—for example, IRBs with jurisdiction in other countries. In the United States, after the 1995 Oklahoma City bombing, the governor of Oklahoma designated the University of Oklahoma Health Sciences Center as the lead IRB for all projects related to research on that bombing, regardless of the institutions and investigators behind them. Although this occurs very rarely, restrictions can also be placed on the ability to collect data after disasters. For example, on February 23, 2011—the day after the most serious earthquake in the Christchurch, New Zealand earthquake sequence of 2010–2011—the government of New Zealand instituted a moratorium on social science research, which was in effect until May 1 of that year. This was done in an effort to reduce burdens on emergency responders and earthquake survivors that the government believed might result from researcher convergence. Another consideration is that, as is the case in other fields, certain kinds of research, such as research involving photographs or videotaping, where participants can be identified, typically require additional privacy waivers.

By their very nature, some disasters can be expected to generate controversy, intense scrutiny, and legal disputes. Under such circumstances, researchers may wish to obtain additional human subjects protection in the form of certificates of confidentiality. These certificates, which are issued by the US National Institutes of Health, are designed to protect research information from various forms of forced disclosure, such as court orders and subpoenas. I obtained a certificate of confidentiality for all the research conducted by the Disaster Research Center on the World Trade Center (WTC) terrorist attacks because I believed there was a high potential for lawsuits and forced disclosure. One of the reasons why I wanted to obtain additional protections for WTC study participants was that I was aware of the many ways in which scholars who had conducted research on the Exxon Valdez oil spill were harassed by Exxon and of the corporation's many efforts to force researchers to disclose data about their study participants (Picou 1996a; 1996b). A caution regarding certificates of confidentiality is that researchers' institutions must be willing to support them if subpoenas are issued. If forced disclosure is a possibility, it is prudent to consult in advance with institutional legal representatives about strategies for research participant protection.

Other practical concerns

In social science research, researchers often offer payment or some other kind of incentive to study participants; and in disaster settings where survivors have suffered material losses this seems especially appropriate. As happens in other types of studies, disaster researchers may have difficulty providing financial incentives if their institutions require personal identification, such as a social security number, in order to release payments. Because researchers typically assure research subjects of confidentiality, they need to work out payment arrangements in advance with their institutions, if they are to fulfill that promise and protect confidentiality. Additionally, care must be taken to ensure that gifts provided to participants are large enough to show appreciation for participation, but not so large that they offer undue encouragement to participate.

Researcher safety is another practical concern in many disaster settings. Widespread criminality is, typically, not a problem in the aftermath of disasters, particularly in the United States, but some countries and communities are more lawless than others, and it is always prudent to be aware of the potential for danger and to manage that risk. Along these lines, cultural competence and sensitivity are required, but this is not a feature exclusive to the disaster field; those who work in this field must be sensitive to norms that center on proper dress and demeanor in different societal settings, out of concern that missteps might trigger negative reactions on the part of residents in disaster-stricken areas, or even on the part of authorities. For example, although my fieldwork in Iran after the 2003 Bam earthquake was largely uneventful, I did experience a few uncomfortable moments in Bam when, in 120 Fahrenheit degrees, I could not stand to wear my long black covering but did not have a lighter replacement; instead I was wearing a long-sleeved white tunic, long khaki pants, and a headscarf. When the much feared morality police headed for me in a public market, an engineer in our team who had grown up mainly in Iran and who spoke the language quickly asked them to direct me to a place in the market where I could purchase an appropriate covering, and all was well. This incident also speaks to the value of working with researchers who are familiar with local cultural norms and practices.

Disaster settings present a variety of other safety challenges. Earthquakes are always followed by aftershocks that can do additional damage and even kill, and hazardous chemicals are invariably found in floodwaters. Drinking water can be contaminated as a consequence of disaster impacts. Debris-covered streets can be hazardous, especially when lighting is lacking as a result of a disaster or never existed in the first place. Technological disasters may lead to unsafe conditions for researchers, just as they do for disaster survivors. For all these reasons, training for researchers should always address safety issues, and IRB protocols should discuss how the safety of researchers as well as that of research subjects will be addressed. Researchers in the field must also monitor authoritative information sources on a regular basis in order to be aware of emerging threats.

Being able to obtain access to places and people is another practical concern that field researchers should not ignore. Sometimes access to hard-hit areas is impossible for a period of time, as happens, for example, when major transportation routes are blocked or airports are shut down as a result of damage. Researchers need up-to-date information on the accessibility of disaster sites, but that information is often difficult to obtain. Simply navigating in disaster-stricken areas is difficult when landmarks and signage have been destroyed. Additionally, authorities typically restrict access to highly damaged areas and may also block entry to emergency shelters and temporary housing sites. Researchers wishing to observe emergency response activities in the field or in emergency operation centers should expect to encounter varying degrees of resistance on the part of authorities. This is doubly true for terrorism-related events, where security is paramount.

There are a number of strategies that can be used when access to sites is being blocked: obtaining approval from the leadership of agencies that are in charge; presenting credentials such as researchers' photos and other identification, which identify the sponsoring funding agency and institution; and, equally if not more importantly, getting in touch with prior contacts in the affected area who can vouch for the legitimacy of the research. For example, the entrée and access that the Disaster Research Center field team was able to achieve after the terrorist attacks of September 11, 2001 in New York were predicated almost entirely on a relationship that had been developed with a high-ranking member of New York's Mayor's Office of Emergency Management before those events. Lead team members Tricia Wachtendorf and James Kendra spent most of the two months after the attacks making observations in the emergency operations center and other sites such as Ground Zero, sitting in on meetings that were held to determine the course of the response and early recovery, shadowing those who were coordinating emergency management activities, and collecting other kinds of perishable data. All this was made possible through the same helpful contact that enabled them to obtain official credentials issued by the city of New York that entitled them to be present in a variety of otherwise restricted settings.

In their book *Children of Katrina*, Alice Fothergill and Lori Peek (2015) include a detailed discussion of the hurdles they had to overcome in gaining access to different settings and in recruiting and retaining study participants after Hurricane Katrina. For example, at one mass shelter, two groups were vying to be in charge of shelter operations. One group gave the researchers permission to enter the shelter and to begin interviewing staff members and disaster survivors, but the second group told them they had to leave. Later on these researchers were told by the first group that they could come back, but found that they still had to do so unobtrusively. In attempting to gain entrée into a school setting, they first approached the school with formal requests. Over a period of months, the school asked them to provide additional documentation regarding their study, then never replied to their requests. Subsequent contacts with schools, made through informal channels, were more successful. Because the study followed children and families over a number of years, these researchers had the additional challenge of tracking study participants often throughout several moves, as parents and children attempted to regain some sense of stability in their lives. A key lesson here is the need to be flexible—and persistent.

Methodological challenges

In addition to practical problems, disaster researchers face methodological and research-related challenges that typically do not arise—or do not arise to the same degree—in other research; and care must be taken to ensure that the difficulties associated with conducting research in the aftermath of disasters do not compromise study results. Displacement is one concern: community residents may no longer be in their homes, and agencies and organizations may also have been forced to operate out of new locations. Those who are displaced are likely to differ in sociologically significant ways from those who are able to remain in or return rapidly to disaster-stricken areas; for example, they may be low-income residents who had been living in substandard or manufactured housing that sustained very severe damage. In the Katrina catastrophe, many New Orleans residents were displaced on a long-term or permanent basis, because they were evacuated to places far from their homes and because the city of New Orleans demolished a lot of low-income housing not long after the hurricane, making it difficult for low-income residents to return. Efforts to track displaced residents may meet with resistance or complete refusal to provide information on the part of emergency management and disaster assistance agencies, and this necessitates appeals and work-arounds.

In discussing efforts to conduct telephone surveys after Hurricane Katrina, Henderson et al. (2009) noted a number of challenges that were related in part to displacement. A phone survey using landlines began six weeks after Katrina and therefore was more likely to reach early returnees. A cell phone survey began three months after the catastrophe, but probably missed potential respondents whose cell phone contracts expired—more likely among lower-income groups. Like other researchers who employ telephone surveys,

these researchers were challenged by other factors, such as the sociodemographic differences between landline and cell phone-only individuals and
households.

Research on businesses affected by disasters was discussed briefly in Chapter
3. Until recently, owing to resource constraints, business-related research
tended to focus on those businesses that could be located and contacted
months or years after a disaster. Put another way, studies mainly focused on
*surviving businesses located in roughly the same geographic areas where they had been
doing business prior to experiencing disaster.* Businesses that had moved to distant
locations or had ceased operating as a result of experiencing a disaster or for
other reasons were left out of such studies, partly because of the difficulty
of tracking them. Recently, however, researchers have improved business
tracking methods. In research on the impacts of Hurricane Katrina on small
businesses in Mississippi, Holly Schrank, Maria Marshall, and their collaborators (Schrank et al. 2013; Marshall and Schrank 2014) developed elaborate
strategies to locate businesses that had moved or had gone out of business
in subsequent years. In order to locate the businesses to be included in their
surveys, they first identified businesses that had featured in the database
of Dun and Bradstreet's study of the area in 2005 but were no longer in the
database in 2009. They then set out to find and make contact with those
missing businesses in order to learn how they fared in the years following
Katrina. They did this through extensive Internet searches intended to locate
businesses that may have moved out of the area but were still operating,
through phone calls meant to show whether they could actually get through
to displaced businesses, and through complex record-linking methods that
brought together information from diverse sources—such as telephone direc-
tories from the intervening years, tax assessors' records, other records that
identified corporate officers and owners' business partners, and state databases on business entities (as distinct from Dun and Bradstreet records). The
researchers even searched through obituaries to find out whether business
owners had died in the years following Katrina. In some cases field workers traveled to disaster-affected areas to locate previous business sites and to
contact personally nearby business owners who might have information on
where businesses and business owners had gone. Clearly these efforts were
highly labor-intensive, but through its painstaking work the research team
was able to develop empirically sound conclusions as to which small businesses were most vulnerable to failure following Katrina and why (for answers
to those questions, see Sydnor et al. 2017 and Chapter 6 here).

Following disasters, efforts to interview or obtain records from agency
and organizational representatives are challenging for several reasons.
Organizations involved directly in responding to disasters are typically so
overwhelmed with simply carrying out their disaster-related functions that
they have little or no time for working with researchers. Agencies providing

services to disaster victims may likewise feel overwhelmed, or may feel a need to withhold information from researchers on the assumption that their clients are already traumatized and overburdened and need to be protected. For a variety of reasons, authorities may actively try to shut down researcher access, for example by telling organizational personnel that they should not talk to researchers.

Many types of research require layers of consent before data can be obtained from research subjects. Studies involving school-age children are a case in point. Obtaining consent typically involves getting permission from school systems, individual schools, parents, and the children themselves. Educational researchers are familiar with these kinds of hurdles, but research in disaster settings is even more fraught than research conducted during non-disaster times. Educational institutions may be overwhelmed as a result of disaster impacts and thus may be less inclined to participate in research. Schools and parents may worry about the negative effects of research on children whose lives have been disrupted. Owing to their own dislocation, parents may be difficult to find and, even when located, may be too overburdened to consider researchers' requests.

Barron Ausbrooks, Barrett, and Martinez-Cosio (2009) conducted a post-Hurricane Katrina study that involved surveys with displaced middle school and high school students, their parents and teachers, school principals, school social workers, and school district personnel. The many challenges they had to overcome included tracking the displaced students to their new homes, assuring ethical protections for children at risk, obtaining the requisite permissions from school districts and individual schools, and obtaining parents' permission and students' consent to participate in the study. Students had to be able to return signed parental permission forms to school—which some did not. Parents themselves were difficult to contact; the researchers noted that, as a result of Katrina, it was sometimes the case that "students were living with relatives while parents looked for work, took care of business back in Louisiana, or had been evacuated elsewhere. The transience of displaced disaster survivors places a distinctive twist on obtaining informed consent" (Barron Ausbrooks et al. 2009: 97). Additionally, student records are protected by federal law, and students cannot be required to participate in studies that touch upon topics such as their psychological well-being (which this study did) without their parents' and their own permission. None of the schools or school districts would give researchers access to the addresses of students who had been relocated as a result of Katrina, so these researchers had to develop alternative ways of locating students. Schools were generally reluctant to work with the research team because they already felt overburdened, and personnel such as school counselors felt the same way. Delays in obtaining necessary permissions and the participation of research subjects meant that the research could not proceed on its planned time schedule.

Henderson et al. (2009) discuss methodological hurdles they encountered in studies conducted after Hurricane Katrina. For example, one study, which commenced in late 2005, involved in-person interviews in New Orleans. Because the study team got into the field soon after the disaster, interviewers had to deal with safety concerns associated with chemical and biological hazards. The interviews were conducted over a four-month period in the city of New Orleans, but that meant that team members were more likely to have interviewed people who had the resources necessary to return to the city during that time frame. The researchers interviewed a disproportionate number of older women; this seemed to have happened because those participants had greater availability than others during daytime hours, when the interviews were conducted, or perhaps because those women were more motivated than other Katrina survivors to return home quickly, and thus were available to be interviewed. The researchers sought to employ a systematic sampling strategy with occupied dwellings, but they were often unable to tell whether dwellings designated as vacant were actually occupied, or whether Federal Emergency Management Agency (FEMA) trailers were occupied or merely being prepared for future occupants. The accounting office at the researchers' university required social security numbers before subjects could be paid for their participation in the study, but the university's IRB specified that social security numbers could not be collected—a problem that was eventually worked out. These were just a few of the many problems these researchers encountered.

As noted earlier, funding agencies are typically more willing to provide research support in the aftermath of severe disasters. This means that most studies that attempt to assess the impacts of disasters on affected populations—for example, studies on the effects or impacts of health and mental health on social networks and social support—do so without the benefit of having baseline pre-disaster data that would make it possible to distinguish disaster-related effects from other factors that could have influenced the outcomes in question. As Galea and colleagues note with respect to mental health research in the disaster context,

> [h]aving to rely on post-only designs means that researchers have limited ability to determine the extent to which disasters caused the mental health consequences being documented after these events . . . absent an assessment of what the population of interest was like before the event, we are limited in our inference as to whether what we see after an event is truly a change or simply a reflection of pre-disaster circumstances. (Galea et al. 2008: S24)

These authors note that there are various strategies for compensating for the lack of baseline data, but those strategies have limitations themselves. For example, researchers can ask study participants to provide information on how they were faring before they experienced a disaster, but participants may have problems with recall or may have a tendency to retrospectively view pre-disaster conditions in light of their current post-disaster situations.

It is not possible to go into greater detail here about the methodological issues and potential biases that accompany research in disaster settings; as noted at the beginning of this chapter, there is a large literature on the challenges associated with applying different methodological approaches to disaster situations. This section was meant to provide a few examples that illustrate the challenging circumstances that surround researchers' attempts to carry out valid, high-quality research in disrupted environments. Similarly, the section that follows is meant to heighten awareness of the distinctive ethical challenges that accompany research in those settings—challenges that may differ from those faced by researchers who conduct studies during non-disaster times.

Ethical challenges

Regarding ethical concerns, disaster researchers come across all the challenges related to informed consent, confidentiality, and protection of the interests of research participants that other sociological and social science researchers encounter; but they often confront additional ones, too. Because some of those who have been affected by disasters, both community residents and emergency responders, have already experienced high levels of stress, special measures may be required to ensure their protection and, as noted earlier, IRBs are likely to require assurances in that regard. Such measures typically include assuring those involved in research that they can withdraw consent at any time or those involved in interview studies that they can refuse to answer particular questions. Supplementary safeguards must be provided for those who could be disproportionately at risk. This category may include people who have lost family members or have been injured, children, frail elderly persons and nursing-home residents, and refugees from disasters and civil wars. Researchers must also be able to refer study participants to local resources such as crisis counselors when necessary. In some cases the participation of professionals qualified to assess the presence of serious negative reactions in research subjects may be warranted.

That said, it is important to consider the kinds of studies that could trigger elevated levels of distress, as well as the kinds of participants who could experience such stress. In some cases, the likelihood of stressful responses is remote or non-existent. For example, research that consists of simply, unobtrusively observing disaster operations or disaster survivors is highly unlikely to place pressure on those who are observed, given its non-intrusive nature. Because of population heterogeneity and variations in disaster experiences, large surveys with randomly selected households in a community that has experienced a disaster are unlikely to induce severe stress in the vast majority of participants. We can contrast them with those examples of hypothetical studies involving face-to-face interviews with first responders who searched for and recovered bodies after a disaster, or with survivors who lost children in a disaster. The potential for creating additional stress for study participants exists on a continuum and, here again, there is no rule of thumb that can be applied to all types of studies and affected populations.

Scholars have also inquired whether those who have gone through disasters, particularly those who have experienced severe impacts, are capable of giving informed consent, in light of the fact that they may be under extreme stress. This raises questions about the decision-making capacity of participants in disaster research as well as in other types of research where stress levels are high. The general consensus in the disaster area is that, just like research participants in comparable studies of other kinds of trauma, those who are involved in disaster research fall somewhere on a continuum between having difficulty with and being fully capable of giving informed consent; those who are truly unable to do it are a very small minority. Put another way, there appears to be nothing about experiencing a disaster that would make survivors uniquely unable to give conscious consent to take part in research (Rosenstein 2004; Collogan et al. 2004; National Institute of Mental Health 2007). Here again, however, researchers must take care to ensure that consent to participate in studies is indeed being given consciously and voluntarily. For example, study participants must be aware that they are taking part in a research study and not, say, in a needs assessment study or in some form of therapy, and they must be informed that taking part in a study, or declining to take part, is in no way related to their eligibility for receiving disaster assistance.

A related ethical issue for researchers is the question of when and how—and even whether—to go into the field in the immediate aftermath of disaster. The logic that undergirds quick-response research is twofold: the data that researchers plan to collect are perishable; and, for reasons of validity, observing activities directly, as they occur in real time, is preferable to hearing about them or reading later accounts. This commitment to "experience-near" research has been part of the field since its inception, but there are also reasons to question whether other sorts of motives may underlie the efforts to get into the field quickly after disasters—motives that could be ethically questionable. The eagerness to collect data and publish them as soon as possible after disasters has been likened to a gold rush (Gomez and Hart 2013; Gaillard and Gomez 2015) in which researchers descend on disaster-stricken areas with little or no coordination and little or no familiarity with the distinctive cultural settings they are attempting to study. Critics suggest that some disaster scholars may be more interested in getting credit from their institutions and professions for publishing study results quickly than for doing high-quality research that has the potential to benefit research subjects.

They also note that convergent researchers represent a draw on resources that could be used more productively in responding to disasters. As Gaillard and Gomez put it,

> one may wonder whether it is appropriate for outsiders less familiar with the affected place, who may lack prior cultural and language skills, to converge on places where people are struggling to rebuild their lives and livelihoods, and have other priorities than answering questions about the recent events. (Gaillard and Gomez 2015: 2)

These authors are referring in particular to culturally insensitive researchers who take advantage of populations in disaster areas, but it is important to recognize that these ethical dilemmas can be present in all types of post-disaster research: researchers must not put their own professional interests before those of research participants. When they go into the field after disasters, they must do so for valid research-related reasons and their timing must reflect legitimate research concerns. The need to collect perishable data does provide a rationale for going into the field as soon as possible after a disaster event. Examples include gathering data on disaster-induced damage at particular locations before debris is cleared or structures are demolished; observing emergency response and sheltering operations while these are under way; collecting samples that indicate exposure to hazardous materials or toxins soon after disaster impact; and capturing data related to early recovery planning that cannot be obtained through other means. Here again, presence in the field at a particular time should be determined by the research questions at stake. Deploying into a disaster area soon after impact may confer a form of "street cred," which some researchers crave; but this can never be a legitimate reason for doing research on a quick-response basis.

Obligations toward study participants

Ethical questions regarding what is owed to participants in research can be especially poignant in the case of disaster studies. The Belmont Report, which provides guidelines for all research with human subjects, emphasizes three critical ethical obligations: respect for persons, beneficence, and justice. *Respect for persons* refers to the obligation to acknowledge and support the decision-making autonomy of research participants and to protect those who may have diminished decision-making capacity. Individuals cannot make autonomous decisions without understanding what taking part in research will mean for them, and thus respect for the autonomy of research subjects necessarily entails the obligation to make clear the parameters of the research being undertaken, including the nature of subjects' participation and potential research risks and benefits. The principle of *beneficence* refers to the obligation to be concerned with the welfare of research subjects. Beneficence requires efforts to maximize potential benefits for research participants while avoiding doing harm. To fulfill this obligation effectively, researchers must be aware of the potential harms that study participants face and must make every effort to mitigate those risks. At the same time, while being concerned with the well-being of research subjects, researchers cannot overpromise with respect to possible direct benefits of participation. *Justice* in research requires researchers to treat all participants fairly. This means, for example, that the burdens of taking part in research must not fall disproportionately on particular individuals or groups.

At a more general level, researchers are ethically obligated not to use whatever power they may have to compel individuals or groups to participate in research, or to make non-participation difficult. This obligation is especially relevant when there are already large power differences between researchers and potential subjects, as happens, for example, when westerners attempt to carry out research in less developed countries. In such circumstances, there is a special obligation to avoid any misunderstandings that could arise regarding study participation. This is a situation in which collaboration with in-country researchers may be essential.

Research carried out in disaster settings must adhere to these standards, and in doing so it must take into account other special circumstances created by those settings. Some disaster survivors may have lost everything and may be so overwhelmed with their own problems that they have no time for taking part in research. Others may believe that participating in a study will help them obtain some needed assistance. Still others may view participation as a form of therapy—a belief termed the "therapeutic misconception." Researchers are required to protect the confidentiality and anonymity of study participants; but, particularly in the immediate aftermath of an event, privacy is often hard to come by in places like emergency shelters and emergency operations centers. Nonetheless, every measure should be taken to secure the privacy of settings in which data are to be collected. There is also the possibility that the research itself disrupts the provision of emergency services (Kelman 2005), which would be ethically unacceptable. To block this possibility, researchers who go into the field immediately after disaster impact often opt for engaging at first only in the observation of response activities, as opposed to carrying out formal or even informal interviewing.

Researchers must also take into account the fact that, in the post-disaster setting, non-research organizations, including ones that provide disaster assistance and media organizations, will be seeking information from those who have been affected. This can both confuse disaster survivors and add to their burdens. Researchers must be able to make clear to potential participants the conditions and protections that accompany research participation—for example, that researchers are not social service workers or journalists, that participation is voluntary, and that the anonymity and confidentiality of participants will be respected.

Particularly in the case of large-scale disasters, researchers from many disciplines—physical scientists, engineers, social scientists, medical researchers, and others, both domestic and international—have a tendency to converge on disaster-stricken communities, which creates the potential for overburdening both the affected population and public officials. Physical scientists and engineers want to be taken on tours of the affected areas in order to collect data. Social scientists want access to members of the public, public officials, and leaders of community institutions, and so on. People with responsibilities for dealing with disaster response and recovery are often forced to field multiple inquiries; and, similarly, victims may be approached by multiple research teams. Concern about convergence and excessive burden was behind the decision to coordinate research after the Oklahoma City bombings in 1995 and the temporary embargo on social science research in Christchurch, New Zealand.

While most scientists and engineers rightly chafe at the notion that a "disaster research czar" should be put in charge of managing researcher convergence, and while, as researchers, we resist measures aimed at exercising prior constraint over research, the potential for excessive burden creates a legitimate ethical concern in disaster settings. The best way to deal with the threat of unacceptable levels of burdensome research is for research teams to communicate and collaborate voluntarily—for example by sharing information on the topics they are studying and on the timing of their research activities, or by exploring ways to consolidate data collection and data-sharing. Funding agencies have an important role to play in encouraging such coordination but should not mandate it.

Regarding other obligations, it is universally accepted that those who conduct research have an obligation to provide feedback on research findings to study participants. This does not mean distributing copies of articles from scholarly journals or jargon-filled technical reports. Rather it means making information available in ways that research subjects can access and understand. This can be done through printed material, a website, community briefings, engaging with the media through interviews or op-ed articles, or a combination of those approaches. Whatever method (or combination of methods) is selected, a paramount concern is to give back to those who have given their time in order to contribute to the success of disaster-related research projects and to provide information that could be useful to their lives and to their communities.

The issue of financially or otherwise compensating study participants was discussed earlier in this chapter but is worth revisiting through the lens of research ethics. Here again, there are no blanket rules or easy solutions. Limits are typically placed on providing compensation for public officials, but there could be conditions under which they would merit compensation—if, for example, they provide consultant services to a research project on their own time and are included as part of the research budget. Regarding members of the general public, provisions for compensation, when deemed appropriate, should be incorporated into research budgets and justified in research proposals through reference to the literature that exists in the area. One simple rule of thumb is that compensation should be commensurate with what is being asked of research participants in terms of the extensiveness of participation and potential inconvenience, as well as in terms of participants' resources and capabilities. Referring back to the principles of respect for persons, beneficence, and justice, compensation arrangements should enable participant agency, cause no harm, potentially provide benefits to those who elect to take part in research activities, and avoid generating unnecessary burdens for some segment(s) of the study population.

As with research in general, common sense and an understanding of the research literature should influence decisions regarding the compensation for research participation in disaster settings. Would taking part in a study involve extra expense or inconvenience for participants? This was the case, for example, in a study I conducted in the San Francisco Bay area, in which focus group participants had to travel to a specific location and pay for parking. The focus groups began in the early evening and lasted for about three hours. Because of the expense and inconvenience involved, this activity was judged to warrant cash payments.

Researchers often face difficult questions about compensation for research participation. Can providing financial compensation possibly serve as an inappropriate inducement to taking part in a research project, as may happen in third-world settings? Would the lack of compensation serve as a disincentive for participation for low-income groups but pose no barrier for the well-off? What constitutes appropriate levels of compensation for different groups in different disaster situations, keeping in mind the key principles of research ethics? These are the kinds of concerns that disaster researchers must confront and address.

Some types of research, such as participatory action research, require the active engagement of research participants during all the phases of a project, from initial problem formulation to the production and dissemination of study results. Additionally, participatory methods have as one of their key aims the empowerment of communities that are engaged in research collaborations so that they can exercise greater agency and press for change. Some critics have questioned whether disaster researchers who claim to be carrying out participatory action research are really following this guidance. These critics point out for example that, particularly in the context of developing countries, concepts such as participation and empowerment are often nothing more than buzzwords that funders expect to hear (Le De, Gaillard, and Friesen 2015). Researchers who wish to employ participatory action research strategies are ethically obliged to do so in good faith, keeping in mind that those strategies require not only collecting and analyzing data but also supporting communities in their efforts to bring about change. Providing such support is, typically, a long-term endeavor.

Community consultation and engagement are also frequently recommended, even for studies that are not explicitly emancipatory in their aims. For example, the guidelines produced by the Working Group on Disaster Research and Ethics, which focus to a great extent on research conducted after disasters in less developed countries, recommend collaboration with the affected communities throughout the research process. The extent to which researchers consult and engage with community members and groups will vary according to study types and objectives. On the one hand, in large-scale surveys that employ modules that have been selected by investigators in advance, as is often the case with post-disaster mental health studies, apart from the actual data collection phase, engagement with members of the community may be minimal or entirely absent. On the other hand, for participant observation research, engagement is essential. In still other cases, such as hazard and disaster research involving citizen science, the main objective of the research is coproduction of knowledge, and engagement with participants is critical to the project's success.

Regardless of level and intensity, to be ethical, consultation and engagement with disaster-affected communities must be authentic. Researchers cannot go into a community with preexisting ideas about exactly how a study should proceed and then pretend to be obtaining community input on the conduct of the study. They may not deceive community members into believing that they are actually having an influence on research when they are not; nor can they say that they have engaged in consultation when they have merely informed the community about their research plans.

Obligations toward those who assist with research

Another related ethical question centers on what "outside" disaster researchers owe to colleagues who reside in disaster zones. Here again, researchers are obligated not to overburden those who are in a position to assist them in their work, for example by providing background information on affected communities and populations and by arranging contacts for them. After Hurricane Katrina, for example, New Orleans- and Gulf-based researchers extended hospitality and provided assistance to many non-local researchers, and later on some felt exploited by ungrateful colleagues. Those who provide valued assistance to disaster researchers should be included as collaborators and given appropriate credit in subsequent papers and publications. In particular, researchers who rely extensively on the expertise of junior scholars, such as graduate students from institutions in disaster-stricken areas, must take care to ensure that the contributions of these students are recognized in appropriate ways.

Outside researchers should keep in mind that colleagues in disaster-stricken areas may themselves be disaster victims or, if not, may have friends, neighbors, relatives, colleagues, and students who have been affected. They may also be involved in assisting and advising local officials on ways of handling disaster-related challenges. Placing demands on them without offering some appropriate, mutually agreed-upon form of reciprocity, compensation, or acknowledgment is a violation of research ethics. As an ethical check, researchers should ask themselves what their responses would be if their own communities experienced a major disaster and how they would expect to be treated by converging outside colleagues.

Lead investigators have other obligations toward colleagues and collaborators, particularly those who have less seniority and experience, such as graduate students and early career researchers working under their direction. It goes without saying that it is unethical to exploit junior colleagues; the obligation to avoid exploitation is explicitly laid out in ethical guidelines such as those provided by the American Sociological Association. Beyond that, senior researchers working in disaster settings have an ethical obligation to attend to the welfare of those who are working for them. First and foremost, this means considering any and all potential safety issues that team members could encounter in the field and addressing those issues prior to deployment. As discussed in the section of this chapter that dealt with practical concerns, carrying out research in disaster settings can be hazardous and the potential for harm to team members should never be taken lightly. Teams going into the field after an earthquake should be instructed on what to do in the event of aftershocks, for example, and any reports of violence or criminal activity in disaster-affected areas should be taken seriously by those who direct research projects. Under some circumstances, it may be advisable for field workers to collect data in pairs, as opposed to going alone. Teams conducting international research must have the kinds of vaccination that are recommended for the areas to which they will be traveling. Protective gear may be required in certain situations.

Conducting research with disaster survivors and with other groups, such as first responders, and particularly research that uses participant observation and face-to-face interviewing methods, can be upsetting and draining even for the most experienced researcher. Empathy is a valued trait in fieldwork, but empathizing can be highly stressful, particularly when researchers spend long hours listening to disaster survivors recount their experiences of pain and loss and when there are physical hardships associated with the conduct of research. Individuals involved in post-disaster studies may find their accommodations and transportation arrangements less than ideal, which further adds to the stress they experience (Mukherji, Ganapati, and Rahill 2014). For these sorts of reasons, lead investigators must be aware of emotional reactions and problems that could arise among team members in the course of research and should consider practices such as regular debriefings during or after trips to the field. When the research requires long-term presence in disaster-affected areas, breaks from engagement should be incorporated into the research plans.

In sum, while on the one hand safety is a practical concern, on the other it is also an ethical concern for those who direct research in disaster settings. It is unethical to ignore the hazardous conditions and situations, physical or emotional, that those who work in the field may face. If ethics is an insufficient motivator for assuming a duty of care in this respect, research leaders should also consider the legal liability, reputational damage, and damage to the scientific enterprise that could result from the failure to address safety concerns.

Concluding Observations

This chapter has focused on the practical, methodological, and ethical aspects of carrying out research in disaster settings and has placed an emphasis on what makes those settings distinctive. The intent has not been to argue that the more general literature on these topics is not relevant to the study of disasters, but rather to emphasize that, while standard practices still apply, adhering to them in disaster settings often requires considerable ingenuity. I have used examples from my own research and lessons identified by other researchers to make that point. At the same time, I have also attempted to show that, as in all types of research, there are no hard and fast rules that can be automatically applied to the conduct of disaster research. Instead researchers are challenged to make numerous judgment calls in their work on the basis of their knowledge, training, past experience, and common sense.

6

Disaster Vulnerability

Introduction

Throughout the history of sociological disaster research, scholars have focused on disasters not as physical phenomena but as social ones. No matter how large, a physical event such as a massive earthquake or a tropical cyclone is not considered a disaster unless it results in losses to human communities and the things they value and in the disruption of the social fabric. Disasters are marked by death and injury, damage to homes and businesses, displacement of populations, short- and longer-term economic losses, and threats to the functioning of social institutions such as educational and healthcare systems. However, the burdens of a disaster are not borne equally; some geographic areas, groups, businesses, and community sectors suffer disproportionately. Understanding how and why these disparities exist is a fundamental question for the sociology of disasters. This chapter provides a partial answer to that question by taking a closer look at the concept of disaster vulnerability and at vulnerable groups.

The Concept of Vulnerability

In an article published in the 1990s, geographer Susan Cutter noted that scholars had advanced a number of definitions of the concept of vulnerability and that those definitions were not necessarily consistent among themselves (Cutter 1996). Since then, there have been additional clarifications but no clear definitional consensus. The United Nations International Strategy for Disaster Reduction (UNISDR) (2017) defines vulnerability as "[t]he conditions determined by physical, social, economic and environmental factors or processes, which increase the susceptibility of a community to the impact of hazards." In a more recent discussion, Bolin and Kurtz (2018: 183) assert that the vulnerability perspective "works to identify an ensemble of sociospatial and political economic conditions and historical as well as current processes which can explain how specific hazard events become disasters." Other definitions take into account both pre-event susceptibility and coping capacity. For Wisner, Blaikie, Cannon, and Davis (2004: 11), vulnerability consists of "the characteristics of a person or group and their situation that influence their capacity to anticipate, cope with, resist, and recover from the impact of a natural hazard." Similarly, Joern Birkmann (2006: 14) argues that vulnerability "has to be seen as the estimation of the wider environment and social circumstances, thus enabling people and communities to cope with the impact of hazardous events or, conversely, limiting their ability to resist the negative impact of the hazardous event ... vulnerability can also take into account the coping capacity and resilience of the potentially affected society."

For our purposes, following Cutter, Boruff, and Shirley (2003) we can begin this discussion by thinking of disaster vulnerability as a set of conditions indicative of the potential for loss: loss of life, physical and mental well-being, the ability to function, physical systems such as buildings and infrastructure, livelihoods and personal assets such as wealth and savings, and environmental diversity and sustainability. The concept of vulnerability has already been introduced in earlier chapters; we learned, for example, that the pioneering volume *At Risk* made the study of vulnerability central to disaster research and provided a model—the pressure and release model—for understanding how vulnerability is produced through macro-, meso-, and microlevel social forces. Earlier discussions in Chapter 4 also highlighted the idea that vulnerability production is a process; vulnerability is not a static entity—a state—but rather an evolving set of conditions driven by a variety of forces, including the dynamics of the world system, processes that marginalize groups on the basis of ideologies such as racism, actions by states and communities that adversely affect particular segments of the population, and other forces that create, maintain, and reproduce inequality. Researchers typically take into account three different dimensions of vulnerability: the hazardousness of different geographic places; built-environment and infrastructure vulnerability; and (our main focus here) social vulnerability.

Drivers of Vulnerability

Hazardousness of place

What is often referred to as "the hazardousness of a place" (Hewitt and Burton 1971) takes into account the fact that particular geographic areas are simply more prone than others to events that arise from hazards. This facet of vulnerability is often referred to as *exposure.* Coastal areas and their residents are exposed to hazards such as hurricanes, places adjacent to rivers and streams are exposed to the potential for riverine and flash floods. Along what is known as the ring of fire, parts of Japan, China, Chile, and New Zealand have experienced a number of devastating earthquakes in the twentieth and twenty-first centuries, a fact that testifies to their high levels of exposure to earthquake hazards. Mexico and countries in Central America such as Nicaragua and El

Salvador have a long history of violent earthquakes and deadly hurricanes. In the United States, exposure to earthquake hazards is high to moderate not only in California but also in Washington, Oregon, the New Madrid Seismic Zone in the Midwest, and even South Carolina and Massachusetts. One of the most hazard-prone places on earth, the Philippines, faces multiple hazards such as tropical cyclones, floods, volcanic eruptions, and earthquakes. Similarly, as seen in the case of Hurricane Maria in 2017, islands in the Caribbean are at risk of being struck by hurricanes that originate in the eastern Atlantic Ocean and are vulnerable to the high winds and flooding that those storms produce. Bangladesh regularly experiences major flooding, and many countries in Africa are prone both to drought and to large-scale flooding.

With respect to technological hazards, as discussed earlier in connection with Hurricane Harvey, Houston is not only prone to hurricanes and floods but also home to the largest chemical complex in the United States, which means that Houston's population is exposed to the risk of impacts from hurricane winds, storm surges, and industrial accidents. Many other communities host numerous facilities that manufacture, process, or store hazardous chemicals. Others are sites of nuclear plants, which makes those communities more vulnerable than others to accidents comparable with the 1979 Three Mile Island disaster, the 1986 Chernobyl disaster, and the 2011 Fukushima triple meltdown. Understanding the different hazards to which communities and societies are exposed is thus an important element in understanding societal vulnerabilities.

As Fordham, Lovekamp, Thomas, and Phillips (2013) emphasize, not all populations and groups that are exposed to hazards are equally vulnerable. Taking earthquake exposure as an example, exposed populations show variation in their capacity for mitigating and preparing for earthquakes, knowledge of what to do in the event of an earthquake, and ability to undertake those self-protective actions. Some groups may be living in dangerous structures, while others live in safer buildings. Evacuation is the most effective self-protective measure when a hurricane threatens, but members of some groups may be unable or unwilling to evacuate for a variety of reasons: lack of transportation, inability to afford gas and stay in a hotel, or concern about potential lost wages. Because of global warming, there will be more heat waves in the future in the United States; but, as we will see later, population groups are differentially vulnerable to extreme heat. Elderly persons, those with preexisting conditions such as asthma and heart problems, and those without access to air conditioning and other cooling options are the ones most at risk.

Built-environment vulnerability

The concept of vulnerability also encompasses the built environment, which includes not only buildings and infrastructure—highways, bridges, electrical systems, ports, and so on—but other constructed systems such as levées, sea-walls, and works that are intended to offer protection against extreme events. Here again, built-environment vulnerability is related to the likelihood of loss through destruction, damage, and functional degradation. Assessments of built-environment vulnerability center on such issues as the overall condition of built-environment elements, when they were built and under what codes and standards, how well the hazards to which the structures are exposed were understood at the time those structures were designed and built, whether they have been adequately maintained, whether, if needed, they have been retrofitted, and whether they are approaching or exceeding the period of time for which they were designed—as is the case, for example, with many US nuclear plants whose permits have nonetheless been extended.

Research by sociologist Charles Perrow (2006) emphasizes the notion that some elements in the built environment are vulnerable simply as a result of the way their components are related to one another and operate. The electrical power grid in North America is an example. Although the power grid normally operates with very high levels of reliability, under certain conditions the grid can be prone to cascading, and even to catastrophic loss of function. This is what happened, for example, in August 2003, when what would have been a minor accident in part of the power grid resulted in a massive blackout that affected the United States and Canada. This blackout was the best-documented case of electrical power service disruption in terms of its effects on safety and health. It began with a series of small mishaps that led to progressive degrading and total failure of the power systems in eight eastern US states and in the Canadian province of Ontario. It started around 2 p.m. on August 14, and it wasn't until the morning of August 17 that the entire affected system was restored and operating reliably. Approximately 50 million people were affected by the blackout, including residents of large cities such as New York City, Toronto, Cleveland, and Detroit.

Several reports and studies have focused on the impacts of the blackout on interdependent infrastructure systems in New York City, where, according to one report,

> Subways were stopped in their tunnels, airports halted operations, and elevators stalled mid-ride. Water systems shut down. The communications network was disrupted; cellular telephones ceased to work; emergency response networks were hampered; and automatic teller machines went dark. Many restaurants and shops shuttered their doors, and streets were rapidly overwhelmed by vehicles and pedestrians trying to find their way home. Without air conditioning, many buildings rapidly became stifling. Stranded commuters spent the night in train stations, hotel lobbies, and emergency shelters. (US Department of Transportation 2004: 2)

When the power failed, 400,000 people were trapped on New York subways. The city lost all of its 11,000 traffic signals, and no mass transit was able to operate except for water ferries and buses. As commuters tried to make their way home, streets, sidewalks, and bridges became increasingly crowded. Eight hundred people trapped in elevators had to be rescued. High-rise buildings lacked water because they lost pumping capacity (US Department of Transportation 2004).

The blackout caused ninety excess deaths in New York City alone, a rise in mortality of 28 percent. Focusing again on differential sensitivity, death rates were highest for those aged between sixty-five and seventy-four (Anderson and Bell 2012). Hospital emergency department visits and admissions due to respiratory problems increased, especially among women, elderly persons, and people suffering from chronic bronchitis (Lin et al. 2011). Food spoiled without adequate refrigeration, which led to an increase in diarrheal illnesses. Calls to 9–11 and other emergency services, including poison control centers, increased sharply (Lin et al. 2011). At the same time, the blackout made the management of illnesses more difficult. Pharmacies were forced to close, making it impossible for people to access prescription drugs, and hospital operations were compromised. On the basis of their research, Anderson and Bell (2012) concluded that the impacts of electrical power outages on mortality and morbidity have been underestimated.

As this example shows, advanced societies are highly vulnerable to power grid disruptions. The grid literally provides the backbone on which societies depend, making it possible to use the Internet and banking services, pump gasoline, or heat and cool structures, to operate transportation and other infrastructure systems, to supply water, to use grocery store checkout systems, and more. Perrow (2006: 213) calls the power grid "the single most vulnerable system in our critical infrastructure," noting that it is vulnerable to attacks by terrorists as well as to extreme weather events such as excessive heat and cold, hurricanes, and floods. The interconnectedness of the global financial and banking infrastructure also makes that system prone to cascading failures. For example, the massive stock market crash in 1987 in the United States and the global financial meltdown in 2007–2008, which ushered in the Great Recession, were related in part to built-in financial infrastructure interdependencies that led to massive losses in the value of financial assets (Tierney 2014).

Social vulnerability

Place-based and built-environment vulnerabilities must be taken into account in developing a full picture of why and in what ways societies and communities are at risk of experiencing disaster losses, because, as we have seen in earlier discussions, community residents become vulnerable to disasters in part because they often live in high-hazard areas and vulnerable structures. For example, in early research on social vulnerability and the built environment, my colleagues and I showed that in Los Angeles persons with disabilities were more likely than able-bodied individuals to be living in older multi-family structures that were vulnerable to damage and even total collapse in earthquakes (Tierney, Petak, and Hahn 1988). In the absence of effective affordable housing policies, many community residents have no choice but to live in unsafe and overcrowded housing units that are physically vulnerable to disaster impacts, for example in manufactured housing and old, poorly maintained apartment buildings. Worldwide, poor people have few options other than to live in slum conditions and in areas that are hazard-prone, such as steep hillsides and flood plains. The association between poverty and unsafe living conditions was highlighted in the *At Risk* volume and is evident in disasters such as the 2010 Haiti earthquake, in which slum dwellings collapsed and slipped *en masse* down the steep hillsides on which they had been constructed.

Sociologists who study hazards and disasters are fundamentally concerned with social vulnerability—that is, with the social origins and aspects of the differential potential of individuals and communities to experience short- and longer-term losses as a consequence of disasters. For the purposes of the discussion in this volume, we can conceptualize social vulnerability to disasters as a condition that can be found at a particular point in time and is the consequence of historical and ongoing societal forces that create a disproportionate potential for loss, and also for experiencing poorer outcomes as a result of loss. Put another way, vulnerable groups are those groups that are more likely to experience a range of negative *impacts* when disasters strike and less likely to experience positive *outcomes* in the aftermath of disasters. A number of publications focus on social vulnerability (see Pelling 2003; Bankoff, Frerks, and Hilhorst 2004; Enarson and Chakrabarti 2009; Thomas, Phillips, Lovekamp, and Fothergill 2013; Enarson and Pease 2016; Enarson, Fothergill, and Peek 2018). Here I distill some of the many insights from these studies while offering a slightly different way of thinking about disaster vulnerability—one that places primary emphasis on the effects of class, race, and gender, as well as on state actions that produce or exacerbate vulnerability.

Some parts of the definition provided in the preceding paragraphs need to be clarified. The first is that social vulnerability has temporal, spatial, and situational dimensions. It exists at particular points in time and in particular locations; while disaster vulnerability is shaped by historical trends, conditions can also evolve and vary in ways that make individuals and groups more or less vulnerable, both in terms of impacts and in terms of outcomes. Regarding impacts, for example, the discussion in Chapter 4 showed how racial and ethnic segregation has resulted in disproportionate exposure to toxic hazards in cities like Phoenix and Los Angeles. Regarding outcomes, vulnerability to experiencing negative outcomes during the post-disaster recovery period results in part from preexisting conditions of vulnerability, but also, importantly, from the resources that are available to survivors in the aftermath of disasters—for example, recovery policies and the extent to which people are able to take advantage of post-disaster relief programs and to take other steps to put their lives back in order. Outcomes for those who lose their homes are shaped in part by policy decisions that can shift over time; but, as we will see later in this chapter when discussing the post-Katrina Road Home program, such policies can reinforce preexisting inequities.

Often the conditions that affect post-disaster recovery outcomes are unrelated to the disaster itself or to disaster relief policies. For example, high rental vacancy rates in one community that experiences a disaster can make it easier for displaced low- to moderate-income renters to find adequate post-disaster housing, rendering them less vulnerable to long-term dislocation, while low vacancy rates in another disaster-stricken community may cause serious difficulties for displaced renters in those same income groups. For a business, disaster recovery can be affected by the overall economic climate; other things being equal, recovery opportunities are likely better during periods of economic growth than when the economy is stagnant, as was the case, for example, for years after the financial crash of 2008. Consequently, vulnerability can best be thought of as a combination of long-term disadvantages such as those typically associated with race and social class and situational conditions that vary over time and across communities.

Another key point is that, while impact and outcome vulnerabilities are often highly correlated, there can also be situations in which losses experienced as a result of disaster impacts can be offset by post-disaster policies that seek to improve outcomes for those affected. To take one example, communities and businesses that depended on the fishing industry suffered significant losses as a result of the 2010 British Petroleum (BP) *Deepwater Horizon* oil rig blowout and oil spill. In the aftermath of the spill, the company quickly devised a compensation scheme and began payouts to victims. In contrast, the long and drawn-out process of compensating fishing-oriented communities and businesses after the 1989 *Exxon Valdez* oil spill, which was caused by Exxon's intransigence in fighting settlement efforts, led to long-term stress for those who were awaiting payouts, as well as to loss of community cohesion and trust in institutions such as the government and the courts (Ritchie 2012; Ritchie, Gill, and Farnham 2013). The Oil Pollution Act of 1990, which was passed after the Exxon spill, clarified the role of so-called responsible parties in compensating those who are negatively affected by oil spills. While the compensation arrangements made after the BP disaster were still a source of community conflict and psychological stress for those affected (Gill, Picou, and Ritchie 2012; Ritchie, Gill, and Long 2018), the 1990 statute at least clarified who should pay for spill-induced losses; and, because compensation came more quickly than in the Exxon disaster, longer-term negative psychological consequences of stress may have been avoided.

Ideally, in the aftermath of disasters efforts should be made to level the playing field so that those who have lost the most in relation to their pre-disaster circumstances should receive the most assistance during the recovery process; but, as we will see in the discussions that follow, this is often not the case. Rather, what happens to those who have experienced losses in disasters is yet another manifestation of what sociologist Robert Merton (1968) referred to as the Matthew effect: those in society who already have advantages tend to accumulate more, while those who lack advantages fall farther behind.[1]

Vulnerable groups? The significance of intersectionality

In both scholarship and public policy, there has been a tendency to characterize a wide range of groups as vulnerable to hazards. A partial list of these groups includes women, poor people, members of racial and ethnic minorities, elderly persons, persons with ongoing health problems and disabilities, and children. Categorizing entire segments of the population in this way can be useful. For example, special disaster-related programs may be developed to target those who live in poverty, or children. Such categorizations also point to characteristics of group members that can make them particularly vulnerable in disaster situations: only women can get pregnant, and women, as opposed to men, are typically victims of domestic violence that occurs in the wake of disasters. While this chapter will shine a spotlight on the ways in which members of different groups are made vulnerable in the context of hazards and disasters, it will also make two related points. First, it is necessary to move away from the kind of essentialism that sees vulnerability as an inherent or intrinsic characteristic of members of particular groups—for example, by arguing that all women, or all children, are vulnerable. To do so would be to ignore the often immense differences that exist within such groups and also the point that, as noted earlier, people are not born vulnerable, they are made vulnerable. Moreover, as we will see in Chapter 7, while individuals and groups are vulnerable differentially, they are also resilient differentially—and high levels of resilience can overcome social deficits that are typically associated with vulnerability.

Second, sociologists have long used the concept of *intersectionality* to refer to the ways in which multiple dimensions of stratification and inequality come together to shape people's life circumstance and life chances. Originally formulated by legal scholar Kimberlé Crenshaw (1991) and developed further by sociologists who study race, class, gender, and other forms of inequality (see, for example, Andersen and Collins 2016; Collins and Bilge 2016), the concept highlights the fact that different axes of inequality combine and interact to form systems of oppression—systems that relate directly to differential levels of social vulnerability, both in normal times and in the context of disaster. Intersectionality calls attention to the need to avoid statements like "women are vulnerable" in favor of a more nuanced view, which asks (in this example): "Which women are more vulnerable or less vulnerable, under what conditions, and why?" There is a vast difference in levels of social vulnerability between a woman who is a recent immigrant of color, non-English-speaking, and working as a night janitor for hourly wages and a Caucasian woman with a PhD who is a high-ranking and hugely compensated executive in a major social media company. Intersecting statuses place people who might otherwise be considered similar—toddlers and teenagers, for example—in very different positions when it comes to their social vulnerability. Thus, even though I will refer to particular groups as vulnerable in these discussions, we must also keep in mind gradations in vulnerability that result from intersecting dimensions of inequality. As Fordham and colleagues put it:

> It is not that children, people with disabilities, women, and other social groups are vulnerable as such; it is a particular amalgamation of factors in place and time that dictates that some groups will be harder hit and less able to recover successfully. (Fordham et al. 2013: 12)

Key Dimensions of Social Vulnerability: Class, Race, and Gender

Social class

The simplest way of thinking about social class is to see class as having three main dimensions: income and wealth, education, and occupation. *Income* consists of what is earned by individuals and households, which can include wages and salaries, dividends on investments, and cash benefits such as social security payments. In contrast, *wealth* is what is owned, or the assets individuals and households possess. Wealth can include equity in a home, savings, stocks, bonds, other financial instruments, and other possessions. The *net worth* of a household consists of its assets minus what it owes, for example in the form of household mortgages and other debt. In the United States, both income and wealth are highly unequal and becoming more so, most of the advantages accruing to those who are extremely well-off, while the income and wealth of other groups remain stagnant or decline. To give just one example, income and wealth are often grouped into quintiles—five tranches that represent, each, 20 percent of the total income and wealth distribution. In 2016, 51.5 percent of all household income was earned by those in the top quintile, while those in the lowest quintile earned only 3.1 percent of the total. In 2016 the average net worth of the top 1 percent of households was around $10,300,000, while the net worth of the lowest 10 percent averaged around $-960 (US Census Bureau 2016).

Education is a second marker of social class membership, which spans both educational attainment and more subtle distinctions, such as where individuals received their educations. High educational attainment is characteristic of the upper-middle and upper classes. Adding to their advantages, members of the wealthiest groups are typically educated at elite primary and secondary schools and colleges—often the schools their parents and grandparents attended—which serves to separate them from members of the lower classes even further.

Occupational status has several dimensions, including the prestige that members of the public assign to an occupation, the amount of independence associated with different occupations, whether individuals earn salaries or hourly wages, and median income levels within occupations. Such differences point to the importance of not only how much individuals earn, but also how they earn that income and the value that others place on particular occupations. For example, physicians and scientists have high occupational prestige, while real estate agents and automobile salespersons are much less admired by members of the public, even if they may earn high incomes through commissions.

Scholars differ in how they distinguish among the different social classes. In the United States, for example, classic research by W. Lloyd Warner (1949) recognized three social classes—upper, middle, and lower—with upper and lower gradations within each class. Currently, the sociologist Dennis Gilbert (2018) divides US society into six classes: the capitalist, upper-middle, middle, and working classes, along with the working poor class and the underclass. Members of the capitalist class are individuals with "old money" that has existed for generations, corporate chief executive officers, and others who have amassed very high net worth. This is the group that is often referred to as "the 1 percent." Members of the capitalist class have very high income and wealth levels, often do not earn their money through actual work, and are likely to have achieved their wealth by inheriting it. This is also the class that possesses the highest amount of political power and influence. Members of the upper-middle class are doing well financially, but not as well as those in the upper class. They have generally attained their class position in their own lifetimes by receiving advanced degrees. They work for a living but, unlike those who are lower in the class hierarchy, their occupations involve little supervision, and they are generally salaried professionals. Doctors, lawyers, and other highly paid professionals fit into this category. Those in the middle class have at least a high school education and can be involved in minor management or supervisory positions. The working class consists of manual workers and many low-paid clerical and retail sales workers. The working poor constitute the lowest-paid manual, clerical, and other workers. These individuals may be working full-time and still fall below the poverty line of $26,104 (2016) as a result of their low wages. The underclass, the lowest group in the class hierarchy, is made up of people who are unemployed, who work part-time for low wages, or who obtain their income through public assistance.

What has come to be called the precariat is a distinctive group that does not fit easily into traditional class categories, which assume that individuals have at least somewhat consistent earnings, even if those earnings are low. As the portmanteau suggests, this group has a precarious economic position, which is highly dependent on the vicissitudes of the market. Members of the precariat are characterized by a lack of predictability in terms of income and employment, along with a lack of the kinds of employment protections and benefits that were traditionally enjoyed by many members of the middle and working classes. This group includes involuntary part-time workers who have little say over the hours they work, participants in the "gig economy," and "private contractors" such as Uber drivers, who may make well below the minimum wage for hours worked. The precariat also includes people who have experienced downward mobility, for example in response to economic downturns, have lost their homes, are unable to live on their meager pension or social security benefits, and may even have been forced into a nomadic existence based on taking advantage of seasonal work in places such as Amazon warehouses. This aspect of precarity was recently captured in the book *Nomadland* (Bruder 2017), which focuses on individuals and groups that are not exactly homeless but are not housed either, and that travel the country in recreational vehicles in search of often backbreaking work.

Social class exerts a profound influence on virtually every aspect of people's lives. Lower-class individuals have lower life expectancies and poorer health outcomes, in part because they are more likely to smoke, to exercise less, and to have poorer diets. Mental health problems are also more common in the lower classes, but despite the higher incidence of these kinds of physical and psychological problems, those in the lower classes are less likely to have adequate medical insurance (Barr 2014). Divorce is more common among the lower social classes, which in part accounts for the higher incidence of female-headed households in these groups (Bureau of Labor Statistics 2013). Members of less privileged groups, especially African American men, are also more likely to be arrested and to find themselves in jail or prison and on parole and probation—circumstances that typically result in poor life chances (Western 2006; Western and Pettit 2010). Home ownership is increasingly less common moving downward in the class hierarchy. Because rents have increased faster than wages in many US cities, working- and lower-class families are finding it increasingly difficult to find affordable housing and often must resort to living in overcrowded conditions (Semple 2016; Kotkin and Cox 2017) and to cutting back on expenditures for basic necessities such as food, transportation, and medical care. Overcrowding is known to have significant negative effects on children, for example higher stress, problems with sleep, and difficulties with school performance and academic achievement (Solari and Mare 2012). The effects of overcrowding on children can persist throughout their lives.

Disasters can add to the everyday injuries associated with being lower in the class hierarchy. Out of necessity, poor people depend a great deal on their place-based networks of social support, which help them overcome poverty by providing free support in the form of childcare, transportation, food, and respites from stressful situations at home. However, because disasters damage or destroy residences and neighborhoods and can result in temporary or permanent residential dislocation, they can disrupt those social support networks. Disasters frequently do the most damage to substandard and rental housing (which is typically made of inferior materials, not generally used in owner-occupied housing), putting poor people at greater risk for residential dislocation.

In addition to damaging support networks and causing displacement, disasters can bring about changes in affected communities that make life even more difficult for those at the lower end of the social hierarchy. To the extent that disasters cause a decline in the availability of rental housing, they cause rents to rise. Increased rents affect displaced people at all income levels, but are most burdensome for those who were struggling before the disaster struck. For example, in 2017, Hurricane Harvey displaced hundreds of thousands of homeowners and renters while also destroying or rendering uninhabitable thousands of rental units. Those forced out of their owner-occupied dwellings, as well as renters, needed to find places to rent in order to achieve some sort of stability in their lives, and so, as a result of this increased demand, rental costs increased (Sarnoff 2017). Temporary federal rental assistance is designed to help displaced residents, but the living conditions many lower-class and underclass people (and others) are forced to endure can threaten their eligibility even for this form of aid. An article that appeared in *Texas Monthly* after Hurricane Harvey in 2017 noted:

> People are denied FEMA [Federal Emergency Management Agency] aid for a wide number of reasons, and in some cases, it might seem, for no reason at all. Aid eligibility rests on being able to prove US citizenship and residence at an address rendered unlivable. This might seem easy, but pitfalls abound: people who lived with roommates or family and might not be listed on a lease or a utility bill; people who lived with too many other applicants; people whose homes could be owned by incarcerated spouses or exes; exchange students, foreigners, and undocumented people who cannot offer proof of citizenship; people who lost their identification in the storm, or their landlord's phone number. The list goes on. (Young 2017)

A look at the US social class system reveals a society that is sharply divided between the haves and the have-nots, between those who are able to live stable lives, have access to a range of amenities, and feel secure in their social class positions and those whose lives are marked by instability, stressful experiences, and other forms of insecurity. Disaster-related burdens fall most heavily on the have-nots. Superimposed on these class disparities are other inequities, which are associated with race and ethnicity; and we turn next to these.

Race and ethnicity

To recal our earlier discussion of racial formation (see pp. 83–4), race is a social construct that is used to mark racialized persons and groups for unequal treatment within society. Racialized categories serve as the basis for practices such as racial segregation, job discrimination, and other forms of social exclusion. Race and ethnicity tend to co-vary with social class, African Americans, Native Americans, and people of Hispanic descent being more likely to have lower-class status than whites. At the same time, however, racial designations bring with them additional disadvantages, which cannot be explained solely by reference to social class markers. For example, in comparison with whites, African Americans and people of Hispanic descent earn less at the same educational levels, amass less wealth at similar income levels, and tend to pay more for equivalent goods and services, largely owing to higher prices in the areas where they live (Williams, Mohammed, Leavell, and Collins 2010). Regardless of their socioeconomic status, racial and ethnic minority group members face unique burdens that are attributable to race alone. These burdens include not only day-to-day expressions of racism but also ongoing disadvantages, such as living in hypersegregated areas, living in close proximity to hazardous facilities, living in "food deserts" that offer limited access to healthy foods, and having reduced access to quality schools and community amenities such as parks and open spaces. Even when we hold the socioeconomic status constant, being a member of a racial or ethnic minority has profound negative effects; for example it contributes to disparities in mortality and other health outcomes (Williams, Priest, and Anderson, 2016).

Income and wealth data reveal the extent of racial disparities in the United States. Data on average incomes tend to mask the extent to which earnings vary as a function of race and ethnicity—and they do so significantly. For example, the most recent census data indicate that the median income for all US households is around $57,230; but the median income for whites is $60,869, while the figures for Hispanics and African Americans are $45,719 and $37,364 respectively. In other words, Hispanic income totals 75 percent of white income, while African American income totals 61 percent. Those of Asian descent earn significantly more than any of these groups: their median income is $78,141.

Since the publication of Melvin Oliver and Thomas Shapiro's (1995) groundbreaking study *Black Wealth, White Wealth*, sociologists have been increasingly focusing on racial and ethnic disparities in wealth, in addition to income disparities. Here the picture is even starker: Hispanics and African Americans possess fewer assets than whites by many orders of magnitude. For example, in 2016, while the median net worth of whites stood at about $171,000, Hispanics and blacks had a median net worth of $20,700 and $17,600 respectively. One in five African American households has zero or negative net worth. Much of this wealth discrepancy can be attributed to lower earnings and less ability to save, lower percentages of home ownership, along with lower housing values for those who do own homes. Adding to these inequities, Hispanics and African Americans have accumulated significantly less than whites in retirement savings, in part because they are less likely to be participating in retirement plans. Whites are five times more likely than Hispanics or blacks to have received large gifts and inheritances that add to their assets (Urban Institute 2017).

The 2008 financial crisis and the Great Recession that followed dealt a massive blow to wealth, employment, and income, both in the United States and worldwide. Between 2007 and 2009, housing prices in major US metropolitan areas lost nearly one third of their value, the Dow Jones stock index lost nearly half of its value, and unemployment increased from 5 to 10 percent (Pfeffer, Danziger, and Schoeni 2013). Minority group members, low-wage workers, and people with less education were more likely to become unemployed and to have their earnings reduced (Hoynes, Miller, and Shaller, 2012).

In the years since the financial crash, wealth losses have been significantly greater for lower-income and minority groups than for those with higher incomes and whites. Controlling for other factors, blacks, Hispanics, and Native Americans lost significantly more wealth than whites and people of Asian descent—impacts that will extend into the future (Pfeffer et al. 2013). The evidence shows that those who had the least to lose before the Great Recession suffered disproportionately and had the greatest difficulty recovering. Race and neighborhood segregation were significant factors in negative outcomes for African Americans in the Great Recession. In a study conducted in Baltimore, Rugh, Albright, and Massey (2015) found that, controlling for other factors such as credit scores and income, blacks were more likely to be victimized by predatory lending (e.g. by being offered risky subprime mortgage loans), paid more for their loans, and experienced more foreclosures, which caused a substantial loss of wealth for members of that group.

What these income and wealth disparities mean in the disaster context is that racial and ethnic minority group members lack the financial "cushions" that whites typically take for granted and that contribute to whites' disaster resilience. Like members of the lower classes, minority group members have fewer financial resources on which to draw when emergencies occur; and, like poor people, they may see their social support networks weakened in the event of disaster. This lowers their access to informal sources of aid.

Gender and vulnerability

As used here and in keeping with sociological treatments of the concept, gender refers not to biological sex but rather to the differential assignment of rights, privileges, and cultural and behavioral expectations that are associated with the designation of persons as male or female, along with the identities that are shaped by those social forces. Gender is the basis not only for signaling differences in expectations regarding "appropriate" behavior, but also and more importantly for producing disparities in such areas as social privilege, socioeconomic status, economic opportunity, and political power.

Like social class and racial–ethnic disparities, gender inequality is pervasive. For women, particularly those in less developed countries, gender inequality can translate into limited personal autonomy, limited access to educational and livelihood-related resources, restrictions on property ownership and the ability to inherit, ongoing threats to physical safety, and lack of access to political power. Worldwide, women bear burdens that are similar to those borne by racialized groups, in the form of actions that are designed to "keep them in their place" and that range from micro-aggressions to the denial of basic human rights and to physical and sexual violence. In the United States, the revelations that began in 2017 regarding the extent of the sexual harassment, assault, and humiliation suffered by women across all walks of life attest to how strongly unequal and exploitive gender relations are part of the social fabric even in highly developed societies. As we will see later in this chapter, individuals who deviate from the traditional gender binary, such as lesbian, gay, bisexual, and transgendered persons, are at risk of similar and even harsher treatment. Indignities rooted in gender-based oppression, like those rooted in race and ethnicity, exert their influence at all levels of the social class hierarchy.

Beginning in 2006, the World Economic Forum has been gathering and disseminating information on the male–female gender gap with the help of a Global Gender Gap Index it developed, which focuses on a collection of variables associated with economic participation and opportunities, educational attainment, survival and health, and political empowerment. Its report for 2017, which contains data on 144 countries, provided both overall rankings and rankings on the four key dimensions of gender achievement. The survey showed that, while no nation on earth has succeeded in eliminating the gender gap, some countries are doing a much better job of addressing it than others. The five countries with the lowest gender gaps were Iceland, Norway, Finland, Rwanda, and Sweden, while those with the largest gaps were Yemen, Pakistan, Syria, Chad, and Iran, in that order. The United States ranks 49th on the index, lower than all wealthy developed countries except for Japan, which ranks 114th. Gender inequities are considered such a serious problem worldwide that the United Nations has included gender equality and the empowerment of women and girls among its major sustainable development goals (World Economic Forum 2017).

Gender inequality is inextricably linked to economic and racialized inequalities. In the United States, women currently earn 80 cents for every dollar earned by men, but African American and Hispanic women earn 63 and 54 cents on the dollar, respectively. Adding further to their burdens, women in the United States lag behind their counterparts in other affluent countries with respect to paid family leave and childcare opportunities. Recent years have also seen their reproductive rights severely curtailed, for example through restrictions on access to contraceptives and abortions (Dastagir 2017).

The US Census set the 2016 poverty line at $24,339 for a family made up of two adults and two children. Poverty rates for 2016 vary considerably across states, from a low of 7.3 percent of the population in New Hampshire to a high of 20.8 percent in Mississippi. States with poverty rates of 18 percent and above are Kentucky, Louisiana, Mississippi, New Mexico, and the District of Columbia. The US territory of Puerto Rico, which experienced catastrophic losses in Hurricane Maria in 2017, had a poverty rate of 43.5 percent in 2016. With the exception of Kentucky, these are also the areas that had the highest percentage of people living in extreme poverty, which is defined as 50 percent of the poverty wage and below.

Poverty in the United States is both gendered and race-based. A report by the National Women's Law Center (Patrick 2017), which is based on 2016 data from the US Census, noted that one in eight women and one in six children were living in poverty and, of this number, two women in five were living in extreme poverty. Women are 38 percent more likely than men to have incomes below the poverty line, and also more likely than men to experience extreme poverty. While 9.7 percent of white non-Hispanic women were living in poverty, those percentages increased significantly for other racial and ethnic groups: 22.88 percent for Native American women, 21.4 percent for African American women, 18.7 percent for women of Hispanic descent, and 10.7 percent for Asian women. Additionally, almost 60 percent of children in poverty live in woman-headed households.

Jennifer Tobin-Gurley and Elaine Enarson (2013) enumerate the many ways in which gender matters in both non-disaster and disaster times. To provide just a few examples, for women, pregnancy creates special needs. For men, expectations regarding masculinity may limit their ability to ask for psychological help when they are experiencing stress, which can lead to self-medication through substance abuse. Women are more risk-averse than men, which means that they may take disaster warnings and evacuation orders more seriously than their male counterparts. In Hurricane Katrina, for example, men were twice as likely as women to resist evacuating (Haney, Elliott, and Fussell 2010). Because of their lack of power and authority, women may be overruled by men when it comes to disaster-related decision-making. Gender is associated with disaster-related mortality, but in complex ways. Some studies find men at greater risk of losing their lives in disasters, while others point to the vulnerability of women and girls. Women's lack of access to needed health services both before and after disasters can put them at risk for adverse health outcomes. Gender role expectations can mean that men experience greater risk of injury during disaster response and recovery periods, while women are exposed to high levels of stress associated with their caring and supportive roles.

In their summary of research on gender and disaster vulnerability, Enarson and colleagues (2018) attribute gender differences in disaster mortality and morbidity to factors such as gender norms, the gendered division of labor in households and workplaces, and other societal practices that result in differential exposure to hazards and their impacts. According to their review, while after disasters men may commit suicide at higher rates than women, women tend to experience more mental health problems than men. Enarson and colleagues also note that research on recent disasters in both less developed and developed nations continues to show that women experience higher risk of violence after disasters, both in the home and in other settings such as temporary shelters.

The Importance of an Intersectional Approach to Vulnerability

As the preceding discussion shows, the intersecting forces of class, race, and gender translate into divergent levels of opportunity and success for individuals and groups. While social class achieves prominence in this respect, race, ethnicity, and gender co-determine class effects, magnifying the benefits that accrue to men and whites to the detriment of non-white racial and ethnic groups and women. At all levels of the class hierarchy, women and the less privileged racial groups fall behind; they do not reap the benefits afforded to members of the dominant group. This means that they have fewer resources available to cope with day-to-day emergencies as well as with disasters.

The social forces that are active and evident in everyday life manifest themselves perhaps even more starkly when it comes to hazard exposure and disaster impacts and outcomes. Those at the lower end of the social class hierarchy are more likely to live in physically vulnerable places and in vulnerable housing types (McCoy and Dash 2013). Lower-income individuals and households must settle for whatever housing they can afford, even if it is unsafe and in poor repair. Renters have little or no leverage over landlords in terms of housing safety. As noted earlier, those with greater financial resources are better able to evacuate and to do so earlier than the less well-off, putting themselves out of harm's way (Elliott and Pais 2006).

Regarding racial differences in vulnerability to disaster impacts, in research that was conducted after Hurricane Katrina, Bevc, Nicholls, and Picou found that African Americans suffered a range of negative effects of that disaster. Summing up their findings, they observed:

> African Americans throughout the primary impact region have suffered disproportionately more problems than other racial or ethnic groups. African Americans were more than twice as likely to have received major damage or have their homes totally destroyed. Large proportions of African Americans had to move out of their residences and proportionately more were separated from family members. Post-Katrina financial problems were most acute for African Americans ... A similar pattern persisted for African Americans in terms of insurance and state grant program claims ... [they] had fewer claims fully settled and had more claims partially settled. (Bevc, Nicholls, and Picou 2010: 155)

After disasters, recovery opportunities are also structured by pre-disaster class, racial, and gender disparities. As the statistics above indicate, social classes, racial and ethnic groups, women and men differ significantly in the degree to which they possess resources that help them prepare for, respond to, and recover from disasters. Those living in poverty, which include many members of racial and ethnic groups and women, typically have little or no discretionary income after paying for housing, food, transportation, and other basic expenses, which means that they are highly unlikely to be able to undertake measures to reduce their disaster risks, such as stockpiling supplies or having the wherewithal to evacuate. Incomes vary significantly across class, race, and gender divides, but the glaring disparities in wealth discussed earlier are perhaps even more indicative of inequities in the ability to cope with disaster-induced problems and to make progress toward recovery.

As we saw in Chapter 4, many of the disadvantages African Americans and other minority group members currently experience, such as racial segregation and barriers to accumulating wealth, are part of the legacy of discriminatory governmental policies. As Bolin and Kurtz observe,

> [t]he state is a major agent in the production, transformation, and enactment of constructions of race ... Through law, policy, and a complex suite of institutional arrangements, racial discrimination in myriad forms is shaped by state-sanctioned practices in civil society. (Bolin and Kurtz 2018: 182)

These inequities can also be found in governmental disaster assistance programs. Individual and household resources are directly related to the ability to gain access to adequate amounts of disaster assistance. In the United States, other than those who have experienced disasters directly, most people are unaware that the major source of federal government recovery assistance for households and businesses comes in the form of loans. Direct assistance of other kinds is quite limited—for example funds for temporary repairs designed to make dwellings livable, or rental vouchers for those who have been displaced. For larger recovery expenditures such as housing reconstruction and major repairs, the main source of assistance is loans from the Small Business Administration—loans that are made on essentially the same basis as private bank loans, that is, by taking into account such factors as a good credit history and an income that permits paying back the loan.

With that information in mind, it is important to consider how different groups might fare in the loan application process. Decisions regarding credit worthiness, including those made by government agencies after disasters, are typically based on a number of criteria, but one of the simplest is consideration of an individual's credit score. However, as of 2015, about 45 million Americans had no credit score at all (Holland 2015). According to the Consumer Financial Protection Bureau, at that time 26 million Americans had no credit history, and of that number, 9 percent of whites and about 15 percent of blacks and Hispanics were without those all-important scores. Another 19 million persons had out-of-date or very sparse credit information, which make them "credit-invisible" or "unscorable." Significantly, 30 percent of the residents of low-income neighborhoods had no credit score. It gets worse. Of those who do have credit scores, about 30 percent have poor scores, which puts them at a disadvantage when they have to qualify for any type of loan (DiGangi 2016).

Recalling other themes discussed in Chapter 4, many of the disadvantages that African Americans and other minority group members currently experience, for instance racial segregation and barriers to accumulating wealth, are part of the legacy of discriminatory practices that were shaped by governmental policies. Credit scores are closely linked to race and ethnicity. A 2007 report to Congress by the Board of Governors of the Federal Reserve System indicated that African Americans and Hispanics have lower scores than whites and Asian Americans and that immigrants have lower scores than they would otherwise merit on the basis of factors such as income. Overall, those with lower scores include blacks, people of Hispanic descent, people under thirty, and residents of low income or from predominantly minority neighborhoods. According to one commentator (Ludwig 2015, n.p.), credit-reporting systems "embed existing racial inequities in our credit system and economy—to the point that a person's credit information serves as a proxy for race." Those inequities can be traced in turn to a history of redlining in minority communities and to the targeting of minority groups for predatory lending practices. In other words, by its very nature, the information that serves as the basis for post-disaster loans is discriminatory.

The same goes for businesses. According to the US Department of Commerce (2010), minority group members applying for business loans are less likely to receive them, more likely to be denied credit, and more likely to pay higher interest rates for their loans than whites. These disparities are thought to be related in turn to minorities' lower levels of wealth that could serve as collateral for loans (Fairlie and Robb 2010). This is yet another example of how long-standing systemic inequalities result in cumulative disadvantage for members of minority groups—the sort of disadvantage that carries over into the disaster context.

Other historical disparities, too, make disadvantaged groups more vulnerable to negative outcomes in the aftermath of disasters. The ability to receive adequate compensation for disaster losses is an important factor in determining which groups are best positioned to experience positive recovery outcomes. However, Peacock and Girard (1997) found that, after Hurricane Andrew, which devastated southern Dade County in Florida in 1992, insurance payouts for disaster recovery were inadequate for Hispanics who were not of Cuban descent, as well as for African Americans. Deficits in insurance payments were in turn related to previous redlining practices in which whites were more likely than other groups to have insurance coverage from one of the country's major insurers (State Farm, Allstate, and Prudential).

Disparities in recovery assistance extended to government compensation as well. At the community level, although they experienced roughly similar levels of damage in Hurricane Andrew, Homestead, a hard-hit majority-white community, received significantly more government assistance than Florida City, a similarly hard-hit majority-African American community. Following the two communities over time, while the value of Homestead single-family homes recovered to pre-Andrew levels within approximately two years, values in Florida City took seven to eight years to recover. By the time of the 2000 census, even as Homestead's household incomes increased and poverty decreased, Florida City's household incomes decreased and poverty increased (Dash and Peacock 2003; see also McCoy and Dash 2013).

Focusing on the individual level, Jessica Pardee studied fifty-one African American women who had been living in public housing before Hurricane Katrina and who were displaced. Relocating was bound to be difficult for this group of women, who "were among the least likely to have savings for rental deposits, funds to purchase basic furniture, or access to job transfers that would ensure a steady stream of income" (Pardee 2012: 68). To make matters worse, of the twenty-one who had been employed before Katrina struck, only four were able to obtain employment afterwards. Almost all of the women received federal government or Red Cross assistance after the hurricane, but they still struggled to find stable housing arrangements, many moving multiple times in the months after the storm. Landlords took advantage of the hurricane to raise rents and place restrictions on those to whom they would rent, further disadvantaging these women. Pardee observed:

> In an ideal scenario, the rehousing process would have been simple—find a place, sign a lease, get an inspection, submit the voucher, and . . .

> Welcome home! In reality, the women in this study faced multiple barri-
> ers imposed by private rental actors and assisting institutions—the people
> charged with 'helping' them after the storm. These women were almost
> always left after Katrina with less money than they had before to pay the
> rent or for other needs. (Pardee 2012: 76–77)

The demolition of four very large public housing projects in New Orleans
narrowed the options for these women in terms of returning to the city, as
did rising rents and cumbersome application requirements and fees for rental
housing. Many women suspected that landlords and city decision-makers
were deliberately trying to make it as difficult as possible for people like them
to return to New Orleans—suspicions that have been largely borne out.

After Superstorm Sandy, the Fair Share Housing Center, a civil rights group,
found evidence of discrimination toward disaster assistance applicants in New
Jersey that adversely affected African American and Hispanic disaster survivors. Around 38 percent of blacks and 20 percent of Hispanics who applied for
resettlement grants were rejected, by comparison with 14.5 percent of whites.
The same pattern was found among applicants for repair and reconstruction assistance: 35 percent of African Americans and 18 percent of Hispanics
were rejected, while the figure was 13.6 percent for whites (New York Times
Editorial Board 2013).

In a volume titled *The Wrong Complexion for Protection*, Robert Bullard and
Beverly Wright argue that the US government has a poor track record when it
comes to the risks faced by African Americans and members of other minority
groups with respect to natural and technological hazards. With regard to the
latter, "[n]umerous bad [government] decisions have turned communities of
far too many low-income people and people of color into 'sacrifice zones' and
toxic dumping grounds, lowering nearby residents' property values (thereby
stealing their wealth) and exposing them to unnecessary environmental
health risks" (Bullard and Wright 2012: 102). Bolstering their argument, they
cite numerous cases in which federal agencies such as the Environmental
Protection Agency acted, or failed to act, to the detriment of minority communities exposed to a range of toxic hazards. In many of those cases, appropriate
governmental responses to toxic hazards had to be forced through class-action
lawsuits.

Native Americans living on reservations are often exposed to toxic
hazards—vulnerability that can also be traced to discriminatory governmental
practices. As Durham and Miller (2010) observe, Native American tribes are
recognized as sovereign nations, but at the same time they are subject to US
government and corporate activities that can put them at risk. Their research
indicates that, of the five hundred Native American nations, more than three
hundred are exposed to toxic hazards. Because of their poverty and powerlessness, Native Americans have been unable to resist corporate and government
actions that increase their vulnerability. Tribal lands such as those inhabited

by the Western Shoshone nation have served as sites for nuclear weapons testing and have been targeted as locations for nuclear waste facilities such as the controversial Yucca Mountain nuclear waste storage site, which has never been implemented and will probably never be. Traditional Mohawk lands in New York state are exposed to pollutants released by nearby industries. Celilo Falls, which was sacred to the Yakama people of the Columbia River plateau, was flooded in 1957 as a result of an Army Corps of Engineers dam-building project on the Columbia River, which forms a border between Washington and Oregon. Jacob (2010) documents how the loss of Celilo Falls constituted a collective trauma for the tribe, destroying as it did its all-important salmon fishery and causing an increase in unemployment. Tribal members were compensated for the loss of the falls in the form of a one-time payment, but tribal representatives had made it clear that money could never compensate for the loss of resources they considered sacred.

There are more than 500 abandoned uranium-mining sites on the Navajo Reservation in Arizona. Those living on the reservation were not aware of uranium-related hazards until 1979, when a dam break released 94 million gallons of mining byproducts and 1,100 tons of radioactive sludge onto reservation land. Tribe members subsequently learned that decades of uranium mining were polluting their soil and their drinking water, exposing them to elevated risks for lung cancer and putting them at risk for kidney damage and various inflammation-related diseases (Arnold 2014). As Bolin and Kurtz observe:

> The casual disregard of Indian miners and their families' health by corporations, the decades of delay in federal compensation for radiation exposure victims and in EPA [Environmental Protection Agency] clean-up and hazard mitigation all speak to the marginality of American Indians. (Bolin and Kurtz 2018: 198)

The Road Home Program, a federally funded Hurricane Katrina recovery program that was the largest of its kind in US history, presents yet another example of how governmental policies and practices reproduce and reinforce racial and class hierarchies. As the name suggests, this program's ostensible purpose was to provide assistance to Louisiana renters and homeowners so that they could avoid long-term displacement and return to their homes. Aid came in the form of forgivable loans to owners of rental properties (so that tenants could return) and to homeowners. Payouts were calculated on the basis of the lower of two numbers: a property's pre-storm market value or the cost of storm-related damages. However, as Kevin Gotham (2014: 783) shows, "African–American applicants for Road Home grants received smaller compensation awards and therefore a fraction of the funds needed to rebuild their homes because they were residents in historically segregated neighborhoods with depressed property values." Gotham explains that about 93 percent of the homes owned by African Americans in New Orleans were valued at less than $150,000, by comparison with 55 percent of white-owned homes. African Americans, particularly those whose homes were extensively damaged, were thus significantly more likely than whites to receive compensation that was far lower than what they required to rebuild or make major repairs. Inequities in Road Home assistance led to protests and a federal class action lawsuit.

Focusing on New Orleans, Elizabeth Fussell (2015) summarizes what is known about the characteristics of Hurricane Katrina evacuees, returnees, and those who experienced long-term displacement. Those with higher incomes and higher educational levels and access to transportation were able to evacuate before Katrina struck, while those with fewer resources either stayed in their homes, to ride out the storm, or sought emergency shelter at the last minute. African Americans, lower-income, and younger residents were displaced farther away from the city, which complicated the recovery process for those groups. One year after the storm, resources again determined who was able to return home, and early returnees were older, better educated, and better off financially. Renters had difficulty returning to New Orleans for several reasons: rental properties had been vulnerable to damage, owners of rental properties may have been unable to make the needed repairs, and, because the supply of rental housing dwindled, rents increased. Again illustrating the impact of governmental decisions on disaster outcomes, as noted earlier, the Housing Authority of New Orleans demolished several low-income housing complexes and then opted for replacing them with mixed-income developments, seriously curtailing rental options for the very poor. To focus on New Orleans neighborhoods in 2010, five years after Katrina, the neighborhoods that lost the most, if we compare their population levels at the time (i.e., in 2010) with pre-storm levels, tended to have larger numbers of minority and low-income residents, renters, residents who lived in subsidized housing prior to Katrina, and residents who received lower levels of FEMA disaster assistance.

After the hurricane struck, there were researchers who hypothesized that those displaced by Katrina might actually be better off by virtue of having been relocated to areas with more job opportunities or higher wages. Could low-income and minority group members actually fare better as a result of having to leave their communities? Vigdor (2007) found that, far from confirming this hypothesis, members of those populations did not benefit from moving, and even when they received temporary government assistance, in the aftermath of Katrina, their overall employment prospects were actually worse. Price (2013) also found that, contrary to research suggesting that moving to better-off neighborhoods improves outcomes such as employment, housing quality, neighborhood quality, health, and mental health for African Americans, those displaced by Katrina were not necessarily better off along those dimensions. The only exception was that African Americans who moved from neighborhoods characterized by extreme poverty to neighborhoods of medium poverty levels did experience some positive outcomes.

Other Aspects of Vulnerability: Children, Older Adults, and Others

The disaster literature indicates that children, elderly persons, people with disabilities, sexual minorities, and other groups, for example people whose language ability is limited and immigrants, both legal and undocumented, are in greater danger of suffering a range of negative outcomes when disasters occur. It is important to remember, however, that vulnerability is conceptually defined as *a potential for loss*. Whether that potential is realized in any given disaster depends on a variety of factors, for example hazard type, whether a disaster affects less developed or developed societies, the severity of disaster impacts, the proximity of at-risk populations to high-impact areas, the extent to which societies and communities have implemented disaster risk reduction strategies, and even situational factors such as the time of day at which a disaster may strike. As shown throughout this chapter, especially in earlier discussions about intersectionality, variables such as age and physical ability are never the sole determinants of negative disaster impacts and outcomes; they exert their influence in combination with other factors.

Additionally, our knowledge of various forms of social vulnerability is not necessarily cumulative. Studies of the differential effects of disasters have used a range of methodologies—some more sophisticated than others—and have defined impacts in different ways, making it difficult to compare impacts across disaster events (Bourque, Siegel, Kano, and Wood 2007). Even concepts as seemingly straightforward as "disaster-related deaths" and "affected populations" are measured in a variety of ways (Guha-Sapir and Hoyois 2015), and the same is the case for other types of impacts, such as those that involve mental health. Further complicating matters, as discussed in Chapter 5, even though disaster impacts are greater in less developed societies, most studies focus on disasters in more developed ones. Ideally, there should be large-scale comparative studies that employ identical definitions of variables of interest and identical state-of-the-art methods across different societies and hazard types, but such studies do not exist at present. Despite such limitations, over time researchers have been able to develop a better understanding of why different groups are vulnerable and have identified patterns and trends in disaster victimization that indicate differential vulnerability. The discussions that follow do not consider all the sources of vulnerability, and even those that are highlighted are not discussed exhaustively. Rather the intention is to focus on the reasons why groups such as children and the elderly can be more vulnerable in disasters and to provide illustrative examples from different types of disasters.

Children and disaster vulnerability

In her review of studies of children and disasters, sociologist Lori Peek (2008) pointed out that children, defined as young individuals up to the age of eighteen years, constitute a significant proportion of those who are worldwide at risk in situations of disasters, and this is so for three main reasons. First, young children are physically vulnerable and dependent on their caregivers for their physical safety. Second, unless they are specifically targeted for help, children are likely to be overlooked by service providers in the aftermath of disasters. Simply the fact that the needs of the adults in a household are met does not guarantee that children's needs will be addressed. Third, disasters have the potential for adversely affecting children's psychological and psychosocial development. When disasters strike, children may lose loved ones and friends, experience residential dislocation, or have their schooling and academic progress interrupted. These types of trauma can have lasting effects. At the same time, on the positive side, Peek also pointed out that children can play a constructive role by encouraging others and by engaging in disaster risk reduction strategies, both in their households and in their communities.

Children are vulnerable to disasters in a variety of ways. A survey of deaths caused by disasters among youths found that very young children—those in their first year of life—present a high risk of mortality in extreme events. While statistics indicate that girls in less developed countries are more at risk of dying as a result of disasters, the picture is different in the United States, where male children and adolescents are more at risk (Peek 2013). Different hazards appear to have differential effects on children; infants are disproportionately affected by extreme heat, while older children are more affected by floods, storms, and extreme cold (Zahran, Peek, and Brody 2008). Bartlett (2008) notes that, worldwide, children in low-income countries are vulnerable to conditions that are being exacerbated by climate change, including more severe droughts, floods, and heat waves, vector-borne diseases, and food insecurity. Children with preexisting respiratory conditions are vulnerable to climate-driven atmospheric conditions such as increase in the levels of ozone and other pollutants (Bartlett 2008).

By comparison with adults, children can be especially vulnerable to the secondary effects of natural disasters, such as the toxic mold and other environmental pollution that typically accompanies flooding, as well as to technological disasters. For example, in the aftermath of the 2010 BP/ *Deepwater Horizon* oil spill, researchers from the National Center for Disaster Preparedness (2013) documented a range of health problems in children in heavily affected communities, including bleeding from noses and ears, skin rashes, gastrointestinal problems, and blurred vision. Depending on such factors as disaster severity, pre-disaster mental health state, and the availability of supportive services, children can be at risk of developing various psychological conditions, for example post-traumatic stress disorder (PTSD), in the aftermath of disasters (Norris, Friedman, Watson et al. 2002; Peek 2008).

In a survey of research, Weissbecker, Sephton, Martin, and Simpson (2008) highlight a number of findings from studies worldwide on the ways in which disasters can affect the psychological and physical well-being of children and adolescents. Disasters can expose children to a variety of stressful life events, such as loss of loved ones, of home, and of educational opportunities, relocation, and changes in family dynamics that result from parental stress. Stress can in turn lead to physiological and neurological changes accompanied by the disruption of sleep patterns, cognitive and memory impairments, and a reduction in immune functioning. Children are at risk of mental health conditions such as PTSD, anxiety, and depression. Because disasters disrupt the social fabric, children's daily routines are altered and they need structure; its absence can lead to behavioral and developmental problems and increased feelings of vulnerability. Children and adolescents are also more susceptible than adults to health problems such as flu-like symptoms that are stress-related and can persist over time. Weissbecker and colleagues also point to research on factors that can reduce or exacerbate the effects of disasters on children. Problems may be more severe for children who were already experiencing stress and having difficulty coping and for children whose parents are exhibiting the effects of pre- and post-disaster stress. Moderating factors include children's coping capacities, social support, and a positive overall family environment. Children's post-disaster difficulties tend to be more severe in less developed countries and in countries that do a poor job of mitigating and preparing for disasters.

The Sandy Child and Family Health (S-CAFH) study was conducted between August 2014 and April 2015, with a randomly selected cohort of respondents in nine New Jersey counties that were most seriously affected by Superstorm Sandy in 2012–those living in areas that experienced storm surge, flooding, and widespread property damage. In that study, 18 percent of parents reported that their children were struggling with anxiety and depression, were having problems sleeping, or having difficulty getting along with their friends. Difficulties were more pronounced for households that experienced damage, particularly minor damage, and for children from homes whose income fell below $20,000 per year. For the latter, the incidence of reported children's problems rose to 35 percent, which is indicative of the effects of social class on children's capacity to cope. Negative effects were also more pronounced when the parents themselves were fighting mental health problems (National Center for Disaster Preparedness 2015).

Being displaced can be particularly hard for children. Five years after Hurricane Katrina, one study found that "[a] startling 60 percent of children displaced by Katrina either have serious emotional disorders, behavioral issues . . . or are experiencing significant housing instability." The same study found that 52 percent of parents believed that their children needed professional help in order to cope with those kinds of problems but were not receiving it for reasons to do with insurance coverage and the shortage of qualified professionals (Children's Health Fund and National Center for Disaster Preparedness 2010: 5). An earlier study had also showed that southern Mississippi and southern Louisiana children from areas affected by Katrina were less likely than unaffected children nationwide to get access to personal healthcare providers. Children who experienced Katrina were also more likely to be African American, to be living in poverty, in single-parent families, and in unsafe neighborhoods, and also to be in fair to poor physical health (Stehling-Ariza, Park, Sury, and Abramson 2012). Here again, it appears that the children who are in the greatest need of health and mental health care after disasters are the ones least likely to receive services. Text Box 1, which accompanies this section, provides more information on what the children went through in the aftermath of Katrina.

As studies like the one conducted by Fothergill and Peek show, simply being young does not predict children's vulnerability to disaster impacts and poor recovery outcomes. Other factors need to be taken into account if we are to understand which children and youths are most vulnerable. These researchers frame children's disaster vulnerability as involving multiple disadvantages:

> Age alone does not make a child vulnerable to disaster. Instead, age interacts with many other factors that may render children particularly at risk. Moreover, vulnerability factors tend to build over time and cluster together, resulting in what we refer to as *cumulative vulnerability* . . . a racial minority child with a physical disability who lives in an impoverished household in a hazard-prone area will experience multiple, intersecting forms of social, environmental, physical, and economic vulnerability that will shape that child's experiences—and likelihood of survival—in a disaster . . . it is not solely age or race or ability status or poverty or hazards exposure, but how these risk factors *accumulate* in a child's life. (Fothergill and Peek 2015: 23)

Elderly persons and disaster vulnerability

Around the world, nations differ considerably in the demographic makeup of their populations. As a general rule, less developed countries "tilt young" in terms of age, with majorities of their populations often under the age of eighteen. In contrast, developed countries "tilt old." Japan, the world's oldest country, is an extreme example: in 2009, the proportion of those aged sixty-five years or older was 23 percent; projections indicate that by 2030 one in three persons will be sixty-five or older, and one in five will be seventy-five or older (Muramatsu and Akiyama 2011). In 2015, one in six people in the world lived in more developed countries, but one third of the world population that

Text Box 1 The Children of Katrina

Alice Fothergill and Lori Peek (2013, 2015) conducted extensive long-term research on New Orleans children and youths who had been displaced by Katrina in order to understand more clearly how that experience affected their lives. They found that these children spent a great deal of time in a sort of limbo, a "permanent temporariness." Many children made more than one move after the hurricane—for example, moving from home to emergency shelters, then to FEMA-provided trailers, and later back to New Orleans or to new communities. While displaced, many continued to miss their former homes. Those who lived with their mothers in single-parent families had typically had the chance to interact with their fathers on a somewhat regular basis before the hurricane, but those opportunities no longer existed in their new homes. Similarly, they lost contact with grandparents, aunts, uncles, and other members of the extended family, who were either left behind or relocated to other communities. Children who were permanently displaced had to adjust to living in new communities and attending new schools, which was stressful for them, while those who returned to New Orleans were under stress because the city had changed so dramatically as a result of Katrina. They were likely to return to different schools, and in many cases the friendship networks they had before the storm no longer existed. Back in New Orleans, they also feared that another hurricane would strike. However, not all children were equally likely to confront such stressors. On the basis of their research, Fothergill and Peek concluded:

> While all the children in our study experienced some degree of permanent temporariness, children who were marginalized, whose families had fewer resources, who were poor, and who were Black, were likely to experience this state more profoundly. Indeed, children's pre- and post-disaster experiences were clearly shaped by their racial background and class status. (Fothergill and Peek 2013: 138)

was sixty-five and older and one half of the world population that was eighty-five and older lived in those countries. These ratios are expected to change over time, as fertility rates continue to decline and life expectancies increase in developed societies (He, Goodkind, and Cowal 2016). What this means is that in the future more and more older adults, including the very old ones, will be exposed to natural and technological hazards.

A large amount of evidence suggests that elderly persons are vulnerable to disasters. In discussing why this is likely the case, Feather (2014) points to several reasons. When disasters threaten, older adults may be limited in their ability to undertake self-protective actions. Just over 40 percent of those over sixty-five have functional limitations that may interfere with their ability to seek safety. Older persons may be reluctant to evacuate when orders are issued, preferring the security and familiarity of their own homes. They may have a greater tendency to base their evacuation decisions on previous experiences with disaster events that did not harm them. A large proportion of older adults have chronic conditions such as high blood pressure, diabetes, and heart disease, which require continual management. If a disaster causes them to stop taking their medication—for example, if their prescriptions go missing as a result of a disaster and they cannot get them refilled—their physical conditions could worsen and become life-threatening. To the extent that elders are socially isolated, they may be overlooked during an emergency and not receive the help they need. The vast majority of elderly persons live at home, but they are increasingly living alone, which may cut them off from sources of social support (Klinenberg 2002; Peek 2012). Social networks can become frayed as people get older; support networks may be especially weak for those who have lost a spouse, are childless, are living in poverty, and are disabled.

Social class and other factors are important in understanding the disaster vulnerability of elderly persons. In the United States, those who are sixty-five and older are better off financially than the youngest members of the population, which potentially offsets some vulnerability factors. For example, in 2015, the poverty rate for the elderly stood at 8.8 percent, which contrasts with a rate of 19.7 percent for children under eighteen. Those sixty-five and older constituted 14.9 percent of the population and 6.9 percent of the very poor (i.e., households earning less than 50 percent of the poverty level), while children represented 23.1 percent of the population and 33.6 percent of the very poor. However, poverty rates for elderly persons differed by gender, older women being more likely than older men to be living in poverty (He et al. 2016). As we saw earlier, race and ethnicity matter: in 2014, among those sixty-five and over, 18 percent of Latinos/as and 19 percent of African Americans were living in poverty, by comparison with 8 percent of non-Hispanic whites (Population Reference Bureau 2015).

Being elderly is typically accompanied by sensory impairments such as decline in visual and hearing capacities and a lessening of cognitive abilities. Mayhorn (2005) notes that these kinds of impairments can interfere with the ability of older adults to pay attention to and comprehend warning messages in disaster situations, as well as to respond appropriately to warnings. After disasters, physical and cognitive limitations may make older individuals less likely to access sources of aid, even if such assistance is badly needed. Weaker social networks may mean that seniors never have the opportunity to learn about recovery programs; and, even for those who are aware, bureaucratic barriers may be difficult to overcome (Peek 2013).

A report on climate change and health documents how the extreme heat that is increasingly resulting from climate change can have a disproportionate impact on elderly persons. Extreme temperatures—defined as 95 degrees Fahrenheit (35 degrees Celsius)—make it impossible for bodies to cool themselves through perspiration alone, and the body's temperature regulation system becomes less effective as people age. Older individuals are also increasingly likely to have chronic conditions that are exacerbated by high heat, such as cardiovascular, respiratory, and renal illnesses and diabetes. Additionally, some of the medications older people take for their health problems can interfere with the body's temperature regulation system (US Global Change Research Program 2016).

A recent report on infrastructure system disruption and disaster vulnerability points to other factors that put older persons at risk in disasters. The power grid is one example. Elders who are dependent on assistive devices that rely on electricity can become endangered if a disaster causes a power outage. Some persons who live in high-rise apartments are unable to go to and from their homes without elevators, but elevators become inoperative when power is disrupted. When Superstorm Sandy struck in 2012, many elderly New York residents were stranded in their apartments when the power went out. With so many medical records now in electronic form, access to medical information can be compromised, which could affect disproportionately older persons in need of medical treatment. As noted, elders are more sensitive to climate change-related hazards like extreme heat, and disruptions of power and water systems can have greater negative effects on them than on younger members of the population (National Institute of Standards and Technology 2016).

Major disasters in the United States and around the world have highlighted the vulnerability of elderly persons. To cite just a few examples, in the 1995 heat wave in Chicago, just under three quarters of those who died were older adults, and social isolation was a significant contributor to their mortality (Klinenberg 2002). In Aceh Province, Indonesia, the hardest hit area in the 2004 Indian Ocean tsunami and the place where the majority of the deaths occurred, women were significantly more likely to be killed, but being elderly, as well as being very young, were also significant risk factors (Doocy et al. 2007). Of those who died in Hurricane Katrina in New Orleans, those over sixty made up 75 percent of the total, those over seventy accounting for 40 percent of that total—even though those over sixty made up only about 15 percent of the population (Adams, Kaufman, Van Hattum, and Moody 2011). The 2011 earthquake and tsunami in Japan killed an estimated 20,000 people. In that disaster, the death rate increased with age, people aged sixty-five and older totaling around 58 percent of those killed. Unlike in the Indian Ocean tsunami, mortality was low for children, and no significant gender differences were found (see Nakahara and Ichikawa 2013). In the wildfires that struck Northern California in October 2017, forty-two people were killed, most of whom were over seventy. The oldest victim was 100 years of age (NBC News

2017). Elderly victims of wildfire died in their homes, which indicates that they were either unwilling or unable to evacuate, as fires spread rapidly.

For reasons discussed earlier, vulnerabilities associated with age are perhaps most evident in extreme heat events. Heat-related deaths are higher for those over sixty, as well as for children under five years of age; mortality risk is higher among older women than among men (Bourque, Siegel, Kano, and Wood 2006). The heat wave that struck Europe in the summer of 2003, which began in June and peaked in August of that year, resulted in approximately 77,000 excess deaths—that is, deaths over and above "normal" and expected levels.[2] A study on mortality in the sixteen most affected countries in the Eurozone found that age as well as gender were major risk factors for dying and that, as age increased, so did death rates. For example, in France, which was especially hard hit, death rates in the over-ninety-five age group increased by 46 percent, as compared with the number that would have been expected had the heat wave not occurred (Robine et al. 2007). In a study of heat-related deaths in 105 cities between 1987 and 2005, Bobb, Peng, Bell, and Dominici (2014) note that, while the risk of dying from extreme heat declined during that period for all age groups, those over seventy-five were most at risk at the beginning of the study. The authors attribute the decline in overall mortality over the eighteen-year period to improvements in responding to heat-related hazards, such as heat–health warning systems and public health programs targeting elderly persons.

While many research findings point to older age as a risk factor for dying in disasters, it should be emphasized that, as in the case of youth, focusing on being elderly alone is insufficient for understanding disaster-related mortality. Indeed, it has been argued that, on its own, age is not associated with the overall risk of dying in various types of disasters (Bourque et al. 2006). For example, although in the Great Hanshin-Awaji (Kobe) earthquake in 1995 in Japan older persons were significantly more likely to die, that was because they tended to live on the lower floors of traditional Japanese residential structures, which collapsed and crushed them when the earthquake struck (Bourque et al. 2006; Wood and Bourque 2018). Like other axes of vulnerability, age exerts its influence when combined with other risk factors; but, even taking those factors into account, the methodological issues discussed in Chapter 5 and earlier in this chapter require us to use caution when reaching conclusions about the risks associated with aging. As Wood and Bourque (2018: 373) note, "[a]n important concern for the study of morbidity and mortality associated with disasters is the generally weak methodology of most studies." Research to date has done a poor job of separating individual risk factors such as age from other potentially confounding factors. For example, focusing again on the 2003 European heat wave, Richard Keller studied nearly 100 deaths that occurred in Paris and found that, while age was a key factor in predicting death, age can also be a proxy for other influences, such as exposure to more

extreme heat conditions and social isolation. Elderly persons in Paris with limited means tended to reside in very tiny apartments on the top floors of classic
Parisian buildings. Those apartments, known as *chambres de bonne* because in
earlier times they housed domestic servants, typically lacked air conditioning
and cross-ventilation. Heat rose and built up in those apartments, exposing
their occupants to temperatures greatly in excess of those in other types of
dwellings. Keller also made the point that, while elderly persons were at high
risk from dying in the heat wave, so were younger marginalized individuals
such as addicts and persons without sources of social support (Keller 2015).

Like Keller, others argue that, to gain a full picture of how and why elderly
persons are at risk in heat waves, a number of other factors have to be taken
into account. The actual amount of heat exposure is one such factor. Extreme
heat is not uniform within communities; environmental conditions such as
building density, paved-over surfaces, and lack of vegetation can create "urban
heat islands," exposing some segments of the population to even higher temperatures during heat waves. Sharon Harlan's research on heat-related deaths
in Maricopa County, Arizona over a nine-year period identified age as a risk
factor, while also singling out other influences on increased mortality such as
the combined effects of being elderly and living alone, living in areas exposed
to urban heat island effects, for example inner-city neighborhoods and places
that lack vegetation, and being vulnerable according to socioeconomic indicators. At the same time, "higher neighborhood income and education, younger
white populations, greener landscapes, AC [air conditioning], and cooler
microclimates were associated with reduced heat vulnerability" (Harlan,
Declet-Barreto, Stefanov, and Petitti 2013: 203). Similarly, a study conducted
on heat-related deaths in cities in Michigan found that deaths from cardiovascular disease were associated with living in zip codes where there were
larger numbers of people over sixty-five and living alone, but also with being
unmarried and living in zip codes with less green space and more homes built
before 1960 (Gronlund et al. 2014). However, that same study noted that the
literature on heat-related deaths is inconsistent in its findings on these kinds
of factors. Here again, as we saw with children and youths, elderly persons
who are most at risk are those who experience cumulative vulnerability.

Elderly persons living in congregate care facilities such as nursing homes
and rehabilitation centers are highly dependent on those institutions
during disasters. While all US nursing homes are required by federal law to
have emergency plans, the quality of those planning efforts is uneven (US
Department of Health and Human Services n.d.). Nursing home emergency
planning tends to focus more on facility-specific emergencies such as fires,
as opposed to large-scale community disasters. Disasters create a range of
problems for nursing homes, for example damage to or complete destruction
of facilities, utility service outages, and the need to evacuate patients on short
notice, when many of them may be frail and dependent on life supports. In

Hurricane Katrina, seventy nursing home residents died in thirteen different facilities. In Hurricane Rita, which occurred shortly after Katrina, twenty-four nursing home residents died when the bus that was being used to evacuate them caught fire (Belli and Falkenberg 2005).

When Hurricane Irma struck Florida in 2017, the storm resulted in approximately ninety deaths, including deaths caused by carbon monoxide poisoning in households where generators were being used, by falls, and by drowning. However, fourteen deaths took place in a single nursing home facility in the community of Hollywood, Florida. The storm resulted in a loss of power to the facility's air conditioning system, causing temperatures inside the facility to skyrocket. Residents began showing symptoms of hyperthermia, but despite their own pleas and those of their family members, their problems were not adequately addressed, even though the nursing home was across the street from a hospital that could have provided emergency care. Twelve of the fourteen deaths in that facility were subsequently ruled to be homicides (Darrah 2017).

Disabilities and disaster vulnerability

Any discussion of disabled persons in the context of disasters has to begin with an understanding of different models or conceptualizations of disability. In their discussion of disability and disaster, Davis et al. (2013) identify three main conceptual formulations that have been applied to the construct of disability: the medical model, the sociopolitical model, and the functional model. The medical model, which was ascendant until well into the late twentieth century, framed disability as an individual-level characteristic associated with medical conditions, diseases, or traumas that cause individuals to deviate from "normal" expectations regarding their physical and mental capabilities. The medical model conceptualizes disability as "real," in the sense that being disabled is thought to be tied to particular diagnosable diseases and conditions that place limitations on individual functioning.

By contrast, the sociopolitical model, which arose out of the disability rights and independent living movements in the latter part of the twentieth century, emphasizes how societies place limitations on differently abled individuals through socially constructed images of disabilities and through policies that create disabling environments. In this view, disability is both socially constructed and socially produced: constructed, because societies develop stereotyped beliefs about those who are defined as disabled; and produced, because policies related to issues such as physical accessibility, educational and occupational opportunities, and the availability of assistive technologies limit what those marked as disabled can accomplish.

Finally, the functional model of disability, which is also consistent with sociological conceptualizations of disability, focuses on the diversity of populations defined as disabled and on abilities as well as on limitations within those populations. Like the sociopolitical model, the functional model focuses on societal barriers to the inclusion of those labeled as disabled and on overcoming those barriers through appropriate policies and assistive technologies. By focusing on functional limitations as opposed to medical diagnoses, this model also brings to the fore the idea that so-called "normal" people can find themselves more or less disabled at various times in their lives: after having an accident that results in mobility, cognitive, or other challenges, after experiencing a severe illness, in some cases while pregnant, after giving birth or having surgery, when suffering the ravages of famine, or when finding oneself in an unfamiliar environment that presents outsized physical challenges. The acronym TAB—temporarily able-bodied—is commonly used in disability rights communities to express the idea that everyone is at risk for becoming disabled at some point in their lives. Recognizing that any one of us can be disabled at one time or another blurs the distinction between being able-bodied and being disabled.

In discussing the vulnerability of disabled persons to disasters worldwide, Stough and Kelman (2018) argue that such persons can be thought of as a minority population in its own right. They have experienced discrimination, been stigmatized, and even been targets of violence. Members of disabled groups are sometimes considered second-class citizens in their own societies; for example, they may face barriers to employment and education and the denial of their human and civil rights. They are frequently stereotyped as incompetent, stupid, and dependent, and their life circumstances are socially constructed as tragic (McDonald, Keys, and Balcazar 2007; Swain and French 2008)—stereotypes that fail to recognize the agency and capabilities of those labeled as disabled. As will be discussed later in this chapter, many of the reasons why people are "disabled" stem from societal policies and practices that place limitations on differently abled groups.

Institutional definitions of disability—that is, the manner in which governments and other institutions quantify, list, and classify disabled persons—can be useful as a way of developing an understanding of the prevalence of disabilities, both in general and in specific population groups. Focusing on the United States, on the basis of 2015 and 2016 census data, Lewis Kraus (2017) provides a picture of the disabled population that includes both general and more specific statistics. The data indicate that an estimated 12.6 percent of the US population are disabled people, but that percentages differ significantly by state, running from a low of 9.9 percent in Utah to a high of 19.4 percent in West Virginia. In ten states, which are mostly located in the southern United States but include Alaska, rates of elderly persons with disabilities reach 40 percent or more. Rates of hearing, vision, and cognitive disabilities, challenges with being ambulatory and with being capable of living independently are positively correlated with age, ranging from less than 1 percent for those under five years of age to 35.4 percent for those who are sixty-five and older. Other census-based statistics provided by Kraus reveal a strong association between disability and economic hardship. In 2015, about 35 percent of disabled persons between the ages of eighteen and sixty-four who were living in communities (as opposed to being institutionalized) were employed, compared with an employment rate of 76 percent for their non-disabled counterparts. The median earnings of people with disabilities aged sixteen and over was $21,571 in 2015, compared with $31,874 for people who were not disabled—a pattern of inequality that has been increasing in magnitude in recent years. Just over one in five persons with disabilities who were of working age, or 21.2 percent, were living in poverty in 2015, whereas the poverty rate in the comparable non-disabled population was 13.8 percent.

Disability rates in the United States vary as a function of social class, race, ethnicity, and gender—which shows the importance of taking an intersectional approach to social vulnerability. Those with higher household incomes and higher levels of education are less likely to be disabled. In contrast, almost half of all adults with household incomes under $15,000 are disabled. African American non-Hispanic adults have higher rates of disability than other groups. Women have higher rates of disability than men. Nearly one in four women have one or more disabilities, by comparison with about one in five men (Courtney-Long et al. 2015). Here again, vulnerability is the result of *cumulative* circumstances, such as being impaired in one or more ways, living in poverty, having lower earnings and less education, and being a member of a racial minority group.

It is easy to understand why having a disability can be a risk factor for experiencing more severe disaster impacts and poorer recovery outcomes. Mobility impairments are the most common disability in the United States (Courtney-Long et al. 2015), and such impairments can make it more difficult to undertake recommended self-protective actions when disaster strikes. For example, earthquakes occur without warning, and when they strike, the recommended self-protective action is to duck (under a table, for example), cover, and hold on. An individual has only a few seconds in which to take cover once the shaking begins; this puts mobility impaired persons at a disadvantage. One study that focused on three US hurricanes (Bonnie, Dennis, and Floyd) found that people with mobility, sensory, and other physical impairments were less likely to evacuate and that some disabled persons were not even aware that evacuation orders had been issued (Van Willigen, Edwards, Edwards, and Hessee 2002). As noted earlier, Mayhorn (2005) found that sensory and cognitive limitations associated with aging can make it difficult for people with those disabilities to perceive and interpret warning messages. As summarized by Stough and Kelman (2018), research on disasters suggests that persons with disabilities have been at greater risk for being killed or injured.

Even though it makes sense that people with disabilities would be at greater risk in disasters than those who are able-bodied, there is a great deal that we do not know when it comes to assessing their vulnerability. Disabilities are many and varied, and within any particular category of disability (e.g., mobility, cognition) impairments can be more or less severe. Some individuals with mild impairments may be able to cope with disasters quite well on their own, while others with the same impairments may be almost totally dependent on others in those situations. Then just as they can be differentially vulnerable, people can also be differentially resilient, depending on their financial resources and their levels of pre-disaster preparedness, for example. Further, there is almost no research that focuses on disability alone, as a risk factor taken in separation from other factors it is associated with, such as race, class, and gender. This is a shortcoming in disaster research, but it is also a shortcoming in disability studies more generally, where axes of diversity and inequality within disabled populations have been given little attention (McDonald et al. 2007). There simply has not been enough well-designed systematic research for us to state definitively that being disabled, in and of itself, is a contributor to disaster victimization and poor recovery outcomes.

It is also important to keep in mind that, following the sociopolitical and functional approaches to disability, the extent to which being disabled leads to disproportionate disaster victimization may have less to do with disabilities themselves than with societal responses to the needs of disabled persons, both in normal times and in disasters. In the United States, for example, as a result of the disability rights movement and of laws such as the Americans with Disabilities Act, the everyday needs of those who are disabled have been recognized and, while much remains to be done, accommodations for those needs have been implemented. At the same time, even with such advances, there is also considerable evidence showing that the US disaster response system has been unprepared to address the needs of disabled persons, particularly those with the greatest needs, in disasters.

After Hurricanes Katrina and Rita, the National Council on Disability (2006) issued a scathing report that documents the difficulties experienced by, and unjust treatment of, disabled residents of affected areas. In the immediate emergency period, people with sensory disabilities lacked access to emergency warnings. For example, those with hearing impairments could not comprehend evacuation instructions or information about emergency shelters because there were no closed-captioned or sign language messages accompanying that guidance. The Federal Communications Commission reminded local broadcasters that they would have to comply with laws requiring communications accessibility, but compliance was spotty. Similarly, informational websites provided by government agencies did not comply with laws regarding access to information for the visually impaired. People with disabilities experienced difficulties regarding evacuation from their homes and from nursing homes and hospitals due to the lack of transportation and assistance personnel. Those who did manage to get to transportation hubs found that many buses lacked ramps and lifts.

The report stated further that the authorities did not seem to be fully aware of the needs of disabled persons in disasters. Mass shelters operated by the Red Cross were not equipped to serve persons with disabilities. Instead, "special needs" shelters were set up; but this often resulted in splitting up families. After the two disasters, information regarding services was not provided in ways that addressed the distinctive needs of people with different disabilities.

Deaths in hospitals and nursing homes tell a similar story of institutional failure. Sheri Fink's (2013) detailed reporting on deaths that occurred among seriously disabled and medically dependent patients in Memorial Hospital in New Orleans reveals that, after Katrina, patients' physical conditions deteriorated rapidly and that, unable to evacuate some patients in the aftermath of the hurricane, medical personnel resorted to "mercy killings," using large doses of major painkillers and tranquillizers. One physician and two nurses were initially accused of second-degree murder, but the grand jury that was subsequently impaneled to investigate the matter declined to indict them. Thirty-five patients died in St. Rita's nursing home in St. Bernard Parish outside New Orleans during Hurricane Katrina. The owners of the nursing home were charged with negligent homicide and cruelty but were found not guilty of those offenses at trial (Cobb 2013). As we learned earlier (p. 152) from the discussion of material concerning Hurricane Irma in 2017, nursing homes continue to be places where patients are largely at the mercy of facility operators and staff, often with tragic consequences when disasters strike. Reports like these reveal the extent to which laws and regulations designed to assist and protect persons with disabilities are often ineffective in disasters. They also point to other ways in which, even in the most prosperous societies, institutions can fail disabled and dependent persons during and after disasters.

Other vulnerable groups

The literature also identifies other groups that can be vulnerable within the context of disasters. The *homeless population* is one of those groups. Ben Wisner was among the first to note that homeless people in high-risk megacities such as Tokyo and Los Angeles are socially invisible; when people encounter them, "the common reaction is to avert the eyes" (Wisner 1998: 32). Consequently, their needs were not being addressed in disaster preparedness planning. Around that same time, Brenda Phillips (1998) argued that almost nothing was known about how those who are homeless fare in disasters. She went on to describe the experiences of homeless people in Santa Cruz, California after the 1989 Loma Prieta earthquake. As a consequence of research conducted in the last twenty years, we now have a better understanding of the disaster vulnerabilities of the homeless population. Some progress is also being made in the development of policies and plans that target the needs of the homeless population in disasters.

Homeless individuals and families are vulnerable to disasters in a number of ways. They live on the margins of society, which can cut them off from information on disaster forecasts, from warnings, and from disaster assistance. Because homelessness is increasingly being criminalized in cities around the United States, for example through ordinances that forbid sleeping in public or living in a vehicle, homeless persons are further stigmatized and often forced into living in marginal places and spaces, such as areas along riverbeds and in forests, which are exposed to flooding and wildfires (Vickery 2017). Many adults and children who are homeless have experienced traumatic events in the past, which makes them especially vulnerable when disasters strike (Bush 2014). Homeless women have often been victims of domestic and sexual violence, and homeless children are likely to have been present during domestic violence episodes (National Center on Family Homelessness 2014). Homeless veterans may also have experienced or been exposed to traumatic events while in the service. Adults and youths may suffer from alcoholism and substance abuse problems (National Coalition for the Homeless 2017). For reasons like these, homeless individuals and families may lack the capacity or the will to seek out assistance during and after disasters. They may also be discriminated against when seeking assistance during disasters, even emergency shelter (Edgington 2009; Vickery 2017). Like community-based organizations more generally, organizations that provide services to homeless individuals and families, for example shelters and transitional living facilities, often lack the capacity to prepare effectively for disasters; they also tend to lack connections to emergency services agencies in their communities (Gin, Kranke, Saia, and Dobalian 2016; Gin et al. 2017; for other discussions of the disaster vulnerability of community-based organizations, see Ritchie, Tierney, and Gilbert 2010).

US government agencies have made some progress in developing guidance toward assisting homeless individuals and families in disasters. For example, in its guidance for service providers, the US Department of Health and Human Services (n.d.) emphasizes the need for a "trauma-informed approach" in planning and response activities that target members of the homeless population. Other resources are available from nonprofit organizations such as the National Health Care for the Homeless Council (Edgington 2009). Some guidance documents specifically target homeless service providers (Tobin and Freeman 2004). What is not known is the extent to which resources like these are actually being used in local communities and, if they are, to what effect.

Those who deviate from societal heteronormal expectations can also be at risk in disasters. *LGBTQ persons* can become targets of discrimination after disasters in a variety of ways. One obvious way is that same-sex unions are not recognized in many countries around the world. Until the landmark 2015 Supreme Court decision in *Obergefell v. Hodges*, same-sex unions were not universally recognized in the United States. Worldwide, disaster aid generally targets "households," but what is considered a household can vary. A family consisting of husband, wife, and children is most likely to meet that definition; but what about an unmarried lesbian or gay couple, with or without children, in a country where being gay is criminalized?

Phillips and Jenkins (2013: 324) note that in disasters "lesbians, gay men, and bisexual or transgendered individuals are among those whose survival, safety, and well-being may be contingent upon finding safe space and sensitized emergency services." Despite these distinctive needs, researchers note that sexual and gender minorities are consistently overlooked in disaster-related laws and policies (Dominey-Howes, Gorman-Murray, and McKinnon 2014; Gaillard, Gorman-Murray, and Fordham 2017). Like those who are homeless, individuals and groups that depart from the established gender binary are typically stigmatized. LGBTQ persons are routinely discriminated against and can become targets of hate crimes, even of deadly attacks. LGBTQ youth may become homeless as a result of their sexual orientations, which compounds their vulnerability. In the United States, right-wing and conservative religious figures have even blamed gays and lesbians for *causing* disasters (Blumenfeld 2016).

Although the topic of sexual minorities in disasters is relatively new, there are already examples of the unequal treatment of them in disasters. For example, in Indian society, the Aravani are males who reject male identity and choose to live as women, while seeing themselves as neither male nor female. The marginalization of the Aravani, who are sometimes referred to as the "third sex," was evident in the aftermath of the 2004 Indian Ocean tsunami. A report on gender issues in that disaster noted:

> Pre-tsunami socio-cultural as well as policy-induced discrimination rendered the Aravani population invisible in the relief, rehabilitation, and reconstruction agenda. There were no official records of deaths and losses incurred by this group or the subsequent trauma and neglect they experienced. Their vulnerabilities were further exacerbated by their systemic exclusion from the mainstream gender discourse and thereby from post-disaster planning exercises. (Pincha 2008: 25)

This pattern repeats itself in other societies. Gays and lesbians are stigmatized in Haiti, and reports concerning their treatment in the aftermath of the catastrophic 2010 Haiti earthquake reveal that in many cases they were denied disaster assistance services and subjected to rape and other forms of violence. They were also blamed for causing the earthquake and sometimes attacked on that basis. Organizations serving LGBTQ persons were also destroyed or damaged in the earthquake (International Gay and Lesbian Human Rights Commission n.d.).

Gaillard et al. (2017) document the disaster experiences of gender minorities in the Philippines, Indonesia, and Samoa. The Bakla in the Philippines are biological males who identify as females and assume both male and female roles in the gendered division of labor. In Indonesia, Waria are men who take on a feminine identity and often work in the beauty industry. In Samoa, the Fa'afafine are biological males who dress as women and who, like the Bakla, perform both male and female tasks. Members of these three groups experience marginalization and stigma every single day; they are "discriminated against, mocked, and deprived of access to resources and the means of protection available to men and women" (Gaillard et al. 2017: 440). Many have experienced various forms of exclusion in disaster situations, such as being denied access to emergency shelters and short-term housing and not being able to obtain sufficient food in the aftermath of disasters.

As often happens in US disasters, fundamentalist Christian clergy blamed the gay community for the Hurricane Katrina catastrophe. After the hurricane, members of the LGBT community faced various kinds of harassment and discrimination. Some faith-based organizations, including churches, were not interested in providing aid to gay hurricane victims. Obtaining support was especially hard for gay African Americans and for persons with AIDS. Louisiana did not recognize same-sex unions at the time of the hurricane, which rendered gay couples ineligible for some forms of aid (Monroe 2016). Prior to the legalization of same-sex marriage in the United States, the LGBTQ advocacy group Human Rights Campaign (2012) published a guide for emergency workers, urging them not to discriminate against gay households and families, but it is unclear how much this advice has been heeded.

In their review of issues related to *language ability and literacy*, Santos-Hernández and Morrow (2013) discuss several widely recognized dimensions of literacy. To touch on just a few of them, literacy means being able to read and understand the meaning of texts (prose literacy); understand signs and images (visual literacy); comprehend documents and have the ability to fill out forms (document literacy); and have access to and be able to use digital devices (digital literacy). Just as in everyday life, the ability to prepare for, respond to, and recover from disasters requires these kinds of skills. Difficulties with achieving competence in these different areas can be a source of social vulnerability when people are exposed to hazards and confront disasters.

The Organization for Economic Cooperation and Development (OECD) consists of the twenty-two most developed countries. The Survey of Adult Skills, which focuses on different forms of literacy, is conducted in the nations that are part of the OECD, plus two other nations. Recognizing that what counts as literacy skills has changed in the twenty-first century, the OECD focuses on three types of literacy among adults aged between sixteen and sixty-five: being able to understand, use, and evaluate written texts in the nation's main language—or what we commonly think of as literacy; numeracy, or the ability to access, use, and interpret mathematical and statistical information; and the ability to access and use digital technology in order to acquire information. Comparing OECD countries, the US population scores well below average in all three areas; it is also distinctive in that younger persons in this country (persons aged between sixteen and twenty-four) do not score better than older persons in literacy and numeracy. (Most countries have seen improvements, as younger generations acquire more skills.) The United States has significant numbers of people—perhaps as many as one third of the adult population—who, by OECD criteria, cannot perform problem-solving tasks even at a minimal level (Organization for Economic Cooperation and Development 2013). This raises questions about the extent to which ordinary Americans can access and understand a range of disaster-related information, including information on hazards and risks, disaster forecasts and warnings, self-protection guidance, and, when disasters strike, information on available relief and recovery services. For example, many of the forms that are required in order to access government assistance after disasters are web-based, favoring those who can navigate the Internet well. After disasters, aid applications can be submitted at physical disaster assistance centers with the help of trained staff, but not everyone can travel to those centers to apply for aid in person.

About 14 percent of the US population is foreign-born, and the literacy rates in this population segment differ from those of native-born Americans. Foreign-born residents make up a high proportion of the population in disaster-prone metropolitan areas such as Miami (37 percent), San Jose, California (36 percent), Los Angeles (34 percent), and San Francisco–Oakland (29 percent). Overall, immigrants have lower prose, document, and quantitative literacy than their native-born counterparts, as measured by the National Assessment of Adult Literacy. Hispanic adults have the lowest literacy scores, followed by blacks and Asians; but there are also large intraracial differences in literacy. There are significant differences in literacy depending on when immigrants arrived in the United States: those who were nineteen or older on arrival having lower literacy levels than those who came at younger ages (US Department of Education 2009). Santos-Hernández and Morrow (2013) note that women immigrants have lower levels of literacy than their male counterparts, which raises concerns about the extent to which they are able to access and comprehend information on disaster risks and recommended preparedness measures.

In New York City, an estimated 192 languages other than English are spoken in residents' homes. The totals for Los Angeles and Houston are 185 and 145 respectively. The US government currently provides various forms of disaster-related online guidance in just over one dozen languages, which is not reflective of the country's linguistic diversity. It is unclear how many people are actually accessing this foreign language information and to what effect. What is clear is that those with high levels of English-language literacy are most advantaged with respect to being able to obtain, understand, and use disaster-related information of all types.

Closely related to immigration, *citizenship* is another factor to consider in understanding social vulnerability. According to the Institute on Statelessness and Inclusion (2014), which notes that data are difficult to obtain in many parts of the world, there are some 10 million people worldwide who are not citizens of any state. This estimated number includes refugees, asylum seekers, internally displaced persons, and residents of countries who for one reason or another lack the privileges of citizenship in those countries. One such group that has recently been in the news is the Rohingya in Myanmar (Burma). The estimated 1 million Rohingya have not been recognized as citizens of Myanmar and have been consistently discriminated against by Burmese institutions. Their communities have been subject to violent attacks, which intensified in 2016, causing hundreds of thousands of Rohingya to flee to neighboring Bangladesh.

Throughout the world, stateless persons are robbed of their human, political, and economic rights, sometimes to the point where, for official purposes, they do not even exist. Depending on the country, stateless persons may be forced to contend with lack of access to the ballot, to education, to health care, to social services, and to employment opportunities; with severe restrictions on travel, both in the country of residence and abroad; and with not having any form of official identification (Institute on Statelessness and Inclusion 2014). Essentially, if citizenship consists of the "right to have rights" (Somers 2008), then those who do not enjoy full citizenship privileges, including stateless persons, are especially vulnerable, both on an everyday basis and in disasters.

In the United States, non-citizens, including both permanent residents ("green-card holders") and undocumented immigrants, have almost the same rights as citizens. Non-citizens face restrictions in areas such as voting and running for office, but otherwise they enjoy the same constitutional protections as citizens. However, with regard to disaster assistance, the situation is different. While the government is required to provide emergency assistance services such as emergency transportation for evacuation and emergency shelter, food, and medical services to non-citizens, the key word here is "emergency." When it comes to other forms of assistance, restrictions do apply. Undocumented immigrants are not eligible for federal programs such as the Individuals and Households Program, which provides short-term recovery assistance such as home repairs and rental vouchers for those who are displaced, nor can they apply for Small Business Administration housing or business loans. However, if some member of a household headed by an undocumented immigrant is a US citizen (e.g. a US-born child), then applications for these forms of assistance can be made on that person's behalf (American Red Cross, National Immigration Law Center, and National Council of La Raza 2007). Nongovernmental organizations (NGOs) can also provide assistance regardless of an applicant's immigration status, or can refrain from asking about citizenship entirely.

Even though undocumented immigrants in the United States do have access to many forms of disaster assistance, there is reason to believe that they will avoid seeking such services, especially in the current political climate. As long ago as the Loma Prieta earthquake, which occurred in 1989, Brenda Phillips (1993) noted that immigrants from Mexico and Central America tended to avoid official disaster shelters as a result of the presence there of military personnel, because the military was widely feared in their native countries: they were scared of being picked up by immigration authorities. Those same kinds of fears caused immigrants along the Gulf Coast to stay behind when evacuation orders were issued for Hurricane Gustav in 2008 (NBC News 2008). In 2017, when Hurricane Harvey was bearing down on Texas, the state indicated that it would be providing services to all residents, regardless of immigration status, but at the federal level the US Customs and Border Control (CBP) was still operating checkpoints that were designed to round up undocumented persons. At the time Harvey struck, Texas had already passed a law permitting police officials to work with CBP and Immigration and Customs Enforcement in apprehending undocumented persons. Although that law had not yet gone into effect at the time of Harvey, its passage had already resulted in declining trust in authorities. Writing about immigrants' plight in Harvey, their lack of trust in government, and their vulnerability, journalist Dara Lind noted:

> Unauthorized immigrants are often wary of seeking government assistance even in the best of circumstances, and their isolation can keep them from finding out important information: Many immigrant residents of Flint, Michigan, for example, found out about the prohibition on drinking the city's lead-contaminated water months after the rest of the city did. High-profile immigration enforcement makes that even harder. (Lind 2017)

In the current political climate, when immigrants are being detained and slated for deportation while taking their children to school, it is not difficult to envision immigrants avoiding shelters and disaster services centers.

Measuring Disaster Vulnerability

Systematic efforts to measure vulnerability began in the early twenty-first century. Just as there is no agreed-upon definition of vulnerability, there is no general consensus as to which set of indicators captures best the different dimensions of vulnerability—social vulnerability included. Vulnerability and its measurement are central to conceptual frameworks that focus on society–environment relations, such as sustainable development, sustainable livelihoods, global environmental change, and hazards and risk (Birkmann 2006: Kok, Narain, Wonink, and Jager 2006; Patt, Schroter et al. 2010). These frameworks have a good deal in common, but they also differ—for example, in the processes on which they focus and in the indicators they employ to measure vulnerability. It will not be possible here to review all these different approaches. Instead, the focus in this section will be on those measurement frameworks that deal most directly with hazards and disasters and, even then, only on the most widely used ones. Readers will notice that the frameworks briefly reviewed below differ in scale as well as in the aspects of vulnerability they address.

The Disaster Deficit Index (DDI) is one in a suite of indicator frameworks that were developed under the auspices of the Inter-American Development Bank to assess vulnerability at the country level for Latin American and Caribbean countries. Its main focus is on economic and financial vulnerability as well as on countries' capacity to obtain resources that may offset disaster losses. The DDI models the degree to which major natural disasters would adversely affect countries' national treasuries and cause them to go into debt, or even to experience economic collapse. A related set of measures, the Local Disaster Index (LDI), focuses on less serious but recurrent disasters that could also affect those same countries. Data on potential deaths, numbers of people affected, and economic losses are measured at the municipal level and then aggregated at the country level. The logic behind the LDI is that, in addition to major disasters, frequent low-level events can negatively affect countries' development trajectories. The Prevalent Vulnerability Index (PVI), a national-level index, is comprised of three sets of indicators and indices, which center on populations and economic activities exposed to hazards; on social and economic vulnerability; and on coping capacity. As an example, Nicaragua, the Dominican Republic, El Salvador, and Honduras have high levels of vulnerability judging from these three indices (see Cardona 2011; also Cardona 2010 for more in-depth discussions of the indices themselves).

The Global Natural Disaster Risk Hotspots project, which was led by Columbia University and the World Bank, focuses on two types of vulnerability at the country level: the risk of disaster-related deaths and the risk of economic losses, each one calculated as a function of population exposed and gross domestic product (GDP). Six natural hazards are considered: earthquakes, volcanoes, landslides, floods, droughts, and cyclones. The goal of the project was to identify "hotspots," or countries and regions with the highest vulnerability to those six hazards. Levels of vulnerability were calculated on the basis of historical data on deaths and economic losses. For the purposes of this project, countries were divided into seven geographic regions and four classes of national wealth: high, upper-middle, lower-middle, and low wealth. According to the measures used in this project, mortality risks are significantly higher in countries with lower levels of wealth, many of which are exposed to multiple natural hazards. Examples of these high-risk countries are Bangladesh, Nepal, El Salvador, the Philippines, Costa Rica, Burundi, and Haiti (Dilley et al. 2005).

The Social Vulnerability Index (SoVI), which was developed at the Hazards and Vulnerability Research Institute (HVRI) at the University of South Carolina (Cutter, Boruff, and Shirley 2003), provides more fine-grained information on vulnerability than the country- and regional-level measures that were just discussed. Based largely on US census data, the SoVI provides measures of vulnerability at the county level; SoVI data can be further disaggregated to focus on smaller geographic areas within counties. When SoVI was originally developed at the start of the twenty-first century, researchers identified variables that were considered important in influencing social vulnerability, and did this on the basis of findings in the disaster research literature. The original index was developed to include forty-two variables; most of these are indicators of population diversity, but they also take into account measures of economic viability and characteristics of the built environment. Using factor analysis, these forty-two variables were reduced to eleven factors that explain differences in vulnerability nationwide. Those factors are personal wealth; proportions of children and elderly persons in the population; race; ethnicity; density of built-environment elements such as housing units and manufacturing and commercial establishments; dependence on one versus multiple economic sectors; quality of the housing stock and percentage of home ownership; occupational makeup of the population; and a measure that takes into account a county's debt level and percentage of the population employed in infrastructure services such as transportation and public utilities.

The newest version of SoVI (2010–2014) reflects recent research on disaster vulnerability. It uses twenty-nine indicators that make up eight different components of social vulnerability: wealth; race and social status; elderly residents; Hispanic ethnicity and residents without health insurance; special needs individuals; service industry employment; Native American populations; and gender.

As an assessment tool, SoVI has several advantages. The data on which the index is based are available for the entire country, which makes it possible to compare counties and communities. Because SoVI uses census data, expenses for costly data collection are largely avoided. Because it takes into account many variables, the index enables researchers and decision makers to understand which variables are most important in influencing social vulnerability in different community contexts, which can in turn help with identifying groups that can be targeted in vulnerability reduction efforts. Because SoVI is based on geographic information systems (GIS), maps can be developed to educate the public and decision makers about the risks their communities face. The index has also proved to be adaptable for use in other societies and communities, such as regions and states in Brazil (de Loyola Hummell, Cutter, and Emrich 2016) and the Lisbon metropolitan area in Portugal (Guillard-Gonçalves, Cutter, Emrich, and Zêzere 2015).

In addition to SoVI, the HVRI developed and regularly updates the Spatial Hazard Event and Loss Database for the United States (SHELDUS). SHELDUS compiles data on fatalities, injuries, and economic losses caused by a wide range of disaster types over the period 1960–2016. Using this database, disaster losses can be aggregated and mapped at the county, state, or regional level, as well as by year.

Concluding Comments

This chapter has focused on three dimensions of vulnerability: hazardousness of place, built-environment vulnerability, and social vulnerability, which has received the strongest emphasis. We learned that social class is perhaps the most important determinant of social vulnerability to disasters, but also that, even within the social class hierarchy, race, ethnicity, and gender are significant predictors of vulnerability. In the United States, being well-off from the standpoint of income and wealth, and also being white and male, all confer advantages; in contrast, a lower position in the social class hierarchy, coupled with being a member of a racial or ethnic minority group and being female, translates into disadvantage, both in normal times and in disasters. Other dimensions of social vulnerability that were explored in this chapter are being young, being elderly, having a disability, being homeless, belonging to a sexual minority, being of limited language ability and literacy, and having less than full citizenship status. A thread running throughout the chapter is that states themselves can set into motion processes that privilege particular groups at the expense of others—for example by institutionalizing redlining practices or by withholding full citizenship rights and access to services from residents within their borders. I have also looked (although in a limited way) at efforts to measure vulnerability at different scales.

Throughout the discussion of the factors that produce social vulnerability, four points have been emphasized. One is that an intersectional approach is essential for understanding vulnerability—that is, a perspective that takes into account the influence of multiple axes of inequality, which combine to make individuals and groups more or less vulnerable. A second and related point is that vulnerability should be thought of as cumulative—the result of a range of social forces that, taken together, shape the fates of individuals and groups on an everyday basis, but also when they confront disasters.

A third point that has been stressed throughout the chapter is that, while research is strong with respect to some predictors of vulnerability such as race, class, and gender, it can be difficult to reach conclusions regarding other factors—age, for example—because the empirical record is less definitive at this time. What is needed is more well-designed, systematically conducted, multivariate, comparative studies on disaster vulnerability that should be capable of teasing out the relative contributions of the various factors that can influence social vulnerability.

Fourth, as indicated at several points in this chapter, focusing on factors that are seen as predicting disaster vulnerability only tells a part of the story. Just as individuals and groups can be differentially vulnerable, they can also be differentially resilient. Social deficits produced by forces such as class, race, and ethnicity can be offset by other factors, such as social support, disaster preparedness, and post-disaster learning. Those whose social positions and capabilities could render them vulnerable also have the capacity to overcome those disadvantages in a variety of ways. Structural forces act on individuals and groups, but agency can modify those forces. It is the combination of structural advantage/disadvantage and resilience that shapes disaster impacts and outcomes. To complete this picture, I turn in the next chapter to the topic of disaster resilience.

7

Disaster Resilience

Concepts, Measures, and Critiques

Introduction

In disaster research and risk reduction policy and practice, it is difficult to find a concept that has achieved so much influence so rapidly as the notion of disaster resilience. Recent scholarship has given the impression that the idea of resilience is relatively new; but, as David Alexander (2013) notes, this general notion has a long history that can be traced back to Roman authors such as Quintilian, Pliny the Elder, and Cicero, the early Christian church, and Tudor England, where resilience was associated with processes of rebounding and elasticity. Its use in the field of engineering mechanics dates back to the mid-nineteenth century—for example as a way of characterizing strength and flexible properties of steel and other materials. The concept began to be used more widely in the twentieth century, but jumped to prominence after 2000.

In academic research, the notion of resilience, like that of vulnerability, is used in a wide range of disciplines. In the mid-twentieth century, the concept began to be employed in the study of complex adaptive systems such as ecological ones, as well as in psychology, where it was advanced to explain why some children and youths who were exposed to stressful situations were able to cope despite those stressors, while others were not (Rutter 1987). With the contributions of scholars like Holling (1973), Adger (2000), Folke et al. (2002), and others, frameworks used in the study of ecological systems began to be applied to social systems—although, as we will see later, there are problems with that analogy. Economists have also focused on the concept of resilience as a way of understanding how individual firms and regional and national economies recover from external shocks such as hikes in the price of energy (Dhawan and Jeske 2006) and production losses (Park, Cho, and Rose 2011). The concept is also prominent in work on environmental and development economics (Perrings 1998; 2006). Again like the concept of vulnerability, resilience has increasingly emerged as a theme in development studies and in research on global environmental change, including climate change (Gallopín 2006; Janssen and Ostrom 2006; Pelling 2011; Denton et al. 2014).

The growing use of the concept in the study of hazards and disasters is a more recent development. Resilience was discussed in the summary volume of the Second Assessment of Research on Natural Hazards (Mileti 1999), but

167

the concept began to rise to prominence a few years later. An article on earth-quake resilience (Bruneau et al. 2003) is an early example of this trend, as are other works published around that time (see Pelling 2003). Since then, there has been an avalanche of books (for example Comfort, Boin, and Demchak 2010; Shaw and Sharma 2011; Miller and Rivera 2011; Kapucu, Hawkins, and Rivera 2013; Ross 2014; Masterson et al. 2014) and hundreds of articles on various aspects of societal resilience in the face of hazards and disasters.

With respect to public policy, the notion of *disaster-resistant communities* was advanced in the United States in the 1990s as part of the Federal Emergency Management Agency (FEMA)'s National Mitigation Strategy; it was part of that agency's sponsorship of a short-lived program called Project Impact, which was designed to provide incentives and guidance to hundreds of communi-ties in order to encourage local-level risk analyses, public communication, and partnership-building activities. The ultimate goal was to reduce disaster-related risks and losses (Cutter et al. 2008; Tierney 2014). However, beginning in the early years of the twenty-first century, the emphasis began to shift away from a conceptual framework that emphasized *disaster resistance* to one that placed priority on *disaster resilience*, thereby taking into account the ability to resist negative disaster impacts while remaining functional, but also the capacity for "bouncing back" after disasters in case resistance strategies failed to contain those impacts.

Resilience has become increasingly dominant in disaster risk reduction discourse and policies. Somewhat arbitrarily, we can associate the beginning of this shift toward resilience in the policy arena with two events: the publica-tion of a US federal government document entitled *Grand Challenges for Disaster Reduction* (Subcommittee on Disaster Reduction 2005), which emphasized the need for measuring and improving disaster resilience; and the United Nations International Strategy for Disaster Reduction's (2007) Hyogo Framework for Action, which was released after a major disaster-related conference in Kobe, Japan in 2005—which in turn marked the tenth anniversary of the Great Hanshin-Awaji (Kobe) earthquake. As I discuss elsewhere (Tierney 2014), in the past ten to fifteen years the concept of disaster resilience has been emphasized in a variety of other publications and policy initiatives, including the 2007 National Strategy for Homeland Security; the 2010 National Security Strategy; the 2010 Quadrennial Homeland Security Review; and the Presidential Policy Directives 8 (National Preparedness) and 21 (Critical Infrastructure Security and Resilience). Many US federal government agencies now have programs that aim at enhancing disaster resilience at different levels—national, regional, statal, and local. Some of those initiatives will be discussed later in this chapter.

Within the nongovernmental sector, the US National Academies of Sciences, Engineering, and Medicine are engaged in a number of activities that focus on community and societal resilience, as evidenced, for example, in a report on public–private partnerships as vehicles for enhancing community resilience (National Research Council 2011). The Academies report entitled *Disaster Resilience: A National Imperative* (National Research Council 2012) pressed for action on resilience conceptualization, measurement, and initiatives. The Community and Regional Resilience Institute (CARRI) has sponsored a series of activities aimed both at resilience conceptualization and measurement and at community-focused resilience-building activities. Both in the United States and around the world, academic centers and think tanks focus on resilience research and policymaking.

A variety of other efforts are indicative of the growing concern with disaster resilience. The World Bank has made resilience in the face of disasters and climate change a key priority in its programs that target developing countries (World Bank Group 2013). The Asia-Pacific Economic Cooperation forum (APEC) also emphasizes disaster resilience as a major concern (Asia-Pacific Economic Cooperation 2015). In the United Kingdom, the influential Department for International Development (DFID) has made enhancing disaster resilience a core approach in its strategy for providing aid to less developed countries (Department for International Development 2011). In 2013 the Rockefeller Foundation launched its 100 Resilient Cities program, which aims at making communities worldwide more resilient in the face of both acute shocks such as disasters and chronic stressors; and recently it teamed up with the US Department of Housing and Urban Development (HUD) on a national competition for enhancing community resilience in the United States. Australia has adopted resilience as a guiding principle in its own humanitarian efforts. New Zealand, which suffered a series of damaging earthquakes in 2010 and 2011, has been developing a national resilience strategy, and many nongovernmental organizations (NGOs) have also been formed in that nation under the resilience rubric. The European Commission prioritizes resilience in its provision of development and humanitarian assistance. The United Nations International Strategy for Disaster Reduction (UNISDR) Hyogo Framework, which ended in 2015, was superseded by the Sendai Framework for Disaster Risk Reduction 2015–2030, which made risk reduction and resilience (taken together) one of its four major priorities.

In this chapter we will explore the meaning of the concept of resilience, look at approaches to measuring resilience, and investigate the applicability of the concept in the study of disaster response and recovery. We will also consider criticisms of the concept and conditions that place limits on resilience capacities. As we did in the previous chapter with vulnerability, we will focus on issues that are relevant to a social–scientific understanding of disaster resilience.

What Is Disaster Resilience?

Conceptualizations and definitions

As is so often the case in academic and policy circles, there is no universally agreed-upon definition of resilience. In a broad overview of the use of the term in various fields, Plodinec (2009) identified no fewer than forty-six different definitions of the concept. Community psychologist Fran Norris and her colleagues (Norris et al. 2008), who focused more on the societal aspects of resilience, listed twenty-one different framings of the concept. Here I offer a few commonly used definitions that provide a sense of how resilience is used in the social science disaster literature. Bruneau et al. (2003: 735) defined earthquake resilience as "the ability of social units (e.g. organizations, communities), to mitigate hazards, contain the effects of disasters when they occur, and carry out recovery activities in ways that minimize social disruption and mitigate the effects of future earthquakes." Similarly, Cutter et al. (2008: 600) define disaster resilience as "the ability to survive and cope with a disaster with minimal impact and damage . . . [along with] the capacity to reduce or avoid losses, contain the effects of disasters, and recover with minimal social disruption."

In a thoughtful review of the social and psychological literature, Norris et al. (2008) refer to the concept of resilience as a metaphor borrowed from non-social science fields, but also as a theory focused on adaptation after shocks and traumas, as a set of capacities, and as a strategy for reducing disaster losses. According to their definition, resilience is "a process linking a set of adaptive capacities to a positive trajectory of functioning and adaptation after a disturbance" (2008: 130).

The 2012 National Academies' report defined disaster resilience as "the ability to prepare and plan for, absorb, recover from and more successfully adapt to adverse events" (National Research Council 2012: 2). A recent World Bank publication defined resilience as "the ability of a system, community, or society exposed to hazards to resist, absorb, accommodate, and recover from the effects of a hazard promptly and efficiently by preserving and restoring essential functions" (Jha, Miner, and Stanton-Geddes 2013: 10).

The current definition of disaster resilience adopted by the UNISDR frames resilience in an almost identical way:

> In the context of disaster risk, the ability of a system, community, or society exposed to hazards to resist, absorb, accommodate, adapt to, transform and recover from the effects of a hazard in a timely and efficient manner, including the preservation and restoration of its essential basic structures and functions through risk management. (United Nations International Strategy for Disaster Reduction 2017)

These definitions convey two ideas that most researchers and practitioners would agree are central to discussions of resilience. The first is that resilience involves *resistance* or *absorptive capacity*; a resilient person, household, organization, community, or built-environment system is one that can experience a major stressor such as a disaster and still function reasonably well, even if part of its functioning has been reduced. Second, resilience involves the ability to *cope and adapt* when disasters strike and to move on to recover. Put another way, depending on the size and severity of a disaster, some or even many resistance measures may fail, but adaptive strategies can help overcome those failures.

The resistive and absorptive aspects of resilience, sometimes referred to as inherent resilience, encompass several types of activities that were previously identified in the literature as "disaster mitigation," or measures that can be taken to reduce the likelihood that a hazard would produce impacts such as death, injury, damage, disruption, and economic loss. Perhaps the best way of minimizing disaster impacts is to avoid dangerous locations in the first place by ensuring that people and structures are not situated in places where they are exposed to hazards—for example, in hazardous coastal zones, floodplains, locations adjacent to active earthquake faults, and places at the wildland–urban interface that present a high risk of wildfires. This is the purpose of hazard-related land use and zoning regulations; but, as we have seen in earlier discussions, such regulations are lacking or are not enforced in many parts of the world and, where they do exist, political and economic actors frequently work to circumvent them. There is also the problem that certain hazards may not have been well understood when human settlements were first established, and this left a legacy of hazard exposure. At the same time, as noted at various points in this volume, the ongoing tendency to develop land even when hazards are recognized is a key contributor to burgeoning disaster losses, as Houston demonstrated in Hurricane Harvey in 2017.

If hazards cannot be avoided entirely, a second line of defense is to ensure that the built environment can resist the forces unleashed by disasters. As more is learned about how elements in the built environment can fail in disasters, this knowledge serves as guidance for improving disaster resistance—for example, through measures such as building codes that encourage or require hazard-resistant design and building practices and through programs that retrofit older structures to make them safer. Around the United States, many communities have steadily improved their requirements for building and infrastructure safety—but many others, typically facing opposition from political and economic interests, have resisted making such changes.

Two earthquakes illustrate the significance of the "resistance" dimension of resilience. On January 12, 2010, a magnitude 7.0 earthquake struck Haiti, causing widespread devastation in the capital of Port au Prince and surrounding areas. The number of deaths attributable to the earthquake is still in dispute; estimates range between tens and hundreds of thousands. Just a few weeks later, on February 27, a massive 8.8 earthquake struck off the coast of Chile, causing intense ground shaking and a tsunami. Although the effects were very severe everywhere, including in Chile's capital, Santiago, estimates suggest that just over 500 people died as a result of the earthquake. A key factor in mortality in Haiti was the lack of earthquake resistance in the built environment; large numbers of people died because they were crushed by collapsed buildings. In Chile, a nation that has a long history of violent earthquakes, the story was different. Many structures survived because they were designed and constructed to resist earthquake forces. Keeping in mind earlier discussions about vulnerability, the quality of the built environment in the two countries was in large measure a reflection of their relative prosperity: Haiti, an island nation that is the poorest in the western hemisphere; and Chile, still a poor country, but well-off enough to be able to invest in higher levels of earthquake safety.

When strategies to resist disaster impacts fail, those affected by disasters must cope and recover. The activities associated with this aspect of resilience, which were formerly termed "preparedness," "response," and "recovery," enable individuals, households, organizations, and communities to address a wide range of needs that result from disasters. Such measures include pre-disaster foresight, planning, and training; warning systems; the mobilization of human and material resources in activities such as search and rescue and the provision of emergency medical care and shelter when disasters strike; efforts to contain secondary threats posed by disasters, such as hurricane-induced hazardous materials spills; and activities aimed at helping affected localities recover as soon as possible—for example debris removal, restoration of utility lifeline services, and the provision of temporary and permanent housing. Disasters can disrupt a range of critical community activities such as economic functioning, livelihoods, schooling, public health and welfare, transportation and other critical infrastructure systems, and housing. The adaptive dimension of resilience seeks to provide temporary and longer-term fixes that address these disruptions. As Paton and Johnston (2006) note, this set of adaptive processes involves not merely a return to the *status quo ante*. Rather adaptation always brings about change of some kind, and successful adaptation should lead to improved resistance and adaptive strategies. In this sense, adaptation after disasters can be seen as "bouncing forward" instead of merely "bouncing back."

Keeping these two aspects of resilience in mind, many discussions of the concept represent resilience graphically, in terms of the degree of degradation of key community and societal functions and the length of time required to restore those functions. Following Bruneau et al. (2003) and taking the community and its various systems (e.g., transportation, lifelines, educational institutions, health care systems) as units of analysis, the graph in Figure 7.1

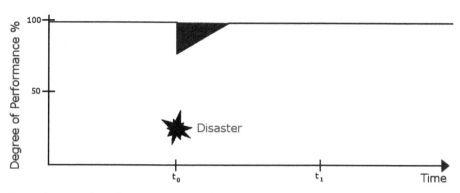

Figure 7.1 Less degradation of system performance, more resilience.
SOURCE: Bruneau et al. 2003.

represents a fictitious community in which effective resistance measures are in place and coping and adaptive strategies are working well enough for the community to overcome disaster-induced disruption. The triangular dark area represents the extent to which systems are not resilient, but in this case the "resilience triangle" is small. In the graph in Figure 7.2, resistance strategies are weaker, leading to a significant loss of system performance, while coping measures are not enacted in a timely way or are insufficient to address disaster impacts and losses. In this case, as indicated by the size of the dark resilience triangle, there is less resilience. The goal of resilience-enhancing measures is to make that loss of performance—that triangle—as small as possible.

While scholars mostly agree on the importance of these two elements of resilience, they diverge on other points. For example, some researchers, such as economist Adam Rose, place more emphasis on the "coping and adapting" dimension of resilience—what he calls dynamic resilience (a notion to be discussed later in this chapter, see pp. 191–2)—than on absorptive capacity.

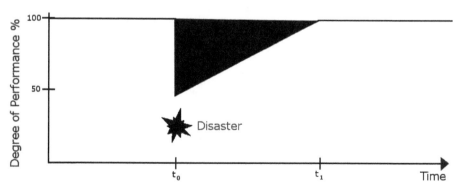

Figure 7.2 Greater degradation of system performance, less resilience.
SOURCE: Bruneau et al. 2003.

They also differ in the ways they envision resilience. As seen in the definitions presented above, some view resilience as a property associated with different units of analysis (e.g., households, communities), while others see it rather as a set of processes that achieve particular resilience-related outcomes. In keeping with the characterization of vulnerability in previous discussions, my approach views resilience not so much as a state but more as a set of processes or activities that societies and communities undertake in their efforts to reduce disaster-related risks.

It is easy to assume that resilience is the opposite of vulnerability—that is, that the most socially vulnerable individuals and groups are the ones who have the greatest difficulty being resilient in the face of disasters. While the two concepts are clearly related, resilience is not the obverse of vulnerability. Vulnerability is indicative of the potential for experiencing disaster losses; but, as we will see later, members of vulnerable groups can be resilient as a consequence of factors such as social support and personal ability to adapt and innovate in the aftermath of disasters.

Resilience domains

The resilience literature and the guidance on becoming resilient point to various aspects of communities that can be the focus of resilience-building strategies. Bruneau et al. (2003) emphasize four resilience domains: technical, organizational, social, and economic. Paton and Johnston (2006) identify five elements of community resilience: knowledge of hazards, shared community values, established social infrastructure, positive social and economic trends, partnerships, and resources and skills. Renschler et al. (2010) identified seven dimensions of community resilience: population and demographics; environmental and ecosystem; organized governmental services; physical infrastructure; lifestyle and community competence; economic development; and social and cultural capital. Geographer Susan Cutter and her collaborators view resilience as having six dimensions: ecological, social, economic, institutional, and infrastructural, as well as community competence (Cutter et al. 2008). Guidance from the World Bank (Jha et al. 2013) points to four dimensions of urban resilience: infrastructural, institutional, economic, and social.

Approaches that are most relevant for the sociological analysis of resilience tend to emphasize the role of different forms of community capital in shaping resilience. Following Bourdieu's (1986) original formulation, capital in this sense is the accumulation, transmission, and reproduction of wealth and monetary value (economic capital), which is the basis for the other forms of capital; credentials such as academic qualifications, along with other symbols of status (cultural capital); and network-based resources gained through connections with others (social capital). If we move now to social class, which is of interest here, social class position is associated with the extent to which members of different social classes possess these three forms of capital. Bourdieu's concept of capital has been influential in sociology and other fields, and this influence can be seen in current approaches to identifying the elements of resilience. For example, sociologists Liesel Ritchie and Duane Gill (2011) base their understanding of the dimensions of community disaster resilience on Flora and Flora's (2018) community capitals framework, which identifies seven types of capital: natural (for example, natural resources and ecosystems), financial, built, political, social, human, and cultural. Similarly, Mayunga (2009) sees resilience as based on social, economic, physical, human, and natural capital. For Norris et al. (2008), the key components of disaster resilience are information and communication, community competence, social capital, and economic development (which can be viewed as economic capital). Also focusing largely on capitals, Kendra, Clay, and Gill (2018) identify nine components of disaster resilience:

- capacity for improvisation in disasters,
- number and quality of physical and infrastructural resources,
- community capital,
- natural resources,
- institutional capital,
- political capital,
- human capital,
- economic capital,
- social capital.

As we saw in Chapter 6 with respect to vulnerability to hazards and disasters, built-environment characteristics need to be taken into consideration in assessing vulnerability. The same is the case with resilience, as indicated by how frequently elements in the built environment are mentioned in efforts to identify key dimensions of resilience such as those just discussed. However, for our purposes we will home in on more societally relevant aspects of resilience. In particular, our focus will be on social capital, because it is closely related to other forms of capital such as economic, political, and cultural and because it is the form that has received the greatest emphasis in the social science disaster literature.

Social capital and disaster resilience

Social capital is fundamentally about social networks and connections. Bourdieu, who originally coined the term, defined social capital as "the aggregate of the actual or potential resources which are linked to possession of a durable network of more or less institutionalized relationships of mutual acquaintance or recognition" (Bourdieu 1986: 248). Robert Putnam, an influential pioneer in social capital research, defines it as "features of social organization such as networks, norms, and social trust that facilitate coordination and cooperation for mutual benefit" (Putnam 1995: 67). Other definitions of the term are similar: "the ability of actors to secure benefits by virtue of membership in social networks or other social structures" (Portes 1998: 6); "friends, colleagues, and more general contacts through whom you receive opportunities to use your financial and human capital" (Burt 1992: 9); and "resources embedded in a social structure which are accessed and/or mobilized in purposive actions" (Lin 1999: 35).

Social capital gives rise to norms, obligations, and a sense of trust among the members of a network and provides channels through which information can flow (Coleman 1988). Belonging to a network entails the expectation of reciprocity: someone does a favor to another individual in her friendship network that the other person will repay at a later point on account of feelings of obligation. Social embeddedness and a sense of belonging are characteristics of social capital, as are civic mindedness and civic engagement. As Putnam's definition indicates, being connected enables network members to engage in collective action to realize their goals—for example, to achieve political or economic objectives.

Scholars generally recognize three forms of social capital that confer different types of benefits. *Bonding* social capital refers to the relationships that exist within a particular group, such as a local group working on issues of homelessness. *Bridging* capital consists of linkages that exist between two or more groups of different types, for instance groups composed of people with different ethnic backgrounds, or entities that were formed for different purposes. In effect, bridging capital widens the network of participants who work toward a common objective, making more resources available. Using the same example, bridging capital would exist if a number of community groups who work on different aspects of the homeless issue (housing, mental and physical health, homeless rights) agreed to join forces and to form a coalition to press for more services for those who are homeless. *Linking* capital involves relationships between groups and centers of power and influence, such as governmental entities. For example, to bring about that linkage, the coalition concerned with addressing the needs of the homeless population might get one of its members elected to city council, establish connections with state or national policymakers, or obtain a large grant from a major foundation. Without bonding social capital, individuals are isolated and lack access to the kinds of resources—for example, financial, informational, and emotional support—that members of cohesive groups enjoy. Without bridging capital, a group's resources may be too limited to address members' needs, or some group members may feel overburdened when asked to provide support. Without linking capital, groups lack connections to more powerful entities that would be in a position to increase their resources in relation to other groups. Where all three forms of capital are present, network members have the best chance of getting access to resources and achieving their goals.

Different approaches to conceptualizing social capital have yielded a variety of measures of the concept. Typical ways of identifying social capital take into account measures of political participation (voting), volunteering, density of and individual or household involvement in community NGOs, embeddedness in social networks, social support, community attachment (e.g., length of residence in a community, home ownership), frequency of participation in social activities, and feelings of trust and belonging. By contrast, low political and community participation, social isolation and marginality, transience, lack of community engagement, and sparse or weak NGOs are associated with low levels of social capital.

In the disaster field, Yuko Nakagawa and Rajib Shaw (2004) were among the first to argue that social capital contributes to disaster resilience. In their research, which involved recovery from the 1995 Great Hanshin-Awaji (Kobe) earthquake and the 2001 Gujarat earthquake in India, they demonstrated a relationship between bonding, bridging, and linking social capital and participation in and satisfaction with response and recovery efforts. Russell Dynes (2006) also linked social capital with disaster resilience, arguing that effective disaster responses both build upon and contribute to the development of social capital. Dynes noted that emergent groups and emergent organizational networks (EMONs), discussed earlier in connection with disaster theory, can be thought of as new forms of social capital that come about in order to address disaster-related challenges. Social capital is also associated with the development of norms—in this case, the altruistic norms that have added force in disaster situations, leading to extensive helping behavior. These points are echoed by writer Rebecca Solnit, whose book *A Paradise Built in Hell: The Extraordinary Communities That Arise in Disaster* (Solnit 2009) details how disasters are accompanied by strong feelings of community solidarity and a variety of forms of pro-social collective action.

In a comprehensive review of the literature on social capital and disasters, Michelle Meyer (2018) identified a number of studies that show that social capital, measured at either the individual or the community level, has a positive impact at various stages of the hazards cycle. For example, social capital is associated with mitigation and adaptation activities, adoption of disaster preparedness measures, evacuation behaviors, disaster responses, and positive recovery outcomes. Meyer also highlights a number of studies that link social capital and disaster resilience. Here I discuss a few such studies, which emphasize the link between social capital and post-disaster outcomes.

Sociologist Eric Klinenberg (2002) conducted research on the factors that contributed to mortality in the 1995 Chicago heat wave, which caused approximately 750 deaths. Selecting two apparently similar Chicago neighborhoods in which heat-related mortality differed significantly, he found that social ties and other variables associated with social capital were key factors associated with low death rates. In the neighborhood where death rates were higher, fear of crime kept people isolated in their homes, many residents were transients, and levels of social interaction and participation in community organizations were low. The neighborhood where mortality was low was a bustling commercial center where people interacted on a daily basis in stores and in the streets. Ties with extended family members were strong in that largely immigrant community and the Catholic Church served as a major community hub. Klinenberg concluded that high levels of social capital had a protective function for otherwise vulnerable community residents.

Brenda Murphy (2007) focused on the role of social capital in two community emergencies that affected the residents of the Canadian province of Ontario. Walkerton, Ontario, a town of about 5,000 residents, was struck with an outbreak of E. coli when its water supply was contaminated. Seven people died of illnesses associated with contamination, and over 2,000 residents—about 40 percent of the population—became ill. Of those interviewed in the wake of the emergency, 60 percent reported providing some form of assistance to their fellow community residents, and 63 percent reported relying on family and friendship networks. Walkerton is a close-knit community with a high rate of participation in local NGOs, and interviewees indicated that their pre-disaster membership in such organizations formed the basis for their involvement in volunteer activities during the incident. In the August 2003 blackout, which was discussed earlier in Chapter 6, Ontario residents who were surveyed reported both anticipating help from and providing help to others in their social networks, particularly those associated with their neighborhoods. In this emergency, mutual aid lowered the burden on public safety agencies, which were then able to turn their attention to other pressing tasks, such as rescuing people trapped in elevators and evacuating disabled persons stranded in high-rise buildings.

Other research reveals the connection between social capital and positive health and mental health outcomes after disasters. Following Hurricane Katrina, Adeola and Picou (2012) employed survey research methods to assess the link between social capital measures (e.g. home ownership, feelings of self-efficacy, involvement with community organizations) and physical health outcomes such as respiratory problems, headaches, nausea, and high blood pressure among Katrina survivors in hard-hit parts of Louisiana and Mississippi. They found that those with high levels of social capital had fewer health problems than those with low social capital. These same researchers looked at long-term patterns of psychological distress following Katrina and found that low levels of social capital were predictive of depression and psychosocial stress, and also that these negative mental health impacts were more common among blacks, older adults, unmarried adults, women, people with less education, and people with weak social networks (Adeola and Picou 2014).

Heid, Pruchno, Cartwright, and Wilson-Genderson (2017) studied the mental health of older New Jersey residents, between the ages of fifty-four and eighty, who were exposed to Hurricane Sandy in 2012. Controlling for other factors that could have influenced outcomes, they found that the severity of storm exposure was associated with more symptoms of post-traumatic stress disorder (PTSD), while respondents' perceptions of neighborhood social cohesion (a measure of social capital) was associated with fewer symptoms. Additionally, even for those with greater exposure to the storm, perceived social cohesion was associated with lower levels of PTSD. (For a review of other studies on social capital and post-disaster health outcomes, see Aida, Kawachi, Subramanian, and Kondo 2013.)

Technological disasters and social capital

Liesel Ritchie's research (Ritchie 2004, 2012; Ritchie, Gill, and Farnham 2013) focuses on the relationship between disasters and social capital. However, in contrast with Dynes, Aldrich, and others, who emphasize how disasters can have a positive effect on social capital and how high social capital facilitates recovery, much of her work documents the ways in which disasters can damage social capital and community cohesiveness, particularly when the disaster agent is technological and the recovery period is protracted and accompanied by litigation-related community conflict. Her research on the long-term impacts of the 1989 *Exxon Valdez* oil spill in one fishing community in Alaska is a case in point. That 11-million gallon spill, the largest in history prior to the 2010 BP *Deepwater Horizon* blowout and oil spill in the Gulf of Mexico, was a catastrophe that had far-reaching consequences not only for the environment, marine life, and fisheries but also for the affected communities. Lawsuits seeking damages from Exxon dragged on for more than twenty-five years, during which the residents of the affected communities were under significant psychological and financial stress and the social fabric became frayed. Attitudes and behaviors associated with social capital, such as dispositions toward trust and goodwill, the willingness to socialize, and feelings of efficacy, declined.

Other researchers who have studied technological disasters also contend that those kinds of events, which involve blame for their occurrence, disputes over the magnitude and severity of impacts, lingering and uncertain effects, and lawsuits, can have a corrosive effect on individual and community social capital (Erikson 1995; Freudenburg 1997; Gill and Picou 1998; Picou, Marshall, and Gill 2004). For example, Mayer, Running, and Bergstrand (2015) studied the residents of four communities affected by the BP *Deepwater Horizon* oil spill and found that, even though the victims of the spill began to be compensated relatively soon after that disaster, many residents were critical of the compensation process, which they saw as random and arbitrary. As a consequence, individual claimants and businesses that had experienced losses felt as if they were in competition with one another for resources, and many avoided interactions where money-related conflicts might surface. The perception that some residents had filed fraudulent claims or profited in a major way from the spill and cleanup created feelings of distrust that also had corrosive effects. The researchers concluded that "residents felt themselves pulled apart rather than together by the claims process during what were already difficult times" (2015: 384).

A note of caution

Findings like these are consistent across a range of studies but, as I have argued elsewhere (see Tierney, Lindell, and Perry, 2001; Tierney 2014, 2018), framing technological disasters as uniquely corrosive glosses over some important points. While some researchers focus on toxic emergencies that result in diminished social capital, others point to situations in which communities have responded to such threats with apathy and denial. For example, Auyero and Swistun (2008) studied an Argentine shantytown called Flammable that is literally located on top of a toxic industrial site. They found that, even though residents suffered a number of health problems, they were doubtful and confused about whether the toxic exposure was harmful, denied the hazard, or blamed their illnesses on sources other than industrial pollution. Gunter, Aronoff, and Joel (1999) studied communities where toxic contamination was present and found in them complacency and an absence of conflict. Kari Norgaard (2011) studied a community in Norway where residents could find evidence of climate change all around them but still engaged in collective climate change denial. Findings like these indicate that, although the literature is replete with studies showing that toxic hazards can lead to community conflict and social capital losses, there can be exceptions.

The downside of social capital

Discussions so far have focused on the ways in which social capital contributes to disaster resilience, but the effects of social capital are not always positive. After all, criminal gangs and mafias are characterized by strong social bonds too. Aldrich (2012) refers to social capital as "Janus-faced"—that is, as a set of resources and capacities that can be used for good or ill. Pioneering researcher Alejandro Portes (1998) provided various examples of what he termed "negative social capital," including ethnically based business monopolies that keep out competitors and groups that control unions and succeed in denying membership to those considered undesirable (typically people of color). He also noted that close-knit groups and communities can exercise strong pressure toward conformity, stifling individual freedom, and that strong ties can pressure group members to remain in deviant lifestyles associated for instance with drug dealing and gang involvement even though they would rather quit. We need to keep in mind that Bourdieu's original interest in social capital centered on how it functioned as a means of distinguishing higher-class "haves" from lower-class "have-nots." For him, social capital was just as much about being able to exclude others as it was about creating in-group solidarity.

Along those same lines, with respect to hazards and disasters, there are a number of examples of how the strong social capital of some groups works to the detriment of others. The environmental justice literature is full of examples of how well-off and well-connected—and typically white—communities succeed in avoiding "environmental bads" such as chemical factories and hazardous landfills, pushing them onto minority communities. When groups with high social capital organize behind the banner of "not in my backyard" (NIMBY), they ensure that environmental bads are thrown into someone else's backyard; and this "someone else" is, typically, a vulnerable group deprived of the capacity and political power to resist.

Daniel Aldrich provides examples of how the strong social capital of some groups can result in the exclusion of others. In a study of the recovery of villages and hamlets in Tamil Nadu, India after the 2004 tsunami (Aldrich 2011), he found that local councils, which had strong bonding social capital, were able to link to external sources of aid such as humanitarian NGOs and higher levels of government. However, he also found that, once those councils obtained recovery resources from the outside, they distributed them in ways that excluded certain groups within the community, such as women (especially female heads of households), elderly residents, and Dalits—members of the lowest caste, formerly known as "untouchables." Communities that did not have local councils received less aid and had difficulty recovering, but at least they had bonding social capital, often in the form of kinship networks, and the aid that was obtained there was distributed more equitably.

The devastation wrought by Hurricane Katrina in New Orleans created a desperate need for temporary housing, and the solution FEMA devised was to provide trailers and trailer parks for displaced residents who remained in the city. A preliminary list of approved sites was developed, and final siting decisions were made by the New Orleans city government. Working with a database of 114 zip codes in and around New Orleans, Aldrich and Crook (2008) documented the number of trailers and trailer parks that actually ended up being located in each zip code. They then looked into the extent to which social capital played a role in where trailers were placed. Using voting rates in the 2004 presidential election as a measure of social capital (because voting rates were closely associated with other forms of civic participation) and controlling for a number of other variables (among them race, income, education, and flood damage), they found that the higher the voting rates in a zip code, the fewer trailers and trailer parks were located in that zip code. Trailers and trailer parks, along with those who live in them, generally come with a certain stigma and are often targeted for NIMBY actions. The authors interpreted their findings as an indication that city leaders were consciously trying to avoid neighborhoods where civically engaged residents were likely to organize in order to resist the siting of trailers.

In September 2013, communities in Colorado's Front Range region experienced massive flooding in what became the costliest disaster in the state's history. Located at the confluence of two rivers, the community of Lyons experienced extensive damage, especially to its infrastructure systems, and the entire town had to be evacuated for a time. Two mobile home parks that had housed mainly low-income and elderly residents were essentially destroyed. Housing costs were already high in the town, a significant proportion of the housing stock was destroyed in the flood, and rents subsequently went up, making it difficult for displaced mobile home residents to return to Lyons. Local advocates of affordable housing and their allies banded together, conducted studies, and developed a proposal for building a sixty-six-unit affordable housing development on six acres of a twenty-five-acre public park. The plan had strong community support, but an opposition faction emerged. That faction, which had backing from major business leaders in the town, claimed to be motivated by the need to preserve parks and open space; but there was also a strong undertone of NIMBYism. An election was held to determine whether the affordable housing development could go forward, and the measure failed. This led to the long-term displacement of mobile home residents who had been flooded out. Sociologist Nnenia Campbell (2016), who studied the aftermath of the flood in Lyons and other communities, noted that, while social capital was high among groups on both sides of the issue, housing advocates were no match when it came to their opponents' economic and political power. Observing that the controversy resulted in bitterness and recriminations on both sides, she also cites the case as an example of the corrosive effects of disasters.

Daly and Silver (2008) point to other problematic aspects of the concept of social capital. They note that the World Bank has embraced the concept and has argued for its importance in economic development and good governance; but they also point out that in the Bank's framing women and the poor are expected to generate social capital as a way of solving their own problems, while the state is assigned a lesser role. These authors express concern that "social capital can provide a rationale for the state to exit poor communities and leave the problem-solving to civil society or individual action" (2008: 553). I will return to this idea later (pp. 210–14), when I discuss critiques of the resilience concept.

Measuring Disaster Resilience

A focus on resilience and its dimensions leads logically to questions about resilience measurement. If improving resilience is a goal, how do we know whether communities and societies are reaching that goal? Which aspects of resilience are functioning well, and which ones need improvement? Do specific elements of resilience need to be prioritized? What baseline data are available that would enable researchers to measure changes in resilience in the aftermath of disasters? Measurement strategies are needed to answer questions like these. The literature on individual, organizational, community, and national resilience is vast. In this section we will consider measurement approaches that explicitly address disaster resilience, as opposed to resilience in general, although the two concepts are obviously related.

When so much attention is being paid to disaster resilience in both research and practice communities, it is not surprising that measurement approaches have also proliferated rapidly. Schipper and Langston (2015) analyzed eighteen sets of indicators that measure resilience at different levels of analysis, some of which focus on disaster resilience. Stevenson et al. (2015) discuss thirteen different resilience assessment frameworks. Cutter (2016) reviewed twenty-seven different measurement schemes that address different resilience domains and units of analysis. Sharifi (2016) identified thirty-six different assessment tools at different analytic levels. The Resilience Measurement Evidence and Learning Community of Practice (2016) has compiled an inventory of thirty-nine resilience measurement approaches and frameworks. These comparative analyses are a good source of information on the details, strengths, and weaknesses of different approaches. Important to note is that, while there is some degree of convergence on key concepts associated with resilience across measurement schemes, concepts are operationalized differently, and at this point there is no general consensus on how disaster resilience should be measured. Frameworks and approaches also vary in terms of the hazards they take into account. Some frameworks, like the three community resilience assessment tools discussed below, are not specific with respect to the hazards considered, or take an all-hazards approach. Others focus on resilience in the face of particular hazards, such as droughts and floods, or on specific dimensions of social life, such as livelihoods and food security.

Measurement approaches can be distinguished in a number of ways. Disaster resilience is a multilevel concept; the resilience of nations, regions, economic sectors, communities, organizations, households, and individuals can all be assessed, which means that measurement schemes should focus on various levels of analysis. A nation as a whole may score one way on resilience criteria, while lower-level social units may score differently. Frameworks can be primarily quantitative or more qualitative. Another aspect on which resilience measurement schemes differ is whether they rely on "objective" data—that is, data that employ social indicators or other objective measures—or on self-reported data or self-assessments. Examples of the latter could include data collected through focus groups and community discussions organized around the concept of resilience, where the perceptions of community members are emphasized. Cutter (2016) makes several further distinctions. Measurements can involve indices made up of quantifiable indicators or variables; scorecards involving assessments of progress toward resilience goals using numerical scores or letter grades; mathematical models of resilience such as those used by economists; or toolkits that provide step-by-step guidance on developing resilience scores. Further, frameworks can either be tailored to focus on individual communities using locally available data or be designed to allow for comparisons across multiple units such as countries or cities. Without attempting to be exhaustive, here I will focus on a few examples of socio-logically relevant resilience measurement approaches of different types, with the goal of providing a general sense of the logics that undergird different frameworks and the types of indicators that are employed. The discussion focuses first on measuring resilience at the community level, then moves on to organizational- and household-level measures.

Community-Level Measurement Frameworks

Baseline resilience indicators for communities (BRIC)

Like the Social Vulnerability Index (SOVI), which was discussed in the previous chapter, BRIC was developed by Susan Cutter and her colleagues (Cutter, Burton, and Emrich 2010; see also Cutter, Ash, and Emrich 2014) at the Hazards and Vulnerability Research Institute. BRIC is a composite measure of inherent disaster resilience comprised of variables drawn from secondary sources such as the US Census and other less costly and widely available data sources. The conceptual framework on which BRIC is based is called the "disaster resilience of place" (DROP) model (Cutter et al. 2008). The unit of analysis is the community, or more specifically the county. BRIC focuses on six resilience domains, also referred to as capitals: social, economic, housing and infrastructure, institutional, community, and environmental. Within each of those domains, multiple variables were selected for inclusion on the basis of findings in the disaster research literature—forty-nine variables in all. For example, the concept of social resilience is measured by variables associated with equality in educational attainment, English language competence within the population, food security, fewer elderly and disabled residents, and the extent to which transportation, telephone service, health insurance, and mental health services are available. The community capital dimension of resilience is made up of variables indicative of place attachment, political engagement, other dimensions of social capital, and residents' disaster preparedness and response training. Institutional resilience is measured by variables related to investments in disaster mitigation, flood insurance coverage, the ability of jurisdictions to coordinate with one another, and disaster experience. Because data are available for all counties in the United States, BRIC allows researchers and decision makers to make cross-county comparisons and to judge how their communities stack up against others. Details of the BRIC framework, including lists of indicators, can be found in Cutter, Burton, and Emrich (2010).

Communities advancing resilience toolkit (CART)

CART is a comprehensive set of resilience assessment and improvement tools that was developed by a group of researchers based primarily in the Terrorism and Disaster Center at the University of Oklahoma; the Geisel School of Medicine at Dartmouth University and the National Center for Post-Traumatic Stress Disorder; and the US Centers for Disease Control and Prevention (Pfefferbaum et al. 2013). The conceptual framework that underpins CART derives from theory and research findings on community capacity and competence from the fields of social psychology, community psychology, and public health. One of the initial publications that laid out this resilience framework was Norris et al. (2008), which was discussed earlier in connection with resilience domains. CART is meant to be applied at the community level, where "community" can also be defined as a neighborhood or some other unit of analysis; participants in the CART process are the ones who decide what the community boundaries are. A core element of the CART assessment, in contrast with that of BRIC, is based on data provided by community stakeholders who take part in a resilience assessment process. Like BRIC, CART uses widely available secondary data sources such as the census (for population, housing, and other community characteristics), the Department of Health and Human Services' Community Health Status Indicators, and other community-level indicators that give a snapshot of community resilience capacities. In this measurement process, the community itself also collects what it considers to be relevant data through strategies such as key informant interviews and what the CART developers call "community conversations." In addition to instructions on how to conduct interviews and community conversations, other components of the toolkit are guidance on stakeholder analysis, capacity and vulnerability assessment, and participatory strategic planning aimed at enhancing resilience.

Although its core concepts and assumptions remain the same, CART has evolved over time in terms of what the research group considers key elements of resilience and how they can be measured. An earlier formulation (Pfefferbaum et al. 2007) specified seven elements that the literature identifies as important for resilience: connectedness, commitment, and shared values; participation; support and nurturance; structure, roles, and responsibilities; resources; critical reflection and skill building; and communication. Further refinement prompted the CART group to reduce these concepts to five: general community resilience; connection and caring; resources; transformative potential; and disaster management. The assessment process involves collecting extensive data in these five areas. Listed below are examples of the interview questions that are associated with each area.

- GENERAL RESILIENCE: Does the community help people in need? What resources are available for disaster and terrorism readiness, response, and recovery?
- CONNECTION AND CARING: Do community members share similar values? Are members committed to the well-being of the community?
- RESOURCES: Are disaster response and recovery services available in the community? Are they available to *all* community members?
- TRANSFORMATIVE POTENTIAL: Does the community have or collect information in order to improve its ability to adapt and learn from crises? Are members able to take part in problem-solving regarding community issues?
- DISASTER MANAGEMENT: What does the community do to prevent disasters and terrorism? Is the community currently doing anything to improve its disaster/terrorism response?

Full details of the CART toolkit are available online (https://www.oumedicine. com/docs/ad-psychiatry-workfiles/cart_online-final_042012.pdf).

Disaster resilience scorecard for cities

This assessment tool was developed by the UNISDR to enable communities to assess their progress toward the "ten essentials for making cities resilient" identified in the Sendai Framework for Action. Different versions of the tool can be used for preliminary assessments, developed through short stakeholder workshops, as well as for more detailed resilience assessments, which would involve longer stakeholder engagement. The detailed tool contains 117 indicators, each measured on a scale of zero to five, covering ten major sets of activities that map onto the "ten essentials." The scorecard enables cities to assess their overall resilience and also to identify areas in which they are performing well and areas that need improvement. Table 7.1 lists the activities scored in the detailed assessment and provides examples of positive indicators for each.

There are many other measurement frameworks that attempt to assess resilience at the city or neighborhood scale. Examples include the Community Disaster Resilience Scorecard, which was developed at the Torrens Resilience Institute at Flinders University, Australia (Arbon et al. 2016), the Rockefeller-supported *City Resilience Index* (Arup 2015), the GOAL's (2015) *Toolkit for Measuring*

Table 7.1 Scorecard activities and selected indicators.

Resilience Essential	Examples of Indicators
Organize for resilience	City plan incorporates risk considerations; stakeholders are included and kept up to date on plans
Identify, understand, and use current and future risk scenarios	Comprehensive risk analyses, updated in last three years and approved by a third party; risk assessments include socioeconomic, spatial, physical, and environmental assets at risk, estimated from most probable and most severe scenarios
Strengthen financial capacity for resilience	Dedicated responsibility within city to access national and international resilience financing; budget for resilience measures exists, is adequate, and is protected
Pursue resilient urban development	No loss of employment from "most severe" disaster scenario; systematic use of design solutions to improve city's resilience, enforced by codes
Safeguard natural buffers to enhance the protective functions offered by natural ecosystems	Critical ecosystem services are identified and monitored annually using key performance indicators; city undertakes transboundary assessments of ecosystem assets and works with neighboring jurisdictions to manage assets
Strengthen the institutional capacity for resilience	Disaster risk reduction stakeholders have memoranda of understanding with relevant NGOs; there are systematic hazard-related public information campaigns using multiple media platforms
Understand and strengthen societal capacity for resilience	In every neighborhood, organizations exist that address the full spectrum of resilience issues; all vulnerable groups confirm that they are regularly engaged in disaster resilience issues
Increase infrastructure resilience	Protective infrastructure is in place to deal with "most severe" disaster scenario with minimal social and economic impacts; no loss of electrical power, even in "most severe" scenarios
Ensure effective disaster response	Comprehensive plans exist in relation to scenarios, and they have been tested in actual emergencies; equipment and relief supplies are defined in relation to scenarios and take into account the use of volunteers
Expedite recovery and "build back better"	Comprehensive plans exist for economic, infrastructure, and community recovery under "most probable" and "most severe" disaster scenarios; stakeholders are involved in "build back better" planning

SOURCE: Compiled from data in United Nations International Strategy for Disaster Reduction (2017).

Community Disaster Resilience, material on conceptualization and measurement provided by the Community and Regional Resilience Institute (www.resilien-tus.org), and draft community resilience indicators developed by the Mitigation Framework Leadership Group (Federal Emergency Management Agency 2017).

Organizational-Level Measurement of Resilience

The literature on organizational resilience mainly focuses on business enter-prises, as opposed to other types of organizations. Many lessons regarding organizational resilience are based on case studies of businesses that have coped and adapted in the face of extreme events (see for example Sheffi 2005, 2017). In contrast with the case study approach, other researchers have developed resilience metrics similar to those discussed above with respect to communities, and these make it possible to assess the resilience of organizations. Other insights on what makes organizations resilient come from post-disaster surveys involving large numbers of businesses. Additional insights on organizational resilience come from research carried out by economists and from bodies that produce standards and engage in resilience assessment.

Resilience measurement for organizations

Resilient Organisations, a research and consulting enterprise based in Christchurch, New Zealand, has developed and implemented a web-based survey questionnaire that enables organizations of all types to measure their resilience (Stephenson, Vargo, and Seville 2010; Lee, Vargo, and Seville 2013). In developing survey items, the Resilient Organisations team drew on several lines of research: studies on organizations that use risky technologies that exhibit nearly error-free performance, research on organizational failures, and inductive research on New Zealand organizations that experienced crises. The survey tool focuses on four main areas: the organization's resilience ethos; sit-uation awareness; management of what is termed "keystone vulnerabilities," or parts of an organization's system that could cripple the whole organization if they failed; and adaptive capacity. The team developed multiple indicators in each of these areas, in the form of statements with which those taking the survey could agree or disagree on a Likert scale. The sum of these items is an overall resilience score. Table 7.2 lists some of these statements, as outlined in one of the group's research papers (Lee et al. 2013).

On the basis of an extensive review of the literature on organizational per-formance in crises, Somers (2009) developed a tool called the Organizational Resilience Potential Scale (ORPS), which was designed to measure what he terms "latent resilience"; and he tested the tool using a survey with a

Table 7.2 Resilience measures developed by Resilient Organisations.

Resilience Component	Examples of Survey Items
Resilience ethos	Our organization has a culture where it is important to make sure that we learn from our mistakes and problems.
	Our organization is able to collaborate with others in our industry to manage unexpected challenges.
Situation awareness	Our organization has clearly defined priorities for what is important during and after a crisis.
	Our organization is able to shift rapidly from business as usual mode to respond to crises.
Management of keystone vulnerabilities	I believe our organization invests sufficient resources in being ready to respond to an emergency of any kind.
	Our organization understands that having a plan for emergencies is not enough and that the plan must be practiced and tested in order to be effective.
Adaptive capacity	People in our organization are known for their ability to use their knowledge in novel ways.
	There is an excellent sense of teamwork and camaraderie in our organization.

SOURCE: Compiled from data in Lee, Vargo, and Seville (2013).

sample of municipal public works managers. Managers were asked to rate their departments on the following factors: goal-directed solution seeking; risk avoidance; critical situational understanding; ability of team members to fill multiple roles; reliance on information sources; and access to resources. Information was gathered on six additional measures: managers' risk perceptions; decentralization of decision making, which is believed to be related to an organization's capacity to respond in crises; extent of continuity of operations planning; managerial information seeking; whether the department had outside accreditation; and the department's involvement in community planning.

Extrapolating from post-disaster business studies

Although not carried out under the rubric of resilience or specifically for measurement purposes, much of my past work has focused on challenges that businesses experience in disasters and on factors that are predictive of positive short-term and long-term business recovery outcomes (see Dahlhamer and Tierney 1998; Webb, Tierney, and Dahlhamer 2000, 2002; Tierney 2007). Those studies had the advantage of employing stratified random sampling methods, as opposed to the methods used in case study approaches, and this made it possible to generalize findings across larger populations of businesses. That body of research led to insights into the pre-disaster characteristics and post-disaster experiences of businesses that tended to fare better than others in the aftermath of disasters—which is one way of thinking about business resilience. One weakness of my research on businesses and disasters was that the samples were limited to businesses that had survived disasters. Other research that also used stratified random sampling methods focused on both surviving businesses and businesses that collapsed after a disaster—in this case, Hurricane Katrina (Marshall, Niehm, Sydnor, and Schrank 2015; Sydnor et al. 2017). Researchers have also employed qualitative methods to delve more deeply into factors that are associated with positive post-disaster outcomes (Alesch, Holly, Mittler, and Nagy 2001); or they have used a combination of quantitative and qualitative approaches (Hall, Malinen, Vosslamber, and Wordsworth 2016). Findings across studies are not entirely consistent, but they do help identify what makes businesses vulnerable to poor recovery outcomes following disasters and to suggest business resilience factors.

Generalizing from these and other, similar studies, we can hypothesize that business disaster resilience is linked to four sets of factors: business characteristics, owner characteristics, disaster impacts, and exogenous economic conditions. Regarding business characteristics, in line with sociological research on organizations, being a large business in terms of number of employees and revenues appears to make those businesses more resilient than small ones. Business type is also important; businesses in economic sectors that are highly regulated, such as financial institutions, are generally more resilient because they are required to be, while businesses in highly competitive sectors where there are higher rates of failure during non-disaster times, for instance in the retail and service sectors, are likely to be more at risk for failure or poor recovery outcomes. Businesses that are involved in post-disaster repair and reconstruction, such as construction companies and hardware stores, may fare better after disasters, with the caveat that those gains are, typically, temporary. Being located in a structure that is owned rather than rented appears to add to resilience. Older businesses, as opposed to recently established ones, appear to be better able to weather stressors brought on by disasters. There is also some evidence that partnerships and other ownership forms, as opposed to sole proprietorships, are more resilient. Businesses that were faring well financially before disaster struck also appear to register more positive outcomes. Finally, there is some evidence that businesses that serve a wide market outside the disaster impact area—for example, by having an Internet sales component or by placing their goods in stores in multiple locations—may have fewer difficulties than businesses with a local focus only, because disasters can create problems with access to businesses or can alter customer behavior.

With respect to business owner characteristics, being male and not being a member of a minority group appear to be associated with greater resilience. Women- and minority-owned businesses tend to have fewer economic resources, which makes them more vulnerable to experiencing difficulties in the aftermath of disasters. The educational attainment level of the business owner is another resilience factor, indicating that an owner's social capital plays a role in business resilience. Resilience is higher when owners have more industry experience and more disaster experience, and there is also an indication that an owner's flexibility, capacity for innovation, and entrepreneurial spirit matter for business recovery.

Disaster impacts are also important for understanding business resilience. Other things being equal, businesses are less likely to be able to cope when disaster damage to structures, inventories, and equipment is very severe and when disruptions of infrastructure services such as electrical power and communications are prolonged—both of which can lead to business closure for longer periods. When a business is located in an area that has been highly damaged—even if the business itself has not—it could face significant recovery challenges. Additionally, where there has been residential damage and dislocation, a business may be in danger of losing its customer base, and this could be especially problematic for businesses that earn their income locally.

Finally, like all businesses, those that have experienced disasters are affected by the overall economic climate and trends within their specific sectors. Generally speaking, resilience levels should be higher in good economic times than in poor ones. Positive economic conditions should favor business recovery, while recessions and periods of high unemployment (and hence less discretionary income for households) should have adverse effects. Disasters typically bring additional funds into affected regions via disaster assistance and insurance payouts, but such funds do not benefit all businesses equally.

Insights from economics

Although economists who do research on disasters tend to focus on disaster effects at the national and regional level, some economists also collect and analyze data on individual businesses. Adam Rose is an economist who has done research on economic impacts and resilience at all three levels. Rose defines and measures business resilience in ways that differ to some degree from previous discussions. He defines *static economic resilience* as the ability of a system—in this case, a business—to maintain functionality when it experiences an external shock such as a disaster. By contrast, *dynamic economic resilience* consists of actions taken to recover from a disaster or some other shock (Rose 2007). Rose also makes a distinction between *inherent* and *adaptive* resilience. Inherent resilience already exists in pre-disaster times; examples include large business inventories and other resources, or arrangements that have been made to ensure that a business can receive the supplies and components it needs even when a disaster occurs. Adaptive resilience consists of strategies that ensure continuity of business operations and recovery after disasters, for instance the ability to continue to operate on generators if the electrical power supply fails, or to relocate the business if needed. Also included in this category is the ability of a business to understand how the disaster has affected the demand for its goods and services, either positively or negatively, and to respond accordingly. Framed in this way, resilience results from a combination of pre-disaster organizational strengths and post-disaster ingenuity (Rose and Krausmann 2013).

Rose's approach to quantitatively assessing business resilience is relatively straightforward and intuitive: as a first step, think of the maximum disruption a business or some other economic unit could experience as the result of a disaster in the form of economic losses, then calculate what percentage of those losses was avoided. That percentage is a measure of resilience. Put another way, resilience is the ratio of losses avoided to potential maximum losses. Rose and his colleagues (Rose, Oladosu, Lee, Asay 2009) demonstrated this resilience metric using the example of businesses affected by the 2001 World Trade Center terrorist attack. Their focal concern was the firms' resilience in the face of business interruption. They obtained a dataset on the 1,134 firms that were forced to relocate after the attack because they had been doing business in the two collapsed Trade Center towers or the immediate vicinity. Between them, these firms employed over 100,000 people. An estimate of the losses that would result if all those businesses ceased to operate (i.e. on an indicator of zero resilience) provided the upper bound of how serious the economic impacts could be. Conversely, estimating losses if all businesses relocated immediately, never experiencing any interruption, provided the lower bound (i.e. an indicator of full resilience). Using data on actual business interruption losses, the researchers determined that 72 percent of potential losses (the upper bound) had in fact been avoided. In their terms, then, the resilience factor for businesses was 72 percent.

Rose's reasoning provides a means of looking at organizational resilience beyond the private sector, with some modifications. For example, without being too simplistic, we can think of the resilience of a hospital, a utility service provider, or a government agency as consisting of the services it is able to provide after a disaster measured against a hypothetical situation in which it is able to provide no services at all. Organizations could then be scored on the basis of their post-disaster performance. A hospital that experiences no decline in its ability to provide services would receive a resilience score of 100 percent, because it managed to avoid all potential disruptions. A utility company that experiences no loss of service provision to any of its customers after disaster would be rated highest on resilience, while companies that experience varying degrees of service disruption to all or to some customers would be scored lower, and so on.

Normative approaches to organizational resilience measurement

In contrast with the empirical approaches to resilience described above, normatively based strategies for assessing organizational resilience take into account how an organization measures up to consensus-based standards for organizational preparedness and crisis response or to other types of standards. Standards developed by the International Organization for Standardization, known as ISO, are widely accepted and used worldwide. A recent standard, ISO 22316: 2017, focuses specifically on organizational resilience. That standard sets out activities that indicate compliance within nine areas of organizational performance:

- shared vision and clarity of purpose,
- an understanding of the context in which the organization operates,
- effective and empowered leadership,
- a supportive organizational culture,
- shared information and knowledge,
- adequate resources,
- development and coordination of management disciplines,
- support for continual improvement,
- the ability to anticipate and manage change.

ISO has also produced a suite of detailed standards associated with risk assessment, risk management, and ensuring the continuity of business operations in the event of disruption that may arise from various sources, such as disasters and terrorist attacks. Compliance with such standards could be taken as indicative of organizational resilience.

The Insurance Institute for Business and Home Safety (IBHS), which receives funding from the insurance industry and other sources, has developed a toolkit called Open for Business (OFB) that consists of guidance aimed at ensuring business continuity after disasters, with a special emphasis on small businesses. IBHS makes this toolkit, called Open for Business EZ (OFB-EZ), available online at no cost and also provides an app that businesses can use to guide their own business continuity planning processes. OFB-EZ recommends best practices in many different areas, including risk assessment and prioritization, operations, finances, human resources, and information technology. Although not framed as a resilience assessment method, OFB-EZ could potentially be converted to one: businesses that have followed all recommendations contained in the toolkit could be given a high resilience score.

Measuring Household Resilience

By comparison with what is available for community-level measures, there are relatively few checklists or toolkits for measuring household resilience to disasters. I begin this section by discussing findings from the disaster research literature that indicate the types of factors likely to be associated with household resilience. I then move on to provide a brief overview of the extensive literature on family psychosocial resilience as it relates to disaster resilience. Finally, I consider some measures that are commonly used to assess household resilience in less developed countries.

Long before the concept of disaster resilience came to the fore, researchers conducted extensive studies on household hazard mitigation and preparedness for a wide range of disasters, as well as for terrorism (for summaries of earlier research, see Drabek 1986 and Tierney et al. 2001; see also Lindell and Perry 2000; Bourque, Mileti, Kano, and Wood 2012). Although it is difficult to generalize because study results are not entirely consistent, we can tentatively identify household characteristics that may be associated with resilience potential, just as we did with businesses. Some studies suggest that minority households are less likely than whites households to adopt mitigation and preparedness measures, and that home ownership and higher levels of income and education are associated with carrying out such measures. Households that actively seek out information about hazards are more likely to prepare, as are households that have previously experienced disasters. Perceived risk tends to be associated with the adoption of protective and preparedness measures, but generally exerts its influence in combination with other factors. Findings such as these need to be put into context: levels of household preparation for disasters are low, even in high-risk areas. Taking into account the many forms of disaster vulnerability that were discussed in the previous chapter, it is not difficult to see why many households would have difficulty coping with a disaster.

The topic of family resilience has been prominent in the psychological sciences for decades, and there are literally hundreds of models that seek to identify family resilience factors, both during normal periods and in the face of stressors (for examples, see Black and Lobo 2008; Becvar 2013; Masten and Monn 2015; Walsh 2016).[1] The vast majority of this work has focused on the psychological well-being of family members, factors associated with psychological vulnerability, and protective factors that help family members avoid negative psychological and social outcomes such as anxiety, depression, and substance abuse. This literature focuses on stressful circumstances of all types, examples of which include illness and bereavement, crime and community violence, wars and civil wars, terrorism, and in some cases disasters. On the basis of the finds presented in this literature, Vogel and the Family Systems

Collaborative Group (2017; see also Vogel and Pfefferbaum 2016) identify four sets of factors that they consider to be associated with family resilience. First, family members should possess a set of beliefs and attitudes that include seeing crises as shared challenges for the family, accepting that distress is to be expected under stressful conditions, having hope, but of the realistic sort, avoiding feelings of blame or guilt, being in touch with religious and other pro-social belief systems, and viewing adversity as a meaningful and even positive experience. Second, under stress, households that are resilient stick to their daily routines and rituals as much as possible, and adapt in situations where that is too difficult. This covers maintaining family roles, for example by ensuring that parents retain their authority. A third set of resilience factors involves communication. In resilient households, family members communicate, but in appropriate ways. For example, adults avoid giving young children more information about a disaster or a stressful situation than they can handle at their developmental level. Household members allow for the expression of a range of emotions, including negative ones, but are also able to find joy under difficult circumstances. Finally, resilient families employ a range of coping and problem-solving skills.

The Social Policy and Evaluation Research Unit (Superu) in New Zealand identifies a range of protective factors that are associated with family resilience. These include family-level factors such as good communication, a secure household income, and effective decision-making processes; family-member factors such as having positive coping skills, behavioral control, and an optimistic outlook; and community connectedness, expressed for instance in having a sense of belonging, creating opportunities for community involvement, and being part of a cohesive community. Also important is the broader community and societal context; for households to thrive, there should be policies that support families, other societal norms that promote household well-being, and a sense of cultural identity and pride (Superu 2015). This framework takes into account not only family characteristics but also the kinds of social capital attributes that were discussed earlier in connection with resilience.

Under the auspices of the United Nations Development Program, Winderl (2014) compiled and conducted a review of a number of measurement approaches and tools at different levels of analysis, the majority of which were formulated for use in less developed countries. The only household-level measurement framework he reviewed, the United Nations Food and Agricultural Organization (FAO) Resilience Index, focuses primarily on food security. The main components of that model are income and food access; access to basic services, such as health services; the existence of social safety nets; household assets; household adaptive capacity, which is reflected in factors such as the diversity of income sources; and household stability in terms of employment, income fluctuations, and the like. The FAO framework or some version of it has been used in other resilience assessments.

There are a number of other measurement frameworks that are used in assessing household resilience in the developing world. The Secure Livelihoods Research Consortium (SLRC) is an alliance composed of researchers from eight institutions in North America, Europe, Asia, and Africa and from the United Nations Food and Agricultural Organization, whose work focuses on household livelihoods and well-being, with an emphasis on household resilience in the face of conflict. The SLRC conducted longitudinal research with households in the Democratic Republic of Congo, Nepal, Pakistan, Sri Lanka, and Uganda. Its measurement tool focuses on three main areas: livelihoods, which consists of food security, income sources, and assets; access to and experience with services, including health and education services and water access; and relationships with governance processes, including civic participation. Through its project Building Resilience and Adaptation to Climate Extremes and Disasters (BRACED), the Overseas Development Institute in the United Kingdom has also developed a suite of instruments for assessing household resilience.

Programs for Enhancing Resilience

Recent years have seen the development of a number of programs aimed at improving resilience. In this section I focus on four such efforts: a program sponsored by the Rockefeller Foundation; resilience planning sponsored by the National Institute of Standards and Technology; activities carried out by ISET-International; and resilience measurement and enhancement efforts at the National Academies of Sciences, Engineering, and Medicine.

As its name indicates, the Rockefeller Foundation's program 100 Resilient Cities (100RC) focuses on urban resilience. This initiative began in 2014. Funding is currently provided to large and small cities on every continent except Antarctica. The program frames resilience as the capacity to respond to two types of problems or stressors that cities face. Chronic stressors, which are ongoing for cities, include problems such as high unemployment, food and water shortages, and climatic change. Acute stressors include natural disasters, disease outbreaks, and terrorist attacks. Each city is required to develop a resilience strategy aimed at reducing the impacts of both types of stressors. One of the key elements of 100RC is the funding of chief resilience officers (CROs) in participating cities. The CRO, who typically reports directly to the city's mayor, is responsible for developing a resilience vision and for bringing together city departments and authorities so that they can coordinate their resilience-related activities. Rather than working in isolation, CROs participate in a global CRO network that enables them to share information on resilience plans and activities. Another key element involves participation by dozens of "platform partners" that can assist cities in developing and implementing their resilience strategies. Partners include technology companies, consulting firms, environmental NGOs, insurance and financial entities, risk-modeling firms, and professional associations. In collaboration with Arup, a London-based consulting firm, Rockefeller developed the Community Resilience Framework, an assessment tool centered on four key elements of urban resilience: leadership and strategy; infrastructure and environment; economy and society, or social and financial systems that contribute to resilience; and health and well-being. Along with other organizations, Rockefeller is also a member of the Global Resilience Partnership (GRP), which seeks to identify innovative resilience-building programs with a focus on highly vulnerable communities in Africa and Asia.

The National Institute of Standards and Technology (NIST) developed the *Community Resilience Planning Guide* to assist communities in assessing and improving their resilience in the face of hazards. The *Guide*, which was released in 2015, provides direction on a six-step planning process that contains the following elements (National Institute of Standards and Technology 2015a, 2015b):

- forming a collaborative planning team,
- understanding the community's social and built environment and their linkages,
- determining community goals and objectives,
- developing a resilience plan and implementation strategy,
- preparing and reviewing the plan and obtaining approval from authorities,
- implementing, evaluating, and updating the plan.

Accompanying the planning guide is a series of planning briefs that instruct communities on how to address various elements in the planning process, for instance how they can characterize their populations and social institutions, set resilience goals, and identify and prioritize resilience shortfalls. NIST also provides funding for the Center for Risk-Based Community Resilience Planning, which is a multidisciplinary consortium of researchers from twelve universities led by Colorado State University.

The Institute for Social and Environmental Transition-International (ISET) is an NGO made up of researchers and practitioners whose activities focus primarily on urban vulnerability reduction and resilience enhancement and emphasize coping and adaptation in the face of climate change and associated extreme events. Although ISET works in developed countries, much of its activity is dedicated to improving the resilience of cities in less developed countries, particularly those in South and East Asia. ISET's programs are typically undertaken in collaboration with partners that specialize in relevant areas of expertise and with local partners, the emphasis being on shared learning. Through its work as part of the Asian Climate Change Resilience Network, ISET developed the Urban Climate Resilience Planning Framework

(UCRPF) (Moench, Tyler, and Lage 2011), which emphasizes understanding vulnerabilities and improving resilience in the following areas:

- URBAN SYSTEMS: ecological systems, critical infrastructure systems (water, power, etc.), food, shelter, energy;
- AGENTS: actors in local communities, including households and governmental and private sector organizations; focus on empowering agents, in particular those that are marginalized;
- INSTITUTIONS: norms, laws, and practices in areas such as land tenure, markets, and rights possessed by different stakeholders (agents), and decision-making processes; and
- EXPOSURE: the direct and indirect effects of climate change on urban systems and agents.

ISET has produced dozens of reports and guidance documents designed to help local actors understand climate change and change-related risks and to devise coping and adaptation strategies. The organization also provides training materials that lead local actors through a planning process that involves establishing basic resilience principles and understanding the UCRPF model; understanding local vulnerabilities and risks through research and stakeholder engagement; and building a resilience action plan.

The National Academies of Sciences, Engineering, and Medicine (the Academies), nonprofit institutions that provide analysis and advice on issues of societal significance in the United States, are also extensively involved in efforts to conceptualize, measure, and improve resilience. Within the Academies, there are a number of groups whose activities focus on building resilience for disasters, disease outbreaks, security threats such as terrorism, and critical infrastructure risks. Academies publications include *Building Community Disaster Resilience through Private–Public Collaboration* (National Research Council 2011) and *Disaster Resilience: A National Imperative* (National Research Council 2012). The Academies Resilient America Roundtable (RAR), which brings together experts from academia, government, and the private sector, has established pilot projects with local partners and stakeholders in four cities: Cedar Rapids Iowa, Charleston South Carolina, Seattle Washington, and Tulsa Oklahoma. Another aspect of RAR is concern with resilience measurement.

Resilient Disaster Responses

As noted earlier in discussions on the history of disaster research, the field began with the study of disaster responses, and the focus on that phase of the hazards cycle remains vital. That research tradition gives many insights into conditions associated with resilient responses to disasters. In its National

Response Framework (NRF), the US Department of Homeland Security (2013) calls for responses that are flexible, scalable, and adaptable—and disaster researchers would agree. These three qualities are seen as important for a variety of reasons. Response operations must be flexible enough to cope with emergencies of different types and sizes and should begin at the local community level; higher-level governmental jurisdictions should join when needs that cannot be met or resources that do not exist at the local level have been identified. Disasters are always dynamic; rather than being discrete events, they *unfold* and new problems invariably emerge. For example, earthquakes can cause tsunamis, landslides, hazardous materials releases, and even nuclear plant emergencies and nuclear emissions, as was seen in Japan in 2011. Flooding also spreads hazardous substances and gives rise to health problems such as toxic mold and waterborne bacteria. Response activities must address the complexities of disasters and be adaptable in the face of changing circumstances. As researcher John Harrald (2006) has pointed out, responding to disasters requires discipline; but it also requires agility.

The Department of Homeland Security also emphasizes that the NRF is a document and a set of principles that can be used by the "whole community"; they guide its response, and, specifically, call for participation not only from governmental agencies but also from the private and NGO sector, for instance from groups of NGOs such as the National Voluntary Organizations Active in Disasters (NVOAD), which exist in many communities. The intention here is to move away from a government-centered approach to a broader one, which incorporates capacities outside government. The NRF also stresses that the needs of vulnerable groups such as children, persons with disability, and non-English speakers should be addressed—that is, disaster responses should be inclusive.

The NRF is not without flaws. For example, it specifies that all organizations that become involved in disasters should use the incident command system (ICS), a specific way of organizing response activities that was developed in the 1980s for responding to wildfires and codified into law after the September 11, 2001 terrorist attacks. The ICS identifies five activities as central to disaster responses: command, operations, planning, logistics, and finance. While it is important that responding organizations and groups have a good sense of how they should operate in a disaster, many will not use the ICS as a means of structuring their activities. The ICS may be rejected as incompatible with the cultures of some organizations, such as NGOs. As discussed in more detail in what follows, disasters inevitably involve actors that emerge spontaneously and that were never involved in pre-disaster planning or training. In other words, responding groups and organizations may not even know that ICS exists. Given the nature of disaster responses, it is essentially impossible to require adherence to a single organizational model (for more discussion, see Kendra and Wachtendorf 2016).

Resilient disaster responses are nonhierarchical. Decisions are made at the appropriate level—usually that of the local incident—and by those who are closest to emerging problems. While responses require coordination, they do not require centralized command. The response to the 1995 Kobe earthquake was slower than it needed to be because local authorities were waiting for the prefectural governor to give orders, while the governor, who was initially unreachable, was waiting for orders from the central government in Tokyo, which were slow in coming. The US Coast Guard is frequently lauded for its performance in disasters, and that is largely because that organization empha-sizes a principle of on-scene initiative. Those in charge of vessels do not wait to be told what to do; they take action on the basis of identified needs (Tierney 2014). As disasters unfold, there are always people who lament the fact that it looks as if no one is in charge and who complain about "chaos." Wanting a centralized structure or a "command and control" model of response flies in the face of what decades of disaster research tell us, namely that disasters are complex and multifaceted, requiring diverse sets of expertise, and that hierarchy is the enemy of rapidity and adaptability.

Along these same lines, resilient responses are able to accommodate emergence. As discussed in Chapter 4, emergent groups are always a part of the response landscape. Organizations may expand in size and may take on tasks they normally do not perform, and volunteers may converge. To focus again on lessons from the Kobe earthquake, hundreds of thousands of people offered volunteer services of all kinds to those in the affected region, but local authorities had difficulty working with volunteer groups. Reasons for their exclusion included Japan's state-centered view of society and its general suspicion of voluntary organizations. In the aftermath of the earthquake, 1995 was referred to as "the first year of the volunteer," VOADs were formed, and laws were changed to make it easier for voluntary groups to function (Tierney 2012).

EMONs are also an invariant feature of disaster responses. Organizations typically cluster around problem-solving tasks, many of which are unique to specific disasters. For example, sociologist Christine Bevc (2010) studied the EMON that developed during the emergency period that followed the terrorist attacks on the World Trade Center in 2001. That EMON consisted of at least 700 different public, private sector, and nonprofit organizations as well as of newly emergent entities, all of which were organized around 42 different tasks. Some of those tasks, such as caring for those who were injured, were typical tasks that are performed in disasters, while others, for example investigating the rubble from the towers as a crime scene, were not typical. Some organizational entities rose to prominence unexpectedly by taking on roles that were not specified in disaster plans, because particular activities were necessary. The Trade Center response was typical of what happens in large-scale disasters.

Butts, Acton, and Marcum (2012) studied EMONs that developed during warning and emergency periods in the multistate area that was struck by Hurricane Katrina. They identified 187 distinct networks that clustered around different tasks and changed over time. Regarding how organizations coordinated their activities, they noted that

> coordination roles in the inner core of the Katrina EMON appear to be filled by a combination of organizations with a standing mandate to bridge diverse groups and organizations whose centrality emerges from tasks and resource considerations that are peculiar to the specific event. (Butts et al. 2012: 25)

Disaster planning seeks to identify and address problems that could emerge during disasters, but disasters always contain an element of the unexpected. This is one of the reasons why emergence is so common. A resilient disaster response is flexible enough to incorporate groups that were not identified in prior planning.

As discussed earlier in Chapter 4, scholars have pointed to the role of improvisation in disaster response (Weick 1998; Kendra and Wachtendorf 2003, 2006; Wachtendorf 2004; Mendonça and Wallace 2007). Because disaster impacts cannot be planned for in totality, disasters almost always create problems that were not envisioned in the original plan. Like jazz pianists and improvisational actors, responders must depart from scores and scripts in order to put together an effective performance. Let us return to the World Trade Center attacks. The Mayor's Office of Emergency Management (OEM) in New York was located in one of the buildings of the World Trade Center complex—a building that caught fire and collapsed on the afternoon of September 11. Surprisingly, the OEM did not have a backup site from which to coordinate emergency operations, which forced the organization to improvise an emergency operations center (EOC) in the middle of a major crisis response. After moving to different locations and not having enough room for all the organizations and personnel that were taking part in the response, the OEM reestablished the EOC in one of the massive piers that line the Hudson River on the west side of Manhattan. The pier accommodated both the entities that had been involved in pre-disaster planning and other organizations, which joined the response team for specific purposes, such as producing maps to show damaged areas and assistance sites, since the OEM had lost its map-making capabilities (Wachtendorf 2004).

Approximately 1 million people were in Lower Manhattan at the time of the attacks, and the subways and trains were not operational. Many people walked uptown and over the Brooklyn Bridge to get home, but an estimated 300,000 people were evacuated by water by means of a spontaneous, improvised system that brought together ferries, tugboats, fishing boats, dinner boats, sightseeing vessels, government watercraft, and other types of vessels. Mariners saw the need that day; they understood the waterways around Manhattan like no one else, so they immediately began a process of self-organizing (Kendra and Wachtendorf 2016). Similarly, in the aftermath of Hurricane Katrina, private boat owners spontaneously organized what they called the Cajun Navy and headed to New Orleans to rescue people who had been trapped by the flood-waters. Some of these same boat operators left Louisiana to perform rescues after Hurricane Harvey in 2017.

Improvising response activities does not mean making up those activities out of whole cloth. Just as students of jazz view improvisation as the out-come of mastering many musical forms, students of disaster responses see improvisation as arising from previously acquired knowledge. In New York, members of the OEM staff had a mental picture of how the EOC needed to be organized and what groups needed to participate. At the same time, they were anxious to make room for new players who had resources and skills to offer. Boat operators had a thorough understanding of the waters surrounding Manhattan, but they also found creative ways of identifying who needed to go where and of labeling origins and destinations in ways that evacuees could understand. As these examples show, improvisation involves retaining pre-disaster knowledge when it makes sense to do so while also using ingenuity to tackle unexpected challenges.

Continuing with this theme, those who are involved in responding to dis-asters must know that they can and should improvise and adapt when the situation calls for it. Organizational practices that confine actors to narrow roles and responsibilities and want things done "by the book" discourage improvisation. Organizational scholars point to conditions that increase the likelihood that disasters can be averted and, when they happen, are managed well. Such conditions include extensive experience on the part of organizational actors; diversity in terms of competencies, experiences, and perspectives; and effective communication among actors. Organizational scholars also point to the importance of nonhierarchical relationships within organizations, such that lower-level staffers know that they have permission to speak up when they see anomalies or signs of impending disaster (Weick and Roberts 1993; Weick, Sutcliffe, and Obstfeld 1999; Sutcliffe and Vogus 2003). Resources are also important. Schulman (1993) refers to the importance of "resource slack," that is, personnel, funds, and material resources that exist over and above what an organization needs for its daily operations and can be rapidly accessed should the need arise. If organizations do not possess those resources themselves, they should have easy ways of obtaining them, which is one reason why various types of mutual aid pacts—for example, among police departments, utility companies, and states—are common in emergency management. Similarly, health and public health organizations have devised ways of increasing their surge capacity in disasters and other emergencies, for instance disease outbreaks.

Resilient disaster response involves anticipating disaster impacts on the built environment and exposed populations while also expecting the unexpected. Pre-disaster hazard assessments, impact and loss estimates, scenarios, and policies designed to identify specific vulnerabilities and vulnerable groups help communities understand the likely consequences of different types of disasters. A knowledge-based planning process increases the chances that the community will be able to respond effectively. At the same time, community leaders and those charged with carrying out response activities should take a critical stance and question their assumptions, both about impacts and about their own response capabilities. What if hazard assessments are based on outdated science? What if community vulnerability analyses overlook important population changes? How current (or outdated) are the resource lists kept by emergency management organizations?

Along with the need to base response plans on sound information, outside-the-box thinking is also required. What if some impacts that have been envisioned do not materialize, but other unanticipated impacts occur? Will the response system be flexible enough to deal with those impacts? Do entities that are planning to respond have significant blind spots, and could they benefit from seeking out external and dissenting perspectives? Regarding the earthquake–tsunami–nuclear-plant meltdowns in Japan in 2011, for example, there was evidence that a major earthquake that occurred hundreds of years ago in the same region had generated a gigantic tsunami, but that information was overlooked by emergency planners. Similarly, Tokyo Power Company, which owned and operated the Fukushima nuclear plants, had been informed that the plants could be disabled by a very large tsunami but did not take steps to enact countermeasures. In the absence of these kinds of blind spots, the catastrophic losses that resulted might have been averted.

Relatedly, disaster response organizations should be learning organizations. They should learn from the disasters they experience, from the experiences of other communities, and from drills and exercises. One reason why after-action reports are developed after disasters and exercises is to identify lessons learned. Equally if not more importantly, however, in order to be resilient, response organizations must incorporate those lessons into their procedures and practices. Sadly, organizations and communities have a tendency to content themselves with pointing out lessons learned and areas in need of improvement, without adapting or changing.

Resilient Disaster Recovery

Although progress has been made in the past few years, recovery remains the least studied of the stages of the hazards cycle—a carryover from the days when disaster response was receiving the lion's share of research. Although not enough is known about disaster recovery processes, researchers—particularly those from the urban planning discipline, but also from sociology—are able to point to factors that predict positive recovery outcomes, which is one way of conceptualizing resilience. Earlier discussions of resilience have focused to some extent on recovery, for example by homing in on conditions that appear to be associated with either positive or negative outcomes for households and businesses. Here we focus on factors that influence community disaster recovery.

Disaster recovery is "the differential process of restoring, rebuilding, and reshaping the physical, social, economic, and natural environment through pre-event planning and post-event actions" (Smith and Wenger 2007: 237). Several aspects of this definition are important to note. First, recovery is differential in the sense that different aspects of disaster-stricken communities recover at different rates, as do different social groups. Second, recovery should be thought of as a process or series of processes, not an end point; and, particularly in cases where disaster impacts are severe, such processes can go on for years, or even for decades. Third, recovery is complex, encompassing multiple aspects of community life. Text Box 2 lists just a few dimensions and domains in which recovery processes operate. As the definition above and the items in the list indicate, disaster recovery involves much more than physical reconstruction and includes social, psychological, cultural, and institutional dimensions.

If we focus on this short list of recovery domains, it is evident that many dimensions of recovery are interdependent and that some aspects of recovery assume priority. For example, it will be difficult to restore housing if major utilities such as power and water are unavailable; and it will be difficult to

---

Text Box 2 What Needs to Recover after Disasters? Examples of Disaster Recovery Domains

Temporary and permanent housing	Household quality of life
Infrastructure: utilities, roads, etc.	Physical well-being
Public buildings	Psychological well-being
Commercial and industrial buildings	"Community spirit" and attachment
Businesses and jobs	Distinctive aspects of community culture
Disrupted economies	Environment, ecosystems, natural resources
Key community institutions: schools, hospitals, etc.	Neighborhoods

restore neighborhoods without homes, schools, and businesses. Similarly, lost jobs and economic activity will not be able to recover unless businesses can reopen; businesses also depend on the availability of utilities and buildings from which to operate, and they need transportation systems to be restored, so that they can receive shipments and customers can reach them. Additionally, transportation systems must be functional and ensure that the supplies needed to repair and rebuild public, commercial, and industrial buildings are available. Household quality of life, psychological well-being, community spirit, and cultural recovery all depend, at least to some degree, on the restoration of the built environment and on the recovery of key community institutions. Researchers have begun to explore these interdependencies through modeling and simulation, with an eye on identifying which pre-disaster measures (e.g. utility-system mitigation measures) and post-disaster actions (e.g. rapid debris removal, utility-system restoration) contribute to better, more resilient recovery outcomes (Miles and Chang 2003, 2006, 2011). To ensure resilient recovery, those in charge of the process must understand interdependencies across domains and scales and guide recovery activities accordingly.

Studies of disasters in the United States and around the world have uncovered a variety of factors that encourage resilient disaster recovery. Laurie Johnson and Robert Olshansky (2016) studied recovery processes after major disasters in six different countries: the 1995 Kobe earthquake and 2011 earthquake and tsunami in Japan; the 2001 World Trade Center attacks; the 2001 Gujurat earthquake in India; the 2004 Indian Ocean earthquake and tsunami in Indonesia; Hurricanes Katrina and Rita in the United States (2005); the 2008 Wenchuan earthquake in China; the 2010–2011 Canterbury earthquake sequence in New Zealand; and Hurricane Sandy in the United States (2012). In some of those cases, such as the 2008 earthquake in China and the 2010–2011 earthquakes in New Zealand, recovery plans and policies were directed by the central government. In others, such as the Japan earthquakes, there was strong central government involvement but also ties with other levels of government. In Indonesia and India the recovery planning and management were more decentralized and balanced; there were multiple entities at different levels that coordinated their activities.

Although these disasters took place in markedly different societies with different forms of governance and systems for providing recovery aid, Johnson and Olshansky saw commonalities across the cases they studied that led to recommendations about how to achieve positive disaster recovery outcomes—what I call here resilient recovery. One key recommendation concerned the locus of recovery decision-making and direction. As we saw with disaster response, centrally controlled recovery activities have a downside. In the Wenchuan earthquake, for example, recovery was directed by China's central State Council and aligned with governmental priorities such as urbanizing the countryside and promoting tourism, as opposed to local concerns and preferences. Rebuilding took place rapidly and entire communities were moved and rebuilt, but in most cases recovery activities were carried out without public involvement and relatively little attention was paid to restoring livelihoods and social networks and addressing community needs. Although the political and economic conditions were different, this same pattern was seen in China following the devastating 1976 Tangshan earthquake, which destroyed 95 percent of the buildings in that city of 500,000 and killed approximately 242,000.[2] As in the Wenchuan case, the central government developed a recovery process for Tangshan that was consistent with its own goals, the emphasis was on physical reconstruction, and public participation was lacking (Zhang, Zhang, Drake, and Olshansky 2014).

Less centralized processes may be more difficult to manage and recovery may take longer, as more actors are involved and there is broader community participation, but the outcomes are likely to be more satisfactory. In addition to recommending that it is important to decentralize recovery decision-making and management to the greatest extent possible, build capacity, and empower the residents of disaster-stricken communities, Johnson and Olshansky (2016) offer the following recommendations:

- obtain and distribute recovery funding efficiently, effectively, and equitably;
- collect and disseminate information to all parties in the recovery process, for example by employing newsletters, websites, paid liaisons, and entities that bring together key personnel from lead agencies and the public;
- support collaboration, both horizontally (across similar types of organizations and at the same level of governance) and vertically (across scales and levels of governance);
- meet immediate, urgent needs in disaster-affected areas while thinking ahead to plan for longer-term community improvements;
- plan and act simultaneously; take actions that are feasible right away while still paying attention to situations that need longer-term deliberation;
- budget for the costs of communication and planning, revise budgets over time, and plan for contingencies in case things go wrong with some aspects of recovery;
- avoid the permanent relocation of residents and affected communities, except when it is clearly necessary, and then take steps to ensure full participation on the part of residents;
- reconstruct quickly, but do not rush; do not sacrifice speed to other important elements of recovery, such as community participation.

Sociologist Brenda Phillips has studied post-disaster recovery extensively. She argues that six principles characterize positive and sustainable disaster recovery: (1) an inclusive, participatory recovery planning and implementation process; (2) a focus on community quality of life; (3) a commitment to economic vitality and diversity; (4) a concern with social and intergenerational equity; (5) a focus on preserving and improving the natural environment and ecosystems; and (6) activities aimed at reducing the impacts of future disasters (Phillips 2009). Other scholars also offer guidance on how to accomplish holistic and sustainable community recovery. Mileti (1999) and Smith and Wenger (2007) point to five conditions that make for better recovery outcomes. Community involvement is essential. Recovery policies should be based on as much relevant information as communities can gather, including details on the population and built environment, the local economy, and available sources of recovery funds. Recovery requires an organizational structure that comprises not only government agencies but also other community organizations, including emergent ones. Attention should be paid to modifying policies in light of the community's disaster experience, for example by changing land use patterns or by upgrading building codes to reduce future losses. There should also be an emphasis on identifying diverse ways of financing recovery.

Coordination among actors around providing assistance is essential for a resilient disaster recovery, but it is often difficult to achieve coordination. This is particularly true in less developed societies, which must rely on outside entities and international NGOs (INGOs) for recovery assistance. Disasters in less developed countries often spur into action various freelancers and organizations that want to demonstrate the efficacy of their particular disaster recovery solutions, with little interorganizational coordination. The 2010 Haiti earthquake is a case in point. Haiti was known as a "republic of NGOs" on account of the extensive involvement of nonprofits in virtually all aspects of community life and the weakness of state institutions. After the earthquake, many of those NGOs sprang into action and were joined by newcomers to Haiti who wanted to assist in any way they could, as well as by for-profit entities that provided assistance. At the same time, many government ministries had been destroyed in the earthquake and many officials were killed, which further eroded government capacity. That scarcely mattered, because NGOs were accustomed to bypassing the state, which they continued to do after the earthquake. The United Nations, which had a large presence in Haiti, was attempting to coordinate INGOs by clustering them together around key recovery tasks such as housing, but those efforts were largely ineffective in Haiti. NGO leaders rotated out of Haiti and were replaced so often that there was little continuity of effort. Decisions were made without input from the residents of the affected areas and, rather than coordinating, officials from different hard-hit jurisdictions competed for aid. The result was a disorganized relief and recovery effort fraught with duplication, service gaps, and ill-informed decision-making—for example, locating temporary housing in areas prone to flooding (Ritchie and Tierney 2011; Katz 2013). United Nations troops that were sent to Haiti from Nepal after the earthquake caused a cholera epidemic that killed thousands. Five years after the earthquake, the National

Public Radio and the investigative journalism group ProPublica documented massive waste and lack of transparency by the Red Cross in Haiti (Elliott and Sullivan 2015). More recently, it was revealed that aid workers from Oxfam International, an INGO, held sex parties with earthquake victims and paid to have sex with residents who were forced into prostitution to make a living.

Social capital and disaster recovery

Political scientist Daniel Aldrich has explored the relationship between social capital and recovery in a range of disaster situations. In *Building Resilience: Social Capital in Post-Disaster Recovery* (Aldrich 2012a), he analyzed the role of social capital in facilitating community recovery in three major disasters: the 1923 Great Kanto (Tokyo) earthquake, the 1995 Great Hanshin-Awaji (Kobe) earthquake, and the 2004 Indian Ocean tsunami. In all three cases, he found that social capital, variously measured as voter turnout, political activism, civic and social movement participation, and "linking" connections to higher governmental levels, was a predictor of recovery outcomes such as a more rapid repopulation of damaged areas. With respect to the Kobe earthquake, Aldrich (2010) also noted that weak or absent social capital ties proved harmful. After that disaster, elderly survivors were randomly assigned to apartments in large complexes, but no consideration was given to keeping their pre-disaster social networks intact. With little opportunity to socialize, receive social support, or have someone to look after them on a regular basis, many of these elders died alone, and suicide was suspected in some of those cases. After the earthquake, the Japanese word *kodokushi*, "lonely death," began to be used to describe these situations (see also Otani 2010).

Aldrich later turned his attention to studying recovery after the 2011 Japan earthquake and tsunami. Among other topics, he focused on the role of community elders and of the concept of *ibasho* in the recovery process. The term *ibasho* designates a place where people come together to interact informally and where they feel at home. In one of the worst affected communities, an NGO called Ibasho established the Ibasho Café as an informal community space, with the intention of building social capital and empowering elderly residents. In its first year, the café served more than 5,000 people and hosted more than fifty community-oriented events. In their research, Aldrich and his collaborators found that, for those who took part in its activities, the café encouraged the formation of social networks and restored a sense of belonging. Elders developed a sense of solidarity, as well as confidence in the progress they were making toward recovery. Moreover, through their participation in café events and activities, elderly disaster survivors found a renewed sense of purpose:

> By demonstrating the knowledge, skills and experience they have to offer [elders] have proven that they are not just a vulnerable population who

needs to be looked after and protected. Rethinking their roles in the community made many elders realize that they still want to be active participants in the community life. (Kiyota, Tanaka, Arnold, and Aldrich 2015: 32)

The Ibasho Café experience illustrates a point made earlier, in Chapter 6: groups that are considered vulnerable by virtue of their social characteristics may still fare well after disasters if they are also resilient.

Researchers affiliated with the Mercatus Center at George Mason University conducted a series of studies and have published extensively on post-Katrina recovery (Chamlee-Wright 2010; Chamlee-Wright and Storr 2009, 2010, 2011). Their research provides a number of examples of how social, cultural, and religious ties influenced rates of return and recovery in the aftermath of Katrina. On the basis of their studies, they argue that financial assistance alone, even if substantial, does little good without the participation of civil society institutions in the recovery process. They also argue that local, bottom-up, non-bureaucratized recovery activities are more likely to be successful than top-down programs, because the former are more closely aligned with the needs and values of those affected by disasters. Like other researchers (Aldrich 2010), the Mercatus Center group argues that, when governmental entities become involved in disaster recovery, they should do so in ways that restore and support social capital ties.

More rapid or, better, more sustainable recovery?

For many years, recovery processes were seen in a positive light if they resulted in a smooth and timely return to the *status quo ante*. Early discussions of the concept of resilience (e.g., Bruneau et al. 2003) also emphasized rapidity as a key dimension of resilience. It is now recognized that, while speed is important in some respects—for example, in getting victims the medical treatment they need and in restoring or replacing critical services such as the provision of water and other lifeline services—it is not necessarily associated with more resilient recovery outcomes. Acting in haste, communities may close off more desirable future options: for example, after a flood they may permit reconstruction in known flood-prone areas when they really should be taking other steps, such as buying out flood-prone properties or revising their land use plans. Community residents and business owners understandably want recovery to take place as swiftly as possible so they can get back to their lives, but there are many aspects of community recovery that require study and deliberation.

The recovery period is a time when communities have an opportunity to take steps that make them more resilient to future disasters and more sustainable overall. The tiny rural town of Greensburg, Kansas is one example. Greensburg experienced a devastating tornado in May, 2007 that almost wiped the town off the map. Facing such ruin, the community developed a long-term recovery plan aimed at making Greensburg a "green community." Recovery policies specified that all public buildings over 4,000 square feet would have to be rebuilt to meet the highest standards established by the US Green Building Council, known as LEED-Platinum, and that they had to use renewable energy sources. Greensburg was successful in carrying out that vision. The idea spread to the private sector, with the result that Greensburg now has what may be the world's only LEED-Platinum tractor dealership. In keeping with the town's vision, the owners of that business went on to set up a wind-energy company. Greensburg attracted attention from around the world for its sustainable recovery practices and became the subject of documentaries, including one narrated by Leonardo di Caprio, as well as books such as *The Greening of Oz: Sustainable Recovery in the Wake of a Tornado* (Fraga 2012). The town is unlikely to experience a direct hit from a tornado in the future (although that cannot be ruled out), but it did seize recovery-period opportunities to build a more sustainable future. Tulsa, Oklahoma is another example of a community that steadily improved its disaster resilience over time as a result of a series of deadly and damaging floods. (See Text Box 3 for details of Tulsa's story.)

Critiques of the resilience concept

The concept of resilience is not without its critics. One problem with the term is that it is so widely used, by so many different constituencies, that its meaning has become increasingly vague. Diverse actors infuse the concept with diverse meanings, with little clarity or consensus on what actually constitutes resilience. In many quarters it has supplanted old disaster terminology that refers to mitigation, preparedness, response, and recovery, subsuming those concepts, which have more concrete meanings, under the "resilience" rubric.

Critics also focus on what they see as the ideological aspects of the concept, noting how it consistently meshes with neoliberal constructions of the state and of social life (for discussions of neoliberalism, see Peck and Tickell 2002; Peck 2010). Neoliberalization, the reigning ideological and practical framing of state–society relations, envisions a diminished role for the state while privileging private sector and civil society solutions for societal challenges. Among other things, the process of neoliberalization presupposes devolution to the private sector of activities formerly performed by the public sector, for instance the delivery of services by private contractors and public–private partnerships as a means of addressing societal problems.

Neoliberalization typically brings about a rollback of state services and the requirement that recipients of assistance meet conditions set out by service providers—for example, by making work a requirement for government aid even if recipients are unable to work. It pressures individuals to

Text Box 3 Building Resilience into Recovery and Beyond: The Case of Tulsa, Oklahoma

Located on the Arkansas River and within the Mingo Creek watershed, Tulsa, Oklahoma has a long history of flood disasters: there were major floods in 1923, 1970, 1974, and 1976, as well as an especially deadly and damaging flood in 1984. Over all that period the city's flood losses increased steadily, in part because the city had relied on levees and dams for flood protection and had allowed intensive development in the floodplain.

In response to repeated floods and other disasters (at one point, Tulsa led the nation in the number of federal disaster declarations), Tulsa devised a range of strategies meant to reduce flood losses. After the flooding in 1974, the city designed and initiated the Mingo Creek Improvement project, which protected approximately 700 homes from future flooding. Following another damaging flood in 1976, the city received federal funds to begin acquiring land in the floodplain. The city also passed a moratorium on building in the floodplain, developed comprehensive floodplain and storm water management programs, and established a flood early alert and warning system. After the 1984 flood, which left fourteen people dead, the city relocated 300 homes and a mobile home park, began a detainment basin project with the Army Corps of Engineers, established a city department of stormwater management, and initiated a stormwater utility fee. Over time, the city acquired 1,000 flood-prone properties, made decisions designed to preserve one quarter of the floodplain as open space, and adopted strict flood-resistant building codes.

Owing to its flood management initiatives, Tulsa received special recognition from the FEMA in 2000 and from the Department of Homeland Security in 2003 for its floodplain management efforts. The city currently receives a rating of 2 on the Community Rating Scale (the second-highest rating) for flood risk reduction, and as a result the flood insurance rates for Tulsa residents are significantly lower than those in other flood-prone communities around the country.

Tulsa is also a national leader in preparedness programs for floods, tornadoes, and other disasters. The city received funding during the 1990s under FEMA's short-lived Project Impact program, which provided support for loss reduction-planning projects, community education, and the development of public–private disaster preparedness partnerships. When that program ended, Tulsa developed a spin-off organization called Tulsa Partners, which continued that work and was especially successful in public–private partnership building. One notable public education project involved a 2003 partnership to distribute disaster preparedness materials in thirty-two McDonald's restaurants in Tulsa. The city also became active in Citizens Corps, a Department of

Homeland Security program that was designed to engage community volunteers in disaster preparedness and response activities. In 2006, Tulsa Partners
joined with the insurance industry-supported Institute of Business and Home
Safety in order to establish a Disaster Resistant Business Council. Another collaboration with the nonprofit organization Save the Children focused on disaster preparedness for day-care centers.

Recent activities and efforts in Tulsa have extended beyond preparedness
for extreme events. For example, in collaboration with the Tulsa Zoo, Tulsa
Partners launched the Millenium Center for Green and Safe Living. The
center, located at the zoo, provides environmental education programs for
the public as well as information on both disaster-resistant and sustainable
building materials and construction practices. The city also participates in the
Mayors' Climate Protection Agreement, a project of the US Conference of
Mayors.

Decisions regarding floodplain management and other disaster loss reduction programs came about in a variety of ways. Repeated flooding made
flood hazards difficult to ignore and led to the formation of citizen groups
that pressured the local government to act. Although community pressure
was initially ignored, flooding in 1976 and the subsequent involvement of
a member of Congress helped gain additional support. The Army Corps of
Engineers was a source of needed technical information, and the passage
of the Water Resources Development Act, which was championed by the
same Congress member, also provided a stimulus for further action. The
1984 floods occurred only nineteen days after the election of a new mayor,
who subsequently organized a flood hazard mitigation team for the city.
The mayor was assisted in these efforts by other committed local officials,
including a city attorney, and by engineering consultants. Later, FEMA Project
Impact funds provided support for coordinated local disaster loss reduction
activities, and local businesses stepped in to continue those efforts when
federal support ended.

Tulsa Partners changed its name to the Disaster Resilience Network in 2016.
The city continues to garner recognition for its resilience-enhancing efforts.
Tulsa recently joined the Rockefeller Foundation's 100 Resilient Cities initiative, which provides support for a chief resilience officer position as well as
various types of technical assistance. (For additional discussions, see Patton
1994; Meo, Ziebro, and Patton 2004; Bullock, Haddow, and Haddow 2008.)

be entrepreneurial by seizing opportunities for themselves; they should be
flexible and adaptable—in other words, they should be resilient. If they are
not, then they are not worthy of receiving support. By putting the onus of
qualifying for assistance on the individual, neoliberalism treats receiving
assistance as a privilege rather than as a right. To be resilient, individuals are

urged to adapt in the face of forces such as rapid urbanization and climate change—forces that are framed as inevitable (see, for example, Rodin 2014). As Julian Reid observes, the pressure to cope in the face of those sorts of chronic and acute stressors produces a resilient subject, "which must permanently struggle to accommodate itself to the world . . . a subject that accepts the disastrousness of the world it lives in as a condition of partaking in that world" (Reid 2013: 355). Resilient subjects are not political subjects with rights, but rather individuals who have "accepted the imperative not to resist or secure themselves from the dangers they face but instead adapt to their enabling conditions" (2013: 355). This view is echoed by other critics, such as Jonathan Joseph, who argues that "the recent enthusiasm for the concept of resilience across a range of policy literature is the consequence of its fit with neoliberal discourse" (2013: 38), which shifts responsibility for public welfare and well-being from the state to the individual. The resilient subject has no choice but to adapt in the face of societal and global changes that are framed as inevitable.

Disaster scholars observe that the diminished role envisioned for the state and the privileging of the private sector in activities such as disaster recovery—both of which are embedded in the neoliberal political economy and resilience discourse—inevitably create problems. In the United States, where neoliberal principles hold sway and shape disaster recovery practices, recovery activities have been increasingly privatized. Services delivered by the private sector are very expensive because private providers have to make a profit, which leads to bloated budgets. Giving private sector actors large amounts of money to perform services like those that are necessary in disaster recovery leads to a decline in transparency and accountability. Without adequate oversight—which is difficult to enact in large-scale disasters—private contractors engage in wasteful practices and are often free to decide for themselves who is worthy of receiving services. Benefits typically accrue to disaster survivors who have the means, connections, and cultural competence to navigate in the disaster assistance landscape—in other words, to survivors who are resilient by virtue of their high levels of social capital. Those who are unable to become "empowered consumers" in the post-disaster environment—the poor, the vulnerable, those who lack bureaucratic savvy—often receive far less than they deserve (Gotham 2012; Adams 2012).

Resilience theorists emphasize that true resilience involves not only adaptation in the face of shocks and stressors, but also transformative activities that overcome those stressors by drastically reducing them. This would mean, for example, shifting from fossil fuels to 100 percent renewable energy as a way of reducing the impacts of climate change (Pelling 2011), or greatly reducing income inequality as a way of reducing disaster vulnerability. These kinds of transformative changes can only be brought about by overcoming systems of power and privilege. However, in part because current resilience formulations rely in great measure on ecological scholarship, resilience discourse is largely silent on issues of power—issues that come to the fore when the focus is on social systems. Species adapt, but human communities can resist. We will return to these ideas in the next chapter.

Concluding Comments

In this chapter we have explored the concept of disaster resilience from a variety of angles: how it is defined, how it is measured at different levels of analysis, what factors contribute to resilience, and what constitutes resilient disaster response and recovery. We have also looked at programs that seek to enhance resilience in the face of hazards and disasters. Additionally, we have considered critical perspectives on resilience, particularly on the way it is framed and practiced in the context of neoliberalism. These critiques are important, but it is also important to recognize that *resilience does exist*. As we have seen, some communities, societies, and groups are simply better than others at mitigating, preparing for, responding to, and recovering from extreme events. This chapter has attempted to show why that is the case by emphasizing the importance of avoiding hierarchical notions of command and control, by insisting on flexibility and adaptability in response and recovery activities, and by understanding the needs of communities that have experienced disasters.

8

What the Future Holds

Greater Risks and Impacts or
Greater Coping Capacity?

Introduction: A Changing Landscape of Risk

Those who try to predict the future are often wrong. Television was first introduced in the 1940s, and in 1946 Darryl Zanuck, an executive at Twentieth Century Fox film company, famously observed that "television won't be able to hold on to any market it captures after the first six months. People will soon get tired of staring at a plywood box every night." In 1977, Ken Olson, the founder of Digital Equipment Corporation, once the second-largest computer company in the United States, opined that "there is no reason anyone would want a computer in their home." Reacting to a prediction that people would soon be using the Internet to buy books and newspapers, purchase airline tickets, and make restaurant reservations, astronomer Clifford Stoll argued in a 1995 *Newsweek* article that those ideas were far-fetched and asked "how come," if "cyberbusiness" was so useful, "my local mall does more business in an afternoon than the entire internet handles in a month?" Only twenty years ago it was almost impossible to foresee a future that would include today's driverless cars, smart phones, 3D printers, and wearable devices. As these examples show, trying to foresee the future is risky. Even so, and with those cautions in mind, enough information exists to provide some idea about the landscape of future disasters. Such projections are not mere opinion or speculation; rather they are based on scientific knowledge and on an understanding of where ongoing environmental and societal trends are heading. Scientists and sociologists who study disasters and other types of crises have offered their views of the disasters to come. In this chapter I employ some of these insights to think about what the future holds in the way of disasters. In addition to considering disasters that could occur in the future, we will also look at known hazards with catastrophic potential. Finally, we will explore the extent to which policies and programs based on the idea of increasing disaster resilience can help with bringing about a safer future.

New Sources of Vulnerability

In a 1996 article, Henry Quarantelli pointed to a number of trends that he claimed would influence twenty-first-century disasters. One of his key points was that, because of the forces of social change, future disasters are likely to be different from those of the past. This didn't mean that the hazards we are accustomed to would go away—only that new and different ones would appear. I summarize just a few of his projections here. He predicted, for example, disasters resulting from failures in ever more interconnected cyber-infrastructures and from accidents in biotechnology facilities. He also noted that the impacts of future disasters would spread far beyond the areas originally affected—as happened, for example, in the 1986 Chernobyl nuclear power plant disaster. Presciently in light of the 2011 catastrophe in Japan, he predicted that natural disaster agents such as floods and tornadoes could cause major accidents in nuclear and chemical facilities. Because of the rapid pace of urbanization, including development and population growth in hazard-prone areas, increasing numbers of people and properties would be put at risk. Changes in the demographic composition of populations around the world would mean that vulnerable populations will increase: in Japan, the problem would be an aging population; in less developed countries with younger demographic profiles, children and youth would be more at risk (Quarantelli 1996).

In later years Quarantelli followed up with additional projections. Once again he expressed the idea that biotechnology is a significant hazard, arguing that "[s]ooner or later there will be the creation of, or the escape from control of, some altered organism that cannot be checked by presently known means ... we are not talking of an unreal movie like *Jurassic Park*, but of real possibilities" (Quarantelli 2001b: 234). He also argued that nation-states are declining in importance with the rise of transnational corporations and international bodies and that globalization requires global hazard and disaster governance systems that have yet to emerge. At the same time, he questioned whether powerful entities such as global corporations would have the legitimacy in the eyes of the world, or even the interest, to manage future crises. Because of a lack of effective global-scale institutions, he argued, disasters that cross borders will be difficult to manage—a point I take up later in this section.

In *The Next Catastrophe*, sociologist Charles Perrow (2006) made an argument as to why the potential for large-scale disasters is growing. Among his main points are that the roots of disasters can be found in *concentrations*, by which he means larger, denser populations living in high-risk geographic areas, as well as larger amounts of dangerous substances being used and stored near population centers. Additionally, for Perrow, the fact that economic power is increasingly concentrated in the hands of ever larger corporations means that decisions regarding safety and security are now made in corporate headquarters by people who are likely to be unfamiliar with conditions at local facilities. Like Quarantelli, Perrow pointed to vulnerabilities associated with our massively interconnected cyber-infrastructure, which leaves open the possibility of cybercrime and malicious hacking that can cause electric power grid failures and the hijacking of the control systems of chemical and nuclear facilities. Perrow recounted a number of past instances in which computer systems were hacked or taken over for nefarious purposes, but from what we currently know such threats loom even larger, and the reality of information warfare is now widely accepted.

One of Quarantelli's key points was that the disasters of the future, although perhaps not seen before, will not be entirely new but rather will have their roots in past and present societal conditions. It is not difficult to see how social change is contributing to risk buildup and setting the stage for disasters. Wildfires in the United States are a case in point. Development has increased in the wildland–urban interface (WUI)–that is, the area where the built environment and the natural environment intermingle. Development is also increasing in exurbia–that is, places that are remote from both cities and suburbs. Population increases in such areas are in part a consequence of a demographic pattern known as amenity migration, or population movement into areas valued for their beauty and recreational opportunities. With incomes rising for some, affluent segments of the population are able to own second (and even third) homes. Even if they are located in wildland areas, those homes are easier to access because of improved transportation systems. At the same time, advances in computer technology have made telecommuting more common, making it possible for residents of the WUI and exurbia to work from those locations (for details on WUI growth, see Radeloff et al. 2018). Institutional forces have also been important in increasing wildfire potential; suppressing fires, as opposed to letting forests burn naturally, as they have throughout history, has led to the buildup of fuels. More people living in wildland areas means more ignition sources in areas that are ripe for burning. As discussed below, climate change is also responsible for the growing incidence of wildfires. The result: more people and structures than ever are exposed to wildfire hazards, and there is more potential for human-induced wildfire ignitions. Another result: the US Department of Agriculture's Forest Service now spends more money annually fighting fires than it spends on forest management (US Department of Agriculture 2015). Those trends are expected to continue.

Similarly, increases in economic losses from hurricanes in the United States are the result of migration and increased development in at-risk coastal areas (Pielke et al. 2008). As seen in Houston when Hurricane Harvey struck in 2017, development in areas that are exposed to flood hazards, coupled with the expansion of impermeable surfaces and the destruction of ecosystems that provide flood protection, is setting the stage for the hurricane and flood disasters of the future. Here again, past conditions and trends have combined to elevate current and future risks.

Both Quarantelli and Perrow warned that technological developments can present new threats, which the public either is unaware of or has only begun to recognize. One such threat that has recently emerged is induced seismicity. As hydraulic fracturing, or fracking, is being employed in oil production, the injection of wastewater from fracking into the earth is resulting in very large increases in the frequency of earthquakes. For example, owing to wastewater injection, the state of Oklahoma has seen a precipitous rise in earthquake activity since 2009 and is now the most seismically active state in the United States, surpassing even California (Hincks, Aspinall, Cooke, and Gernon 2018). Most of those earthquakes are relatively small, but in 2016 a magnitude 5.8 earthquake in Oklahoma caused injuries and did significant damage. Other states that have seen increases in the frequency of earthquakes are Arkansas, Colorado (where a magnitude 5.3 earthquake struck in 2011), Kansas, New Mexico, and Texas (Ellsworth et al. 2015). As later discussions concerning the New Madrid Seismic Zone will show, earthquakes are certainly not unknown in the central United States, but what is different now is how frequently they are occurring. Scientists have pointed out that "[g]oing forward, the most probable risks in areas of increased seismicity include life-threatening injuries caused by falling objects and economic loss from damage to structures with low capacity to absorb moderate earthquake shaking" (Ellsworth et al. 2015: 625).

Induced earthquakes present significant societal challenges. Because deepwater injection often causes earthquakes in places where they have not occurred before, residents of affected areas are generally unfamiliar with earthquakes and with recommended self-protective actions. What kinds of information does the public need? As the quote above indicates, the frequency of earthquakes is increasing in parts of the country where structures were not built to resist earthquake damage, and such damage represents a life-safety hazard. Should new codes be adopted for earthquake-resistant construction and for retrofitting existing buildings, and, if so, how strict should the codes be, which types of structures require such measures, and which party or parties should pay for those upgrades?

The problem of induced earthquakes also raises important legal and regulatory questions. Should corporations be liable for damages done by induced earthquakes? In the Netherlands, for example, companies that caused increased seismicity through natural gas extraction are required to compensate property owners, not only for damage but also for the loss of value of their homes (Muir-Wood 2017). In the United States such issues have typically been dealt with at the state level, and approaches are inconsistent. For example, legal scholar Emery Richards (2016) observes that laws in Ohio, which has experienced fracking-induced earthquakes, assign liability to corporations that are found culpable for damage. Ohio also strengthened regulations relating to fracking in 2012 after a series of earthquakes, including a magnitude 4 temblor that struck in Youngstown in 2011. In Colorado, the law also upholds liability for induced earthquake damage. In contrast, Texas and Oklahoma—two states whose economies are heavily dependent on oil and gas—have neither strict liability for damage nor strong regulatory regimes (Richards 2016).

As Quarantelli also noted, future disasters are likely to have an impact on multiple nation-states and regions.[1] Disaster scholars (see Quarantelli, Lagadec, and Boin 2006; Wachtendorf 2009; Boin 2009; Boin, Busuioc, and Groenleer 2013) have observed that disasters that affect two or more different societies—a phenomenon often called "transboundary (or transborder) social ruptures"—are becoming increasingly common. To give just a few examples of transborder crises, in 1997 the Red River floods caused major impacts in the United States and Canada. In Europe in 2000, a break in a dam holding toxic waste at a gold mine in Baia Mare, Romania sent large quantities of cyanide into the Someş River and then into the Tisa River, the second largest river in Hungary, and on into the Danube River, affecting Serbia and Bulgaria. The spill poisoned drinking water for millions of people and resulted in massive fish kills. In early 2003, an outbreak of severe acute respiratory syndrome (SARS) began in the Pearl River Delta region in China and ultimately spread to thirty-seven countries, with major impacts in places as far apart geographically as Hong Kong and Toronto, Canada. In August of that year, as discussed earlier, the electrical power grid failed in parts of the northeastern and Midwestern United States and in the province of Ontario, Canada, leaving major cities such as New York City and Toronto completely without power for days. In 2004, the Indian Ocean earthquake and tsunami killed people in fourteen countries in the Indian Ocean region. In the fall of 2017, Hurricane Irma cut a swathe through the Caribbean and the United States, affecting island nations and territories within the jurisdictions of the United States, the United Kingdom, France, and the Netherlands, along with the nations of Cuba, the Dominican Republic, and Haiti, as well as the United States itself. Then Hurricane Maria proceeded to devastate some of those same places, the US territory of Puerto Rico, and other nations, such as Dominica and Turks and Caicos.

Scholars tell us that transboundary disasters have several attributes. One of them, obviously, is that they cross national borders. Additionally, they may begin with small accidents or failures, but subsequently their effects spread more broadly, often in unexpected ways. For example, as we saw earlier, the 2003 failure of the electrical power grid in the United States and Canada disrupted subway and air travel, caught people in elevators who then had to be rescued, shut down water systems, affected communications and cell phone service, degraded the emergency response system, and caused widespread health problems.

Globalization in areas such as finance and industry means that crises have increasingly far-reaching effects. The financial crisis of 2008 began in the United States but spread rapidly worldwide, nearly collapsing the global financial system. More recently, earthquakes in Taiwan, floods in Thailand, and the 2011 Japan triple disaster caused major disruptions in global supply chains, affecting trade in such products as semiconductors, hard drives, and auto parts and causing substantial losses to such iconic companies as Honda, Toyota, Nissan, Samsung, Western Digital, Seagate, and Lenovo.

Another characteristic of transboundary disasters is that, as they unfold, officials in the affected or potentially affected countries have difficulty getting a full picture of what is actually happening, in part because of the uncertainties associated with such crises, but also because those officials may never have communicated with one another before in a crisis context. Additionally, there can be legal or political barriers to information-sharing across borders, or nations may outright deny or cover up major transborder threats, as happened in 1986 with the Chernobyl nuclear disaster in what was then the Soviet Union, or in 2003 with SARS.

Large-scale disasters that affect individual societies are difficult to manage, but when several societies are affected communication and coordination challenges increase exponentially. Further, it may be only after a major transboundary event has occurred that preexisting vulnerabilities become clear, as happened, for example, after the 2011 Japan triple disaster, when Toyota realized that its worldwide business was disrupted because suppliers of materials necessary for making its vehicles were concentrated in the impact area. Finally, these kinds of disruptions have the potential for creating legitimacy crises for the governments and institutions involved. We saw this, for example, with the SARS outbreak, where the credibility and crisis-management capability of the Chinese government was so widely criticized that the Chinese leadership was forced to revamp the country's emergency management system (Lim 2014).

Disasters that affect multiple nations are of course not new. The Lisbon earthquake of 1755 was felt all over Europe as well as in northern Africa, and tsunamis created by the earthquake affected places as far away as England and Ireland. The earthquake had wide-ranging social, economic, and cultural impacts. For example, it struck a blow to Portugal's imperial ambitions and had a profound effect on moving European societies toward a less religious, more scientific view of the origins of disasters. However, what is new is that we are now beginning to understand the special challenges that societies face in our specific twenty-first-century social and economic context. With respect to transboundary disasters, this social and economic context has two key characteristics. First, we live in an increasingly globalized, high-technology world that can amplify societal and infrastructural vulnerabilities. And, second, we lack transnational governance structures to manage the risks associated with transboundary disasters.

Globalization means that societies and economies are more interconnected and interdependent than ever before, and frequently in ways that are not well understood—as we saw, for example, in the case of global supply chains that are disrupted by distant disaster events. Our complex, interconnected global system of travel means that viruses like SARS and Ebola could spread before authorities in the affected societies are even aware of what is going on. In a globalized world, corporations and other enterprises have to be extremely large in order to compete. Size is usually considered an advantage in terms of the ability to prepare for and respond to crises, but this is not always true, because, as noted earlier, large global entities may lack an understanding of more localized hazards and risks in the places where they do business. They may not care enough about those hazards and risks to take action, either. For example, having experienced deadly accidents in its US plants, British Petroleum professed to be improving its safety record, but the corporation actually cut off funds that would make that possible—right up until the catastrophic 2010 *Deepwater Horizon* blowout and oil spill (Tierney 2014). Global integration can also mean that risky and even criminal practices spread more widely across borders, as happened in the run-up to the 2008 financial meltdown.

Governance mechanisms for managing transboundary risks and crises are nascent, weak, or entirely lacking. Hazards and disasters cross borders, but often the capacity to manage them does not. Global efforts like the United Nations International Strategy for Disaster Reduction are primarily nation-state-focused and are voluntary. As Cameron (2017) indicates, "[u]nlike armed conflict, natural disasters have no legally binding set of regulations to govern the actions of those involved in aid and recovery." Feldman and Fish (2015) also point out that transnational legal regimes for disaster management are poorly developed. Entities such as the International Federation of Red Cross and Red Crescent Societies and the United Nations Office for the Coordination of Humanitarian Assistance have developed nonbinding guidelines for aid provision, but that guidance mainly relates to donor countries that provide disaster assistance to less developed ones, as opposed to two or more nations that collaborate to manage a transboundary crisis. Agreements that do exist tend to focus on responding to particular types of hazards. Examples include the Joint Contingency Plan, which provides for cooperation between the United States and Mexico in situations involving oil and hazardous materials spills along their shared border; Europe's Directive 2007/60/EC on the Assessment and Management of Flood Risk; and the Arctic Council's Agreement on Cooperation on Marine Oil Pollution, Preparedness, and Response in the Arctic (Tierney 2012; Feldman and Fish 2015).

John Hannigan refers to the parties that are involved one way or another in the management and politics of hazards and disasters within and across borders as a "global policy field" consisting of

national states and local governments; regional organizations, international finance institutions (IFIs); United Nations disaster agencies and other
international governmental organizations (IGOs); non-governmental
organizations (NGOs); multi-actor initiatives and partnerships; scientific,
technical, and academic communities; private actors; and the mass
media. (Hannigan 2012: 22)

Typically, there is only weak or sporadic coordination among such entities,
and even within specific sectors, such as the NGO sector, there is often a lack
of coordination. Hannigan notes, for example, that the United Nations High
Commission for Refugees, the United Nations Office for the Coordination of
Humanitarian Affairs, and similar agencies have attempted to coordinate the
many entities involved in activities such as the provision of temporary housing in a "cluster" system, but with limited success.

The Evil We Know: Hazards with Catastrophic Potential

In an earlier publication (Tierney 2014), I called attention to some hazards
that are recognized as having the potential to cause major and even catastrophic disasters. Here I discuss some of those hazards briefly. Focusing on
earthquakes, the Great Tohoku earthquake and tsunami of 2011 caused massive amounts of death and destruction, but it was not the true "big one" that
Japan has been awaiting for decades. Scientists argue that what is called the
Great Tokai earthquake—a magnitude 8 event—is overdue and that the likelihood of such an event in the next twenty-five years approaches 90 percent. The
Tokai magnitude 8 earthquake will strike not far from Tokyo, in the Nankai
Trough, where the Philippine Sea Plate is sliding under the Eurasian Plate.
When it occurs, this earthquake will cause a major tsunami and, like the
2011 mega-disaster, the tsunami will threaten nuclear power plants in the
region. Direct property damage from that event is conservatively estimated
at $310 billion. This total does not take into account indirect losses that
could result, for example, from the disruption of economic activities in the
densely populated impact region. Following Perrow's reasoning, the deaths
and massive damages waiting to be caused by the Great Tokai earthquake will
be a consequence of concentrations—of people, economic activity, and built
environment and infrastructure.

A major earthquake in the New Madrid Seismic Zone (NMSZ) in the central
United States, although much less likely than the Great Tokai earthquake,
would also have devastating impacts. The earthquakes that occurred in the
NMSZ in the winter of 1811–1812 were the largest seismic events ever to
strike in the contiguous United States. Scenarios suggest that a 7.7 magnitude
earthquake in the NMSZ could kill as many as 86,000, displace 7.2 million
people, damage over half a million homes, and disrupt bridges, highways,

and pipelines in an eight-state area, the most severe disruption occurring in Tennessee, Arkansas, and Missouri. A major earthquake in the NMSZ would be a truly catastrophic event.

Both the 2004 Indian Ocean tsunami and the 2011 Japan triple disaster were caused by subduction-related seismic events—that is, geologic conditions in which one tectonic plate was sliding beneath another—and the same will be true for the coming Great Tokai earthquake. Another area of concern in this respect is the Cascadia Subduction Zone (CSZ) in the Pacific Northwest. The CSZ is about 700 miles long, stretching from northern California to southern British Columbia in Canada. Researchers have only begun to get a clear idea of the hazards that are associated with the CSZ in the past thirty-odd years, and much of the information they have developed is unfamiliar to the public. To complicate matters further, since awareness of the magnitude of the threat associated with this seismic zone is relatively recent, buildings and infrastructure in the region were not designed to resist the kinds of forces a large CSZ earthquake could generate. According to a scenario developed by the Cascadia Region Earthquake Workgroup (CREW) in 2013, the CSZ is capable of producing earthquakes in the 9.0 range, as well as tsunamis—all comparable to the events that occurred in Japan in 2011. The zone is close to the shore in many areas, so a tsunami could strike some communities as soon as fifteen minutes after the earthquake occurs. Those living, working, and traveling in tsunami inundation zones would have to evacuate immediately or lose their lives. A large CSZ earthquake will significantly damage ports, airports, highways, and bridges and will do extensive damage to buildings, especially those constructed before current seismic codes (Cascadia Region Earthquake Workgroup 2013).

Climate Change-Related Threats

A multidimensional hazard

Climate change is already affecting societies around the world, and as it progresses its impacts will be even more profound, influencing virtually every aspect of human life: agriculture and food security, water supplies, human health, and the critical infrastructure—to name just a few. Analyzing and synthesizing the research record on climate change and extreme events, the Intergovernmental Panel on Climate Change (IPCC) (Field, Barros, Stocker, and Dahe 2012) concluded that climate change will affect the frequency, intensity, spatial extent, timing, and duration of weather and climate events while at the same time increasing vulnerability and damaging coping and adaptive capacity among affected populations. The wind speeds of tropical cyclones will increase, as we have already seen in 2013 with typhoon Hayian, the strongest storm ever to make landfall. Droughts are expected to increase in some parts of the world, and overall there will be an increase in the number of warm days and nights, raising the potential for heat-related death and illness. We can expect also to see more precipitation events of the very severe variety, like the extreme rainfall that accompanied Hurricane Harvey in 2017, and scientists affiliated with the IPCC tell us that the future has in store "unprecedented weather and climate effects" (Field et al. 2012: 7).

Focusing on the health impacts of climate change, according to the US Global Change Research Program (2016), in the future we can expect to see changes such as these:

- an increase in temperature-related deaths and illness such as heat stroke and cardiovascular disease;
- greater incidence and severity of air quality-related health conditions such as asthma;
- increases in vector-borne diseases such as malaria, dengue fever, West Nile, and Lyme disease;
- increased exposure to water-related contamination from chemicals and bacteria;
- threats to food security.

These kinds of health threats will be most significant for groups that are already vulnerable. In Chapter 6, for example, we saw how extreme heat disproportionately affects those who are elderly and socially isolated. Higher daytime and nighttime temperatures and heat waves will make life more difficult for poor residents in places like Phoenix and Las Vegas in the United States and in large cities in India, as well as for those whose jobs require them to work outdoors. The demand for air conditioning will soar during heat waves, putting an excessive strain on power systems. Asthma and other respiratory problems are prominent in inner-city neighborhoods, and climate change will result in a worsening of those conditions.

The Third National Climate Assessment (2014) pointed to these and other looming threats, noting also that because so much damage is being done to ecosystems as a result of climatic change, "the capacity of ecosystems to buffer the impacts of extreme events like fires, floods, and severe storms is being overwhelmed" (2014: 14). Global warming has cascading effects. For example, climate change affects the health of forests, increasing wildfire risks; and, as the frequency and severity of wildfires increase, the particulate emissions from these fires will cause respiratory problems. Fires also scour out landscapes, practically ensuring that subsequent rainfall events (which will be more intense in some areas) will cause flash flooding and mudslides. A recent report (Miller 2018) indicates that California will experience this type of a "whiplash" cycle, in which drought and subsequent wildfires will be followed by heavy-rainfall years flooding, and debris flows—a cycle that will lead to escalating social impacts and losses. Climate change is contributing to ocean acidification, which in turn threatens marine ecosystems; and these are a source of food for millions and offer protection from extreme events. We have already seen in Superstorm Sandy in 2012 that rising sea levels caused by climate change will give rise to higher storm surges, endangering megacities like New York and Miami and countries like Bangladesh, which already experiences recurrent major floods.

Climate change and coastal flooding

Focusing on floods, Hallegatte, Green, Nicholls, and Corfee-Morlot (2013) conducted research to assess future economic losses from climate change-related coastal flooding by 2050 in the 136 largest urban agglomerations worldwide. Currently, average annual losses for those cities are approximately $6 billion; that amount is expected to increase at least tenfold, to something between $60 and $63 billion by 2050. This study ranked urban areas in terms of the size of projected losses for 2050, taking into account anticipated social and economic trends, environmental changes such as subsidence and sea-level rise, and investments that cities have made in adaptation. The study also took into account annualized annual flood losses in relation to the gross domestic product (GDP) of each of the 136 cities and urban agglomerations. Table 8.1 lists the ten cities with the highest projected economic losses from coastal flooding in 2050 along with changes in loss projection from a baseline year of 2005, as well as the share of GDP that future losses will represent.

Table 8.1 Cities with the highest projected economic losses from coastal flooding-related hazards in 2050.

Urban Agglomeration	Average Annualized (AA) Losses in US $million	Percent Increase over 2005 AA Losses	Losses as a Percentage of City GDP
Guangzhou, China	13,200	11%	1.46%
Mumbai, India	6,414	5%	0.49%
Kolkata, India	3,350	24%	0.26%
Guyaquil, Ecuador	3,189	13%	1.08%
Shenzhen, China	3,136	7%	0.40%
Miami, United States	2,549	21%	0.36%
Tianjin, China	2,276	26%	0.30%
New York-Newark, United States	2,056	5%	0.08%
Ho Chi Minh City, Vietnam	1,953	12%	0.83%
New Orleans, United States	1,864	18%	1.42%

SOURCE: Compiled from data in Hallegatte, Green, Nicholls, and Corfee-Morlot 2013.

As the table indicates, and in agreement with our earlier discussion, two cities in China's Pearl River Delta, Guangzhou and Shenzen, are in the top ten in terms of projected flood losses; losses are expected to be highest in Gangzhou, which is also the city with the highest losses in proportion to its GDP. Three urban agglomerations—Tianjin, Kolkata, and Miami—will see the largest increases vis-à-vis the losses measured in 2005. In some areas, such as New York–Newark, losses will be high but will constitute small percentages of their overall GDPs. Even so, the numbers are significant. Cities in less developed countries predominate on this list; and, with the exception of New Orleans and Miami, these are also the cities that will see the highest losses in proportion to their GDPs. Coastal flooding is merely one of many consequences of climate change with which future generations will have to contend.

Can Resilience-Centered Approaches Reduce Future Disaster Impacts?

In this volume I have explored how long-term global and societal trends contribute to the buildup of risk and set the stage for the occurrence of disasters when some force of nature or technological failure serves as a trigger. In the present chapter we have taken a brief look at what the future holds, in order to see how social and environmental processes and anthropogenic threats created by humans, such as climate change and cyber-insecurity, are setting the stage for future disasters. In the face of looming threats like those discussed here, societies and communities have essentially two options: business as usual; or the adoption of measures that can dramatically reduce vulnerability and contain losses.

In the light of what has been discussed in earlier chapters, business as usual will have predictable effects. Disaster-related losses in the form of death, injury, illness, and economic costs will continue to rise. Those effects will be borne disproportionately by the poorer countries of the world and by the most vulnerable groups, in both developed and less developed countries. In countries at the periphery and semi-periphery of the world system, disasters will drive more people into poverty, will prevent the poor from escaping poverty, and will slow or reverse development efforts. Disaster events will interact with other social ills, such as wars and civil wars, to produce severe humanitarian crises. As weather extremes become more common as a consequence of climate change, floods, droughts, and other perils will increase food insecurity and will threaten livelihoods. Conflicts over resources will become more frequent. An already poorly functioning international disaster relief system will face mounting challenges.

In developed countries, business as usual will become increasingly costly and disruptive. Many wealthy countries, or communities and regions in those countries, have adopted and implemented disaster risk reduction measures, but even with such measures in place losses will continue to rise, because historical practices of development have put more people and property in harm's way and because construction and population growth continue in hazardous areas. Similarly, greenhouse gas mitigation and climate adaptation programs have been adopted by many nations, communities, and sectors, but their implementation has likely come too late to slow the rate of global climate change and to head off its consequences.

Under a business-as-usual scenario, political and economic forces will continue to operate in ways that magnify burgeoning risks. As seen in the case of the 2014 repeal of the Biggart-Waters Act, which encouraged charging risk-based premiums for flood insurance, neither the general public nor elites find reality-based insurance costs acceptable. With business as usual, artificially low hazard insurance rates will prevail, and members of the public living outside hazardous areas will increasingly subsidize others' risky choices. Then, as losses increase, insurance premiums will rise for everyone. Disaster assistance costs will continue to escalate, and worldwide disaster losses will climb. Annual losses such as those experienced in 2017—an estimated $330 billion—will become more common. While such losses might not seem particularly large considering the size of major economies worldwide, they represent opportunities that must be forgone; dollars spent responding to and recovering from disasters cannot be invested elsewhere.

Climate change adaptation projects will proceed as planned in a business-as-usual scenario, but retreat and relocation will increasingly be coping strategies of choice, as life in coastal areas and other disaster-prone zones becomes more and more untenable. Property values will plummet in hazardous areas, and insuring at-risk properties will become prohibitively expensive or impossible at some point, wiping out homeowners' investments. Jurisdictions worldwide will face the challenge of extensively retrofitting, relocating, or abandoning critical infrastructure elements such as ports, highways, and power plants. Distinctive local and regional cultures threatened by disasters and climate change, such as cultures that are dependent on fishing and other subsistence activities, will weaken or disappear.

There will of course be winners as well as losers in our business-as-usual scenario. Rebuilding after increasingly destructive disasters will provide jobs for developers and those in the design and construction trades, and financial institutions in stricken communities will benefit from an influx of disaster assistance funds. Consulting companies that manage the disbursement of disaster assistance monies will thrive, as will professionals with expertise in areas such as land use planning, risk analysis, catastrophic risk modeling, and risk securitization. Coastal residents displaced by climate change will have to move somewhere, which will be beneficial for sectors of the economy that rely on property development and construction. Healthcare-related institutions should see their fortunes improve as larger numbers of people experience the adverse effects of disasters and climate change—provided that those victims are adequately insured. Similarly, institutions and professions that offer psychological first aid and mental health and other forms of support will see the demand for their services increase in tandem with disaster-related losses and disruption.

A Resilient Future?

As we saw in Chapter 7, the concept of resilience currently represents the holy grail of disaster risk reduction. Embraced in many parts of the developed world, in particular in the United States, and framed as a broad set of measures addressing pre- and post-disaster protections and services, the disaster resilience construct promises an alternative to an increasingly dismal business-as-usual future. But can it achieve that objective? Given what we already know, there is reason for skepticism. As noted at various points in this book, many of the activities that are subsumed under the rubric of disaster resilience are the same activities that have been advocated for many decades under the rubric of the disaster cycle: mitigation, preparedness, response, and recovery. Despite impressive progress in many jurisdictions, disaster losses continue to increase. If resilience discourse is merely a repackaging of older concepts associated with the disaster cycle, how effective can it be?

As I noted earlier and have discussed elsewhere (Tierney 2015), at the individual and household levels, becoming more resilient is an attractive idea for those who are already capable of choosing among risk reduction options and exercising agency. Such groups include well-off households with equity in their homes, adequate savings, insurance to cover their losses, and an understanding of how to access the disaster aid to which they are entitled. Those lacking in such assets are at a disadvantage in terms of becoming disaster resilient. What does it mean to be disaster resilient if you are a single mother who is already paying more than half your income to rent a unit in a poorly constructed, poorly maintained apartment complex? To what extent can a woman become more resilient if she is living in a male-dominated society governed by patriarchal norms? How resilient can you be if you are an elderly person living on a fixed income in a house with a paid-off mortgage who cannot afford to (or chooses not to) purchase hazard insurance? We would do well to remember points made in Chapter 6 about the root causes of vulnerability and their relationship to social inequality.

If resilience has been framed as the holy grail of disaster risk reduction, then in some views social capital is the holy grail of disaster resilience. Social capital, we are told, is a resource that is available to all who wish to become resilient in the face of disasters, even (or perhaps especially) the poor. Yet social capital is unevenly distributed within the social order, those at the upper end of the class hierarchy possessing not only high levels of bonding and bridging capital, but also the all-important linking form, which connects them to those with political and economic power. Those on the disadvantaged side of the class divide can rely on their bonding networks of social support for problem-solving on an everyday basis, but they typically lack the access to power that the linking ties represent—the very kinds of connections that can matter most when disasters strike. We already have evidence that after disasters social capital works differently for the well-off, who can mobilize support from geographically distant sources, and for the poor, whose more localized networks may be frayed and unable to function well in the aftermath of disasters (Elliott, Haney, and Sams-Abiodun 2010). How will those who are disadvantaged recover if their ongoing support networks are damaged or destroyed by disaster, or if post-disaster policies and programs do further damage to their networks of support?

Among the many criticisms that have been launched against the concept of resilience in recent years, perhaps the most compelling arguments center on its negative implications for political agency. Too often, discourses on resilience take for granted the assumption that individuals, families, communities, and other social actors have no choice but to adapt to a world in which hazards that are beyond their control—atmospheric, geologic, technological, and climate-related forces—wreak havoc. In this view, resilience requires adaptability and adjustment. Too often, discussions about ways of increasing resilience turn people's attention away from the need to reverse the social, political, and economic processes that combine to produce vulnerability and disasters. As Béné and colleagues observe with respect to the resilience of cities,

> what is missing in the present literature on urban resilience is the social justice and political dimensions of the concept and a clearer understanding of the advantages but also the dangers of adopting such a concept as a new policy narrative without specifically acknowledging the political economy dimension of urbanization. (Béné et al. 2018: 129)

An emphasis on resilience as currently framed in mainstream disaster discourse ignores the fact that people are political actors who can seize opportunities to create substantial social change that reduces their vulnerability to disasters and other stressors. Viewing potential victims as having no choice but to adapt to inevitable hazards in a resilient fashion obscures this point. Accepting the mainstream view of resilience means that we seek to improve our ability to respond to catastrophic oil spills and to adapt to climate change, rather than engaging in political activity that would reduce our reliance on fossil fuels while working toward an alternative-energy future. We look for social capital-based solutions to disaster preparedness rather than demanding, as political actors, that the poor not be housed in buildings that will kill them if an earthquake or hurricane should occur.

With respect to climate change, under the resilience rubric, those who live in affluent societies expect the populations of low-income countries to become more resilient to climate-induced stressors and events. However, as Cannon and Müller-Mahn (2010: 633) state bluntly, "[w]ith climate change, it is impossible to ignore the fact that the expected increase in poverty of hundreds of millions of people in developing countries is being caused by the behavior of the economies of richer countries." Or, as Friend and Moench (2015: 648) put it, what is needed is a "fundamental social transformation not just on supporting people who are already poor to cope with various shocks and crises, but addressing the factors determining why such people are poor in the first place and setting agendas of enhancing wellbeing and prosperity."

However, rather than shouldering the burden of causing projected increases in poverty and advancing transformative strategies, well-off nations carry on with business as usual and urge the poor and the powerless to become more resilient.

Resilience has a lot in common with the earlier concept of sustainable development, which promised a pathway to the improvement of living conditions in less well-off societies. Like sustainable development, resilience has its origins in the Global North and likely finds little resonance in the Global South (Aguirre 2002; Tierney 2015). Here again, disaster resilience frameworks underemphasize the extent to which reducing disaster vulnerability necessitates reducing social inequality, empowering those who are vulnerable, and taking actions that diminish the burdens placed on poor nations and communities.

Even as discourses in the United States and other parts of the Global North extoll the virtues of disaster resilience, neoliberal policies that roll back social provisions and benefit the 1 percent at the expense of the others (who rank lower in the social class hierarchy) undermine the very support networks that make social resilience possible. If policymakers were genuinely committed to helping individuals, households, businesses, and communities to become more resilient in the face of disasters, they would champion policies that promote a living wage, access to health care, high-quality education, community cohesion, and community empowerment. Such measures constitute the starting point for achieving durable, effective disaster resilience programs and outcomes. Studies such as those discussed in this volume emphasize a basic but profound point: those who cannot provide decent living conditions and food and clothing for their families cannot and will not commit time and resources to becoming disaster resilient. Without a social and economic infrastructure to support it, disaster resilience is nothing more than a hollow promise.

Throughout this book I have explored the nexus between power and vulnerability: the power of local growth machines to act as boosters for development that ignores hazards; the power to relegate people of color to hazardous areas and sacrificial zones; the power of nation-states to promote activities that contribute to risk buildup; the power of international financial institutions to determine the fates of nations in the developing world; and the power that makes it possible for nations at the core of the world system to export hazards to dependent states at the periphery. Because the exercise of these kinds of power constitutes the social, political, and economic driver of disaster risk, vulnerability, and victimization, it follows logically that reducing risk requires challenges to hegemonic power—challenges that are organized, systematic, and persistent.

Notes

NOTES TO CHAPTER 1

1 Efforts have been under way for decades to predict earthquakes or, failing that, to issue short-term warnings, advisories, and real-time warnings—that is, warnings issued to distant areas at the time when earthquakes begin to occur. Without going into detail about the success—or lack of it—of such initiatives, suffice it to say that, at this point in time, the ability to foresee earthquakes remains elusive.
2 This definition of hazard mitigation should not be confused with the way the term is used in climate change circles, where mitigation refers to efforts to limit greenhouse gas emissions and reduce global warming.

NOTES TO CHAPTER 2

1 White and his collaborators later acknowledged this blind spot, noting that "[a]long with growth of interest in the concept of vulnerability has come a recognition of the role of broader, deeper and more powerful social forces which constrain choice and which cannot be countered with technical or social fixes" (White, Kates, and Burton 2001: 91).

NOTES TO CHAPTER 3

1 WEA was developed in a collaboration among the Federal Communications Commission, the FEMA, and cell phone service providers.

NOTES TO CHAPTER 4

1 The report was produced as part of the National Climate Assessment (NCA). A federal law, the Global Change Research Act of 1990, makes it mandatory for the participating agencies to develop an updated NCA every four years.
2 More information on the non-disclosure of hazards in Texas can be found in the 2016 *Houston Chronicle* series "Chemical Breakdown."
3 SOVI scores and publications that employ SOVI in vulnerability assessment can be found on the website of the University of South Carolina's Hazards and Vulnerability Research Institute (http://artsandsciences.sc.edu/geog/hvri/front-page).
4 This happened under the presidency of Bill Clinton, who promoted the

export of Arkansas-grown rice to Haiti and later apologized for doing so in view of its impact on Haiti's economy.

5 It should be noted, however, that "growth" doesn't always mean more construction. Capital accumulation can also take place when limits on growth, whether natural or legally enforced, cause housing prices to soar, as seen, for example, in the city of San Francisco.

6 At the time of that race riot, Tulsa was home to the wealthiest African American community in the United States and to what was then called "Black Wall Street."

NOTES TO CHAPTER 6

1 The term "Matthew effect" is based on the biblical gospel of Matthew, which states (13:12): "Whoever has will be given more . . . Whoever does not have, even what they have will be taken from them." Merton's original use of the concept referred to the fact that, in science, scientists who already have high status are given more credit for their discoveries than less eminent researchers, even if the latter made more substantive contributions to discoveries. As a consequence, resources accrue to more famous senior scientists at the expense of equally creative and accomplished junior ones.

2 This number includes both people who died during the heat wave (70,000) and subsequent deaths that were attributed to exposure to extreme heat (7,000). The study also includes deaths that occurred during periods of extreme heat in June, as well as during high-heat periods in August.

NOTES TO CHAPTER 7

1 This literature refers to "families," but I prefer "households," which can include unrelated members, so I will use both terms interchangeably.

2 At the time when the Tangshan earthquake took place, China was much more of a centralized, Soviet-style state, with strong governmental control over most aspects of its social and economic life. China was poorer, more rural, and much less developed. Like the Soviet Union, China did not permit the dissemination of information about the disasters that took place within its borders. The outside world learned about the Tangshan catastrophe only gradually, over a period of years.

NOTES TO CHAPTER 8

1 Recall that recent decades have seen growth in the number of nation-states. Former regions in the Soviet Union are now sixteen separate nation-states. Additionally, other entities have declared independence, breaking off into smaller national units; for example, the former Yugoslavia is now five separate countries, and the former Czechoslovakia is now two countries: the Czech Republic and Slovakia.

Bibliography

Adams, V. (2012) The other road to serfdom: Recovery by the market and the affect economy in New Orleans. *Public Culture* 24(1), 185–216.

Adams, V. (2013) *Markets of Sorrow, Labors of Faith: New Orleans in the Wake of Katrina*. Duke University Press, Durham, NC.

Adams, V., Van Hattum, T., and English, D. (2009) Chronic disaster syndrome: Displacement, disaster capitalism, and the eviction of the poor from New Orleans. *American Ethnologist* 36(4), 615–636.

Adams, V., Kaufman, S.R., Van Hattum, T., and Moody, S. (2011) Aging Disaster: Mortality, vulnerability, and long-term recovery among Katrina survivors. *Medical Anthropology* 30(3), 247–270.

Adeola, F.O. and Picou, J.S. (2012) Race, social capital, and the health impacts of Katrina: Evidence from the Louisiana and Mississippi Gulf Coast. *Human Ecology Review* 19(1), 10–24.

Adeola, F.O. and Picou, J.S. (2014) Social capital and the mental health impacts of hurricane Katrina: Assessing long-term patterns of psychosocial distress. *International Journal of Mass Emergencies and Disasters* 32(1), 121–156.

Adger, W.N. (2000) Social and ecological resilience: Are they related? *Progress in Human Geography* 24, 347–364.

Adger, W.N. (2003) Social capital, collective action, and adaptation to climate change. *Economic Geography* 79(4), 387–404.

Aerts, J.C.J.H., Botzen, W.J.W., Emanuel, K., Lin, N., de Moel, H., and Michel-Kerjan, E.O. (2014) Evaluating flood resilience strategies for coastal megacities. *Science* 344(6183), 473–475.

Aguirre, B.E. (2002) Can sustainable development sustain us? *International Journal of Mass Emergencies and Disasters* 20, 111–125.

Aguirre, B.E., Wenger, D., and Vigo, G. (1998) A test of the emergent norm theory of collective behavior. *Sociological Forum* 13(2), 301–320.

Agyeman, J., Bullard, R.D., and Evans, B. (2003) *Just Sustainabilities: Development in an Unequal World*. Earthscan: London.

Aida, J., Kawachi, I., Subramanian, S.V., and Kondo, K. (2013) Disaster, social capital, and health. In I. Kawachi, S. Takao, and S.V. Subramanian, eds., *Global Perspectives on Social Capital and Health*. Springer: New York, 167–187.

Albala-Bertrand, J.M. (1993) *Political Economy of Large Natural Disasters*. Clarendon: Oxford.

Albala-Bertrand, J.M. (2006) The unlikeliness of an economic catastrophe: Localization and globalization. Working Paper 576, Queen Mary University of London, School of Economics and Finance, London.

Albright, E.A. and Crow, D.A. (2015) Learning processes, public and stakeholder engagement: Analyzing responses to Colorado's extreme flood events of 2013. *Urban Climate* 14, 79–93.

Albright, E.A. and Crow, D.A. (2016) Learning in the aftermath of extreme floods: Community damage and stakeholder perceptions of future risk. *Risk, Hazards & Crisis in Public Policy* 6(3), 308–328.

Aldrich, D.P. (2010) Fixing recovery: Social capital in post-crisis resilience. *Journal of Homeland Security*, http://works.bepress.com/daniel_aldrich/7.

Aldrich, D.P. (2011) The externalities of strong social capital: Post-tsunami recovery in Southeast India. *Journal of Civil Society* 7(1), 81–99.

Aldrich, D.P. (2012a) *Building Resilience: Social Capital in Post-Disaster Recovery.* University of Chicago Press, Chicago, IL.

Aldrich, D.P. (2012b) Social capital in post disaster recovery: Towards a resilient and compassionate East Asian community. In Y. Sawada and S. Oum, eds., *Economic and Welfare Impacts of Disasters in East Asia and Policy Responses.* ERIA: Jakarta, 157–178.

Aldrich, D.P. (2012c) Social, not physical, infrastructure: The critical role of civil society after the 1923 Tokyo earthquake. *Disasters* 36(3), 398–419.

Aldrich, D.P. and Crook, K. (2008) Strong civil society as a double-edged sword: Siting trailers in post-Katrina New Orleans. *Political Research Quarterly* 61(3), 379–389.

Aldrich, D.P. and Meyer, M.A. (2015) Social capital and community resilience. *American Behavioral Scientist* 59(2), 254–269.

Alesch, D.J., Arendt, L.A., and Petak, W.J. (2005) *Seismic Safety in California Hospitals: Assessing an Attempt to Accelerate the Replacement or Seismic Retrofit of Older Hospital Facilities.* Multidisciplinary Center for Earthquake Engineering Research, SUNY: Buffalo.

Alesch, D.J., Arendt, L.A., and Petak, W.J. (2012) *Natural Hazard Mitigation Policy Implementation, Organizational Choice, and Contextual Dynamics.* Springer: Dordrecht.

Alesch, D.J. and Holly, J.N. (1998) Small business failure, survival, and recovery: Lessons from the January 1994 Northridge Earthquake. In *Proceedings of the NEHRP Conference and Workshop on Research on the Northridge, California Earthquake of January 17, 1994.* Consortium of Universities for Research in Earthquake Engineering: Richmond, CA, 48–55.

Alesch, D.J., Holly, J.N., Mittler, E., and Nagy, R. (2001) *Organizations at Risk: What Happens When Small Businesses and Not-for-Profits Encounter Natural Disasters.* Public Entity Risk Institute: Fairfax, VA.

Alesch, D.J. and Petak, W.J. (1986) *The Politics and Economics of Earthquake Hazard*

Mitigation: Unreinforced Masonry Buildings in Southern California. Institute of Behavioral Science, University of Colorado: Boulder.

Alexander, D.E. (2013) Resilience and disaster risk reduction: An etymological journey. *Natural Hazards and Earth System Sciences* 13(11), 2707–2716. doi: 10.5194/nhess-13-2707-2013.

Allen, B.L. (2007) Environmental justice, local knowledge, and after-disaster planning in New Orleans. *Technology in Society* 29, 153–159.

American Red Cross, National Immigration Law Center, and National Council of La Raza (2007) *Fact Sheet: Immigration Eligibility for Disaster Assistance,* http:// www.nilc.org/wp-content/uploads/2015/11/disasterassist_immeligibility_20 07-062.pdf.

American Society of Civil Engineers Hurricane Katrina External Review Panel (2007) *The New Orleans Hurricane Protection System: What Went Wrong and Why.* ASCE: Reston, VA.

Andersen, M.L. and Collins, P.H. (2016) *Race, Class, and Gender: An Anthology,* 9th edn. Cengage Learning: Boston, MA.

Anderson, G.B. and Bell, M.L. (2012) Lights out: Impact of the August 2003 power outage on mortality in New York, NY. *Epidemiology* 23, 189–193.

Anderson, W.A. (2014) The Great Alaska Earthquake and the dawn of US social science earthquake research. In *Proceedings of the 10th National Conference in Earthquake Engineering.* Earthquake Engineering Research Institute: Anchorage, AK. https://datacenterhub.org/resources/12948/download/10 NCEE-001678.pdf.

Ansell, C., Boin, A., and Keller, A. (2010) Managing transboundary crises: Identifying the building blocks of an effective response system. *Journal of Contingencies and Crisis Management* 18(4), 195–207.

Applied Technology Council (2016) *Critical Assessment of Lifeline System Performance: Understanding Societal Needs in Disaster Recovery.* National Institute of Standards and Technology: Gaithersburg, MD.

Arbon, P., Steenkamp, M., Cornell, V., Cusack, L., and Gebbie, K. (2016) Measuring disaster resilience in communities and households: Pragmatic tools developed in Australia. *International Journal of Disaster Resilience in the Built Environment* 7, 201–215.

Arif, A., Robinson, J., Stanek, S., Fichet, E.S., Townsend, P., Worku, Z., and Starbird, K. (2017) A closer look at the self-correcting crowd: Examining corrections in online rumors. *Proceedings of the ACM 2017 Conference on Computer-Supported Cooperative Work and Social Computing (CSCW '17).* ACM: Portland, OR, 155–168.

Arnold, C. (2014) Once upon a mine: The legacy of uranium on the Navajo nation. *Environmental Health Perspectives* 122, A44–A49.

Aronoff, M. and Gunter, V. (1992) Defining disaster: Local constructions for recovery in the aftermath of chemical contamination. *Social Problems* 39, 345–365.

Arup (2015) *City Resilience Index*. London, http://www.arup.com/projects/city-resilience-index.

Arvai, J. and Rivers, L., eds. (2014) *Risk Communication: Learning From the Past, Charting a Course for the Future*. Taylor & Francis: London.

Ash, K.D., Cutter, S.L., and Emrich, C.T. (2013) Acceptable losses? The relative impacts of natural hazards in the United States, 1980–2009. *International Journal of Disaster Risk Reduction* 5, 61–72.

Asia-Pacific Economic Cooperation (2015) *Annex A: APEC Disaster Risk Reduction Framework*. APEC, http://www.apec.org/Meeting-Papers/Annual-Ministerial-Meetings/2015/2015_amm/annexa.

Auyero, J. and Swistun, D. (2008) The social production of toxic uncertainty. *American Sociological Review* 73, 357–379.

Bankoff, G., Frerks, G., and Hilhorst, D. (2004) *Mapping Vulnerability: Disasters, Development and People*. Earthscan: London.

Barr, D.A. (2014) *Health Disparities in the United States: Social Class, Race, Ethnicity, and Health*. Johns Hopkins University Press: Baltimore, MD.

Barrios, R.E. (2017) What does catastrophe reveal for whom? The anthropology of crises and disasters at the onset of the Anthropocene. *Annual Review of Anthropology* 46, 151–166.

Barron Ausbrooks, C.Y., Barrett, E.J., and Martinez-Cosio, M. (2009) Ethical issues in disaster research: Lessons from Hurricane Katrina. *Population Research and Policy Review* 28(1), 93–106.

Barrows, H.H. (1923) Geography as human ecology. *Annals of the Association of American Geographers* 13, 1–14.

Barry, J. (1997) *Rising Tide: The Great Mississippi Flood of 1927 and How It Changed America*. Simon & Schuster: New York.

Bartlett, S. (2008) The implications of climate change for children in lower-income countries. *Children, Youth, and Environments* 18(1), 71–98, http://www.jstor.org/stable/10.7721/chilyoutenvi.18.1.0071.

Bates, K.A. and Swan, R.S. (2010) *Through the Eye of Katrina: Social Justice in the United States*. Carolina Academic Press: Durham, NC.

Beamish, T.D. (2002a) *Silent Spill: The Organization of an Industrial Crisis*. MIT Press: Cambridge, MA.

Beamish, T.D. (2002b) Waiting for crisis: Regulatory inaction and ineptitude and the Guadalupe dunes oil spill. *Social Problems* 49, 150–177.

Bean, H., Liu, B.F., Madden, S., Sutton, J., Wood, M.M., and Mileti, D.S. (2016) Disaster warnings in your pocket: How audiences interpret mobile alerts for an unfamiliar hazard. *Journal of Contingencies and Crisis Management* 24(3), 136–147.

Bean, H., Sutton, J., Liu, B.F., Madden, S., Wood, M.M., and Mileti, D.S. (2015) The study of mobile public warning messages: A research review and agenda. *Review of Communication* 15(1), 60–80. doi: 10.1080/15358593.2015.1014402.

Becvar, D.S. (2013) *Handbook of Family Resilience*. Springer: New York.

Belli, A. and Falkenberg, L. (2005) 24 nursing home evacuees die in bus fire. *Houston Chronicle*, September 24, http://www.chron.com/news/hurricanes/article/24-nursing-home-evacuees-die-in-bus-fire-1946742.php.

Béné, C., Mehta, L., McGranahan, G., Cannon, T., Gupte, J., and Tanner, T. (2018) Resilience as a policy narrative: Potentials and limits in the context of urban planning. *Climate and Development* 10(2), 116–133, http://dx.doi.org/10.1080/17565529.2017.1301868.

Benson, C. and Twigg, J. (2004) *Measuring Mitigation: Methodologies for Assessing Natural Hazard Risks and the Net Benefits of Mitigation: A Scoping Study*. ProVention Consortium and the International Federation of Red Cross and Red Crescent Societies: Geneva.

Berger, P.L. (1963) *Invitation to Sociology: A Humanistic Perspective*. Doubleday: New York.

Berger, P.L. and Luckmann, T. (1966) *The Social Construction of Reality: A Treatise in the Sociology of Knowledge*. Anchor Books: New York.

Berke, P., Newman, G., Lee, J., Combs, T., Kolosna, C., and Salvesen, D. (2015) Evaluation of networks of plans and vulnerability to hazards and climate change: A resilience scorecard. *Journal of the American Planning Association* 81(4), 287–302.

Berliner, P.F. (1994) *Thinking in Jazz: The Art of Improvisation*. University of Chicago Press: Chicago, IL.

Bevc, C.A. (2010) *Working on the Edge: Examining Covariates in Multi-Organizational Networks on September 11th Attacks on the World Trade Center*. Doctoral dissertation, University of Colorado, Boulder.

Bevc, C.A., Nicholls, K., and Picou, J.S. (2010) Community recovery from Hurricane Katrina: Storm experiences, property damage, and the human condition. In D.L. Brunsma, D. Overfelt, and J.S. Picou, eds., *The Sociology of Katrina: Perspectives on a Modern Catastrophe*, 2nd edn. Rowman & Littlefield, Lanham, MD, 135–156.

Birkland, T.A. (1997) *After Disaster: Agenda Setting, Public Policy, and Focusing Events*. Georgetown University Press: Washington, DC.

Birkland, T.A. (2007) *Lessons of Disaster: Policy Change after Catastrophic Events*. Georgetown University Press: Washington, DC.

Birkmann, J. (2006) Measuring vulnerability to promote disaster-resilient societies: Conceptual frameworks and definitions. In J. Birkmann, ed., *Measuring Vulnerability to Natural Hazards: Towards Disaster Resilient Societies*. United Nations University Press: Tokyo, 9–54.

Black, K. and Lobo, M. (2008) A conceptual review of family resilience factors. *Journal of Family Nursing* 14(1), 33–55.

Blaikie, P., Cannon, T., Davis, I. and Wisner, B. (1994) *At Risk: Natural Hazards, People's Vulnerability, and Disasters*. Routledge: London.

Blumenfeld, W.J. (2016) God and natural disasters: It's the gays' fault? *Huffington*

Post, February 2, https://www.huffingtonpost.com/warren-j-blumenfeld/god-and-natural-disasters-its-the-gays-fault_b_2068817.html.

Blumer, H. (1939) Collective behavior. In R.E. Park, ed., *Principles of Sociology*. Barnes and Noble, New York, 219–280.

Blumer, H. (1969) *Symbolic Interactionism: Perspective and Method*. Prentice-Hall: Englewood Cliffs, NJ.

Bobb, J.F., Peng, R.D., Bell, M.L., and Dominici, F. (2014) Heat-related mortality and adaptation to heat in the United States. *Environmental Health Perspectives* 122(8), 811–816.

Boin, A. (2009) The new world of crises and crisis management: Implications for policy and research. *Review of Policy Research* 26(4), 367–377.

Boin, A., Busuioc, M., and Groenleer, M. (2013) Building European union capacity to manage transboundary crises: Network or lead-agency model? *Regulation & Governance* 8(4), 1–20.

Boin, A. and 't Hart, P. (2012) Aligning executive action in times of adversity: The politics of crisis co-ordination. In M. Lodge and K. Wegrich, eds., *Executive Politics in Times of Crisis*. Palgrave: Basingstoke, 179–196.

Bolin, B., Grineski, S., and Collins, T. (2005) The geography of despair: Environmental racism and the making of South Phoenix, Arizona, USA. *Human Ecology Review* 12(2), 156–168.

Bolin, B. and Kurtz, L.C. (2018) Race, class, ethnicity, and disaster vulnerability. In H. Rodríguez, W. Donner, and J.E. Trainor, eds., *Handbook of Disaster Research*, 2nd edn. Springer: Cham, Switzerland, 181–203.

Bolin, R.C. and Stanford, L. (1990) Shelter and housing issues in Santa Cruz county. In R.C. Bolin, ed., *The Loma Prieta Earthquake: Studies of Short-Term Impacts*. Institute of Behavioral Science, University of Colorado: Boulder.

Bolin, R.C. and Stanford, L. (1993) Emergency sheltering and housing of earthquake victims: The case of Santa Cruz county. In P.A. Bolton, ed., *The Loma Prieta, California, Earthquake of October 17, 1989: Public Responses*. US Government Printing Office: Washington, DC., B43–B50.

Bolin, R.C. and Stanford, L. (1998) *The Northridge Earthquake: Vulnerability and Disaster*. Routledge: London.

Bonanno, G.A., Brewin, C.R., Kaniasty, K., and LaGreca, A.M. (2010) Weighing the costs of disaster: Consequences, risks, and resilience in individuals, families, and communities. *Psychological Science in the Public Interest* 11, 1–49.

Bondi, L. (1990) Feminism, postmodernism, and geography: Space for Women? *Antipode* 22(2), 156–167.

Boscarino, J.A., Kirchner, H.L., Hoffman, S.N., Sartorius, J., and Adams, R.E. (2011) PTSD and alcohol use after the World Trade Center attacks: A longitudinal study. *Journal of Traumatic Stress* 24(5), 515–525.

Bostrom, A., Fischhoff, B., and Morgan, M.G. (1992) Characterizing mental models of hazardous processes: A methodology and an application to radon. *Journal of Social Issues* 48(4), 85–100.

Bosworth, S.L. and Kreps, G.A. (1986) Structure as process: Organization and role. *American Sociological Review* 51, 699–716.

Bourdieu, P. (1986) The forms of capital. In J.G. Richardson, ed., *Handbook of Theory and Research for the Sociology of Education*. Greenwood Press: New York, 241–258.

Bourque, L.B., Mileti, D.S., Kano, M., and Wood, M.M. (2012) Who prepares for terrorism? *Environment and Behavior* 44(3), 374–409, http://dx.doi.org/10.1177/0013916510390318.

Bourque, L.B., Siegel, J.M., Kano, M., and Wood, M.M. (2006) Weathering the storm: The impact of hurricanes on physical and mental health. *The Annals of the American Academy of Political and Social Science* 604(1), 129–151.

Bourque, L.B., Siegel, J.M., Kano, M., and Wood, M.M. (2007) Morbidity and mortality associated with disasters. In H. Rodríguez, E.L. Quarantelli, and R.R. Dynes, eds., *Handbook of Disaster Research*. Springer: New York, 97–112.

Bours, D., McGinn, C., and Pringle, P. (2014a) *Guidance Note 1: Twelve Reasons Why Climate Change Adaptation M&E Is Challenging*. Sea Change, Phnom Penh, Cambodia & UKCIP: Oxford.

Bours, D., McGinn, C., and Pringle, P. (2014b) *Guidance Note 3: Theory of Change Approach to Climate Change Adaptation Programming*. Sea Change, Phnom Penh, Cambodia & UKCIP: Oxford.

Boykoff, M.T. and Boykoff, J.M. (2004) Balance as bias: Global warming and the US prestige press. *Global Environmental Change* 14, 125–136.

Brackbill, R.M., Stellman, S.D., Perlman, S.E., Walker, D.J., and Farfel, M.R. (2013) Mental health of those directly exposed to the World Trade Center disaster: Unmet mental health care need, mental health treatment service use, and quality of life. *Social Science & Medicine* 81, 110–114.

Bragg, R. (1999) Storm over South Florida building codes. *New York Times*, May 27.

Brody, S.D., Kang, J.E., and Bernhardt, S.P. (2010) Identifying factors influencing flood mitigation at the local level in Texas and Florida: The role of organizational capacity. *Natural Hazards* 52, 167–184, http://dx.doi.org/10.1007/s11069-009-9364-5.

Brody, S.D., Kang, J.E., Zahran, S., and Bernhardt, S.P. (2009) Evaluating local flood mitigation strategies in Texas and Florida. *Built Environment* 35(4), 492–515.

Brouillette, J.R. and Quarantelli, E.L. (1971) Types of patterned variation in bureaucratic adaptations to organizational stress. *Sociological Inquiry* 41, 39–46.

Brown, P. (1995) Race, class, and environmental health: A review and systemization of the literature. *Environmental Research* 69(1), 15–30.

Brown, P. (2007) *Toxic Exposures: Contested Illnesses and the Environmental Health Movement*. Columbia University Press: New York, NY.

Browne, K.E. (2015) *Standing in Need: Culture, Comfort, and Coming Home after Katrina.* University of Texas Press: Austin, TX.

Browne, K.E. and Peek, L. (2014) Beyond the IRB: An ethical toolkit for long-term disaster research. *International Journal of Mass Emergencies and Disasters* 32(1), 82–120.

Bruder, J. (2017) *Nomadland: Surviving America in the Twenty-First Century.* Norton: New York.

Brulle, R.J. and Pellow, D.N. (2006) Environmental justice: Human health and environmental inequalities. *Annual Review of Public Health* 27, 103–124, http://dx.doi.org/10.1146/annurev.publhealth.27.021405.102124.

Bruneau, M., Chang, S.E., Eguchi, R.T. et al. (2003) A framework to quantitatively assess and enhance the seismic resilience of communities. *Earthquake Spectra* 19, 733–752. doi: 10.1193/1.1623497.

Bryant, B. and Mohai, P. (1992) *Race and the Incidence of Environmental Hazards: A Time for Discourse.* Westview Press: Boulder, CO.

Bullard, R.D. (1990) *Dumping in Dixie: Race, Class, and Environmental Quality.* Westview Press: Boulder, CO.

Bullard, R.D. and Wright, B., eds. (2009) *Race, Place, and Environmental Justice After Hurricane Katrina.* Westview Press: Boulder, CO.

Bullard, R.D. and Wright, B. (2012) *The Wrong Complexion for Protection: How the Government Response to Disaster Endangers African American Communities.* NYU Press: New York.

Bullock, J.A., Haddow, G.D., Haddow, K.S. (2008) *Global Warming, Natural Hazards, and Emergency Management.* CRC Press: Boca Raton, FL.

Burby, R.J., ed. (1998) *Cooperating with Nature: Confronting Natural Hazards with Land-Use Planning for Sustainable Communities.* Joseph Henry Press: Washington, DC.

Burby, R.J. (2006) Hurricane Katrina and the paradoxes of government disaster policy: Bringing about wise governmental decisions for hazardous areas. *Annals of the American Academy of Political and Social Science* 604, 171–191.

Bureau of Labor Statistics (2013) Marriage and divorce: Patterns by gender, race, and educational attainment. *Monthly Labor Review.* doi: 10.21916/mlr.2013.32.

Burt, R. (1992) *Structural Holes: The Social Structure of Competition.* Harvard University Press: Cambridge, MA.

Burton, C. and Cutter, S.L. (2008) Levee failures and social vulnerability in the Sacramento-San Joaquin Delta area, California. *Natural Hazards Review* 9(3), 136–149. doi: 10.1061/(ASCE)1527–6988(2008)9:3(136).

Burton, C., Mitchell, J.T., and Cutter, S.L. (2011) Evaluating post-Katrina recovery in Mississippi using repeat photography. *Disasters* 35(3), 488–509.

Burton, I., Kates, R.W., and White, G.F. (1978) *The Environment as Hazard.* Oxford University Press: New York.

Bush, E.M. (2014) Homeless individuals and families are especially vulnerable during disasters and emergencies. *Michigan State University Extension*, July 7, http://msue.anr.msu.edu/news/homeless_individuals_and_families_are_especially_vulnerable_during_disaster.

Button, G. (2016) *Disaster Culture: Knowledge and Uncertainty in the Wake of Human and Environmental Catastrophe.* Routledge: New York.

Butts, C.T., Acton, R.M., and Marcum, C.S. (2012) Interorganizational collaboration in the Hurricane Katrina response. *Journal of Social Structure* 13, 1–17, http://www.cmu.edu/joss/content/articles/volume13/ButtsActonMarcum.pdf.

Butts, C.T., Petrescu-Prahova, M., and Cross, B.R. (2007) Responder communication networks in the World Trade Center disaster: Implications for modeling of communication within emergency settings. *Journal of Mathematical Sociology* 31(2), 121–147. doi: 10.1080/00222500601188056.

Cable, S., Shriver, T.E., and Mix, T.L. (2008) Risk society and contested illness: The case of nuclear weapons workers. *American Sociological Review* 73, 380–401.

Cameron, E. (2017) Natural disasters and international law. Peace Palace Library, September 14, https://www.peacepalacelibrary.nl/2017/09/natural-disasters-and-international-law.

Campbell, N. (2016) *Trial by flood: Experiences of older adults in disaster.* Doctoral dissertation, Department of Sociology, University of Colorado, Boulder.

Cannon, T. and Müller-Mahn, D. (2010) Vulnerability, resilience and development discourses in context of climate change. *Natural Hazards* 55, 621–635.

Cardona, O.D. (2010) *Indicators of Disaster Risk and Risk Management: Summary Report, Program for Latin America and the Caribbean.* Washington, DC: Inter-American Development Bank.

Cardona, O.D. (2011) Disaster risk and vulnerability: Concepts and measurement of human and environmental insecurity. In H.G. Brauch, U.O., Spring, C., Mesjasz, et al. *Coping with Global Environmental Change, Disasters and Security.* Springer-Verlag, Berlin, Germany, 107–121.

Cardona, O.D., Ordaz, M.G., Marulanda, M.C., Barbat, A.H., and Carreño, M.L. (2010) Earthquake risk from the financial protection perspective: A metric for fiscal vulnerability evaluation in the Americas. Paper presented at the 14th European Conference on Earthquake Engineering, Ohrid, Macedonia.

Cardona, O.D., Ordaz, M.G., Marulanda, M.C., Carreño, M.L., and Barbat, A.H. (2010) Disaster risk from a macroeconomic perspective: A metric for fiscal vulnerability evaluation. *Disasters* 34(4), 1064–1083.

Carpenter, S., Walker, B., Anderies, J.M., and Abel, N. (2001) From metaphor to measurement: Resilience of what to what? *Ecosystems* 4, 765–781.

Carr, L.J. (1932) Disaster and the sequence-pattern concept of social change. *American Journal of Sociology* 38(2), 207–218, http://www.jstor.org/stable/2766454.

Cartlidge, E. (2014) Updated: Appeals court overturns manslaughter convictions of six earthquake scientists. *Science*, November 10, http://www.sci encemag.org/news/2014/11/updated-appeals-court-overturns-manslaughter-convictions-six-earthquake-scientists.

Cascadia Region Earthquake Workgroup (2013) Cascadia Subduction Zone Earthquakes: A Magnitude 9.0 Earthquake Scenario. CREW: Seattle, WA.

Centers for Disease Control and Prevention (2004) Mental health status of World Trade Center rescue and recovery workers and volunteers: New York City, July 2002–August 2004. *Center for Disease Control and Prevention Morbidity and Mortality Weekly Report* 53(35), 812–815.

Centre for Research on the Epidemiology of Disasters (CRED) (2016) *Poverty and Death: Disaster Mortality 1996–2015*. CRED, Institute of Health and Society, Université catholique de Louvain: Brussels.

Cerulo, K. (2008) *Never Saw It Coming: Cultural Challenges to Envisioning the Worst*. University of Chicago Press: Chicago, IL.

Chakraborty, J., Collins, T.W., Montgomery, M.C. and Grineski, S.E. (2014) Social and spatial inequities in exposure to flood risk in Miami, Florida. *Natural Hazards Review* 15(3). doi: 10.1061/(ASCE)NH.1527–6996.0000140.

Chamlee-Wright, E.L. (2010) *The Cultural and Political Economy of Recovery: Social Learning in a Post-Disaster Environment*. Routledge: London.

Chamlee-Wright, E.L. and Storr, V.H. (2009) "There's no place like New Orleans": Sense of place and community recovery in the ninth ward after Hurricane Katrina. *Journal of Urban Affairs* 31, 615–634.

Chamlee-Wright, E.L. and Storr, V.H., eds. (2010) *The Political Economy of Hurricane Katrina and Community Rebound*. Edward Elgar: Cheltenham.

Chamlee-Wright, E.L. and Storr, V.H. (2011) Social capital as collective narratives and post-disaster community recovery. *Sociological Review* 59(2), 266–282.

Chang, S.E. (2000) Disasters and transport systems: Loss, recovery, and competition at the port of Kobe after the 1995 earthquake. *Journal of Transport Geography* 8(1), 53–65.

Chang, S.E. (2010) Urban disaster recovery: A measurement framework with application to the 1995 Kobe Earthquake. *Disasters* 34(2), 303–327.

Chang, S.E. and Rose, A.Z. (2012) Towards a theory of economic recovery from disasters. *International Journal of Mass Emergencies and Disasters* 32(2), 171–181.

Chauhan, A. and Hughes, A.L. (2017) Providing online crisis information: An analysis of official sources during the 2014 Carlton Complex wildfire. In *Proceedings of the 25th International Conference on Human Factors in Computing Systems (CHI 2017)*. ACM, New York, NY, 399–408.

Chen, W., Cutter, S.L., Emrich, C.T., and Shi, P. (2013) Measuring social vulnerability to natural hazards in the Yangtze River Delta region, China. *International Journal of Disaster Risk Science* 4(4), 169–181.

Children's Health Fund and National Center for Disaster Preparedness (2010) *Legacy of Katrina: The Impact of a Flawed Recovery on Vulnerable Children of the Gulf*

Coast: A Five-Year Status Report: Significant Emotional Distress, Behavioral Problems and Instability Persist among Children Affected by the 2005 Disaster. Columbia University: New York.

Chung, B., Jones, L., Campbell, L.X., Glover, H., Gelberg, L. and Chen, D.T. (2008) National recommendations for enhancing the conduct of ethical health research with human participants in post-disaster situations. *Ethnicity & Disease* 18, 378–383.

Clark, B. and Jorgenson, A.K. (2012) The treadmill of destruction and the environment impacts of militaries. *Sociology Compass* 6(7), 557–569.

Clarke, L. (1993) The disqualification heuristic: When do organizations misperceive risk? In W.R. Freudenburg and T.I.K. Youn, eds., *Research in Social Problems and Public Policy*. JAI Press: Greenwich, CT, vol. 5, 289–312.

Clarke, L. (2002) Panic: Myth or reality? *Contexts* 1, 21–26.

Cobb, J.A. (2013) *Flood of Lies: The St. Rita's Nursing Home Tragedy*. Pelican: Gretna, LA.

Coleman, J.S. (1988) Social capital in the creation of human capital. *American Journal of Sociology* 94, S95–S120.

Collins, P.H. and Bilge, S. (2016) *Intersectionality*. Polity: Malden, MA.

Collins, T. (2010) Marginalization, facilitation, and the production of unequal risk: The 2006 Paso del Norte floods. *Antipode* 42, 258–288.

Collins, T. and Bolin, B. (2009) Situating hazard vulnerability: negotiating wildfire hazard in the US southwest. *Environmental Management* 44, 441–459.

Collogan, L.K., Tuma, F., Dolan-Sewell, R., Borja, S., and Fleischman, A.R. (2004) Ethical issues pertaining to research in the aftermath of disaster. *Journal of Traumatic Stress* 17(5), 363–372.

Comfort, L.K., Boin, A., and Demchak, C.C. (eds.) (2010) *Designing Resilience: Preparing for Extreme Events*. University of Pittsburgh Press: Pittsburgh, PA.

Commission on Racial Justice (1987) *Toxic Wastes and Race in the United States: A National Report on the Racial and Socio-Economic Characteristics on Communities with Hazardous Waste Sites*. United Church of Christ: New York.

Community and Regional Resilience Institute (2013) *Building Resilience in America's Communities: Observations and Implications of the CRS Pilots*. CARRI: Washington, DC.

Coppola, D.P. (2007) *Introduction to International Disaster Management*. Elsevier: Boston, MA.

Courtney-Long, E.A., Carroll, D.D., Zhang, Q.C., Stevens, A.S., Griffin-Blake, S., Armour, B.S., and Campbell, V.A. (2015) Prevalence of disability and disability type among adults, United States, 2013. *Centers for Disease Control and Prevention: Morbidity and Mortality Weekly Report* 64(29), 777–808.

Crenshaw, K. (1991) Mapping the margins: Intersectionality, identity politics, and violence against women of color. *Stanford Law Review* 43(6), 1241–1299, http://www.jstor.org/stable/1229039.

Cummings, C.L., Berube, D.M., and Lavelle, M.E. (2013) Influences of individual-level characteristics on risk perceptions to various categories of environmental health and safety risks. *Journal of Risk Research* 16(10), 1277–1295. doi: 10.1080/13669877.2013.788544.

Cutter, S.L. (1996) Vulnerability to environmental hazards. *Progress in Human Geography* 20(4), 529–539.

Cutter, S.L., ed. (2001) *American Hazardscapes: The Regionalization of Hazards and Disasters.* Joseph Henry Press: Washington, DC.

Cutter, S.L. (2003) The vulnerability of science and the science of vulnerability. *Annals of the Association of American Geographers* 93(1), 1–12. doi: 10.1111/1467–8306.93101.

Cutter, S.L. (2016) The landscape of disaster resilience indicators in the USA. *Natural Hazards* 80, 741–758.

Cutter, S.L. (2017) The forgotten casualties redux: Women, children, and disaster risk. *Global Environmental Change* 42, 117–121.

Cutter, S.L., Ash, K.D., and Emrich, C.T. (2014) The geographies of community disaster resilience. *Global Environmental Change* 29, 65–77.

Cutter, S.L., Ash, K.D. and Emrich, C.T. (2016) Urban-rural differences in disaster resilience. *Annals of the American Association of Geographers* 106(6), 1236–1252. doi: 10.1080/24694452.2016.1194740.

Cutter, S.L., Barnes, L., Berry, C., Burton, C., Evans, E., Tate, E., and Webb, J. (2008) A place-based model for understanding community resilience to natural disasters. *Global Environmental Change* 18, 598–606. doi: 10.1016/j.gloenvcha.2008.07.013.

Cutter, S.L., Boruff, B.J., and Shirley, W.L. (2003) Social vulnerability to environmental hazards. *Social Science Quarterly* 84(2), 242–261.

Cutter, S.L., Burton, C., and Emrich, C.T. (2010) Disaster resilience indicators for benchmarking baseline conditions. *Journal of Homeland Security and Emergency Management* 7(1), 1–22.

Cutter, S.L., Emrich, C.T., Mitchell, J.T., Piegorsch, W.W., Smith, M.M. and Weber, L. (2016) *Hurricane Katrina and the Forgotten Coast of Mississippi.* Cambridge University Press: New York.

Cutter, S.L., Schumann, R.L., and Emrich, C.T. (2014) Exposure, social vulnerability and recovery disparities in New Jersey after Hurricane Sandy. *Journal of Extreme Events* 1(1). doi: 10.1142/S234573761450002X.

Dahlhamer, J.M. and Tierney, K. (1998) Rebounding from disruptive events: Business recovery following the Northridge earthquake. *Sociological Spectrum* 18(2), 121–141.

Daly, M. and Silver, H. (2008) Social exclusion and social capital: A comparison and critique. *Theory and Society* 37(6), 537–566.

Darrah, N. (2017) Florida nursing home deaths during Hurricane Irma ruled homicides. *Fox News*, November 22, http://www.foxnews.com/us/2017/11/22/florida-nursing-home-deaths-during-hurricane-irma-ruled-homicides.html.

Dash, N. and Peacock. W.G. (2003) Long-term recovery from Hurricane Andrew: A comparison of two ethnically diverse communities. Paper presented at the annual meeting of the Southwestern Sociological Association, San Antonio.

Dastagir, A.E. (2017) What do men get that women don't? Here are a few things. *USA Today*, March 1.

Davis, E.A., Hansen, R., Kett, M., Mincin, J., and Twigg, J. (2013) Disability. In D.S.K. Thomas, B.D. Phillips, W.E. Lovekamp, and A. Fothergill, eds., *Social Vulnerability to Disasters*, 2nd edn. CRC Press: Boca Raton, FL, 199–234.

Davis, M. (1999) *Ecology of Fear: Los Angeles and the Imagination of Disaster*. Henry Holt: New York.

Davis, M. (2006) *Planet of Slums*. Verso: London.

De Loyola Hummell, B.M., Cutter, S.L., and Emrich, C.T. (2016) Social vulnerability to natural hazards in Brazil. *International Journal of Disaster Risk Science* 7, 111–122.

Denton, F., Wilbanks, T.J., Abeysinghe, A.C., Burton, I., Gao, Q., Lemos, M.C., Masui, T. et al. (2014) Climate-resilient pathways: Adaptation, mitigation, and sustainable development. In C.B. Field, V.R. Barros, D.J. Dokken, K.J. Mach, M.D. Mastrandrea, T.E. Bilir, M. Chatterjee et al., eds., *Climate Change 2014: Impacts, Adaptation, and Vulnerability, Part A*. Cambridge University Press: Cambridge, 1101–1131.

Department of Health and Human Services (2012) *Gaps Continue to Exist in Nursing Home Preparedness and Response During Disasters, 2007–2010*. Office of the Inspector General: Washington, DC.

Department for International Development (2011) *Defining Disaster Resilience: A DFID Approach Paper*. DFID: London.

Dhawan, R. and Jeske, K. (2006) How resilient is the modern economy to energy price shocks? *Economic Review (Federal Reserve Bank of Atlanta)*, January, https://www.researchgate.net/publication/5025718.

DiGangi, C. (2016) How many Americans have bad credit? *Credit*, February 12, http://blog.credit.com/2016/02/how-many-americans-have-bad-credit-136868.

Dilley, M., Chen, R.S., Deichmann, U., Lerner-Lam, A.L., Arnold, M., Agwe, J., Buys, P. et al. (2005) *Natural Disaster Hotspots: A Global Risk Analysis* [English]. World Bank: Washington, DC.

Dominey-Howes, D., Gorman-Murray, A., and McKinnon, S. (2014) Queering disasters: On the need to account for LGBTI experiences in natural disaster contexts. *Gender, Place & Culture* 21(7), 905–918. doi: 10.1080/0966369X.2013.802673.

Doocy, S., Gorokhovich, Y., Burnham, G., Balk, D., and Robinson, C. (2007) Tsunami mortality estimates and vulnerability mapping in Aceh, Indonesia. *Research and Practice* 97(S1), S146–S151.

Downey, L. (2006a) Environmental inequality in metropolitan America in 2000. *Sociological Spectrum* 26(1), 21–41.

Downey, L. (2006b) Environmental racial inequality in Detroit. *Social Forces* 85(2), 771–796.

Downey, L. (2006c) Using geographic information systems to reconceptualize spatial relationships and ecological context. *American Journal of Sociology* 112(2), 567–612.

Downey, L. (2015) *Inequality, Democracy, and the Environment.* NYU Press: New York.

Downey, L., DuBois, S., Hawkins, B. and Walker, S. (2008) Environmental inequality in metropolitan America. *Organization & Environment* 21(3), 270–294.

Downey, L. and Hawkins, B. (2008) Race, income, and environmental inequality in the United States. *Sociological Perspectives* 51(4), 759–781.

Drabek, T.E. (1985) Managing the emergency response. *Public Administration Review* 45, 85–92.

Drabek, T.E. (1986) *Human System Responses to Disaster: An Inventory of Sociological Findings.* Springer-Verlag: New York.

Drabek, T.E. (1987) Emergent structures. In R.R. Dynes, B. DeMarchi, and C. Pelanda, eds., *Sociology of Disasters: Contribution of Sociology to Disaster Research.* Franco Angeli: Gorizia, 190–259.

Drabek, T.E. (1989) Disasters as non-routine social problems. *International Journal of Mass Emergencies and Disasters* 7, 253–264.

Drabek, T.E. (1996) *Sociology of Disaster: Instructor's Guide.* Federal Emergency Management Agency, Emergency Management Institute: Emmitsburg, MD.

Drabek, T.E. (2007) Social problems perspectives, disaster research, and emergency management: Intellectual contexts, theoretical extensions, and policy implications. Paper presented at the annual meeting of the American Sociological Association, New York.

Drabek, T.E. and Haas, J.E. (1969) Laboratory simulation of organizational stress. *American Sociological Review* 34, 223–238.

Drabek, T.E. and Hoetmer, G. (1991) *Emergency Management: Principle and Practice for Local Government.* International City and County Management Association: Washington, DC.

Drabek, T.E. and McEntire, D.A. (2003) Emergent phenomena and the sociology of disaster: Lessons, trends and opportunities from the research literature. *Disaster Prevention and Management: An International Journal* 12(2), 97–112. doi: 10.1108/09653560310474214.

Drabek, T.E., Tamminga, H.L., Kilijanek, T.S., and Adams, C.R. (1981) *Managing Multiorganizational Emergency Responses: Emergent Search and Rescue Networks in Natural Disaster and Remote Area Settings.* Natural Hazards Center, University of Colorado: Boulder.

Dunlap, R.E. and McCright, A.M. (2015) Challenging climate change: The denial countermovement. In R.E. Dunlap and R.J. Brulle, eds., *Climate Change and Society: Sociological Perspectives.* Oxford University Press: New York, 300–322.

Durham, C. and Miller, D.S. (2010) Native Americans, disasters, and the U.S. government: Where responsibility lies. In J.D. Rivera, and D.S. Miller, eds., *How Ethnically Marginalized Americans Cope with Catastrophic Disasters: Studies in Suffering and Resilience.* Edwin Mellen Press: Lampeter, Wales, 17–49.

Dynes, R.R. (1970) *Organized Behavior in Disasters.* DC Health: Lexington, MA.

Dynes, R.R. (1988) Cross-cultural international research: Sociology and disaster. *International Journal of Mass Emergencies and Disasters* 6, 101–129.

Dynes, R.R. (1993) Disaster reduction: The importance of adequate assumptions about social organization. *Sociological Spectrum* 13, 175–192.

Dynes, R.R. (1994) Community emergency planning: False assumptions and inappropriate analogies. *International Journal of Mass Emergencies and Disasters* 12(2), 141–158.

Dynes, R.R. (2000) The dialogue between Voltaire and Rousseau on the Lisbon earthquake: The emergence of a social science view. *International Journal of Mass Emergencies and Disasters* 18(1), 97–115.

Dynes, R.R. (2006) Social capital: Dealing with community emergencies. *Homeland Security Affairs* 2(2), 1–26, http://hdl.handle.net/10945/25095.

Dynes, R.R., De Marchi, B., and Pelanda, C., eds. (1987) *Sociology of Disasters: Contribution of Sociology to Disaster Research.* Franco Angeli: Milan.

Eden, L. (2004) *Whole World on Fire: Organizations, Knowledge, and Nuclear Weapons Devastation.* Cornell University Press: Ithaca, NY.

Edgington, S. (2009) *Disaster Planning for People Experiencing Homelessness.* National Health Care for the Homeless Council: Nashville, TN.

Elliott, J.R., Haney, T.J., and Sams-Abiodun, P. (2010) Limits to social capital: Comparing network assistance in two New Orleans neighborhoods devastated by Hurricane Katrina. *Sociological Quarterly* 51, 624–648.

Elliott, J.R. and Howell, J. (2017) Beyond disasters: A longitudinal analysis of natural hazards' unequal impacts on residential instability. *Social Forces* 95(3), 1181–1207. doi: 10.1093/sf/sow086.

Elliott, J.R. and Pais, J. (2006) Race, class, and Hurricane Katrina: Social differences in human responses to disaster. *Social Science Research* 35(2), 295–321.

Elliott, J.R. and Sullivan, L. (2015) How the Red Cross raised half a billion dollars for Haiti and built six homes. *ProPublica,* https://www.propublica.org/article/how-the-red-cross-raised-half-a-billion-dollars-for-haiti-and-built-6-homes.

Ellsworth, W.L., Llenos, A.L., McGarr, A.F., Michael, A.J., Rubenstein, J.L., Mueller, C.S., Petersen, M.D. et al. (2015) Increasing seismicity in the US mid-continent: Implications for earthquake hazard. *Leading Edge* 34(6), 618–626. doi: 10.1190/tle34060618.1.

Emrich, C.T. and Cutter, S.L. (2011) Social vulnerability to climate-sensitive hazards in the southern United States. *Weather, Climate, and Society* 3, 193–208.

Enarson, E. and Chakrabarti, P.G.D., eds. (2009) *Women, Gender and Disaster: Global Issues and Initiatives.* SAGE: Thousand Oaks, CA.

Enarson, E., Fothergill, A., and Peek, L. (2018) Gender and disaster: Foundations and new directions for research and practice. In H. Rodríguez, W. Donner, and J.E. Trainor, eds., *Handbook of Disaster Research*, 2nd edn. Springer: Cham, Switzerland, 205–223.

Enarson, E. and Morrow, B.H. (1997) A gendered perspective: The voices of women. In W.G. Peacock, B.H. Morrow, and H. Gladwin, eds., *Hurricane Andrew: Ethnicity, Gender and the Sociology of Disasters.* Routledge, London, 115–140.

Enarson, E. and Morrow, B.H., eds. (1998) *The Gendered Terrain of Disaster: Through Women's Eyes.* Praeger: Westport, CT.

Enarson, E. and Pease, B., eds. (2016) *Men, Masculinities, and Disaster.* Routledge: New York.

Engle, N.L. (2011) Adaptive capacity and its assessment. *Global Environmental Change* 21(2), 647–656.

Erikson, K.T. (1976) *Everything in Its Path.* Simon & Schuster: New York.

Erikson, K.T. (1995) *A New Species of Trouble.* Norton: New York.

Eyerman, R. (2015) *Is This America? Katrina as Cultural Trauma.* University of Texas Press: Austin.

Fairlie, R.W., and Robb, A.M. (2010) *Disparities in Capital Access Between Minority and Non-Minority-Owned Businesses: The Troubling Reality of Capital Limitations Faced by MBEs.* US Department of Commerce, Minority Business Development Agency: Washington, DC.

Farazmand, A., ed. (2014) *Crisis and Emergency Management*, 2nd edn. CRC Press: Boca Raton, FL.

Fatemi, F., Ardalan, A., Aguirre, B., Mansouri, N. and Mohammadfam, I. (2017) Social vulnerability indicators in disasters: Findings from a systematic review. *International Journal of Disaster Risk Science* 22, 219–227. doi: 10.1016/j.ijdrr.2016.09.006.

Feather, J. (2014) Why older adults face more danger in natural disasters. Huffington Post, February 17, https://www.huffingtonpost.com/entry/why-older-adults-face-mor_b_4461648.html.

Federal Emergency Management Agency (2017) *Draft Interagency Concept for Community Resilience Indicators and National-Level Measures.* FEMA, Mitigation Framework Leadership Group, US Department of Homeland Security: Washington, DC.

Feldman, E.A. and Fish, C. (2015) Natural disasters, nuclear disasters, and global governance. Paper 1552, University of Pennsylvania, Philadelphia, 1–54, http://scholarship.law.upenn.edu/faculty_scholarship/1552.

Field, C.B., Barros, V., Stocker, T.F., and Dahe, Q., eds. (2012) *Managing the Risks of Extreme Events and Disasters to Advance Climate Change Adaptation: Special Report of the Intergovernmental Panel on Climate Change.* Cambridge University Press: Cambridge.

Finch, C., Emrich, C.T., and Cutter, S.L. (2010) Disaster disparities and differential recovery in New Orleans. *Population and Environment* 31(4), 179–202, http://www.jstor.org/stable/40587588.

Fink, S. (2013) *Five Days at Memorial: Life and Death in a Storm-Ravaged Hospital.* Crown: New York.

Finucane, M.L., Slovic, P., Mertz, C.K., Flynn, J., and Satterfield, T.A. (2000) Gender, race, and perceived risk: The "white male" effect. *Health, Risk & Society* 2(2), 159–172. doi: 10.1080/713670162.

Fischhoff, B. (2005) A hero in every aisle seat. *New York Times*, August 7, http://www.nytimes.com/2005/08/07/opinion/a-hero-in-every-aisle-seat.html.

Fischhoff, B. (2012) Risk perception and communication. In B. Fischhoff, ed., *Risk Analysis and Human Behavior*. Earthscan: London, 3–32.

Fitzhugh, S.M., Gibson, C.B., Spiro, E.S., and Butts, C.T. (2016) Spatio-temporal filtering techniques for the detection of disaster-related communication. *Social Science Research* 59, 137–154. doi: 10.1016/j.ssresearch.2016.04.023.

Flora, C.B. and Flora, J. (2008) *Rural Communities: Legacy and Change*, 3rd edn. Westview Press: San Francisco, CA.

Flynn, J., Slovic, P., and Mertz, C.K. (1994) Gender, race, and the perception of environmental health risk. *Risk Analysis* 14, 1101–1108.

Folke, C., Carpenter, S., Elmqvist, T., Gunderson, L., Holling, C.S., and Walker, B. (2002) Resilience and sustainable development: Building adaptive capacity in a world of transformations. *Ambio* 31(5), 437–440.

Fordham, M. (1998) Making women visible in disasters: Problematising the private domain. *Disasters* 22, 126–143.

Fordham, M., Lovekamp, W.E., Thomas, D.S.K., and Phillips, B.D. (2013) Understanding social vulnerability. In D.S.K. Thomas, B.D. Phillips, W.E. Lovekamp, and A. Fothergill, eds., *Social Vulnerability to Disasters*, 2nd edn. CRC Press: Boca Raton, FL, 1–29.

Fortun, K. and Frickel, S. (2013) Making a case for disaster science and technology studies. An STS Forum on the East Japan Disaster. Online forum, https://fukushimaforum.wordpress.com/online-forum-2/online-forum/making-a-case-for-disaster-science-and-technology-studies.

Foster, J.B. and Holleman, H. (2014) The theory of unequal ecological exchange: A Marx–Odum dialectic. *Journal of Peasant Studies* 41(2), 199–233.

Fothergill, A. (1996) Gender, risk, and disaster. *International Journal of Mass Emergencies and Disasters* 14(1), 33–56.

Fothergill, A. (1998) The neglect of gender in disaster work: An overview of the literature. In E. Enarson and B.H. Morrow, eds., *The Gendered Terrain of Disaster: Through Women's Eyes*. Praeger: Westport, CT, 11–25.

Fothergill, A., Maestas, E.G., and Darlington, J.D. (1999) Race, ethnicity and disasters in the United States: A review of the literature. *Disasters* 23(2), 156–173.

Fothergill, A. and Peek, L. (2004) Poverty and disasters in the United States: A review of recent sociological findings. *Natural Hazards* 32, 89–110.

Fothergill, A. and Peek, L. (2013) Permanent temporariness: Displaced children in Louisiana. In L. Weber and L. Peek, eds., *Displaced: Life in the Katrina Diaspora*. University of Texas Press: Austin, 119–43.

Fothergill, A. and Peek, L. (2015) *Children of Katrina*. University of Texas Press: Austin.

Foucault, M. (1965) *Madness and Civilization*. Pantheon: New York.

Fraga, R. (2012) *The Greening of Oz: Sustainable Architecture in the Wake of a Tornado*. Wasteland Press: Shelbyville, KY.

Frank, A.G. (1966) *The Development of Underdevelopment*. Monthly Review Press: New York.

Frank, A.G. (1969) *Capitalism and Underdevelopment in Latin America: Historical Studies of Chile and Brasil*. Modern Reader Paperbacks: New York.

Frank, A.G. (1979) *Dependent Accumulation and Underdevelopment*. Monthly Review Press: New York.

Freudenburg, W.R. (1997) Contamination, corrosion and the social order: An overview. *Current Sociology* 45(3), 19–39.

Freudenburg, W.R., Gramling, R., Laska, S., and Erikson, K.T. (2009) *Catastrophe in the Making: The Engineering of Katrina and the Disasters of Tomorrow*. Island Press: Washington, DC.

Frickel, S. and Vincent, M.B. (2007) Hurricane Katrina, contamination, and the unintended organization of ignorance. *Technology in Society* 29(2), 181–188.

Friedman, L. (2017) Scientists fear Trump will dismiss blunt climate report. *New York Times*, August 7.

Friend, R. and Moench, M. (2015) Rights to urban climate resilience: Moving beyond poverty and vulnerability. *WIREs Climate Change* 6(6), 643–651.

Fritz, C.E. (1961) Disasters. In R.K. Merton and R.A. Nisbet, eds., *Contemporary Social Problems*. Harcourt: New York, 651–694.

Fussell, E. (2015) The long-term recovery of New Orleans' population after Hurricane Katrina. *American Behavioral Scientist* 59(10), 1231–1245.

Fussell, E., Sastry, N., and Van Landingham, M. (2010) Race, socioeconomic status, and return migration to New Orleans after Hurricane Katrina. *Population and Environment* 31, 20–42.

Gaddis, E.B., Miles, B., Morse, S., and Lewis, D. (2007) Full-cost accounting of coastal disasters in the United States: Implications for planning and preparedness. *Ecological Economics* 63(2 &3), 307–318.

Gaillard, J.C. and Gomez, C. (2015) Post-disaster research: Is there gold worth the rush? *Jàmbá: Journal of Disaster Risk Studies* 7(1), a120. doi: 10.4102/jamba. v7i1.120.

Gaillard, J.C., Gorman-Murray, A., and Fordham, M. (2017) Sexual and gender minorities in disaster. *Gender, Place & Culture* 24(1), 18–26. doi: 10.1080/0966369X.2016.1263438.

Gaillard, J.C., Sanz, K., Balgos, B.C., Dalisay, S.N.M., Gorman-Murray, A., Smith, F., and Toelupe, V. (2017) Beyond men and women: A critical perspective on gender and disaster. *Disasters* 41(3), 429–447.

Galea, S., Maxwell, A.R. and Norris, F. (2008) Sampling and design challenges in studying the mental health consequences of disasters. *International Journal of Methods in Psychiatric Research* 17(S2), 21–28.

Galea, S., Vlahov, D., Resnick, H., Ahern, J., Susser, E., Gold, J. Bucuvalas, M., and Kilpatrick, D. (2003) Trends of probable post-traumatic stress disorder in New York City after the September 11 terrorist attacks. *American Journal of Epidemiology* 158(6), 514–524. doi: 10.1093/aje/kwg187.

Gallopín, G.C. (2006) Linkages between vulnerability, resilience, and adaptive capacity. *Global Environmental Change* 16, 293–303.

Gauchat, G. (2012) Politicization of science in the public sphere: A study of public trust in the United States, 1974 to 2010. *American Sociological Review* 77(2), 167–187.

Ghuman, S.J., Brackbill, R.M., Stellman, S.D., Farfel, M.R., and Cone, J.E. (2014) Unmet mental health care need 10–11 years after the 9/11 terrorist attacks, 2011–2012 results from the World Trade Center Health Registry. *BMC Public Health* 14(491). doi: 10.1186/1471-2458-14-491.

Gilbert, D.L. (2018) *The American Class Structure in an Age of Growing Inequality*, 10th edn. SAGE: Thousand Oaks, CA.

Gilbert, S.W., Burtry, D.T., Helgeson, J.F., and Chapman, R.E. (2015) *Community Resilience Economic Decision Guide for Buildings and Infrastructure Systems*. NIST Special Publication 1197, National Institute of Standards and Technology, US Department of Commerce.

Gill, D.A. and Picou, J.S. (1998) Technological disaster and chronic community stress. *Society & Natural Resources* 11(8), 795–815.

Gill, D.A., Picou, J.S. and Ritchie, L.A. (2012) The 2010 BP oil spill and 1989 Exxon Valdez oil spill: A comparison of initial social impacts. *American Behavioral Scientist* 56(1), 3–23.

Gin, J.L., Eisner, R.K., Der-Martirosian, C., Kranke, D., and Dobalian, A. (2017) Preparedness is a marathon, not a sprint: A tiered maturity model for assessing preparedness in homeless residential organizations in Los Angeles. *Natural Hazards Review* 19(1). doi: 10.1061/(asce)nh.1527-6996.0000276

Gin, J.L., Kranke, D., Saia, R. and Dobalian, A. (2016) Disaster preparedness in homeless residential organizations in Los Angeles county: Identifying needs, assessing gaps. *Natural Hazards Review* 17(1), 1–8. doi: 10.1061/(ASCE) NH.1527-6996.0000208.

Glassman, J. (2010) Critical geography II: Articulating race and radical politics. *Progress in Human Geography* 34(4), 506–512.

GOAL (2015) *Toolkit for Measuring Community Disaster Resilience: Guidance Manual*. GOAL, https://www.goalglobal.org/images/GOAL_Toolkit_Disaster_ Resilience_Guidance_Manual_May_2015.compressed.pdf..

Godschalk, D.R. (2003) Urban hazard mitigation: Creating resilient cities. *Natural Hazards Review* 4(3), 136–143.

Goldberg, D. (2002) *The Racial State*. Blackwell: Oxford.

Gomez, C. and Hart, D.E. (2013) Disaster gold rushes, sophisms and academic neocolonialism: Comments on "earthquake disasters and resilience in the global North." *Geographical Journal* 179(3), 272–277.

Gosling, M. and Hiles, A. (2010) Business continuity statistics: Where myth meets fact. Continuity Central, http://www.continuitycentral.com/feature0660.html.

Gotham, K.F. (2012) Disaster, Inc.: Privatization and post-Katrina rebuilding in New Orleans. *Perspectives on Politics* 10(3), 633–646.

Gotham, K.F. (2014) Racialization and rescaling: Post-Katrina rebuilding and the Louisiana Road Home program. *International Journal of Urban and Regional Research* 38(3), 773–790.

Gould, K.A., Pellow, D.N., and Schnaiberg, A. (2004) Interrogating the treadmill of production: Everything you wanted to know about the treadmill but were afraid to ask. *Organization & Environment* 17(3), 296–316.

Gould, K.A., Pellow, D.N., and Schnaiberg, A. (2008) *Treadmill of Production: Injustice and Unsustainability in the Global Economy*. Routledge: New York.

Government Accountability Office (2015a) *Hurricane Sandy: An Investment Strategy Could Help the Federal Government Enhance National Resilience for Future Disaster*. GAO: Washington, DC.

Government Accountability Office (2015b) *An Investment Strategy Could Help the Federal Government Enhance National Resilience for Future Disasters*. GAO: Washington, DC.

Grineski, S.E., Collins, T.W., Chakraborty, J., and Montgomery, M. (2015) Hazardous air pollutants and flooding: A comparative interurban study of environmental injustice. *GeoJournal* 80(1), 145–158.

Grineski, S.E., Collins, T.W., Romo Aguilar, L., and Aldouri, R. (2010) No safe place: Environmental hazards and injustice along Mexico's northern border. *Social Forces* 88, 2241–2266.

Gronlund, C.J., Zanobetti, A., Schwartz, J.D., Wellenius, G.A., and O'Neill, M.S. (2014) Heat, heat waves, and hospital admissions among the elderly in the United States, 1992–2006. *Environmental Health Perspectives* 122(11), 1187–1192.

Guha-Sapir, D. and Hoyois, P. (2015) *Estimating populations affected by disasters: A review of methodological issues and research gaps*. Centre for Research on the Epidemiology of Disasters, Institute of Health and Society, Université catholique de Louvain: Brussels.

Guillard-Gonçalves, C., Cutter, S.L., Emrich, C.T., and Zêzere, J.L. (2015) Application of social vulnerability index (SoVI) and delineation of natural risk zones in Greater Lisbon, Portugal. *Journal of Risk Research* 18(5), 651–674, http://dx.doi.org/10.1080/13669877.2014.910689.

Gunter, V.J., Aronoff, M., and Joel, S. (1999) Toxic contamination and communities: Using an ecological–symbolic perspective to theorize response contingencies. *Sociological Quarterly* 40(4), 623–640.

Gupta, A. and Ferguson, J. (1997) *Culture, Power, Place: Explorations in Critical Anthropology*. Duke University Press: Durham, NC.

Haas, J.E., Kates, R.W. and Bowden, M.J., eds. (1977) *Reconstruction Following Disaster*. MIT Press: Cambridge, MA.

Haddow, G.D., Bullock, J.A., and Coppola, D.P. (2016) *Introduction to Emergency Management*, 6th edn. Elsevier: Oxford.

Hall, C.M., Malinen, S., Vosslamber, R., and Wordsworth, R., eds. (2016) *Business and Post-Disaster Management: Business, Organisational, and Consumer Resilience and the Christchurch Earthquakes*. Routledge: New York.

Hallegatte, S., Green, C., Nicholls, R.J., and Corfee-Morlot, J. (2013) Future flood losses in major coastal cities. *Nature Climate Change* 3, 802–806.

Haney, T.J., Elliott, J.R., and Fussell, E. (2010) Families and hurricane response: Risk, roles, resources, race and religion. In D. Brunsma, D. Overfelt, and J.S. Picou, eds., *The Sociology of Katrina: Perspectives on a Modern Catastrophe*, 2nd edn. Rowman & Littlefield, Lanham, MD, 77–102.

Hannigan, J. (2012) *Disasters without Borders*. Polity: Cambridge.

Harlan, S.L., Brazel, A.J., Prashad, L., Stefanov, W.L., and Larsen, L. (2006) Neighborhood microclimates and vulnerability to heat stress. *Social Science & Medicine* 63, 2847–2863.

Harlan, S.L., Declet-Barreto, J.H., Stefanov, W.L., and Petitti, D.B. (2013) Neighborhood effects on heat deaths: Social and environmental predictors of vulnerability in Maricopa County, Arizona. *Environmental Health Perspectives* 121(2), 197–204.

Harrald, J.R. (2006) Agility and Discipline: Critical success factors in disaster response. *Annals of the American Academy of Political and Social Science* 604, 256–272.

Harvey, D. (1973) *Social Justice and the City*. University of Georgia Press: Athens, GA.

Harvey, D. (1993) *Justice, Nature, and the Geography of Difference*. Blackwell: Oxford.

Harvey, D. (2001) *Spaces of Capital: Toward a Critical Geography*. Routledge: New York.

Hawkins, R.L. and Maurer, K. (2010) Bonding, bridging and linking: How social capital operated in New Orleans following Hurricane Katrina. *British Journal of Social Work* 40, 1777–1793.

Hawley, K., Moench, M., and Sabbag, L. (2012) *Understanding the Economics of Flood Risk Reduction: A Preliminary Analysis*. Institute for Social and Environmental Transition-International: Boulder, CO.

He, W., Goodkind, D., and Kowal, P. (2016) *An Aging World: 2015* (International Population Reports). US Department of Commerce, US Census Bureau: Washington, DC, https://www.census.gov/content/dam/Census/library/publications/2016/demo/p95-16-1.pdf.

Healy, A. and Malhotra, N. (2009) Myopic voters and natural disaster policy. *American Political Science Review* 103(3), 387–406, http://dx.doi.org/10.1017/S0003055409990104.

Heid, A.R., Pruchno, R., Cartwright, F.P., and Wilson-Genderson, M. (2017) Exposure to Hurricane Sandy, neighborhood collective efficacy, and post-traumatic stress symptoms in older adults. *Aging & Mental Health* 21(7), 742–750. doi: 10.1080/13607863.2016.1154016.

Helliwell, J.F. and Putnam, R.D. (1995) Economic growth and social capital in Italy. *Eastern Economic Journal* 21(3), 295–307.

Henderson, T.L., Sirois, M., Chen, A.C.-C., Airriess, C., Swanson, D.A., and Banks, D. (2009) After a disaster: Lessons in survey methodology from Hurricane Katrina. *Popular Research and Policy Review* 28(1), 67–92.

Henry, C.S., Morris, A.S., and Harrist, A.W. (2015) Family resilience: Moving into the third wave. *Family Relations* 64, 22–43.

Hewitt, K. (1983a) The idea of calamity in a technocratic age. In K. Hewitt, ed., *Interpretations of Calamity: From the viewpoint of human ecology.* Allen & Unwin: Boston, MA, 3–32.

Hewitt, K. (1983b) *Interpretations of Calamity: From the Viewpoint of Human Ecology.* Allen & Unwin: Boston, MA.

Hewitt, K. and Burton, I. (1971) *The Hazardousness of a Place: A Regional Ecology of Damaging Events.* University of Toronto Press: Toronto.

Highfield, W. and Brody, S.D. (2013) Evaluating the effectiveness of local mitigation activities in reducing flood losses. *Natural Hazards Review* 14(4), 229–236.

Hilgartner, S. and Bosk, C.L. (1988) The rise and fall of social problems: A public arenas model. *American Journal of Sociology* 94, 53–78.

Hincks, T., Aspinall, W., Cooke, R., and Gernon, T. (2018) Oklahoma's induced seismicity strongly linked to wastewater injection depth. *Science* 359(6381), 1251–1255. doi: 10.1126/science.aap7911.

Hinshaw, R.E. (2006) *Living with Nature's Extremes: The Life of Gilbert Fowler White.* Johnson Books: Boulder, CO.

Hiroi, O., Mikami, S., and Miyata, K. (1985) A study of mass media reporting in emergencies. *International Journal of Mass Emergencies and Disasters* 3, 21–49.

Hochrainer, S. (2009) Assessing the macroeconomic impacts of natural disasters: Are there any? Policy Research Working Paper 4968, World Bank, Global Facility for Disaster Reduction and Recovery, Washington, DC.

Hoffman, S.M. (1998) Eve and Adam among the embers: Gender patterns after the Oakland Berkeley firestorm. In E. Enarson and B.H. Morrow, eds., *The Gendered Terrain of Disaster: Through Women's Eyes.* Praeger: Westport, CT, 55–61.

Hoffman, S.M. and Oliver-Smith, A, (eds.) (2002) *Catastrophe and Culture: The Anthropology of Disaster.* School for Advanced Research Press: Santa Fe, NM.

Holland, K. (2015) 45 million Americans are living without a credit score.

CNBC, http://www.cnbc.com/2015/05/05/credit-invisible-26-million-have-no-credit-score.html.

Holling, C.S. (1973) Resilience and stability of ecological systems. *Annual Review of Ecology and Systematics* 4, 1–23, http://www.jstor.org/stable/2096802.

Hooks, G. (1994) Regional processes in the hegemonic nation: Political, economic, and military influences on the use of geographic space. *American Sociological Review* 59(5), 746–772, http://www.jstor.org/stable/2096446.

Hooks, G. and Smith, C.L. (2004) The treadmill of destruction: National sacrifice areas and Native Americans. *American Sociological Review* 69(4), 558–575, http://www.jstor.org/stable/3593065.

Hooks, G. and Smith, C.L. (2005) Treadmills of production and destruction: Threats to environment posed by militarism. *Organization & Environment* 18(1), 19–37.

Horney, J., Dwyer, C., Aminto, M., Berke, O., and Smith, G. (2017) Developing indicators to measure post-disaster community recovery in the United States. *Disasters* 41(1), 124–149.

HoSang, D., LaBennett, O., and Pulido, L., eds. (2012) *Racial Formation in the 21st Century*. University of California Press: Berkeley, CA.

Hoynes, H., Miller, D.L., and Schaller, J. (2012) Who suffers during recessions? *Journal of Economic Perspectives* 26, 27–48.

Hughes, A. and Chauhan, A. (2015) Online media as a means to affect public trust in emergency responders. In L. Palen, M. Buscher, T. Comes, and A. Hughes, eds., *Proceedings of the ISCRAM 2015 Conference, May 24–27, Kristiansand, Norway*. ISCRAM: Kristiansand, 171–181.

Hughes, A., Palen, L., Sutton, J., Liu, S.B., and Vieweg, A. (2008) "Site-seeing" in disaster: An examination of on-line social convergence. In F. Friedrich and B. Van De Walle, eds., *Proceedings of the 5th International ISCRAM Conference*. Academic Press: Washington, DC. http://www.amandaleehughes.com/OnlineConvergenceISCRAM08.pdf.

Hughes, A., St. Denis, L., Palen, L., and Anderson, K.M. (2014) Online public communications by police and fire services during the 2012 Hurricane Sandy. In *Proceedings of the SIGCHI 2014 Conference on Human Factors in Computing Systems*. ACM: New York, 1505–1514.

Human Rights Campaign (2012) *Working with the Lesbian, Gay, Bisexual and Transgender Community: A Cultural Guide for Emergency Responders and Volunteers*. HRC: Washington, DC.

Hunt, M., Tansey, C.M., Anderson, J., Boulanger, R.F., Eckenwiler, L., Pringle, J., and Schwartz, L. (2016) The challenge of timely, responsive and rigorous ethics review of disaster research: Views of research ethics committee members. *PLoS ONE* 11(6), 1–15.

Hurlbert, J.S., Haines, V.A., and Beggs, J.J. (2000) Core networks and tie activation: What kinds of routine networks allocate resources in nonroutine situations? *American Sociological Review* 65, 598–618.

Institute on Statelessness and Inclusion (2014) *The World's Stateless*. ISI: Eindhoven, Netherlands.

Interagency Performance Evaluation Task Force (2008) *Performance Evaluation of the New Orleans and Southeast Louisiana Hurricane Protection System: Final Report of the Interagency Performance Evaluation Task Force*. US Army Corps of Engineers: Washington, DC.

Internal Displacement Monitoring Center (2017) *Recovery Postponed: The Long-Term Plight of People Displaced by the 2011 Great East Japan Earthquake, Tsunami and Nuclear Radiation Disaster*. Internal Displacement Monitoring Center: Geneva.

International Gay and Lesbian Human Rights Commission (n.d.) *The Impact of the Earthquake, and Relief and Recovery Programs on Haitian LGBT People*. IGLHRC: New York.

Jacob, M. (2010) Ethnography, memory, and culture: Healing the soul wound of technological disaster. In J.D. Rivera and D.S. Miller, eds., *How Ethnically Marginalized Americans Cope with Catastrophic Disasters: Studies in Suffering and Resilience*. Edwin Mellen Press, Lampeter, Wales, 37–49.

Jaeger, C.C., Renn, O., Rosa, E.A., and Webler, T. (2001) *Risk, Uncertainty, and Rational Action*. Earthscan: London.

Janoske, M., Liu, B.F., and Sheppard, B. (2012) *Understanding Risk Communication Best Practices: A Guide for Emergency Managers and Communicators*. National Consortium for the Study of Terrorism and Responses to Terrorism, University of Maryland, College Park, MD.

Janssen, M.A. and Ostrom, E. (2006) Resilience, vulnerability, and adaptation: A cross-cutting theme of the international human dimensions programme on global environmental change. *Global Environmental Change* 16, 237–239.

Jensen, J. (2011) *Preparedness: A Principled Approach to Return on Investment*. International Association of Emergency Managers: Falls Church, VA.

Jensen, J. and Thompson, S. (2016) The incident command system: A literature review. *Disasters* 40, 158–182.

Jha, A.K., Miner, T.W., and Stanton-Geddes, Z., eds. (2013) *Building Urban Resilience: Principles, Tools, and Practice*. World Bank: Washington, DC.

Johnson, C. (2004) *The Sorrows of Empire: Militarism, Secrecy, and the End of the Republic*. Metropolitan Books: New York.

Johnson, L.A. and Olshansky, R.B. (2016) *After Great Disasters: An In-Depth Analysis of How Six Countries Managed Community Recovery*. Lincoln Institute of Land Policy: Cambridge, MA, 1–72.

Johnson, N.R. (1987) Panic at "the Who concert stampede": An empirical assessment. *Social Problems* 34, 362–373.

Johnson, N.R. (1988) Fire in a crowded theater: A descriptive analysis of the emergence of panic. *International Journal of Mass Emergencies and Disasters* 6, 7–26.

Johnson, N.R., Feinberg, W.E., and Johnston, D.M. (1994) Microstructure and panic: The impact of social bonds on individual action in collective flight from the Beverly Hills Supper Club fire. In R.R. Dynes and K. Tierney, eds., *Disasters, Collective Behavior, and Social Organization*. University of Delaware Press: Newark, 168–189.

Johnston, B. (2007) Half-lives, half-truths, and other radioactive legacies of the Cold War. In B. Johnson, ed., *Half-Lives and Half-Truths: Confronting the Radioactive Legacies of the Cold War*. SAR Press: Santa Fe, NM, 1–24.

Jorgenson, A.K. (2006) Unequal ecological exchange and environmental degradation: A theoretical proposition and cross-national study of deforestation, 1990–2000. *Rural Sociology* 71(4), 685–712.

Kahn, M.E. (2005) The death toll from natural disasters: The role of income, geography, and institutions. *Review of Economics and Statistics* 87(2), 271–284.

Kahneman, D. (2011) *Thinking, Fast and Slow*. Farrar, Straus & Giroux: New York.

Kahneman, D., Slovic, P., and Tversky, A. (1982) *Judgements under Uncertainty: Heuristics and Biases*. Cambridge University Press: London.

Kahneman, D. and Tversky, A. (1972) Subjective probability: A judgement of representativeness. *Cognitive Psychology* 3, 430–454.

Kahneman, D. and Tversky, A. (1979) Prospect theory: An analysis of decision under risk. *Econometrica* 47, 263–291.

Kang, J.E., Peacock, W.G., and Husein, R. (2010) An assessment of coast zone hazard mitigation plans in Texas. *Journal of Disaster Research* 5(5), 526–534.

Kapucu, N. and Garayev, V. (2016) Structure and network performance: Horizontal and vertical networks in emergency management. *Administration & Society* 48(8), 931–961.

Kapucu, N., Hawkins, C.V., and Rivera, F.I. (2013) *Disaster Resiliency: Interdisciplinary Perspectives*. New York: Routledge.

Kates, R.W. (2011) *Gilbert F. White, 1911–2006: A Biographical Memoir*. National Academy of Sciences: Washington, DC.

Katz, J.M. (2013) *The Big Truck that Went by: How the World Came to Save Haiti and Left Behind a Disaster*. St. Martin's Press: New York.

Keating, A., Campbell, K., Mechler, R., Michel-Kerjan, E., Mochizuki, J., Kunreuther, H., Bayer, J. et al. (2014) *Operationalizing Resilience against Natural Disaster Risk: Opportunities, Barriers, and a Way Forward*. Zurich Flood Resilience Alliance: Zurich.

Keating, J.P., Loftus, E.F., and Manber, M. (1983) Emergency evacuations during fires: Psychological considerations. In R.F. Kidd and M.J. Saks, eds., *Advances in Applied Social Psychology*. Lawrence Erlbaum Associates: Hillsdale, NJ, 83–99.

Keller, C., Bostrom, A., Kuttschreuter, M., Savadori, L., Spence, A., and White, M. (2012) Bringing appraisal theory to environmental risk perception: A review of conceptual approaches of the past 40 years and suggestions for future research. *Journal of Risk Research* 15(3), 237–256. doi: 10.1080/13669877.2011.634523.

Keller, R.C. (2015) *Fatal Isolation: The Devastating Paris Heatwave of 2003.* Chicago: University of Chicago Press.

Kelman, I. (2005) Operational ethics for disaster research. *International Journal of Mass Emergencies and Disasters* 23(3), 141–158.

Kempner, J., Merz, J.F., and Bosk, C.L. (2011) Forbidden knowledge: Public controversy and the production of nonknowledge. *Sociological Forum* 26(3), 475–500.

Kendra, J.M., Clay, L.A., and Gill, K.B. (2018) Resilience and disasters. In H. Rodríguez, W. Donner, and J.E. Trainor, eds., *Handbook of Disaster Research,* 2nd edn. Springer: Cham, Switzerland, 87–107.

Kendra, J.M. and Wachtendorf, T. (2003) Elements of community resilience in the World Trade Center attack. *Disasters* 27(1), 37–53.

Kendra, J.M. and Wachtendorf, T. (2006) The waterborne evacuation of lower Manhattan on September 11: A case of distributed sensemaking. Preliminary paper no. 355, Disaster Research Center, University of Delaware, Newark, DE.

Kendra, J.M. and Wachtendorf, T. (2016) *American Dunkirk: The Waterborne Evacuation of Manhattan on 9/11.* Temple University Press: Philadelphia, PA.

Kessler, R.C., Galea, S., Gruber, M.J., Sampson, N.A., Ursano, R.J., and Wessely, S. (2008) Trends in mental illness and suicidality after Hurricane Katrina. *Molecular Psychiatry* 13(4), 374–384.

Kilpatrick, D.G. (2004) The ethics of disaster research: A special section. *Journal of Traumatic Stress* 17(5), 361–362.

Kingdon, J. (1995) *Agendas, Alternatives, and Public Policies.* Addison-Wesley: Boston, MA.

Kingdon, J. (2011) Agendas, Alternatives, and Public Policies: Update Edition, with an Epilogue on Health Care. Pearson Education: New York.

Kiyota, E., Tanaka, Y., Arnold, M., and Aldrich, D.P. (2015) Elders leading the way to resilience. *SSRN Electronic Journal.* doi: 10.2139/ssrn.2575382.

Klein, R.J.T., Nicholls, R.J., and Thomalla, F. (2003) Resilience to natural hazards: How useful is this concept? *Global Environmental Change Part B: Environmental Hazards* 5(1 & 2), 35–45.

Kleindorfer, P., Kunreuther, H., and Ou-Yang, C. (2012) Single-year and multi-year insurance policies in a competitive market. *Journal of Risk and Uncertainty* 45, 51–78.

Klinenberg, E. (2002) *Heat Wave: A Social Autopsy of Disaster in Chicago.* University of Chicago Press: Chicago, IL.

Knoke, D. (1990) *Political Networks: The Structural Perspective.* Cambridge University Press, Cambridge, MA.

Knowles, S.G. (2011) *The Disaster Experts: Mastering Risk in Modern America.* University of Pennsylvania Press: Philadelphia.

Knox, R. (2016) A $1 pill that could save thousands of lives: Research suggests cheap way to avoid U.N.-caused cholera. WBUR CommonHealth, http://www.wbur.org/commonhealth/2016/02/05/antiobiotic-pill-cholera-united-nations.

Kok, M.T.J., Narain, V., Wonink, S., and Jager, J. (2006) Human vulnerability to environmental change: An approach for UNEP's global environmental outlook (GEO). In J. Birkmann, ed., *Measuring Vulnerability to Natural Hazards: Towards Disaster Resilient Societies*. United Nations University Press: Tokyo, 128–147.

Koks, E.E., Carrera, L., Jonkeren, O., Aerts, J.C.J.H., Husby, T.G., Thissen, M., Standardi, G. et al. (2016) Regional disaster impact analysis: Comparing input–output and computable general equilibrium models. *Natural Hazards and Earth System Sciences*, 16, 1911–1924.

Kopp, R.J., Krupnick, A.J., and Toman, M.A. (1997) Cost–benefit analysis and regulatory reform: An assessment of the science and art. RFF Discussion Paper 97–19, Resources for the Future, Washington, DC.

Korten, T. (2015) In Florida, officials ban term "climate change." *Miami Herald*, March 8.

Kotkin, J. and Cox, W. (2017) Rising rents are stressing out tenants and heightening America's housing crisis. *Forbes*, October 19.

Kousky, C. (2014) Informing climate adaptation: A review of the economic costs of natural disasters. *Energy Economics* 46, 576–592.

Kraus, L. (2017) *2016 Disability Statistics Annual Report*. Institute of Disability, University of New Hampshire: Durham, NH.

Kreps, G.A. (1984) Sociological inquiry and disaster research. *Annual Review of Sociology* 10, 309–330.

Kreps, G.A. (1985) Disaster and the social order. *Sociological Theory* 3(1), 49–64, http://www.jstor.org/stable/202173.

Kreps, G.A., ed. (1989) *Social Structure and Disaster*. University of Delaware Press: Newark.

Kreps, G.A. and Bosworth, S.L. (1993) Disaster, organizing, and role enactment: A structural approach. *American Journal of Sociology* 99, 428–463.

Kreps, G.A., Bosworth, S.L., Mooner, J.A., Russell, S.T., and Myers, K.A. (1994) *Organizing, Role Enactment, and Disaster: A Structural Theory*. University of Delaware Press: Newark.

Kreps, G.A. and Drabek, T.E. (1996) Disasters are nonroutine social problems. *International Journal of Mass Emergencies and Disasters* 14, 129–153.

Kroll-Smith, S., Baxter, V., and Jenkins, P. (2015) *Left to Chance: Hurricane Katrina and the Story of Two New Orleans Neighborhoods*. University of Texas Press: Austin.

Kuligowski, E.D. (2011) *Terror Defeated: Occupant Sensemaking, Decision-Making and Protective Action in the 2001 World Trade Center Disaster*. Doctoral Dissertation, Department of Sociology, University of Colorado: Boulder.

Kull, D., Mechler, R., and Hochrainer-Stigler, S. (2013) Probabilistic cost-benefit analysis of disaster risk management in a development context. *Disaster* 37(3), 374–400.

Kunreuther, H.C., Pauly, M.V., and McMorrow, S. (2013) *Insurance and Behavioral*

Economics: Improving Decisions in the Most Misunderstood Industry. Cambridge University Press: New York.

Kunreuther, H.C. and Rose, A.Z., eds. (2004a) *The Economics of Natural Hazards,* vol. 1. Edward Elgar: Cheltenham.

Kunreuther, H.C. and Rose, A.Z., eds. (2004b) *The Economics of Natural Hazards,* vol. 2. Edward Elgar: Cheltenham.

Kunreuther, H.C. and Roth, R.J., Sr., eds. (1998) *Paying the Price: The Status and Role of Insurance Against Natural Disasters in the United States.* Joseph Henry Press: Washington, DC.

Kunreuther, H.C. and Slovic, P. (1986) Decision making in hazard and resource management. In R.W. Kates and I. Burton, eds., *Geography, Resources, and Environment,* vol. 2: *Themes from the Work of Gilbert F. White.* University of Chicago Press: Chicago, IL, 153–187.

Kurokawa, K. (2012) The Official Report of the Fukushima Nuclear Accident Independent Investigation Committee. National Diet of Japan: Tokyo.

Kurtz, H. (2009) Acknowledging the racial state: An agenda for environmental justice research. *Antipode* 41(4), 684–704.

Laditka, S.B., Laditka, J.N., Xirasagar, S., Cornman, C.B., Davis, C.B., and Richter, J.V.E. (2008) Providing shelter to nursing home evacuees in disasters: Lessons from Hurricane Katrina. *American Journal of Public Health* 98(7), 1288–1293.

Lasswell, H.D. (1948) The structure and function of communication in society. In L. Bryson, ed., *Communication of Ideas.* Harper: New York, 37–51.

Le De, L., Gaillard, J.C., and Friesen, W. (2015) Academics doing participatory disaster research: How participatory is it? *Environmental Hazards* 14(1), 1–15. doi: 10.1080/17477891.2014.957636.

Lee, A.V., Vargo, J., and Seville, E. (2013) Developing a tool to measure and compare organizations resilience. *Natural Hazards Review* 14, 29–41. doi: 10.1061/(ASCE)NH.1527–6996.0000075.

Lerner, J.S. and Keltner, D. (2001) Fear, anger, and risk. *Journal of Personality and Social Psychology* 81(1), 146–159. doi: 10.1037//0022–3514.81.1.146.

Levine, C. (2004) The concept of vulnerability in disaster research. *Journal of Traumatic Stress* 17(5), 395–402.

Lim, W.K. (2014) *Field Work: Constructing a New Emergency Management Organizational Field in China in the Post-SARS Era.* Doctoral dissertation, Department of Sociology, University of Colorado Boulder.

Lin, N. (1999) Building a network theory of social capital. *Connections* 22(1), 28–51.

Lin, R., Xia, R., and Smith, D. (2014) UC releases list of 1,500 buildings: Big step for LA quake safety. *Los Angeles Times,* January 25, http://articles.latimes.com/2014/jan/25/local/la-me-ln-concrete-buildings-list-20140125.

Lin, S., Fletcher, B.A., Luo, M., Chinery, R., and Hwang, S. (2011) Health impact in New York City during the Northeast blackout of 2003. *Public Health Reports* 126(3), 384–393.

Lind, B.E., Tirado, M., Butts, C.T., and Petrescu-Prahova, M. (2008) Brokerage roles in disaster response: Organisational mediation in the wake of Hurricane Katrina. *International Journal of Emergency Management* 5(1 & 2), 75–99.

Lind, D. (2017) Fear of deportation could keep Texans from evacuating for Harvey—and Trump is making it worse. *Vox*, August 25, http://www.vox.com/policy-and-politics/2017/8/25/16205040/hurricane-harvey-checkpoints-immigration-border.

Lindell, M.K., Alesch, D., Bolton, P.A., Greene, M.R., Larson, L.A., Lopes, R., May, P.J. et al. (1997) Adoption and implementation of hazard adjustments. *International Journal of Mass Emergencies and Disasters* 15 (special issue), 327–453.

Lindell, M.K., Arlikatti, S., and Prater, C.S. (2009) Why people do what they do to protect against earthquake risk: Perceptions of hazard adjustment attributes. *Risk Analysis* 29, 1072–1088.

Lindell, M.K. and Perry, R.W. (1992) *Behavioral Foundations of Community Emergency Management*. Hemisphere Publishing Corporation: Washington, DC.

Lindell, M.K. and Perry, R.W. (2000) Household adjustment to earthquake hazard: A review of research. *Environment and Behavior* 32, 590–630.

Lindell, M.K. and Perry, R.W. (2004) *Communicating Environmental Risk in Multiethnic Communities*. SAGE: Thousand Oaks, CA.

Lindell, M.K. and Perry, R.W. (2012) The protective action decision model: Theoretical modifications and additional evidence. *Risk Analysis* 32(4), 616–632.

Liu, S.B. and Palen, L. (2010) The new cartographers: Crisis map mashups and the emergence of neogeographic practice. *Cartography and Geographic Information Science* 37(1), 69–90.

Liu, S.B., Palen, L., Sutton, J., Hughes, A.L., and Vieweg, S. (2008) In search of the bigger picture: The emergent role of on-line photo sharing in times of disaster. In F. Friedrich and B. Van De Walle, eds., *Proceedings of the 5th International ISCRAM Conference*. Academic Press: Washington, DC. https://works.bepress.com/vieweg/11.

Logan, J. and Molotch, H. (1987) *Urban Fortunes: The Political Economy of Place*. University of California Press: Berkeley.

Ludwig, S. (2015) Credit scores in America perpetuate racial injustice. Here's how. *Guardian*, October 13. www.theguardian.com/commentisfree/2015/oct/13/your-credit-score-is-racist-heres-why.

Lundgren, R. and McMakin, A. (2009) *Risk Communication: A Handbook for Communicating Environmental, Safety, and Health Risks*, 4th edn. John Wiley & Sons, Inc.: Hoboken, NJ.

Lyles, L.W., Berke, P., and Smith, G. (2014a) A comparison of local hazard mitigation plan quality in six states, USA. *Landscape and Urban Planning* 122, 89–99.

Lyles, L.W., Berke, P., and Smith, G. (2014b) Do planners matter? Examining factors driving incorporation of land use approaches into hazard mitigation plans. *Journal of Environmental Planning and Management* 57(5), 792–811.

Marlon, J., Howe, P., Mildenberger, M., and Leiserowitz, A. (2016) *Yale climate opinion maps, US 2016.* Yale Program on Climate Communication, Yale University: New Haven, CT.

Marlowe, J.M., Lou, L., Osman, M., and Zeba Alam, Z. (2015) Conducting post-disaster research with refugee background peer researchers and their communities. *Qualitative Social Work* 14(3), 383–398.

Marshall, M.I., Niehm, L.S., Sydnor, S.B., and Schrank, H.L. (2015) Predicting small business demise after a natural disaster: An analysis of pre-existing conditions. *Natural Hazards* 79, 331–354.

Marshall, M.I. and Schrank, H.L. (2014) Small business disaster recovery: A research framework. *Natural Hazards* 72(2), 597–616.

Marshall, S. and McCormick, K. (2015) *Returns on Resilience: The Business Case.* Urban Land Institute: Washington, DC.

Massey, D.S. and Denton, N.A. (1998) *American Apartheid: Segregation and the Making of the Underclass.* Harvard University Press: Cambridge, MA.

Masten, A.S. and Monn, A.R. (2015) Child and family resilience: A call for integrated science, practice, and professional training. *Family Relations* 64, 5–21. doi: 10.1111/fare.12103.

Masterson, J.H., Peacock, W.G., Van Zandt, S.S., Grover, H., Schwarz, L.F., and Cooper Jr., J.T. (2014) *Planning for Community Resilience: A Handbook for Reducing Vulnerability to Disasters.* Island Press: Washington, DC.

Matejowsky, T. (2015) Merchant resiliency and climate hazard vulnerability in the urban Philippines: Anthropological perspectives on 2011 typhoons Nesat and Nalgae. In D.C. Wood, ed., *Climate Change, Culture, and Economics: Anthropological Investigations* (Research in Economic Anthropology 35). Emerald Group Publishing Limited: Bingley, UK, 239–262.

Matthewman, S. (2015) *Disasters, Risks and Revelation.* Palgrave Macmillan: New York.

May, P.J. (1991) Reconsidering policy design: Policies and publics. *Journal of Public Policy* 11(2), 187–206.

May, P.J. (1992) Policy learning and failure. *Journal of Public Policy* 12(4), 331–354, http://www.jstor.org/stable/4007550.

May, P.J. (1999) Fostering policy learning: A challenge for public administration. *International Review of Public Administration* 4(1), 21–31. doi: 10.1080/12294659.1999.10804920.

May, P.J. and Feeley, T.J. (2000) Regulatory backwaters: Earthquake risk reduction in the Western United States. *State & Local Government Review* 32(1), 20–33, http://www.jstor.org/stable/4355248.

May, P.J., Jochim, A.E., and Sapotichne, J. (2011) Constructing homeland security: An anemic policy regime. *The Policy Studies Journal* 39(2), 285–307.

Mayer, B., Running, K., and Bergstrand, K. (2015) Compensation and community corrosion: Perceived inequalities, social comparisons, and competition following the *Deepwater Horizon* oil spill. *Sociological Forum* 30(2), 369–390.

Mayhorn, C.B. (2005) Cognitive aging and the processing of hazard information and disaster warnings. *Natural Hazards Review* 6(4), 165–170.

Mayunga, J.S. (2009) *Measuring the Measure: A Multidimensional Scale Model to Measure Community Disaster Resilience in the US Gulf Coast Region*. Doctoral dissertation, Urban and Regional Sciences, Texas A&M University, College Station.

McCoy, B. and Dash, N. (2013) Class. In D.S.K. Thomas, B.D. Phillips, W.E. Lovekamp, and A. Fothergill, eds., *Social Vulnerability to Disasters*, 2nd edn. CRC Press: Boca Raton, FL, 83–112.

McDonald, K.E., Keys, C.B., and Balcazar, F.E. (2007) Disability, race/ethnicity and gender: Themes of cultural oppression, acts of individual resistance. *American Journal of Community Psychology* 39, 145–161.

McEntire, D.A. (2007) *Disciplines, Disasters, and Emergency Management*. Charles C. Thomas: Springfield, IL.

McGoey, L. (2012a) The logic of strategic ignorance. *British Journal of Sociology* 63(3), 553–576.

McGoey, L. (2012b) Strategic unknowns: Towards a sociology of ignorance. *Economy and Society*, 41(1), 1–16. doi: 10.1080/03085147.2011.637330.

McNamara, D.E., Rubinstein, J.L., Myers, E., Smoczyk, G., Benz, H.M., Williams, R.A., Hayes, G. et al. (2015) Efforts to monitor and characterize the recent increasing seismicity in central Oklahoma. *Leading Edge* 34(6), 628–639. doi: 10.1190/tle34060628.1.

McPhee, J. (1989) *The Control of Nature*. Farrar, Straus & Giroux: New York.

Melamed, J. (2015) Racial capitalism. *Critical Ethnic Studies* 1(1), 76–85, http://www.jstor.org/stable/10.5749/jcritethnstud.1.1.0076.

Mendonça, D. and Wallace, W.A. (2007) A cognitive model of improvisation in emergency management. *IEEE Transactions on Systems, Man and Cybernetics, Part A: Systems and Humans* 38(4), 547–561.

Mendonça, D., Webb, G., Butts, C. and Brooks, J. (2014) Cognitive correlates of improvised behaviour in disaster response: The cases of the Murrah Building and the World Trade Center. *Journal of Contingencies and Crisis Management* 22(4), 185–195.

Meo, M., Ziebro, B., and Patton, A. (2004) Tulsa turnaround: From disaster to sustainability. *Natural Hazards Review* 5, 1–9.

Merton, R.K. (1957) The role-set: Problems in sociological theory. *British Journal of Sociology* 8(2), 106–120.

Merton, R.K. (1968) The Matthew effect in science. *Science*, 159(3810), 56–63.

Meyer, M.A. (2018) Social capital in disaster research. In H. Rodríguez, W. Donner, and J.E. Trainor, eds., *Handbook of Disaster Research*, 2nd edn. Springer: Cham, Switzerland, 263–286.

Michel-Kerjan, E., Hochrainer-Stigler, S., Kunreuther, H., Linnerooth-Bayer, J., Mechler, R., Muir-Wood, R., Ranger, N. et al. (2013) Catastrophe risk models from evaluating disaster risk reduction investments in developing countries. *Risk Analysis* 33(6), 984–999.

Miles, S.B. and Chang, S.E. (2003) *Urban Disaster Recovery: A Framework and Simulation Model.* Multidisciplinary Center for Earthquake Engineering Research, University at Buffalo: Buffalo, NY.

Miles, S.B. and Chang, S.E. (2006) Modeling community recovery from earthquakes. *Earthquake Spectra* 22(2), 439–458.

Miles, S.B. and Chang, S.E. (2011) ResilUS: A community disaster resilience model. *Cartography and GIS* 38, 36–51.

Mileti, D.S. (1975) *Natural Hazards Warning Systems in the United States.* Institute of Behavioral Science, University of Colorado: Boulder.

Mileti, D.S. (1999) *Disasters by Design: A Reassessment of Natural Hazards in the United States.* Joseph Henry Press: Washington, DC.

Mileti, D.S. and Darlington, J.D. (1997) The role of searching in shaping reactions to earthquake risk information. *Social Problems* 44, 89–103.

Mileti, D.S., Drabek, T.E., and Haas, J.E. (1975) *Human Systems in Extreme Environments.* Institute of Behavioral Science, Program on Environment and Behavior, University of Colorado: Boulder.

Mileti, D.S. and Fitzpatrick, C. (1993) *The Great Earthquake Experiment: Risk Communication and Public Action.* Westview Press: Boulder, CO.

Mileti, D.S., Fitzpatrick, C., and Farhar, B.C. (1990) *Risk Communication and Public Response to the Parkfield Earthquake Prediction Experiment.* Hazards Assessment Laboratory and Department of Sociology, Colorado State University: Fort Collins.

Mileti, D.S. and O'Brien, P. (1992) Warnings during disaster: Normalizing communicated risk. *Social Problems* 39, 40–57.

Mileti, D.S. and Peek, L. (2000) The social psychology of public response to warnings of a nuclear power plant accident. *Journal of Hazardous Materials* 75, 181–194.

Mileti, D.S. and Sorensen, J.H. (1987) Natural hazards and precautionary behavior. In N.D. Weinstein, ed., *Taking Care: Understanding and Encouraging Self-Protective Behavior.* Cambridge University Press: Cambridge, 189–207.

Miller, B. (2018) Climate change could leave Californians with "weather whiplash." CNN, http://www.cnn.com/2018/04/23/us/climate-change-california-whiplash-wxc/index.html.

Miller, D.S. and Rivera, J.D. (2011) Tragedy has brought us together: Responding to new and emerging regional catastrophes. In D.S. Miller and J.D. Rivera, eds., *Comparative Emergency Management: Examining Global and Regional Responses Disasters.* CRC Press: Boca Raton, FL, xxix–xliii.

Mitchell, B.C. and Chakraborty, J. (2015) Landscapes of thermal inequity: Disproportionate exposure to urban heat in the three largest US cities. *Environmental Research Letters* 10(11), http://iopscience.iop.org/arti cle/10.1088/1748–9326/10/11/115005/meta.

Moench, M., Tyler, S., and Lage, J., eds. (2011) *Catalyzing Urban Climate Resilience: Applying Resilience Concepts to Planning Practice in the ACCCRN Program*. Institute for Social and Environmental Transition-International: Boulder, CO.

Mohai, P., Pellow, D., and Roberts, J.T. (2009) Environmental Justice. *Annual Review of Environment and Resources* 34, 405–430. doi: 10.1146/ann urev-environ-082508-094348.

Molotch, H. (1976) The city as a growth machine: Toward a political economy of place. *American Journal of Sociology* 82(2), 309–332, http://www.jstor.org/ stable/2777096.

Monroe, I. (2016) Hurricane Katrina's struggling black gay community. Huffington Post, September 2, https://www.huffingtonpost.com/irene-monroe/hurricane-katrinas-strugg_b_8074408.html.

Montgomery, M.C. and Chakraborty, J. (2015) Assessing the environmental justice consequences of flood risk: A case study in Miami, Florida. *Environmental Research Letters* 10, 1–11.

Moore, S., Daniel, M., Linnan, L., Campbell, M., Benedict, S., and Meier, A. (2004) After Hurricane Floyd passed: Investigating the social determinants of disaster preparedness and recovery. *Family & Community Health* 27(3), 204–217.

Morgan, M.G., Fischhoff, B., Bostrom, A., and Atman, C.J. (2002) *Risk Communication: A Mental Models Approach*. Cambridge University Press: Cambridge.

Moss, P. and Falconer Al-Hindi, K., eds. (2008) *Feminisms in Geography: Rethinking Space, Place, and Knowledges*. Rowman & Littlefield: Lanham, MD.

Mueller, J. and Stewart, M.G. (2011a) Balancing the risks, benefits, and costs of homeland security. *Homeland Security Affairs* 7, 1–27.

Mueller, J. and Stewart, M.G. (2011b) *Terror, Security, and Money: Balancing the Risks, Benefits, and Costs of Homeland Security*. Oxford University Press: New York.

Mueller, J. and Stewart, M.G. (2012) The terrorism delusion: America's over-wrought response to September 11. *International Security* 37, 81–110.

Muir-Wood, R. (2017) Billions in liabilities: Man-made earthquakes at Europe's biggest gas field. RMS, http://www.rms.com/blog/2017/01/26/ billions-in-liabilities-man-made-earthquakes-at-europes-biggest-gas-field

Mukherji, A., Ganapati, N.E., and Rahill, G. (2014) Expecting the unexpected: Field research in post-disaster settings. *Natural Hazards* 73(2), 805–828.

Multihazard Mitigation Council (2004) *Natural Hazard Mitigation Saves*. National Institute of Building Sciences: Washington, DC.

Multihazard Mitigation Council (2005) *Natural Hazard Mitigation Saves: An Independent Study to Assess the Future Savings from Mitigation Activities*, vol. 2: Study Documentation. National Institute of Building Sciences: Washington, DC.

Muramatsu, N. and Akiyama, H. (2011) Japan: Super-aging society preparing for the future. *Gerontologist* 51(4), 425–432. doi: 10.1093/geront/gnr067.

Murphy, B.L. (2007) Locating social capital in resilient community-level emergency management. *Natural Hazards* 41, 297–315.

Nakagawa, Y. and Shaw, R. (2004) Social capital: A missing link to disaster recovery. *International Journal of Mass Emergencies and Disasters* 22(1), 5–34.

Nakahara, S. and Ichikawa, M. (2013) Mortality in the 2011 tsunami in Japan. *Journal of Epidemiology* 23(1), 70–73.

National Center for Disaster Preparedness (2010) *Impact on Children and Families of the Deepwater Horizon Oil Spill: Preliminary Findings of the Coaster Population Impact Study*. Columbia University: New York.

National Center for Disaster Preparedness (2013) *Children's Health and Disasters: Children's Health After the Oil Spill: A Four-State Study Findings from the Gulf Coast Population Impact Project*. Columbia University: New York.

National Center for Disaster Preparedness (2015) *The Hurricane Sandy Person Report: Disaster Exposure, Health Impacts, Economic Burden, and Social Well-Being* (The Sandy Child and Family Health Briefing Report Series). Columbia University: New York.

National Center on Family Homelessness (2014) *America's Youngest Outcasts: A Report Card on Child Homelessness*. American Institutes for Research: Waltham, MA.

National Coalition for the Homeless (2017) *Substance Abuse and Homelessness*. National Coalition for the Homeless: Washington, DC.

National Council on Disability (2006) *The Impact of Hurricanes Katrina and Rita on People with Disabilities: A Look Back and Remaining Challenges*. National Council on Disability: Washington, DC.

National Institute of Mental Health (2007) Ethical issues to consider in developing, evaluating, and conducting research post-disaster. National Institutes of Health: Bethesda, MD, http://www.nimh.nih.gov/funding/grant-writing-and-application-process/ethical-issues-to-consider-in-developing-evaluating-and-conducting-research-post-disaster.shtml.

National Institute of Standards and Technology (2015a) *Community Resilience Planning Guide for Buildings and Infrastructure Systems*, vol. 1 (NIST Special Publication 1190). NIST: US Department of Commerce.

National Institute of Standards and Technology (2015b) *Community Resilience Planning Guide for Buildings and Infrastructure Systems*, vol. 2 (NIST Special Publication 1190). NIST: US Department of Commerce.

National Institute of Standards and Technology (2016) *Critical Assessment of Lifeline System Performance: Understanding Societal Needs in Disaster Recovery*. NIST: US Department of Commerce.

National Preparedness Leadership Initiative (n.d.) *Investing in Resilience, Investing in the Whole Community*. National Preparedness Leadership Initiative, Harvard Kennedy School, Harvard School of Public Health: Cambridge, MA.

National Research Council (1989) *Improving Risk Communication*. National Academies Press: Washington DC.

National Research Council (1996) *Understanding Risk: Informing Decisions in a Democratic Society*. National Academies Press: Washington, DC.

National Research Council (2006) *Facing Hazards and Disasters: Understanding Human Dimensions*. National Academy Press: Washington, DC.

National Research Council (2011) *Building Community Disaster Resilience through Public–Private Collaboration*. National Academies Press: Washington, DC.

National Research Council (2012) *Disaster Resilience: A National Imperative*. Committee on Increasing National Resilience to Hazards and Disasters, Committee on Science, Engineering, and Public Policy, and National Academies Press: Washington, DC.

National Research Council (2013a) *Geotargeted Alerts and Warnings: Report of a Workshop on Current Knowledge and Research Gaps*. National Academies Press: Washington, DC.

National Research Council (2013b) *Public Response to Alerts and Warnings Using Social Media: Report of a Workshop on Current Knowledge and Research*. National Academies Press: Washington, DC.

NBC News (2008) Illegal immigrants opted to stay during Gustav. *NBC News*, September 2, http://www.nbcnews.com/id/26513677/ns/us_news-life/t/illegal-immigrants-opted-stay-during-gustav/#.WwhQhYoh2Uk.

NBC News (2017) Majority of northern California fire victims were senior citizens. *NBC News*, October 21, https://www.nbcbayarea.com/news/local/North-Bay-Fires-Victims-451678753.html

Neal, D.M. and Phillips, B.D. (1990) Female-dominated local social movement organizations in disaster-threat situations. In G. West, G. and R.L. Blumberg, eds., *Women and Social Protest*. Oxford University Press: New York, 243–255.

Neria, Y., DiGrande, L., and Adams, B.G. (2011) Posttraumatic stress disorder following the September 11, 2001, terrorist attacks: A review of the literature among highly exposed populations. *American Psychologist* 66(6), 429–446.

Newman, E. and Kaloupek, D.G. (2004) The risks and benefits of participating in trauma-focused research studies. *Journal of Traumatic Stress* 17(5), 383–394.

Newsome, B.O. and Jarmon, J.A. (2016) *A Practical Introduction to Homeland Security and Emergency Management: From Home to Abroad*. CQ Press: Thousand Oaks, CA.

New York Times Editorial Board (2013) Hurricane Sandy and New York's poor. *New York Times*, December 23.

Ngo, E.B. (2001) When disasters and age collide: Reviewing vulnerability of the elderly. *Natural Hazards Review* 2(2), 80–89.

Nigg, J.M., Riad, J.K., Wachtendorf, T., Tweedy, A., and Reshaur, L. (1998) Disaster resistant communities initiative: Evaluation of the pilot phase. Final Project Report #40, University of Delaware Disaster Research Center, Newark, DE.

Norgaard, K.M. (2006) "People want to protect themselves a little bit": Emotions, denial, and social movement nonparticipation. *Sociological Inquiry* 76(3), 372–396.

Norgaard, K.M. (2011) *Living in Denial: Climate Change, Emotions, and Everyday Life.* MIT Press: Cambridge, MA.

Norris, F.H. (2006) Disaster research methods: Past progress and future directions. *Journal of Traumatic Stress* 19(2), 173–184.

Norris, F.H., Friedman, M.J., and Watson, P.J. (2002) 60,000 disaster victims speak, part ii: Summary and implications of the disaster mental health research. *Psychiatry: Interpersonal and Biological Processes* 65(3), 240–260. doi: 10.1521/psyc.65.3.240.20169.

Norris, F.H., Friedman, M.J., Watson, P.J., Byrne, C.M., Diaz, E., and Kaniasty, K. (2002) 60,000 disaster victims speak, part i: An empirical review of the empirical literature, 1981–2001. *Psychiatry: Interpersonal and Biological Processes* 65(3), 207–239. doi: 10.1521/psyc.65.3.207.20173.

Norris, F.H., Galea, S., Friedman, M.J., and Watson, J., eds. (2006) *Methods for Disaster Mental Health Research.* Guilford Press: New York.

Norris, F.H., Stevens, S.P., Pfefferbaum, B., Wyche, K.F., and Pfefferbaum, R.L. (2008) Community resilience as a metaphor, theory, set of capacities, and strategy for disaster resilience. *American Journal of Community Psychology* 41, 127–150. doi: 10.1007/s10464-007-9156-6.

O'Brien, P. and Mileti, D.S. (1992) Citizen participation in emergency response following the Loma Prieta earthquake. *International Journal of Mass Emergencies and Disasters* 10, 71–89.

Okuyama, Y. (2007) Economic modeling for disaster impact analysis: Past, present, and future. *Economic Systems Research* 19(2), 115–124.

Oliver, M. and Shapiro, T.M. (1995) *Black Wealth/White Wealth: A New Perspective on Racial Inequality.* Routledge: New York.

Oliver-Smith, A. (1996) Anthropological research on hazards and disasters. *Annual Review of Anthropology* 25, 303–328, http://www.jstor.org/stable/2155829.

Oliver-Smith, A. (2010) Haiti and the historical construction of disasters. *NACLA Report on the Americas* 43(4), 32–36. doi: 10.1080/10714839.2010.11725505.

Oliver-Smith, A. and Hoffman, S.M. (1999) *The Angry Earth.* University of Florida: Routledge, New York.

Olshansky, R.B. and Johnson, L.A. (2010) *Clear as Mud: Planning for the Rebuilding of New Orleans.* Routledge: New York.

Omi, M. and Winant, H. (1994) *Racial Formation in the United States: From the 1960s to the 1990s,* 2nd ed. Routledge, New York, NY.

Organization for Economic Cooperation and Development (2013) *OECD Skills Outlook 2013: First Results from the Survey of Adult Skills.* OECD Publishing. doi: 10.1787/9789264204256-en.

Otani, J. (2010) *Older People in Natural Disasters: The Great Hanshin Earthquake of 1995*. Kyoto University Press/Trans Pacific Press: Kyoto/Victoria, Australia.

Palen, L. and Hughes, A. (2018) Social media in disaster communication. In H. Rodríguez, W. Donner, and J.E. Trainor, eds., *Handbook of Disaster Research*, 2nd edn. Springer: Cham, Switzerland, 497–518.

Palen, L. and Liu, S.B. (2007) Citizen communications in crisis: Anticipating a future of ICT-supported public participation. *Proceedings of the CHI Conference: Emergency Action*. ACM: New York, 727–736.

Palen, L., Vieweg, S., Liu, S.B., and Hughes, A. (2009) Crisis in a networked world: Features of computer-mediated communication in the April 16, 2007 Virginia Tech event. *Social Science Computing Review* 27, 467–480.

Palen, L., Vieweg, S., Sutton, J., Liu, S.B., and Hughes, A. (2007) Crisis informatics: Studying crisis in a networked world. Paper presented at the Third International Conference on E-Social Science, October 7–9, Ann Arbor, Michigan, http://citeseerx.ist.psu.edu/viewdoc/download?doi=10.1.1.113.57 50&rep=rep1&type=pdf.

Pardee, J.W. (2012) Living through displacement: Housing insecurity among low-income evacuees. In L. Weber and L. Peek, eds., *Displaced: Life in the Katrina Diaspora*. University of Texas Press: Austin, 63–78.

Park, J., Cho, J. and Rose, A. (2011) Modeling a major source of economic resilience to disasters: Recapturing lost production. *Natural Hazards* 58(1), 163–182.

Park, R.E. (1936) Human ecology. *American Journal of Sociology* 42, 1–15.

Parrott, W.G. (2017) Role of emotions in risk perception. In G. Emilien, R. Weitkunat, and F. Lüdicke, eds., *Consumer Perception of Product Risks and Benefits*. Springer: Cham, 221–232.

Paton, D. and Johnston, D., eds. (2006) *Disaster Resilience: An Integrated Approach*. Charles C. Thomas: Springfield, IL.

Patrick, K. (2017) Income security, National snapshot: Poverty among women and families, 2016. National Women's Law Center, https://nwlc.org/wp-content/uploads/2017/09/Poverty-Snapshot-Factsheet-2017.pdf.

Patt, A.G., Tadross, M., Nussbaumer, P., Asante, K., Metzger, M., Rafael, J., Goujon, A. et al. (2010) Estimating least-developed countries' vulnerability to climate-related extreme events over the next 50 years. *Proceedings of National Academy of Sciences* 107(4), 1333–1337. doi: 10.1073/pnas.0910253107.

Patt, A.G., Schroter, D., Klein, R.J.T., and de la Vega-Leinert, A.C., eds. (2010) *Assessing Vulnerability to Global Environmental Change*. Earthscan: London.

Patterson, O., Weil, F., and Patel, K. (2010) The role of community in disaster response: Conceptual models. *Population Research and Policy Review* 29(2), 127–141.

Patton, A., ed. (1994) *From Rooftop to River: Tulsa's Approach to Floodplain and Stormwater Management*. Department of Public Works: Tulsa, OK.

Peacock, W.G. (2003) Hurricane mitigation status and factors influencing mitigation status among Florida's single-family homeowners. *Natural Hazards Review* 4(3), 149–158.

Peacock, W.G. and Girard, C. (1997) Ethnic and racial inequalities in disaster damage and insurance settlements. In W.G. Peacock, B.H. Morrow, and H. Gladwin, eds., *Hurricane Andrew: Ethnicity, Gender and Sociology of Disasters*. Routledge: London, 171–190.

Peacock, W.G., Morrow, B.H., and Gladwin, H. (1997) *Hurricane Andrew: Ethnicity, Gender and the Sociology of Disasters*. Routledge: London.

Peake, L. and Sheppard, E. (2014) The emergence of radical/critical geography within North America. *ACME: An International E-Journal for Critical Geographies* 13(2), 305–327.

Peck, J. (2010) *Constructions of Neoliberal Reason*. Oxford University Press: Oxford.

Peck, J. and Tickell, A. (2002) Neoliberalizing space. *Antipode* 34(3), 380–404.

Peek, L. (2008) Children and disasters: Understanding vulnerability, developing capacities, and promoting resilience: An introduction. *Children, Youth, and Environments* 18(1), 1–29, http://www.jstor.org/stable/10.7721/chilyoutenvi.18.1.0001.

Peek, L. (2010) Age. In B.D. Phillips, D.S.K. Thomas, A. Fothergill, and L. Blinn-Pike, eds., *Social Vulnerability to Disasters*. CRC Press: Boca Raton, FL, 155–185.

Peek, L. (2012) They call it "Katrina fatigue": Displaced families and discrimination in Colorado. In L. Weber and L. Peek, eds., *Displaced: Life in the Katrina Diaspora*. University of Texas Press: Austin, 31–46.

Peek, L. (2013) Age. In D.S.K. Thomas, B.D. Phillips, W.E. Lovekamp, and A. Fothergill, eds., *Social Vulnerability to Disasters*, 2nd edn. CRC Press: Boca Raton, FL, 167–198.

Peek, L. and Fothergill, A. (2009) Using focus groups: Lessons from studying daycare centers, 9/11, and Hurricane Katrina. *Qualitative Research* 9(1), 31–59.

Pelling, M. (2003) *The Vulnerability of Cities: Natural Disasters and Social Resilience*. Routledge: New York.

Pelling, M. (2011) *Adaptation to Climate Change: From Resilience to Transformation*. Routledge: New York.

Pellow, D. (2000) Environmental inequality formation: Toward a theory of environmental justice. *American Behavioral Scientist* 43(4), 581–601.

Pellow, D. (2007) *Resisting Global Toxics: Transnational Movements for Environmental Justice*. MIT Press: Cambridge, MA.

Perrings, C. (1998) Resilience in the dynamics of economy-environment systems. *Environment and Resource Economics* 113(3 & 4) 503–520.

Perrings, C. (2006) Resilience and sustainable development. *Environmental and Development Economics* 11, 417–427. doi: 10.1017/S1355770X06003020.

Perrow, C. (1984) *Normal Accidents: Living with High-Risk Technologies*. Basic Books: New York.

Perrow, C. (2006) *The Next Catastrophe: Reducing our Vulnerabilities to Natural, Industrial, and Terrorist Disasters*. Princeton University Press: Princeton, NJ.

Perry, R.W. and Hirose, H. (1983) *Volcano Management in the United States and Japan.* JAI Press, Greenwich, CT.

Perry, R.W. and Lindell, M.K. (1991) The effects of ethnicity on evacuation. *International Journal of Mass Emergencies and Disasters* 9, 47–68.

Perry, R.W. and Lindell, M.K. (2007) *Emergency Planning.* John Wiley & Sons, Inc.: Hoboken, NJ.

Petrescu-Prahova, M. and Butts, C.T. (2005) Emergent coordination in the World Trade Center disaster. Paper No. 36, Institute for Mathematical Behavioral Sciences, University of California, Irvine, http://citeseerx.ist.psu.edu/viewdoc/summary?doi=10.1.1.59.8310

Pfeffer, F.T., Danziger, S., and Schoeni, R.F. (2013) Wealth disparities before and after the Great Recession. *Annals of the American Academy of Political and Social Science* 650(1), 98–123.

Pfefferbaum, B., Reissman, D.B., Pfefferbaum, R.L., Klomp, R.W., and Gurwitch, R.H. (2007) Building resilience to mass trauma events. In L.S. Doll, S.E. Bonzo, J.A. Mercy, D.A. Sleet, and E.N. Haas, eds., *Handbook of Injury and Violence Prevention.* Springer: New York, 347–358.

Pfefferbaum, R.L., Pfefferbaum, B., and Van Horn, R.L. (2011) *Communities Advancing Resilience Toolkit (CART): The Cart Integrated System.* Terrorism and Disaster Center at the University of Oklahoma Health Sciences Center: Oklahoma City.

Pfefferbaum, R.L., Pfefferbaum, B., Van Horn, R.L., Klomp, R.W., Norris, F.H., and Reissman, D.B. (2013) The communities advancing resilience toolkit (CART): An intervention to build community resilience to disasters. *Journal of Public Health Management & Practice* 19(3), 250–258.

Pfefferbaum, R.L., Pfefferbaum, B., Zhao, Y.D., Van Horn, R.L., McCarter, G.S., and Leonard, M.B. (2016) Assessing community resilience: A CART survey application in an impoverished urban community. *Disaster Health* 3(2), 45–56.

Phillips, B.D. (1993) Cultural diversity in disasters: Sheltering, housing, and long term recovery. *International Journal of Mass Emergencies and Disasters* 11, 99–110.

Phillips, B.D. (1998) Sheltering and housing of low-income and minority groups in Santa Cruz county after the Loma Prieta earthquake. In J.M. Nigg, ed., *The Loma Prieta, California, Earthquake of October 17, 1989: Recovery, Mitigation, and Reconstitution* (US Geological Survey Professional Paper 1553-D), US Government Printing Office: Washington, DC, 17–28.

Phillips, B.D. (2009) *Disaster Recovery.* CRC Press: Boca Raton, FL.

Phillips, B.D. (2014) Qualitative disaster research. In P. Leavy, ed., *The Oxford Handbook of Qualitative Research.* Oxford University Press: Oxford. doi: 10.1093/oxfordhb/9780199811755.013.010.

Phillips, B.D. and Jenkins, P. (2013) Violence. In D.S.K. Thomas, B.D. Phillips, W.E. Lovekamp, and A. Fothergill, eds., *Social Vulnerability to Disasters*, 2nd edn. CRC Press: Boca Raton, FL, 311–340.

Phillips, B.D., Thomas, D.S.K., Fothergill, A. and Blinn-Pike, L., eds. (2010) *Social Vulnerability to Disasters*. CRC Press: Boca Raton, FL.

Philo, C. (2005) The geographies that wound. *Population, Space and Place* 11, 441–454.

Picou, J.S. (1996a) Compelled disclosure of scholarly research: Some comments on "high stakes litigation." *Law & Contemporary Problems* 59(3), 149–157.

Picou, J.S. (1996b) Sociology and compelled disclosure: Protecting respondent confidentiality. *Sociological Spectrum* 16(3), 209–237.

Picou, J.S. (1996c) Toxins in the environment, damage to the community: Sociology and the toxic tort. In P. Jenkins and S. Kroll-Smith, eds., *Witnessing for Sociology: Sociologists in Court*. Greenwood Press: Westport, CT, 210–223.

Picou, J.S., Marshall, B.K., and Gill, D.A. (2004) Disaster, litigation, and the corrosive community. *Social Forces* 82(4), 1493–1522, doi: 10.1353/sof.2004.0091.

Pielke, R.A. (1999) Who decides? Forecasts and responsibility in the 1997 Red River flood. *Applied Behavior Science Review* 7(2), 83–101.

Pielke, R.A., Gratz, J., Landsea, C.W., Collins, D., Saunders, M.A., and Musulin, R. (2008) Normalized hurricane damage in the United States: 1900–2005. *Natural Hazards Review* 9(1), 29–42.

Pielke, R.A. and Landsea, C.W. (1998) Normalized hurricane damages in the United States: 1925–1995. *Weather and Forecasting* 13(3), 621–631.

Pincha, C. (2008) Indian Ocean Tsunami Through the Gender Lens: Insights from Tamil Nadu, India. Earthworm Books: Mumbai.

Plodinec, J.M. (2009) *Definitions of Resilience: An Analysis*. Community and Regional Resilience Institute, Oak Ridge National Laboratory: Oak Ridge, TN.

Polsky, C., Neff, R., and Yarnal, B. (2007) Building global change vulnerability assessments: The vulnerability scoping diagram. *Global Environmental Change* 17, 472–485.

Population Reference Bureau (2015) *2015 World Population Data Sheet*. PRB: Washington, DC.

Portes, A. (1998) Social capital: Its origins and applications in modern sociology. *Annual Review of Sociology* 24, 1–24. doi: 10.1146/annurev.soc.24.1.1.

Poursanidis, D. and Chrysoulakis, N. (2017) Remote sensing, natural hazards and the contribution of ESA Sentinels missions. *Remote Sensing Applications: Society and Environment* 6, 25–38. doi: 10.1016/j.rsase.2017.02.001.

Price, G.N. (2013) Hurricane Katrina as an experiment in housing mobility and neighborhood effects: Were the relocated poor black evacuees better-off? *Review of Black Political Economy* 40, 121–143.

Prince, S.H. (1920) *Catastrophe and Social Change: Based upon a Sociological Study of the Halifax Disaster*. Columbia University Press: New York.

Proctor, B.D., Semega, J.L. and Kollar, M.A. (2016) *Income and Poverty in the United States: 2015: Current Population Reports*. United States Census Bureau: Washington, DC.

Proctor, R.N. and Schiebinger, L., eds. (2008) *Agnotology: The Making and Unmaking of Ignorance*. Stanford University Press: Palo Alto, CA.

Pulido, L. (2000) Rethinking environmental racism: White privilege and urban development in southern California. *Annals of the Association of American Geographers* 90(1), 12–40.

Pulido, L. (2016) Flint, environmental racism, and racial capitalism. *Capitalism Nature Socialism* 27(3), 1–16. doi: 10.1080/10455752.2016.1213013.

Pulido, L. (2017) Geographies of race and ethnicity II: Environmental racism, racial capitalism and state-sanctioned violence. *Progress in Human Geography* 41(4), 1–10. doi: 10.1177/0309132516646495.

Putnam, R.D. (1995) Bowling alone: America's declining social capital. *Journal of Democracy* 6(1), 65–78.

Putnam, R.D. (2000) *Bowling Alone: The Collapse and Revival of American Community*. Simon & Schuster: New York.

Putnam, R.D. (2001) Social capital: Measurement and consequences. *Isuma: Canadian Journal of Policy Research* 2, 41–51.

Quarantelli, E.L. (1954) The nature and conditions of panic. *American Journal of Sociology* 60, 267–275.

Quarantelli, E.L. (1974) Weaknesses in disaster planning. *Proceedings of the Human Factors and Ergonomics Society Annual Meeting* 18(3), 321–322.

Quarantelli, E.L. (1977) Panic behavior: Some empirical observations. In D.J. Conway, ed., *Human Response to Tall Buildings*. Dowden, Hutchinson, and Ross, Inc.: Stroudsburg, PA, 336–350.

Quarantelli, E.L. (1987) Disaster studies: An analysis of the social historical factors affecting the development of research in the area. *International Journal of Mass Emergencies and Disasters* 5, 285–310.

Quarantelli, E.L. (1988) The NORC research on the Arkansas tornado: A fountainhead study. *International Journal of Mass Emergencies and Disasters* 6, 283–310.

Quarantelli, E.L. (1995) Emergent behaviors and groups in the crisis time of disasters. Preliminary Paper #226, Disaster Research Center, University of Delaware, Newark.

Quarantelli, E.L. (1996) The future is not the past repeated: Projecting disasters of the 21st century from present trends. Preliminary Paper #229, Disaster Research Center, University of Delaware, Newark.

Quarantelli, E.L. (1998) *What Is a Disaster? Perspectives on the Question*. Routledge: London.

Quarantelli, E.L. (2001a) Another selective look at future social crises: Some aspects of which we can already see in the present. *Journal of Contingencies and Crisis Management* 9(4), 233–237.

Quarantelli, E.L. (2001b) Sociology of panic. In N.J. Smelser and P.B. Baltes, eds. *International Encyclopedia of the Social and Behavioral Sciences*. Pergamon Press: Oxford, 11020–11023.

Quarantelli, E.L. and Dynes, R.R. (1970) Property norms and looting: Their patterns in community crises. *Phylon* 31, 168–182.

Quarantelli, E.L. and Dynes, R.R. (1972) When disaster strikes (it isn't much like what you've heard and read about). *Psychology Today* 5, 66–70.

Quarantelli, E.L., Lagadec, P., and Boin, R.A. (2007) A heuristic approach to future disasters and crisis: New, old, and in-between types. In H. Rodríguez, E.L. Quarantelli, and R.R. Dynes, eds., *Handbook of Disaster Research*. Springer: New York, 16–41.

Quarantelli, E.L., Taylor, V.A., and Tierney, K. (1977) Delivery of emergency medical services in disasters. Preliminary Paper #46, Disaster Research Center, University of Delaware, Newark.

Quarantelli, E.L., Wenger, D., Mikami, S., and Hiroi, O. (1993) The reporting of news in disaster: A comparative study of Japanese and American communities. Historical and Comparative Series #8. Disaster Research Center, University of Delaware, Newark.

Radeloff, V.C., Helmers, D.P., Kramer, H.A., Mockrin, M.H., Alexandre, P.M., Bar-Massada, A., Butsic, V. et al. (2018) Rapid growth of the US wildland–urban interface raises wildfire risk. *Proceedings of the National Academy of Sciences USA* 115(13), 3314–3319.

Rayner, S. (2012) Uncomfortable knowledge: The social construction of ignorance in science and environmental policy discourses. *Economy and Society* 41(1), 107–125. doi: 10.1080/03085147.2011.637335.

Red Cross (2012) *Understanding Community Resilience and Program Factors That Strengthen Them: A Comprehensive Study of Red Cross Red Crescent Societies Tsunami Operation*. International Federation of Red Cross and Red Crescent Societies: Geneva, http://www.ifrc.org/PageFiles/96984/Final_Synthesis_Characteristics_Lessons_Tsunami.pdf.

Reid, J. (2013) Interrogating the neoliberal biopolitics of the sustainable development-resilience nexus. *International Political Sociology* 7, 353–367.

Reininger, B.M., Rahbar, M.H., Lee, M. et al. (2013) Social capital and disaster preparedness among low income Mexican Americans in a disaster prone area. *Social Science & Medicine* 83, 50–60.

Renschler, C.S., Frazier, A.E., Arendt, L.A., Cimellaro, G.P., Reinhorn, A.M. and Bruneau, M. (2010) Developing the "peoples" resilience framework for defining and measuring disaster resilience at the community scale. *Proceedings of the 9th US National and 10th Canadian Conference on Earthquake Engineering, July 25–29, Toronto*. Earthquake Engineering Research Institute: Oakland, CA, 1152–1161.

Resilience Measurement Evidence and Learning Community of Practice (2016) *Analysis of Resilience Measurement Frameworks and Approaches*. Overseas Development Institute: London.

Richards, E.G. (2016) Finding fault: Induced earthquake liability and regulation. *Field Report: Columbia Journal of Environmental Law*, 1–33, http://www.

columbiaenvironmentallaw.org/finding-fault-induced-earthquake-liability-and-regulation-2.

Risk to Resilience Study Team (2009) *Catalyzing Climate and Disaster Resilience: Processes for Identifying Tangible and Economically Robust Strategies*. Risk to Resilience Study: Kathmandu, Nepal.

Ritchie, L.A. (2004) *Voices of Cordova: Social Capital in the Wake of the Exxon Valdez Oil Spill*. Doctoral dissertation, Mississippi State University, Department of Sociology, Anthropology, and Social Work, Starkville.

Ritchie, L.A. (2012) Individual stress, collective trauma, and social capital in the wake of the Exxon Valdez oil spill. *Sociological Inquiry* 82(2), 187–211.

Ritchie, L.A. and Gill, D.A. (2007) Social capital theory as an integrating theoretical framework in technological disaster research. *Sociological Spectrum* 27(1), 103–129. doi: 10.1080/02732170601001037.

Ritchie, L.A. and Gill, D.A. (2011) The role of community capitals in disaster recovery. Paper presented at the PERI Symposium "Community Recovery from Disaster." http://www.riskinstitute.org/peri/content/view/1118/5.

Ritchie, L.A., Gill, D.A., and Farnham, C. (2013) Recreancy revisited: Beliefs about institutional failure following the Exxon Valdez oil spill. *Society and Natural Resources: An International Journal* 26, 655–671. doi: 10.1080/08941920.2012.690066.

Ritchie, L.A., Gill, D.A., and Long, M.A. (2018) Mitigating litigating: An examination of psychosocial impacts of compensation processes associated with the 2010 BP *Deepwater Horizon* Oil Spill. *Risk Analysis*. doi: 10.1111/risa.12 969.

Ritchie, L.A. and Tierney, K. (2011) Temporary housing planning and early implementation in the 12 January 2010 Haiti earthquake. *Earthquake Spectra* 27(S1), S487–S507.

Ritchie, L.A., Tierney, K., and Gilbert, B. (2010) Disaster preparedness among community-based organizations in the city and county of San Francisco: Serving the most vulnerable. In D. Miller and D.J. Rivera, eds., *Community Disaster Recovery and Resiliency: Exploring Global Opportunities and Challenges*. CRC Press: Boca Raton, FL, 251–280.

Robbins, P. (2012) *Political Ecology*. Routledge: New York.

Roberts, K.H. (1989) New challenges in organizational research: High-reliability organizations. *Industrial Crisis Quarterly* 3, 111–125.

Roberts, P.S. (2016) *Disasters and the American state: How politicians, bureaucrats, and the public prepare for the unexpected*. Cambridge University Press: New York.

Roberts, P.S., Ward, R., and Wamsley, G. (2012) The evolving federal role in emergency management: Policies and processes. In C.B. Rubin, ed., *Emergency Management: The American Experience, 1900–2010*, 2nd edn. CRC Press: Boca Raton, FL, 247–276.

Roberts, P.S., Ward, R., and Wamsley, G. (2014) The evolution of emergency management in America: From a troubling past to an uncertain future. In A. Farazmand, ed., *Crisis and Emergency Management: Theory and Practice*, 2nd edn. CRC Press: Boca Raton, FL, 167–187.

Robine, J.A. (2017) When climate change encounters the revolution in adult longevity. *Aging Clinical and Experimental Research* 29(6), 1073–1074.

Robine, J.M., Cheung, S.L., Le Roy, S., Van Oyen, H., and Herrmann, F.R. (2007) *Report on Excess Mortality in Europe during Summer 2003* (2003 Heat Wave Project). Inserm: Paris.

Rodin, J. (2014) *The Resilience Dividend: Being Strong in a World Where Things Go Wrong*. Rockefeller Foundation: New York.

Rose, A.Z. (1995) Input–output economics and computable general equilibrium models. *Structural Change and Economic Dynamics* 6(3), 295–304.

Rose, A.Z. (2007) Economic resilience to natural and man-made disasters: Multidisciplinary origins and contextual dimensions. *Environmental Hazards* 7(4), 383–398.

Rose, A.Z. (2009) *Economic Resilience to Disasters*. Community and Regional Resilience Institute, Oak Ridge National Laboratory: Oak Ridge, TN.

Rose, A.Z. and Krausmann, E. (2013) An economic framework for the development of a resilience index for business recovery. *International Journal of Disaster Risk Reduction* 5, 73–83. doi: 10.1016/j.ijdrr.2013.08.003.

Rose, A.Z. and Liao, S. (2005) Modeling regional economic resilience to disasters: A computable general equilibrium analysis of water service disruptions. *Journal of Regional Science* 45(1), 75–112.

Rose, A.Z., Oladosu, G., Lee, B., and Asay, G.B. (2009) The economic impacts of the September 11 terrorist attacks: A computable general equilibrium analysis. *Peace Economics, Peace Science and Public Policy* 15(2), 1554–8597.

Rose, G. (1993) *Feminism and Geography: The Limits of Geographical Knowledge*. Polity: Cambridge.

Rose-Redwood, R.S. (2006) Governmentality, geography, and the geo-coded world. *Progress in Human Geography* 30(4), 469–486.

Rosenstein, D.L. (2004) Decision-making capacity and disaster research. *Journal of Traumatic Stress* 17(5), 373–381.

Ross, A.D. (2014) *Local Disaster Resilience: Administrative and Political Perspectives*. Routledge: New York.

Rossi, P.J., Wright, J.D., and Weber-Burdin, E. (1982) *Natural Hazards and Public Choice: The State and Local Politics of Hazard Mitigation*. Academic Press: Cambridge.

Rubin, C.B. (2012) An introduction to 110 years of disaster response and emergency management. In C.B. Rubin, ed., *Emergency Management: The American Experience, 1900–2010*, 2nd edn. CRC Press: Boca Raton, FL, 1–12.

Rudel, T.K., Timmons, R.J., and Carmin, J. (2011) Political economy of the environment. *Annual Review of Sociology* 37, 221–238. doi: 10.1146/annurev.soc.012809.102639.

Rugh, J.S., Albright, L., and Massey, D.S. (2015) Race, space, and cumulative disadvantage: A case study of the subprime lending collapse. *Social Problems* 62(2), 186–218.

Rutter, M. (1987) Psychosocial resilience and protective mechanisms. *American Journal of Orthopsychiatry* 57(3), 316–331. doi: 10.1111/j.1939–0025.1987. tb03541.x.

Samuelson, W. and Zeckhauser, R.J. (1988) Status quo bias in decision making. *Journal of Risk and Uncertainty* 1, 7–59.

Sandman, P.M. (2012) *Responding to Community Outrage: Strategies for Effective Risk Communication*. American Industrial Hygiene Association, http://www.psand man.com/media/RespondingtoCommunityOutrage.pdf.

Santos-Hernández, J. and Morrow, B.H. (2013) Language and literacy. In B. Phillips, D.S.K. Thomas, A. Fothergill, and L. Blinn-Pike, eds., *Social Vulnerability to Disasters*, 2nd edn. CRC Press: Boca Raton, FL.

Sarnoff, N. (2017) Apartment rents rising in Harvey's wake. *Houston Chronicle*, October 5.

Sassen, S. (2012) *Cities in the World Economy*, 4th edn. Pine Forge Press: Thousand Oaks, CA.

Scanlon, J. (1997) Human behaviour in disaster: The relevance of gender. *Australian Journal of Emergency Management* 11, 2–7.

Schipper, E.L.F. and Langston, L. (2015) A comparative overview of resilience measurement frameworks. Working Paper 422, Overseas Development Institute, London.

Schnaiberg, A. (1980) *The Environment: From Surplus to Scarcity*. Oxford University Press: New York.

Schnaiberg, A. and Gould, K.A. (1994) *Environment and Society: The Enduring Conflict*. St. Martin's Press: New York.

Schrank, H.L., Marshall, M.I., Hall-Phillips, A., Wiatt, R.F., and Jones, N.E. (2013) Small-business demise and recovery after Katrina: Rate of survival and demise. *Natural Hazards* 65, 2353–2374.

Schroeder, A., Wamsley, G.L., and Ward, R. (2001) The evolution of emergency management in America: From a painful past to a promising but uncertain future. In A. Farazmand, ed., *Handbook of Crisis and Emergency Management*. CRC Press: Boca Raton, FL, 357–418.

Schulman, P.R. (1993) The negotiated order of organizational reliability. *Administration and Society* 25, 353–372.

Schweinberger, M., Petrescu-Prahova, M., and Vu, D.Q. (2014) Disaster response on September 11, 2001 through the lens of statistical network analysis. *Social Networks* 37, 42–55.

Semple, K. (2016) When the kitchen is also a bedroom: Overcrowding worsens in New York. *New York Times*, February 29.

Sharifi, A. (2016) A critical review of selected tools for assessing community resilience. *Ecological Indicators* 69, 629–647. doi: 10.1016/j.ecolind.2016.05.023.

Sheffi, Y. (2005) *The Resilient Enterprise: Overcoming Vulnerability for Competitive Advantage*. MIT Press: Cambridge, MA.

Sheffi, Y. (2017) *The Power of Resilience: How the Best Companies Manage the Unexpected*. MIT Press: Cambridge, MA.

Silver, R.C., Holman, E.A., McIntosh, D.N., Poulin, N., and Gil-Rivas, V. (2002) Nationwide longitudinal study of psychological responses to September 11. *Journal of the American Medical Association* 288(10), 1235–1244.

Shaw, R. and Sharma, A. (2011) *Climate and Disaster Resilience in Cities*. Emerald Group: Bingley, UK.

Slovic, P. (1999) Trust, emotion, sex, politics, and science: Surveying the risk-assessment battlefield. *Risk Analysis* 19(4), 689–701.

Slovic, P. (2010) *The Feeling of Risk: New Perspectives on Risk Perception*. Earthscan: London.

Slovic, P., Finucane, M.L., Peters, E., and MacGregor, D.G. (2004) Risk as analysis and risk as feelings: Some thoughts about affect, reason, risk, and rationality. *Risk Analysis* 24(2), 311–322.

Slovic, P., Finucane, M.L., Peters, E., and MacGregor, D.G. (2007) The affect heuristic. *European Journal of Operational Research* 177, 1333–1352.

Slovic, P., Fischhoff, B., and Lichtenstein, S. (1978) Judged frequency of lethal events. *Journal of Experimental Psychology: Human Learning and Memory* 4(6), 551.

Slovic, P., Fischhoff, B., and Lichtenstein, S. (1979) Rating the risks. *Environment* 21(3), 14–39.

Slovic, P., Fischhoff, B., and Lichtenstein, S. (1981) Facts and fears: Societal perception of risk. In K.B. Monroe, ed., *NA: Advances in Consumer Research*, vol. 8. Association for Consumer Research: Ann Arbor, MI, 497–502.

Smelser, N.J. (1962) *Theory of Collective Behavior*. Free Press: New York.

Smith, G. and Wenger, D. (2007) Sustainable disaster recovery: Operationalizing an existing agenda. In H. Rodríguez, E.L. Quarantelli, and R.R. Dynes, eds., *Handbook of Disaster Research*. Springer: New York, 234–257.

Soden, R. and Palen, L. (2014) From crowdsourced mapping to community mapping: The post-earthquake work of OpenStreetMap Haiti. In C. Rossitto, L. Ciofi, D. Martin, and B. Conein eds, *COOP 2014: Proceedings of the 11th International Conference on the Design of Cooperative Systems, 27–30 May 2014, Nice (France)*, 311–326.

Soja, E.W. (1989) *Postmodern Geographies: The Reassertion of Space in Critical Social Theory*. Verso: New York.

Soja, E.W. (2000) *Postmetropolis: Critical Studies of Cities and Regions*. Blackwell: Malden, MA.

Soja, E.W. (2009) The city and spatial justice. Paper prepared for presentation at the Spatial Justice Conference, Nanterre, Paris, France, March 12–14.

Solari, C.D. and Mare, R.D. (2012) Housing crowding effects on children's well-being. *Social Science Research* 41(2), 464–476.

Solnit, R. (2009) *A Paradise Built in Hell: The Extraordinary Communities That Arise in Disaster*. Viking: New York.

Somers, M.R. (2008) *Genealogies of Citizenship: Markets, Statelessness, and the Right to Have Rights*. Cambridge University Press: Cambridge.

Somers, S. (2009) Measuring resilience potential: An adaptive strategy for organizational crisis planning. *Journal of Contingencies and Crisis Management* 17(1), 12–23.

Spiro, E.S., Acton, R.M., and Butts, C.T. (2013) Extended structures of mediation: Re-examining brokerage in dynamic networks. *Social Networks* 35, 130–143. doi: 10.1016/j.socnet.2013.02.001.

Staeheli, L.A., Kofman, E., and Peake, L.J., eds. (2004) *Mapping Women, Making Politics: Feminist Perspectives on Political Geography*. Routledge: New York.

Stallings, R.A. (1995) *Promoting Risk: Constructing the Earthquake Threat*. Aldine de Gruyter: Hawthorne, NY.

Stallings, R.A. (1997) Methods of disaster research: Unique or not? *International Journal of Mass Emergencies and Disasters* 15(1), 7–19.

Stallings, R.A., ed. (2002) *Methods of Disaster Research*. International Research Committee on Disasters: Newark, DE.

Stallings, R.A. (2007) Methodological issues. In H. Rodríguez, E.L. Quarantelli, and R.R. Dynes, eds., *Handbook of Disaster Research*. Springer: New York, 55–82.

Stallings, R.A. and Quarantelli, E.L. (1985) Emergent citizen groups and emergency management. *Public Administration Review* 45, 93–100.

Starbird, K., Spiro, E.S., Edwards, I., Zhou, K., Maddock, J., and Narasimhan, S. (2016) Could this be true? I think so! Expressed uncertainty in online rumoring. In *Proceedings of the 2016 CHI Conference on Human Factors in Computing Systems*. ACM: New York, 360–371.

Stehling-Ariza, T., Park, Y.S., Sury, J.J., and Abramson, D. (2012) Measuring the impact of Hurricane Katrina on access to a personal healthcare provider: The use of the National Survey of Children's Health for an external comparison group. *Maternal and Child Health Journal* 16(S1), S170–S177.

Stellman, J.M., Smith, R.P., Katz, C.L., Sharma, V., Charney, D.S., Herbert, R., Moline, J. et al. (2008) Enduring mental health morbidity and social function impairment in World Trade Center rescue, recovery, and cleanup workers: The psychological dimension of an environmental health disaster. *Environmental Health Perspectives* 116(9), 1248–1253.

Stevenson, J.R., Vargo, J., Ivory, V., Bowie, C., and Wilkinson, S. (2015) *Resilience Benchmarking and Monitoring Review*. Ministry of Business, Innovation, and Employment: Wellington, NZ.

Stephenson, A., Vargo, J., and Seville, E. (2010) Measuring and comparing organisational resilience in Auckland. *Australian Journal of Emergency Management* 25(2), 27–32.

Stocking, S. and Holstein, L. (2009) Manufacturing doubt: Journalists' roles and the construction of ignorance in a scientific controversy. *Public Understanding of Science* 18, 23–42.

Stough, L.M. and Kelman, I. (2018) People with disabilities and disasters. In H. Rodríguez, W. Donner, and J.E. Trainor, eds., *Handbook of Disaster Research*, 2nd edn. Springer: Cham, Switzerland, 225–242.

Stryckman, B., Grace, T.L., Schwarz, P., and Marcozzi, D. (2015) An economic analysis and approach for health care preparedness in a substate region. *Disaster Medicine and Public Health Preparedness* 9(4), 344–348. doi: 10.1017/dmp.2015.37.

Subcommittee on Disaster Reduction (2005) *Grand Challenges for Disaster Reduction*. Office of Science and Technology Policy: Washington, DC.

Substance Abuse and Mental Health Services Administration (2016) *Disaster Technical Assistance Center Supplemental Research Bulletin: Challenges and Considerations in Disaster Research*, www.samhsa.gov/sites/default/files/dtac/supplemental-research-bulletin-jan-2016.pdf.

Superu (2015) Family resilience. *In Focus*, August, http://thehub.superu.govt.nz/assets/Uploads/In-Focus-Family Resilience-2015.pdf.

Susman, P., O'Keefe, P., and Wisner, B. (1983) Global disasters: A radical interpretation. In K. Hewitt, ed., *Interpretations of Calamity: From the Viewpoint of Human Ecology*. Allen & Unwin: Boston, MA, 263–283.

Sutcliffe, K.M. and Vogus, T.J. (2003) Organizing for resilience. In K. Cameron, J.E. Cutton, and R.E. Quinn, eds., *Positive Organizational Scholarship*. Berrett-Koehler Publishers: San Francisco, CA, 94–110.

Sutton, J. (2010) Twittering Tennessee: Distributed networks and collaboration following a technological disaster. In *Proceedings of the 7th International ISCRAM Conference*. Information Systems for Crisis Response and Management: Brussels, http://citeseerx.ist.psu.edu/viewdoc/download?doi=10.1.1.701.9623&rep=rep1&type=pdf.

Sutton, J. (2012) When online is off: Public communications following the February 2011 Christchurch, NZ earthquake. In L. Rothkrants, J. Ristvej, and Z. Franco, eds., *Proceedings of the 9th International ISCRAM Conference, April, Vancouver, Canada*. http://www.iscram.org/legacy/ISCRAM2012/proceedings/ISCRAM2012_proceedings.pdf

Sutton, J., Gibson, C.B., Phillips, N.E., Spiro, E.S., League, C., Johnson, B., Fitzhugh, S.M. et al. (2015) A cross-hazard analysis of terse message retransmission on Twitter. *Proceedings of the National Academy of Sciences* 112(48), 14793–14798. doi: 10.1073/pnas.1508916112.

Sutton, J., Gibson, C.B., Spiro, E.S., League, C., Fitzhugh, S.M., and Butts, C.T. (2015) What it takes to get passed on: Message content, style, and structure as predictors of retransmission in the Boston marathon bombing response. *PLoS ONE* 10(8), 1–19. doi: 10.1371/journal.pone.0134452.

Sutton, J., League, C., Sellnow, T. and Sellnow, D. (2015) Emergency public health messaging in a disaster event: Content and style factors for terse messages. *Health Communication* 30(2), 135–143.

Sutton, J., Palen, L., and Shklovski, I. (2008) Back-channels on the front-lines: Emerging use of social media in the 2007 Southern California wildfires. In F. Friedrich and B. Van De Walle, eds., *Proceedings of the 5th International ISCRAM Conference*. Academic Press: Washington, DC, 624–631, http://cmci. colorado.edu/~palen/Papers/iscram08/BackchannelsISCRAM08.pdf.

Sutton, J., Spiro, E.S., Butts, C.T., Fitzhugh, S.M., Johnson, B.A., and Greczek, M. (2013) Tweeting the spill: Online informal communications, social networks, and conversational microstructures during the *Deepwater Horizon* oilspill. *International Journal of Information Systems for Crisis Response and Management* 5(1), 58–76.

Sutton, J., Spiro, E.S., Greczek, M., Johnson, B., Fitzhugh, S.M., and Butts, C.T. (2012) Connected communications: Network structures of official communications in disaster. In L. Rothkranz, J. Ristvej, and Z. Franco, eds., *Proceedings of the 9th International ISCRAM Conference, April, Vancouver, Canada*. ISCRAM: Vancouver, 1–10.

Sutton, J., Spiro, E.S., Johnson, B.A., Fitzhugh, S.M., Gibson, C.B., and Butts, C.T. (2014a) Terse message amplification in the Boston bombing response. In S.R. Hiltz, M.S. Pfaff, L. Plotnick, and P.C. Shih, eds., *Proceedings of the 11th International Conference on Information Systems for Crisis Response and Management, May 24*. Pennsylvania State University: University Park, 612–621.

Sutton, J., Spiro, E.S., Johnson, B.A., Fitzhugh, S.M, Gibson, C.B., and Butts, C.T. (2014b) Warning tweets: Serial transmission of warning messages during a disaster event. *Information, Communication, and Society* 17(6), 765–787.

Sutton, J. and Woods, C. (2016) Tsunami warning message interpretation and sense making: Focus group insights. *Weather, Climate, and Society* 8, 389–398.

Swain, J. and French, S. (2008) *Disability on Equal Terms*. SAGE: Thousand Oaks, CA.

Swidler, A. (1986) Culture in action: Symbols and strategies. *American Sociological Review* 51(2), 273–286, http://www.jstor.org/stable/2095521.

Swiss Reinsurance (2014) *Mind the Risk: A Global Ranking of Cities Under Threat from Natural Disasters*. Swiss Re: Zurich.

Sydnor, S., Niehm, L., Lee, Y., Marshall, M.I., and Schrank, H.L. (2017) Analysis of post-disaster damage and disruptive impacts on the operating status of small businesses after Hurricane Katrina. *Natural Hazards* 85(3), 1637–1663.

Sylves, R. (2015) *Disaster Policy and Politics*, 2nd edn. CQ Press: Thousand Oaks, CA.

Szasz, A. and Meuser, M. (1997) Environmental inequalities: Literature review and proposals for new directions in research and theory. *Current Sociology* 45(3), 99–120.

Sze, J. (2006) *Toxic soup redux: Why environmental racism and environmental justice matter after Katrina*. Understanding Katrina: Social Science Research Council, http://understandingkatrina.ssrc.org/Sze.

Szentes, T. (1971) *The Political Economy of Underdevelopment*. Budapest: Akadémiai Kiadó.

Tang, Z., Brody, S.D., Quinn, C., and Chang, L. (2010) Moving from agenda to action: Evaluating local climate change action plans. *Journal of Environmental Planning and Management* 53(1), 41–62.

Tanner, T. and Rentschler, J. (2015) *Unlocking the "Triple Dividend" of Resilience: Why Investing in Disaster Risk Management Pays Off*. Overseas Development Institute/World Bank: London/Washington, DC.

Tapia, A.H., Lalone, N., and Kim, H. (2014) Run amok: Group crowd participation in identifying the bomb and bomber from the Boston Marathon bombing. In S.R. Hiltz, M.S. Pfaff, L. Plotnick, and P.C. Shih, eds., *Proceedings of the 11th International ISCRAM Conference, May 24*. Pennsylvania State University: University Park, 265–274.

Taylor, V.A. (1977) Good news about disasters. *Psychology Today*, October, 93–96.

Taylor, V.A., Ross, G.A., and Quarantelli, E.L. (1977) *Delivery of Mental Health Services in Disasters: The Xenia Tornado and Some Implications*. Disaster Research Center, University of Delaware: Newark.

Tchouakeu, M.N., Maitland, C., Tapia, A., and Kvasny, L. (2013) Humanitarian inter-organizational collaboration network: Investigating the impact of network structure and information and communication technology on organisation performance. *International Journal of Services Technology and Management* 19(1, 2, 3), 19–43.

Thaler, R. (2015) Misbehaving: The Making of Behavioral Economics. Norton: New York.

Thaler, R. and Sunstein, C. (2008) *Nudge: Improving Decisions about Health, Wealth, and Happiness*. Penguin Books: London.

Third National Climate Assessment (2014) *Climate Change Impacts in the United States*. US National Climate Assessment, US Global Change Research Program: Washington, DC.

Thomas, D.S.K., Phillips, B.D., Lovekamp, W.E., and Fothergill, A., eds. (2013) *Social Vulnerability to Disasters*, 2nd edn. CRC Press: Boca Raton, FL.

Tierney, K. (1994) Property damage and violence: A collective behavior analysis. In M. Baldassare, ed., *The Los Angeles Riots: Lessons for the Urban Future*. Westview Press: Boulder, CO, 149–173.

Tierney, K.J. (1999) Toward a critical sociology of risk. *Sociological Forum* 14, 215–242.

Tierney, K. (2007) From the margins to the mainstream? Disaster research at the crossroads. *Annual Review of Sociology* 33, 503–525.

Tierney, K. (2008) Hurricane Katrina: Catastrophic impacts and alarming lessons. In J.M. Quigley and A. Rosenthal, eds., *Risking House and Home: Disasters, Cities, Public Policy*, 119–136.

Tierney, K. (2009) *Disaster Response: Research Findings and Their Implications for*

Resilience Measures (CARRI Research Report 6). Natural Hazards Center, University of Colorado: Boulder.

Tierney, K. (2012) Critical disjunctures: Disaster research, social inequality, gender, and Hurricane Katrina. In E. David and E. Enarson, eds., *The Women of Katrina: How Gender, Race, and Class Matter in an American Disaster*. Vanderbilt University Press: Nashville, TN, 245–258.

Tierney, K. (2014) *The Social Roots of Risk: Producing Disasters, Promoting Resilience*. Stanford University Press: Palo Alto, CA.

Tierney, K. (2015) Resilience and the neoliberal project: Discourses, critiques, practices—and Katrina. *American Behavioral Scientist* 59(10), 1327–1342. doi: 10.1177/0002764215591187.

Tierney, K. (2018) Disaster as social problem and social construct. In A. Treviño, ed., *The Cambridge Handbook of Social Problems*. Cambridge University Press: Cambridge, 79–94.

Tierney, K. and Bruneau, M. (2007) Conceptualizing and measuring resilience: A key to disaster loss reduction. *TR News* 250, 14–17.

Tierney, K., Lindell, M.K., and Perry, R.W. (2001) *Facing the Unexpected: Disaster Preparedness and Response in the United States*. Joseph Henry Press: Washington, DC.

Tierney, K. and Oliver-Smith, A. (2012) Social dimensions of disaster recovery. *International Journal of Mass Emergencies and Disasters* 30, 122–146.

Tierney, K., Petak, W.J., and Hahn, H. (1988) *Disabled Persons and Earthquake Hazards*. Institute of Behavioral Science, Natural Hazards Center, University of Colorado: Boulder.

Tierney, K. and Taylor, V.A. (1977) EMS delivery in mass emergencies: Preliminary research findings. *Mass Emergencies* 2, 151–157.

Tobin, K. and Freeman, P. (2004) Emergency preparedness: A manual for homeless service providers. Center for Social Policy Publications 6. University of Massachusetts: Boston, MA, http://scholarworks.umb.edu/csp_pubs/30.

Tobin-Gurley, J. and Enarson, E. (2013) Gender. In D.S.K. Thomas, B.D. Phillips, W.E. Lovekamp, and A. Fothergill, eds., *Social Vulnerability to Disasters*, 2nd edn. CRC Press: Boca Raton, FL, 139–165.

Turner, R.H. and Killian, L.M. (1987) *Collective Behavior*. Prentice Hall: Englewood Cliffs, NJ.

Tversky, A. and Kahneman, D. (1973) Availability: A heuristic for judging frequency and probability. *Cognitive Psychology* 5(2), 207–232.

Tversky, A. and Kahneman, D. (1974) Judgement under uncertainty: Heuristics and biases. *Science* 185(4157), 1124–1131.

Tversky, A. and Kahneman, D. (1981) The framing of decisions and the psychology of choice. *Science* 211(4481), 453–458.

United Nations International Strategy for Disaster Reduction (2007) Hyogo Framework for Action 2005–2015: Building the resilience of nations and communities to disasters. UNISDR, https://www.unisdr.org/2005/wcdr/inter gover/official-doc/L-docs/Hyogo-framework-for-action-english.pdf.

United Nations International Strategy for Disaster Reduction (2017) Terminology, https://www.unisdr.org/we/inform/terminology#letter-v.

Urban Institute (2017) Nine charts about wealth inequality in America (updated), http://apps.urban.org/features/wealth-inequality-charts.

US Army Corps of Engineers (2015) *Memorandum for Planning Community of Practice* (Economic Guidance Memorandum 16–01). Federal Interest Rates for Corps of Engineers Projects for Fiscal Year 2016, Department of the Army, US Army Corps of Engineers: Washington, DC.

US Census Bureau (2016) *Income and Earnings Summary Measures by Selected Characteristics: 2015.* Department of Commerce, Census Bureau: Washington, DC.

US Census Bureau (2017) *Income and Earnings Summary Measures by Selected Characteristics: 2016.* Department of Commerce, Census Bureau: Washington, DC.

US Department of Commerce (2010) *Disparities in Capital Access between Minority and Non-Minority-Owned Businesses: The Troubling Reality of Capital Limitations Faced by MBEs.* US Department of Commerce, Minority Business Development Agency: Washington, DC.

US Department of Education (2009) *Issue Brief: English Literacy of Foreign-Born Adults in the United States: 2003.* US Department of Education: Jessup, MD.

US Department of Health and Human Services (n.d.) *Disaster Response for Homeless Individuals and Families: A Trauma-Informed Approach.* Office of the Assistant Secretary for Preparedness and Response, https://www.phe.gov/Preparedness/planning/abc/Documents/homeless-trauma-informed.pdf.

US Department of Homeland Security (2013) *National Response Framework.* Homeland Security: Washington, DC.

US Department of Transportation (2004) *Effects of Catastrophic Events on Transportation System Management and Operations: August 2003 Northeast Blackout New York City* (Report no. DOT_VNTSC-FHWA-04-04). John A. Volpe National Transportation Systems Center: Cambridge, MA.

US General Accounting Office (1983) *Siting of Hazardous Waste Landfills and Their Correlation with Racial and Economic Status of Surrounding Communities.* US Printing Office: Washington, DC.

US Global Change Research Program (2016) *The Impacts of Climate Change on Human Health in the United States.* US Global Change Research Program: Washington, DC.

Uscher-Pines, L., Chandra, A., Acosta, J., and Kellerman, A. (2012) Citizen preparedness for disasters: Are current assumptions valid? *Concepts in Disaster Medicine* 6(2), 170–173.

Van der Elst, N.J., Page, M.T., Weiser, D.A., Goebel, T.H.W., and Hosseini,

S.M. (2016) Induced earthquake magnitudes are as large as (statistically) expected. *Journal of Geophysical Research: Solid Earth* 121, 4575–4590.

Van Willigen, J. *Applied Anthropology: An Introduction*. Greenwood: Santa Barbara, CA.

Van Willigen, M., Edwards, T., Edwards, B., and Hessee, S. (2002) Riding out the storm: Experiences of the physically disabled during Hurricanes Bonnie, Dennis, and Floyd. *Natural Hazards Review* 3, 98–106.

Vickery, J. (2017) *Every day is a disaster: Homelessness and the 2013 Colorado floods.* Doctoral Dissertation, University of Colorado, Department of Sociology, Boulder.

Vieweg, S., Hughes, A., Starbird, K., and Palen, L. (2010) A comparison of microblogging behavior in two natural hazard events: What Twitter may contribute to situational awareness. *Proceedings of the ACM 2010 Conference on Human Factors in Computing Systems, Atlanta, GA*. ACM: New York, 1079–1088.

Vieweg, S., Palen, L., Liu, S.B., Hughes, A., and Sutton, J. (2008) Collective intelligence in disaster: Examination of the phenomenon in the aftermath of the 2007 Virginia Tech shooting. In F. Friedrich and B. Van De Walle, eds., *Proceedings of the 5th International ISCRAM Conference*. Academic Press: Washington, DC, 44–54.

Vigdor, J.L. (2007) The Katrina effect: Was there a bright side to the evacuation of greater New Orleans? Working Paper 13022, National Bureau of Economic Research, Cambridge, MA.

Vogel, J.M. and the Family Systems Collaborative Group (2017) *Family Resilience and Traumatic Stress: A Guide for Mental Health Providers*. National Center for Child Traumatic Stress: Los Angeles, CA, https://www.nctsn.org/sites/default/files/resources//family_resilience_and_traumatic_stress_providers.pdf

Vogel, J.M. and Pfefferbaum, P. (2016) Family resilience after disasters and terrorism. In R. Pat-Horenczyk, D. Brom and J.M. Vogel, eds., *Helping Children Cope with Trauma: Individual, Family and Community Perspectives*. Routledge: New York, 81–100.

Wachtendorf, T. (2004) *Improvising 9/11: Organizational improvisation in the World Trade Center disaster*. Doctoral dissertation, University of Delaware, Department of Sociology, Newark.

Wachtendorf, T. (2009) Trans-system social ruptures: Exploring issues of vulnerability and resiliency. *Review of Policy Research* 26, 379–393.

Wachtendorf, T. and Kendra, J.M. (2006) Improvising disaster in the city of jazz: Organizational response to Hurricane Katrina. Social Science Research Council, http://http://understandingkatrina.ssrc.org/Wachtendorf_Kendra.

Walaski, P.F. (2011) *Risk and Crisis Communications: Methods and Messages*. John Wiley & Sons, Inc.: Hoboken, NJ.

Walker, G. and Burningham, K. (2011) Flood risk, vulnerability and environmental justice: Evidence and evaluation of inequality in a UK context. *Critical Social Policy* 31(2), 216–240.

Walker, T.D. (2015) Enlightened absolutism and the Lisbon earthquake: Asserting state dominance over religious sites and the church in Eighteenth-century Portugal. *Eighteenth-Century Studies* 48(3), 307–328.

Walsh, F. (2016) *Strengthening Family Resilience*, 3rd edn. Guilford Press: New York.

Warmbrodt, Z. and Meyer, T. (2017) How Washington lobbyists fought flood insurance reform. *Politico*, September 2.

Warner, W.L. (1949) *Social Class in America: A Manual of Procedure for the Measurement of Social Status*. Science Research Associates: Chicago, IL.

Waters, M.C. (2016) Life after Hurricane Katrina: The resilience in survivors of Katrina (RISK) project. *Sociological Forum* 31, 750–769.

Webb, G.R., Tierney, K., and Dahlhamer, J.M. (2000) Businesses and disasters: Empirical patterns and unanswered questions. *Natural Hazards Review* 1(2), 83–90.

Webb, G.R., Tierney, K., and Dahlhamer, J.M. (2002) Predicting long-term business recovery from disaster: A comparison of the Loma Prieta Earthquake to Hurricane Andrew. *Environmental Hazards* 4(2) 45–58. doi: 10.3763/ehaz.2002.0405.

Weber, L. and Peek, L., eds. (2012) *Displaced: Life in the Katrina Diaspora*. University of Texas Press: Austin.

Weick, K.E. (1993) The collapse of sensemaking in organizations: The Mann Gulch disaster. *Administrative Science Quarterly* 38, 628–652.

Weick, K.E. (1998) Improvisation as a mindset for organizational analysis. *Organization Science* 9(5), 543–555.

Weick, K.E. and Roberts, K.H. (1993) Collective mind in organizations: Heedful interrelating on flight decks. *Administrative Science Quarterly* 38, 357–381.

Weick, K.E., Sutcliffe, K.M., and Obstfeld, D. (1999) Organizing for high reliability: Processes of collective mindfulness. In R. Sutton and B. Staw, eds., *Research in Organizational Behavior*. Jai Press: Greenwich, CT, 81–123.

Weick, K.E., Sutcliffe, K.M., and Obstfeld, D. (2005) Organizing and the process of sensemaking. *Organization Science* 16(4), 409–421.

Weinstein, N.D. (1980) Unrealistic optimism about future life events. *Journal of Personality and Social Psychology* 39, 806–820.

Weinstein, N.D. (1989) Optimistic biases about personal risks. *Science* 246, 1232–1233.

Weissbecker, I., Sephton, S.E., Martin, M.B., and Simpson, D.M. (2008) Psychological and physiological correlates of stress in children exposed to disaster: Current research and recommendations of intervention. *Children, Youth and Environments* 18(1), 30–70, http://www.jstor.org/stable/10.7721/chilyoutenvi.18.1.0030.

Wenger, D.E. (1987) Collective behavior and disaster research. In R.R. Dynes, B. DeMarchi, and C. Pelanda, eds., *Sociology of Disasters: Contributions of Sociology to Disaster Research*. Franco Angeli: Milan, 213–237.

Wenger, D.E., Dykes, J.D., Sebok, T.D., and Neff, J.L. (1975) It's a matter of myths: An empirical examination of individual insight into disaster response. *Mass Emergencies* 1, 33–46.

Wenger, D.E. and James, T.F. (1994) The convergence of volunteers in a consensus crisis: The case of the 1985 Mexico City earthquake. In R.R. Dynes and K. Tierney, eds., *Disasters, Collective Behavior, and Social Organization*. University of Delaware Press: Newark, 229–243.

Western, B. (2006) *Punishment and Inequality in America*. Russell Sage Foundation: New York.

Western, B. and Pettit, B. (2010) Incarceration and social inequality. *Daedalus* 139, 8–19.

White, C.M. (2011) *Social Media, Crisis Communications, and Emergency Management: Leveraging Web 2.0 Technologies*. CRC Press: Boca Raton, FL.

White, G.F. (1945) Human adjustment to floods. Research Paper 29, Department of Geography, University of Chicago, IL.

White, G.F., ed. (1974) *Natural Hazards: Local, National, Global*. Oxford University Press: New York.

White, G.F. and Haas, J.E. (1975) *Assessment of Research on Natural Hazards*. MIT Press: Cambridge, MA.

White, G.F., Kates, R.W., and Burton, I. (2001) Knowing better and losing even more: The use of knowledge in hazards management. *Environmental Hazards* 3, 81–92.

Wilhelmi, O.V. and Hayden, M.H. (2010) Connecting people and place: A new framework for reducing urban vulnerability to extreme heat. *Environmental Research Letters* 5(1), http://iopscience.iop.org/article/10.1088/1748-9326/5/1/014021/meta.

Williams, D.R., Mohammed, S.A., Leavell, J., and Collins, C. (2010) Race, socioeconomic status and health: Complexities, ongoing challenges and research opportunities. *Annals of the New York Academy of Sciences* 1186, 69–101.

Williams, D.R., Priest, N., and Anderson, N. (2016) Understanding associations between race, socioeconomic status and health: Patterns and prospects. *Health Psychology* 35(4), 407–411.

Williams, J. (2011) A sustainable return on investment. In S. Coyle, *Sustainable and Resilient Communities: A Comprehensive Actions Plan for Towns, Cities, and Regions*. John Wiley & Sons: Hoboken, NJ.

Williams, S. (2008) Rethinking the nature of disaster: From failed instruments of learning to a post-social understanding. *Social Forces* 87(2), 1115–1138.

Winderl, T. (2014) *Disaster Resilience Measurements: Stocktaking of Ongoing Efforts in Developing Systems for Measuring Resilience*. United Nations Development Program: New York, https://www.preventionweb.net/files/37916_disaster-resiliencemeasurementsundpt.pdf.

Wisner, B. (1998) Marginality and disaster vulnerability: Why the homeless of Tokyo don't "count" in disaster preparations. *Applied Geography* 18(1), 25–33.

Wisner, B., Blaikie, P., Cannon, T., and Davis, I. (2004) *At Risk: Natural Hazards, People's Vulnerability, and Disasters*, 2nd edn. Routledge: London.

Wisner, B. and Walker, P. (2005) *The Making and Unmaking of Whiteness*. Duke University Press: Durham, NC.

Wood, M.M. and Bourque, L.B. (2018) Morbidity and mortality associated with disaster. In H. Rodríguez, W. Donner, and J.E. Trainor, eds., *Handbook of Disaster Research*, 2nd edn. Springer: Cham, Switzerland, 357–383.

Wood, M.M., Mileti, D.S., Bean, H., Liu, B.F., Sutton, J., and Madden, S. (2018) Milling and public warnings. *Environment and Behavior* 50(5), 535–566.

World Bank Group (2013) *Building Resilience: Integrating Climate and Disaster Resilience into Development: The World Bank Group Experience*. Global Facility for Disaster Risk Reduction, World Bank: Washington, DC.

World Bank Group (2017) *Unbreakable: Building the Resilience of the Poor in the Face of Natural Disasters*. Climate Change and Development Series, World Bank: Washington, DC.

World Economic Forum (2017) *The Global Gender Gap Report*. World Economic Forum: Geneva.

Wozniak, K., Davidson, G., and Ankersen, T. (2012) *Florida's Coastal Hazards Law: Property Owner Perceptions of the Physical and Regulatory Environment with Conclusions and Recommendations*. Florida Sea Grant, National Oceanic and Atmospheric Administration, University of Florida: Gainesville.

Young, A.L. (2017) Displaced by the storm: Texas evacuees without options. *Texas Monthly*, October 6, https://www.texasmonthly.com/articles/displ aced-by-the-storm-texas-evacuees-without-options.

Zahran, S., Peek, L., and Brody, S.D. (2008) Youth mortality by forces of nature. *Children, Youth and Environments* 18(1), 371–388, http://www.jstor.org/ stable/10.7721/chilyoutenvi.18.1.0371.

Zaval, L. and Cornwell, J.M. (2016) Cognitive biases, non-rational judgements, and public perceptions of climate change. In M.C. Nisbet, M. Schafer, E. Markowitz, S. Ho, S. O'Neill, and J. Thaker, eds., *The Oxford Encyclopedia of Climate Change Communication*. Oxford University Press: Oxford. doi: 10.1093/ acrefore/9780190228620.013.304.

Zavestoski, S. and the Contested Illness Research Group (2012) *Contested Illnesses: Citizens, Science, and Health Social Movements*. University of California Press: Oakland.

Zeng, L., Starbird, K., and Spiro, E.S. (2016) Rumors at the speed of light? Modeling the rate of rumor transmission during crisis. In *The 49th Hawaii International Conference on System Sciences*. Institute of Electrical and Electronics Engineers (IEEE): Piscataway, NJ, 1969–1978. doi: 10.1109/HICSS.2016.248.

Zhang, Y., Zhang, C., Drake, W., and Olshansky, R. (2014) Planning and recovery following the great 1976 Tangshan earthquake. *Journal of Planning History* 14(3), 224–243. doi: 10.1177/1538513214549435.

Zhang, Y., Drake, W., Xiao, Y., Olshansky, R., Johnson, L., and Song, Y. (2016)

Disaster recovery planning after two catastrophes: the 1976 Tangshan earthquake and the 2008 Wenchuan earthquake. *International Journal of Mass Emergencies and Disasters* 34(2), 174–203.

Zottarelli, L.K. (2008) Post-Hurricane Katrina employment recovery: The interaction of race and place. *Social Science Quarterly* 89(3), 592–607.

Index